REMEMBERING
THE
COVENANT
A COMMENTARY ON
THE BOOK OF MORMON

VOLUME 5

Denver C. Snuffer, Jr.

Published in the United States by Mill Creek Press.
Mill Creek Press is a registered trademark of Mill Creek Press, LLC.
www.millcreekpress.com

ISBN-10: 0-9891503-4-8
ISBN-13: 978-0-9891503-4-7

Printed in the United States of America on acid-free paper.

First Edition

Cover design by Mill Creek Press.

CONTENTS

VOLUME 5

UNITY OR HIERARCHY

Virtue and Righteousness

There is a difference between virtue and righteousness. Virtue is laudable, required and necessary, but righteousness has priority. Virtue surrenders to righteousness, not vice-versa. The point can be illustrated from scripture:

It is not virtuous to kill. Nephi was repulsed at the idea, but the Lord required it, and Nephi complied. The doctrinal reasons justifying the killing are set out in *The Second Comforter*, and there were sufficient reasons both under the Law of Moses and the Lord's standards of judgment to vindicate the Lord's decision to kill Laban. The killing was offensive to virtue, but it was righteous.

It is not virtuous to mockingly taunt others. Yet Elijah was pursuing a righteous course against the priests of Baal when he did just that:

> "And it came to pass at noon, that Elijah mocked them, and said, Cry aloud: for he is a god; either he is talking, or he is pursuing, or he is in a journey, or peradventure he sleepeth, and must be awaked." (1 Kings 18:27)

Mocking is both unvirtuous and uncouth, and in this context would qualify only as righteous.

It is not virtuous to rail against the religious leaders of any faith. Yet John the Baptist rebuked the Scribes and Pharisees as a generation of vipers:

> "Then said he to the multitude that came forth to be baptized of him, O generation of vipers, who hath warned you to flee from the wrath to come?" (Luke 3:7)

This term of derision, "generation of vipers" is graphic and in context it is both offensive and uncouth. Yet he was a righteous man, moreso than any other apart from Christ.[1979]

It was not virtuous for Christ to rebuke His accusers:

> "Woe unto you, scribes and Pharisees, hypocrites! . . . for a pretense make long prayer: therefore ye shall receive the greater damnation. Woe unto you, scribes and Pharisees, hypocrites! for ye compass sea and land to make one proselyte, and when he is made, ye make him twofold more the child of hell than yourselves. Woe unto you, ye blind guides, . . . ye fools and blind . . . " (Matthew 23:14–17)

The language of the Lord here is quite blunt, uncouth and in the context of that language, guttural. It was righteous, but not an example of virtuous language.

It was worse still for Christ to call Herod "that fox." This is a term of derision comparable in our own language to calling someone a "son of a bitch."[1980] Yet it was righteous, justified and appropriate.

[1979] Luke 7:28 "For I say unto you, Among those that are born of women there is not a greater prophet than John the Baptist: but he that is least in the kingdom of God is greater than he."

[1980] Luke 13:32 "And he said unto them, Go ye, and tell that fox, Behold, I cast out devils, and I do cures to day and to morrow, and the third *day* I shall be perfected."

It was blunt and threatening for Joseph to tell his guards in Liberty Jail:

> "SILENCE, ye fiends of the infernal pit. In the name of Jesus Christ I rebuke you, and command you to be still; I will not live another minute and hear such language. Cease such talk, or you or I die THIS INSTANT!" (from *The Autobiography of Parley P. Pratt,* emphasis in original.)

Calling another a "fiend of the infernal pit" is quite abrasive and offensive; it was intended to be so.

Those who prefer virtue to righteousness will handicap their ability to work for the Lord's ends. He will always require righteousness to be done. When someone prefers virtue and neglects righteousness, or condemns the righteous for their lack of virtue, their inappropriate standard serves only one purpose. It gets applied against the one proposing to use it. They get to be measured by the standard they apply.[1981]

I choose to look at Elijah, John the Baptist, Christ and Joseph Smith, as well as any other person moved to rebuke me or anyone else by the power of the Holy Ghost as fully justified and Christlike. I do not resist the challenge of a righteous rebuke. I welcome them. No one should feel they cannot "damn" me. I'll consider it important and will respond with my defense, or an apology if I think it is warranted.

It is important for you to know that I do not think Christ is a limp-wristed, lisping chap who dotes on us and has nothing but bouquets of flowers to dispense to us. I think He's about to return in judgment, dressed in red to burn the wicked. He has said that is who He is and I believe Him. I would like to have as many people take

---

[1981] Matthew 7:22 "Many will say to me in that day, Lord, Lord, have we not prophesied in thy name? and in thy name have cast out devils? and in thy name done many wonderful works?"

that seriously and consider repenting. We are mistaken in our belief that we are chosen. We are mistaken when we think we are too good to be in need of continual repentance. We are nothing before God. We are about to see His judgments. I know these ideas make me irritating.

As Hugh Nibley put it, "there is nothing so irritating as being awakened from a sound sleep." But my hope is to awaken some few. Therefore, it is worth offending a great number if the result benefit a few. That is the way things work here and I am quite realistic about it all.

It is also important to be clear about some things. First, the Strengthening the Members Committee is a real group, although its existence was denied for a while by the church. Second, they are not supposed to be pressuring local leaders to harass church members. When they do, it is considered a violation of the process because all church discipline is supposed to be 1) local and 2) independent. When they interfere it is inappropriate. Third, I WANT them to know there are leaks, and they have spilled onto the Internet. They should do what they need to do to plug them. It should be noted that there have been several forum discussions related to me shut down and deleted since my earlier post. Fourth, I want everyone to know if there is a problem which has offended a distant and imperial committee, it is not because I believe too little in the Lord, but too much in Him and too little in men. Fifth, they are misbehaving in a cowardly, unmanly way by this stealth attack. It would be far better, if they want to be credible, for them to address it openly. Do as I have invited them to do. Show me where I'm wrong. Let me respond. Let some sunlight on the matter. It is shameful, even cowardly, to avoid and accuse from a shadow, only to later pretend they weren't involved. Pressuring local, reluctant leaders who know better from personal experience with their local members is manipulative.

I consider the words chosen by me to be measured, appropriate and inspired by the right reaction to a cowardly and shameful act by this subversive committee. They are wrong to behave this way. They have probably engaged in illegal activity by leaking onto the Internet what should be kept confidential. I have done them a service by alerting them to this misconduct. Surely, no matter how misguided their deliberations may be, they intend to preserve their legal protection to claim to have privileges under the law. That protection is forfeited when they act this way.

Organizational Changes

I teach a Business Leadership class in an MBA program. One of the trends in modern business is "flattening of the structure" because a top-heavy management structure is no longer needed. It is possible, with new technology, for the top to be a single layer, and middle-management to be eliminated entirely.

I've thought about the possibility this presents for a religious movement. As I've written in several of my books, the origin of Mormonism makes it much more suited as a "movement" than as a controlled institution. However, the history Mormonism originated in made it impossible for the religion to survive separate from the institution created to perpetuate it. If it were not for Brigham Young taking the extraordinary steps he took to preserve the faith restored through Joseph Smith, it would have died. Brigham Young did act, reaffirmed the institutional structure, argued it could NOT exist without the bulwark of ordered offices and holders of authority, and as a result, the institution remained. More importantly, through the institution the religion has been able to stay. The religion was altered in form because of the merger of religion and institution, now having no life independent of the institution. The interplay between these two (the religion and the organized structure), has been that the religion has been dominated by the institution. Indeed, it has stayed around only because of the institutional power to keep it here.

However, new social and technological advances have given the religion an opportunity to assume life on its own, unlinked to an institution. When Ronald Poelman gave his talk separating the "Gospel" and the "Church" in general conference,[1982] the talk was censored and re-written. A comparison between the original talk and the replacement is available on-line.[1983] However, in the last general conference, Elder Hallstrom's talk[1984] dealt with the subject again, this time making the distinction without being censored. The advances in social and technological management of information and people between the 1984 and 2012 have been more than significant.

The possibility exists now for an entire religious body to become "one" in heart and in belief, not because of periodic visits from a distant hierarchy, but because they are in constant communication amongst themselves. Though they are in India or Mexico or Russia or the US, they can stay abreast of the very latest through direct communication with each another.

This global change is the harbinger of changes coming to every organization on earth, including the church. The church has been an early adopter of technology for decades. As they continue to adapt to new technical capabilities, it will not be long before, once again, we can "live in the same small village." Just as Joseph Smith would answer questions over the fence in his yard with his neighbors in Nauvoo, the possibility is coming for all of us to log into a continuing, flattened structure with no middle management. The top and the bottom of the organization becoming one. No longer any lofty

---

[1982] Poelman, "The Gospel and the Church", General Conference, October 1984.

[1983] http://www.lds-mormon.com/poelman.shtml

[1984] Hallstrom, "Converted to His Gospel through His Church", General Conference, April 2012.

branches, exalted to the sky, with the lesser members confined to the shade, but a uniform and equal access among one another from top to bottom.

In Joseph's day there was no technology that would allow Joseph to be in contact with converts or members worldwide. There was an absolute need for a vertical, hierarchical organization with Presidency, Twelve, Seventy, Stake, Ward, and Quorum leadership levels interfacing between the top and bottom. In contrast, today if the president of the church wanted to address you and I, he could send an email, or post a message on a board where we could all visit and hear directly from him. He could record a MP3 message for us to download. Just like the rest of the world, the church itself could now be "flattened" without any of the difficulties Joseph would have encountered.

Although we tend to think the structure is absolutely essential, it isn't. For example, the revelation giving the overall church structure was not followed by the church from the time if was received (March 28, 1835) until 1975 when President Spencer W. Kimball organized the First Quorum of the Seventy. Between those times, the Seventies had an on-again off-again existence at the general level of the church, with only the Seven Presidents regarded as General Authorities for almost all of that time. Needs arose, the Quorum was activated, and it has been in existence since then. Is that a one-way street? Could the expansion that happens at one moment because of global needs be reversed at another time? Could the structure be simplified if it isn't required just as it was expanded after 140 years?

As technology expands capabilities, it should not surprise us to find one day that the many layers of the church's organization will increasingly be shortened, condensed, consolidated and simplified. It is now possible, for example, for the Lord to return and speak to us all at the same moment, no matter where located, using existing off-the-shelf means. I use that to illustrate a point, not to suggest the Lord will use those means. However, the economy of heaven is such that miracles are not employed when simple physical means will accomplish the needed work. The Lord prefers "small means" because they conform to a law.[1985]

The idea the church could be "flattened" while the Gospel remains unaffected is an idea that can only occur if you think of the church as separate from the Gospel. The church opposed that idea just a few years ago. Now it is taught in general conference. We should not be surprised if other, presently unlikely ideas one day soon are part of our religious practices.

How can the people of God become "one" if they entertain the idea there must be a hierarchy in control? In fact, Zion and a hierarchy are mutually exclusive. You can have one, or the other, but not both. Hence the Lord's frequent assertion that HE will bring again

---

[1985] Alma 37:7 "And the Lord God doth work by means to bring about his great and eternal purposes; and by very small means the Lord doth confound the wise and bringeth about the salvation of many souls."
2 Nephi 2:11 "For it must needs be, that there is an opposition in all things. If not so, my first-born in the wilderness, righteousness could not be brought to pass, neither wickedness, neither holiness nor misery, neither good nor bad. Wherefore, all things must needs be a compound in one; wherefore, if it should be one body it must needs remain as dead, having no life neither death, nor corruption nor incorruption, happiness nor misery, neither sense nor insensibility."

Zion (not us).[1986] Removing all the barriers between the top and bottom, and establishing only a great equality between His people, is a likely prerequisite for the return of Zion.[1987] The technical environment exists and the pressure will grow to flatten the church's organizational structure. The only reason to resist that pressure would be a deliberate desire to keep distance between the top and bottom of the structure.

The Church of Jesus Christ of Latter-day Saints is never spoken of in scripture as the Lord's elect in heaven. There is another body called the Church of the Firstborn. This group is equal in earthly and

---

[1986] D&C 84:99–100 "The Lord hath brought again Zion;
    The Lord hath redeemed his people, Israel,
    According to the election of grace,
    Which was brought to pass by the faith
    And covenant of their fathers.
    The Lord hath redeemed his people;
    And Satan is bound and time is no longer.
    The Lord hath gathered all things in one.
    The Lord hath brought down Zion from above.
    The Lord hath brought up Zion from beneath."
Mosiah 12:22 "Thy watchmen shall lift up the voice; with the voice together shall they sing; for they shall see eye to eye when the Lord shall bring again Zion;"
Mosiah 15:29 "Yea, Lord, thy watchmen shall lift up their voice; with the voice together shall they sing; for they shall see eye to eye, when the Lord shall bring again Zion."
3 Nephi 16:18 "Thy watchmen shall lift up the voice; with the voice together shall they sing, for they shall see eye to eye when the Lord shall bring again Zion."

[1987] D&C 78:5–7 "That you may be equal in the bonds of heavenly things, yea, and earthly things also, for the obtaining of heavenly things. For if ye are not equal in earthly things ye cannot be equal in obtaining heavenly things; For if you will that I give unto you a place in the celestial world, you must prepare yourselves by doing the things which I have commanded you and required of you."

heavenly things.[1988] This will not be some fundamentalist group taking multiple wives, calling themselves by that name. It will instead be called that by the Lord. [I have little confidence in self-identifying individuals or groups. The Lord calls and sends whomsoever He elects; they make few claims to authority. Instead their message is their credential, like the Lord before them.] The Church of the Firstborn is likely to be comprised of members of The Church of Jesus Christ of Latter-day Saints who have taken their faith seriously and used the scriptures as their guide. They will be those who are not sleeping when the Lord, as a thief in the night, returns unwanted.

The Church of the Firstborn will be humble, obscure members of the church. Those are the ones the Lord associated with during His ministry. It was scandalous how He mingled with the bottom of the social order—prostitutes, tax collectors, lepers, and outcasts. His people were and are "the least" in this world. So have been His messengers. It is almost amusing to think of Isaiah or Nephi or Jeremiah getting an honorary degree, or humanitarian award for their valuable contributions to society. Indeed, when society celebrates a messenger by heaping acclaim on them, it strongly suggests they have too much

---

[1988] D&C 76:54–57 "They are they who are the church of the Firstborn. They are they into whose hands the Father has given all things— They are they who are priests and kings, who have received of his fulness, and of his glory; And are priests of the Most High, after the order of Melchizedek, which was after the order of Enoch, which was after the order of the Only Begotten Son."
D&C 88:4–5 "This Comforter is the promise which I give unto you of eternal life, even the glory of the celestial kingdom; Which glory is that of the church of the Firstborn, even of God, the holiest of all, through Jesus Christ his Son—"
D&C 93:20–22 "For if you keep my commandments you shall receive of his fulness, and be glorified in me as I am in the Father; therefore, I say unto you, you shall receive grace for grace. And now, verily I say unto you, I was in the beginning with the Father, and am the Firstborn; And all those who are begotten through me are partakers of the glory of the same, and are the church of the Firstborn."

of the world about them to have chosen rightly.[1989] Mormon was alarmed to see this penetrating into the Holy Church of God in the last days.[1990]

Well, the point is technology and communication are making organizations everywhere "flatter" and without the complex hierarchies once necessary to manage them. From multi-national to local organizations, the trends are accelerating in that direction. It will not be surprising to me if the prophetic promise of Zion's return is made possible, at last, because there is no longer any necessity for hierarchical organization as we speed along in new communication and information development. Today a single person sitting at a keyboard can send a message to millions of people by posting on a blog or message board. What a marvel that is! Imagine how that would have changed Joseph Smith's mission had it been available then!

Imagine how futile it is in this new connected world to attempt to force people into believing things about doctrine, history, and truth. I suspect only the foolish will attempt it and only for so long as it begins to produce widespread failure and rejection by the better informed worldwide audience.

I expect the next Enoch sent to cry repentance before the return of the final Zion will have little more than "a red guitar, three chords and the truth." (Bob Dylan) There will no longer be a need for "the words of the prophets to be written on the subway walls and tenement halls" because they will be available on everyone's handheld.

[1989] 3 Nephi 12:10–12 "And blessed are all they who are persecuted for my name's sake, for theirs is the kingdom of heaven. And blessed are ye when men shall revile you and persecute, and shall say all manner of evil against you falsely, for my sake; For ye shall have great joy and be exceedingly glad, for great shall be your reward in heaven; for so persecuted they the prophets who were before you."

[1990] Mormon 8:38 "O ye pollutions, ye hypocrites, ye teachers, who sell yourselves for that which will canker, why have ye polluted the holy church of God? Why are ye ashamed to take upon you the name of Christ? Why do ye not think that greater is the value of an endless happiness than that misery which never dies—because of the praise of the world?"

(Simon & Garfunkel) The question is, of course, whether anyone can distinguish between the truth and error. That has always been the challenge. Flattening the structure, or even eliminating it altogether, does not remove the burden upon us to choose correctly between the invitation to repent and humble ourselves and the temptation to think ourselves justified by our religion. The return of "natural fruit" will come from conversion to truth, not commitment to organizational behavior.

We should not seek to be a manufactured product, but individuals who all know God. Our destiny lies somewhere other than putting ourselves inside little boxes. Mormonism today is working on a model of management which is about to be abandoned by the world. Strong, central organizations, tend to flatten people. Inspired people only need a flattened organization, because they govern themselves.

Today

Today I was told there are some people growing impatient at not achieving an audience with the Lord. I replied:

It is not a goal to be achieved, but a mercy to be received.

I AM A MORMON

The rant by the MSNBC reporter denigrating Mormonism, provoked by the political season we are in, has inspired the following response:

By faith I self-identify as "Mormon" because that was what we called ourselves when I joined The Church of Jesus Christ of Latter-day Saints. I believe the faith, accept the Book of Mormon as scripture, and have received the ordinances offered by the church, including the temple rites. I appreciate and respect these rites and trust in them as a covenant between myself and God.

It is as silly a proposition for someone from my faith to "interpret" my beliefs and say I'm "not a good Mormon" or that I'm "not a faithful Mormon" as it is for the larger "Christian" community to say that Latter-day Saints aren't "Christian." (I'll get to that in Part 3) In this, however, I want to look at the criticism of Mormonism by the self-identifying "Christians."

I'll concede that Mormons don't accept Historic Christianity. I don't accept it. I think it is riddled with errors, believes in a falsely constructed set of mental gyrations which produce an incoherent definition of the Godhead that even self-proclaimed "Christians" admit they can't understand. I am not sure they could even say they actually believe it. At least those who have it explained to them don't believe it. What does "uncreate" and "of the same substance" and "not dividing the parts" of the three members of the Godhead give us, anyway? It produces a God who is "wholly other" and therefore as alien to me as the stuff living in tubes beside the volcanic openings on the bottom of the Pacific. That God (or those Gods) or whatever sense you want to make of it, is something I reject. Not only do I reject it, it repulses me. It makes me think the Historic Christian God is a complete fabrication, unscriptural in origin, incomprehensible in form, the product of such contradictory assertions that only a fool could trust in the existence of such a thing. I reject it. Period. It is damned foolish for anyone to trust in it and think it will save them. It won't. It is a complete fabrication and utter nonsense. Now, having said that, I have no interest in questioning their "Christianity." If *they* want to believe that, they are free to do so and call themselves Christians.

On the other hand, I do believe in Jesus Christ. Not in the sense that He's everywhere and nowhere, but that He at one time occupied an actual manger on the evening of His birth. He was baptized in water by John the Baptist in the Jordan River. His Father witnessed it; *not* from "inside Jesus" because they were commingled; instead the Father (a separate Being occupying a separate location) looked down, saw His Son baptized, and then sent a sign to testify of the Son while speaking in a voice heard by John the Baptist. I believe in Jesus who was crucified, died, was laid to rest in a borrowed tomb, and then rose from the dead. I believe in the man whose body was torn and had the prints of nails in His hands and feet, and who then returned to life. I believe in that Jesus. He showed those hands to 11 surviving Apostles and then to a crowd gathered in the Americas. All of them touched His physical, wounded hands. I believe in Him. Because of my belief in Him, I have done whatever I have come to understand He wanted from me. As a result, I have obtained faith in Him.

Moreover, because of the things I have offered in obedience to Him, and by making an acceptable sacrifice, and enduring what others apparently are not willing in this day to endure, I know Him. I know His hands have wounds, His arms are open to welcome those who will come to Him, and He embraces those whom He saves. He is not a God of the dead or the distant, but the God of the Living. Real. Tangible. Resurrected and living now.

So when Historic Christianity presumes to judge my faith and relegate me to non-Christian, I'm absolutely willing to say I do not believe as you do. I reject, outright, what you say about Christ. It is nonsense to me, and I refuse to be included among those who claim to follow Historic Christianity. It is powerless to save. It is the doctrines of men, mingled with scripture. Your creeds are an abomination to God. He has said so. I believe Him. Consequently I MUST reject your creeds. But despite this, I still have faith in Christ. Not as you do, but as I do.

If your inauthentic, incomprehensible, creedal God wants to damn me because I do not accept the creeds of Historic Christianity, then I'm pleased to go into a lake of fire and brimstone and enjoy the heat. I think it is stupid to think that kind of flimsy and man-concocted God exists. And even more foolish to think your pious condescension is going to bind God to accept your opinions about my faith. I am Christian. Just not dazzled by your creedal nonsense.

I've studied the pre-Nicene debates, am acquainted with the political and social arguments leading up to standardizing the disputes of then-extant Christianity, and know why they returned again to adopt the follow-on creeds of the Apostles and Athenasian Creed. Here, for you good Historic Christian readers, is what your creeds say I must believe to be saved:

We worship one God in Trinity and Trinity in Unity. Neither confounding the Persons, nor dividing the Substance. For there is one

Person of the Father, another of the Son, and another of the Holy Ghost. But the Godhead of the Father, of the Son and of the Holy Ghost is all One, the Glory Equal, the Majesty Co-Eternal. Such as the Father is, such is the Son, and such is the Holy Ghost. The Father Uncreate, the Son Uncreate, and the Holy Ghost Uncreate. The Father Incomprehensible, the Son Incomprehensible, and the Holy Ghost Incomprehensible. The Father Eternal, the Son Eternal, and the Holy Ghost Eternal and yet they are not Three Eternals but One Eternal. As also there are not Three Uncreated, nor Three Incomprehensibles, but One Uncreated, and One Incomprehensible. So likewise the Father is Almighty, the Son Almighty, and the Holy Ghost Almighty. And yet they are not Three Almighties but One Almighty.

So the Father is God, the Son is God, and the Holy Ghost is God. And yet they are not Three Gods, but One God. So likewise the Father is Lord, the Son Lord, and the Holy Ghost Lord. And yet not Three Lords but One Lord. For, like as we are compelled by the Christian verity to acknowledge every Person by Himself to be God and Lord, so are we forbidden by the Catholic Religion to say, there be Three Gods or Three Lords. The Father is made of none, neither created, nor begotten. The Son is of the Father alone; not made, nor created, but begotten. The Holy Ghost is of the Father, and of the Son neither made, nor created, nor begotten, but proceeding.

So there is One Father, not Three Fathers; one Son, not Three Sons; One Holy Ghost, not Three Holy Ghosts. And in this Trinity none is afore or after Other, None is greater or less than Another, but the whole Three Persons are Co-eternal together, and Co-equal. So that in all things, as is aforesaid, the Unity is Trinity, and the Trinity is Unity is to be worshipped. He therefore that will be saved, must thus think of the Trinity.

To me this is not merely confusion, it is complete crap. Undiluted and unfiltered. I agree there is not "three incomprehensibles" here, but dozens. And there are not "one uncreated" thing going on here, but instead many foolish mental creations launched in a torrent of contradictory and nonsensical gibberish. It is worthy of Lewis Carroll. They multiply as soon as you begin to read them. It is nothing I can, do or ever would accept; and certainly not something to be worshipped. The better approach might be to adopt Through the Looking Glass in its place. At least that nonsense is interrupted occasionally by brilliant prose. This "Christian" creedal stuff is neither prosaic nor sensible. And, all the worse, to be saved you "must thus think of the Trinity!" Well, there you go. You've set the bar too high for me. I cannot pass over. I cannot get to "Go." I surrender in my inability to manage this capacity to "thus think of the Trinity" because my mind requires something "comprehensible" rather than "incomprehensible." Or "Incomprehensible."

Christ said it was "eternal life to know" God.[1991] Your God is by your own definition "Incomprehensible," and therefore cannot be known. So you see, you're damned too if you take this stuff seriously. Because you can't "think thus of the Trinity" and comprehend, much less "know" the only true God. So you are as damned as I in your profession of the "Incomprehensible" God of your creed.

However, I allow you the privilege of believing this stuff. I trust your sincerity when you say you do believe it. I do not question whether you are in your right mind for claiming to believe and to "think thus of the Trinity." After all, you have a whole lot of history on your side. I respect that. But I'd ask that you not presume to speak for God when you try to speak about Him. Unless He has said it, then I'm not particularly interested in what men have to say about Him. Furthermore, I do not believe Historic Christian Councils are

---

[1991] John 17:3 "And this is life eternal, that they might know thee the only true God, and Jesus Christ, whom thou hast sent."

entitled to any respect in their compromises and voting to establish the "truth" about God.

Either you've met with Him, have a message from Him, and can tell me what He said to you, or you have a political rally and you've produced merely more noise, like any political convention does.

This creedal system has resulted in a history of excesses designed to protect it from criticism and to coerce skeptics. I will touch upon that in the next post.

I Am a Mormon, Part 2

The "Historic Christian" faith fragmented because of centralized control seeking to govern even the thoughts of "Christian" believers. The creed I quoted in Part 1 says Christians "must think thus" about God. The rulers of the church were not content to claim they held the keys, but wanted to micromanage even the minds of their followers.

On November 1, 1478, Pope Sixtus IV issued his edict titled "*Exigit sincere devotionis*" which authorized the appointment of "inquisitors" to assure the thoughts of faithful "Christians" were doctrinally pure. This authorization allowed the Catholic kings of Europe to not merely preach the religion, but also to police and compel orthodoxy. Those who were regarded as non-conforming were to be treated as heretics and to be persecuted, even destroyed.

If what they were doing was good, then in the eyes of the hierarchy no deed done in pursuit of the "true Christian faith" was to be avoided; even if the means used involved treachery, deceit and torture. The "truth" was just so important that it justified whatever needed doing to accomplish it.

To incentivize the inquiries, the kings were allowed to confiscate heretics' property. Thus it was financially beneficial to the kings to determine there were heretics among them. In the extremity of torture, almost any person would confess they were heretical to end their pain.

The Inquisition was made possible from the work done two centuries earlier by the man now known as "St. Dominic." He envisioned the idea of moving from persuasion to excommunication to compel conformity among "Christians." If that failed to reform, then he thought it well to engage in even more coercive means, such as confiscation of property and corporeal punishment. This would allow the wayward to be reclaimed. After all, if the church held the keys to save people, then using those keys in coercive ways was justified by the ultimate goal of saving souls. Pope Pius XII would cooperate with Hitler in the Balkans using the same justification.

St. Dominic conceived of a religious order that would be devoted solely to the duty to combatting heresy and propagating the "true Catholic faith." This order, now known as the Dominicans, was known by other, earlier nicknames. They were initially the Militia of Christ. They took St. Dominic's name only after his death. Much later, after they headed the effort to eradicate heresy by policing the Inquisition, they were known as the "hounds of God" or the "dogs of God" because of their zeal in shedding the blood of heretics.

When a religion abandons the obligation to persuade, and resorts to intimidation and coercion, it has lost the battle. Whenever this happens, the faith declines. "Christianity" was already losing its grip when the Pope Sixtus IV Bull was issued. The Inquisition that followed guaranteed there would be protests against the greatly altered church which benefitted and promoted the Inquisition.

In Mormonism there is a doctrinal bulwark in place to prevent this kind of historic error from being repeated. Our scriptures decry the use of any means, however slight, to compel conformity. We have no "orthodox" creed in Mormonism. We welcome all truth, from whatever source. We have the following statements in our scriptures:

"We claim the privilege of worshiping Almighty God according to the dictates of our own conscience, and allow all men the same privilege, let them worship how, where, or what they may." (Article of Faith 11)

We condemn those "whose hearts are so set upon the things of this world, and aspire to the honors of men, that they do not learn this one lesson—That the rights of the priesthood are inseparably connected with the powers of heaven, and that the powers of heaven cannot be controlled nor handled only upon the principles of righteousness . . . [W]hen we undertake to cover our sins, or gratify our pride, our vain ambitions, *or to exercise control or dominion or compulsion upon the souls of the children of men, in any degree of unrighteousness, behold, the heavens withdraw themselves*; the Spirit of the Lord is grieved; and when it is withdrawn, Amen to the priesthood or the authority of that man." (D&C 121:35–37, emphasis added.)

Our faith permits one means to *"control"* members:

"[O]nly by persuasion, by long-suffering, by gentleness and meekness, and by love unfeigned; By kindness, and pure knowledge, which shall greatly enlarge the soul." (D&C 121:41)

We are hemmed in, curtailed and cannot behave as St. Dominic deemed necessary, and as the Holy Inquisition performed. We are relegated to use only persuasion. If we hold a truth as correct, then the burden rests on us to advance it persuasively and to bring others to voluntarily accept it. Our only power, as a church, is in the meek advancement of truth by our persuasion and example. Force, dominion and control is not ours to use. So in this sense also Mormonism departs dramatically from Historic Christianity.

Furthermore, a well respected official LDS Church Historian published an article in the BYU Studies magazine titled, "*I Don't Have A Testimony of Church History.*" In it, Assistant LDS Church Historian

Davis Bitton explained that when it comes to the LDS Church's history, we are free as church members to believe and express our beliefs on any topic because we do not have an official version. For example, he remarked specifically he did not have a "testimony" of the Mountain Meadows Massacre.

One of the great strengths of my religion is the open willingness to allow freedom of thought, and to require the better view to be established only by persuasion, and never by coercion.

We should never lapse into the darkness of policing the thoughts of Mormons by a central hierarchy bent on extinguishing different thought among Mormons. We have no "orthodox" criteria which can be used to carve some believers out and relegate them to the status of "apostate" or "heretic," and thereby dismember the membership. Our faith was established on a scriptural and doctrinal foundation which precludes it. Each Mormon is responsible for what they believe and to provide reasons to persuade others of the correct view.

This necessarily requires a good deal of work for Mormons. We are required to research and gather the information for ourselves. We are free to believe as we will, but to defend our religion we must undertake some work to find it. Therefore, the most devout members of the religion are also among the most studious of the church. We are permitted to believe as we will, but the church is under no obligation to do the work for us. We study, research and ponder this faith individually. For we believe salvation is individual, not collective.

I Am a Mormon, Part 3

I am a Mormon. That is because I believe in this faith. Through-and-through, I am convinced Joseph Smith really was called of God, translated the Book of Mormon—an authentic new volume of scripture telling the account of a fallen people.

What I believe and why I believe it has been the subject of eight books to date. I've made no secret of my thoughts, experiences and reasons for becoming and remaining a Mormon. There are a handful of fellow-Mormons who resent or question my views. This is quite odd, since I do not question theirs. Apparently they do not know Mormonism is non-creedal, and respects every person's right to worship as they wish. There should be very little "control" over beliefs in Mormonism, and a great deal of freedom for its converts. As shown in the prior post, even an Assistant LDS Church Historian claimed *he* didn't have a testimony of church history. We are free to reach our own conclusions. Those who criticize are apparently unaware of the contours of the religion they espouse.

I do not question church leaders' good-faith, or their right to make decisions, even ones I disagree with. It is not a sin, nor apostasy to have an opinion different than the leaders. They alone have the right to lead and I believe they do so to the best of their ability. Their right is upheld by the common consent of the church. Until someone is dismissed by the common consent, we all sustain them in our prayers and actions. At least if you are an active Mormon, as I am.

The church's leaders are empowered by the common consent of the church, according to a pattern established by God. I work to make their job easier by doing whatever is asked of me in donating church service. Yet now I find myself the object of fellow-Mormon's ire, and judging from leaks on the Internet also from the Strengthening the Members Committee of the Church of Jesus Christ of Latter-day Saints. I absolutely disagree that I am not allowed to believe as I do and also be a faithful, active Mormon. I have explained what I believe and why, and discussed problems in church history from a faithful, but candid view.

Fortunately Mormonism is not Historic Christianity. Historic Christianity splintered into the Protestant and Catholic divisions because the church hierarchy attempted to suppress freedom to believe the truth among the members. That inappropriate overreaching created the Lutheran Church, then all the others, as believers in the Gospel of Christ were unable to believe or trust a hierarchy determined to suppress thought and limit discussion. Mormonism has the advantage of knowing this history, and can avoid making that kind of foolish error. That does not mean we will avoid it, only that we are well enough informed by history to be able to avoid it.

I am a "Mormon" whether another church member thinks my faith is consistent with his or not. This is because I am converted, and sincerely do accept these teachings originated from God when He once again intervened directly in mankind's affairs. The Lord was able to intervene because a young man, following a promise in the Bible, asked in faith which church he should join. The Lord answered him, and set that young man on a course in which the Gospel of Jesus Christ was returned to the earth. The return began with God's direct involvement, and included a return of angels to minister to and teach Joseph Smith things *worth every person's time to investigate.*

I investigated Joseph's claims. In fact, I continue to investigate them, searching deeper and deeper into understanding this great, final work by God. It was begun by the Lord through Joseph Smith. But it was not finished then, and our new scriptures promise yet greater things still in the future (see 9th Article of Faith). When anyone asks God in humility about this work, they can get an answer from God.[1992] In fact, at the core of Mormonism is the obligation of every believer to study, ponder, pray and ask God for themselves.[1993]

[1992] James 1:5 "If any of you lack wisdom, let him ask of God, that giveth to all *men* liberally, and upbraideth not; and it shall be given him."

[1993] Moroni 10:4–5 "And when ye shall receive these things, I would exhort you that ye would ask God, the Eternal Father, in the name of Christ, if these things are not true; and if ye shall ask with a sincere heart, with real intent, having faith in Christ, he will manifest the truth of it unto you, by the power of the Holy Ghost. And by the power of the Holy Ghost ye may know the truth of all things."

Every Mormon is supposed to know God by hearing from Him. Then, once having secured a testimony that Mormonism is true, we have an obligation to testify to others about this new work of God in our day.[1994]

I have been doing that for many years. Elder Ballard has told us all to go to the Internet to defend our religion, and I have done that too. I have been dutiful in observing what I've understood my obligations to be as a faithful Mormon.

There is a claim made by some uninformed fellow-Mormons that as a result of what I've written in *Passing the Heavenly Gift*, I have caused unintended "collateral damage" to some people's faith. Meaning, they want to condemn my efforts because they think there might be some few who were discouraged by that book. There have been dozens of letters and emails I have received by those who, after reading it, were strengthened in their faith. There are many who had been inactive or disaffected from the church and returned to activity after reading the book, and yet there are allegedly some few who have been so challenged by the book that they have left the church. I have to say, first, I am honestly unaware of and have never heard any credible account of someone leaving the church because of what I've written. If there is someone who has, or if you know of someone who has, then I'd appreciate it if you would post a comment giving me some information about that. But I want names of those who have "left the church" because of the book. I don't want rumors, or fictitious personas or pseudonyms adopted by someone concealing their identity. That kind of dishonest "AstroTurf" is not proof of anything. You know who I am because I'm being honest. I'm exposed to view, accountable and honest. The fake community of posters and commen-

---

[1994] D&C 38:41 "And let your preaching be the warning voice, every man to his neighbor, in mildness and in meekness."
D&C 88:81 "Behold, I sent you out to testify and warn the people, and it becometh every man who hath been warned to warn his neighbor."

tators are, in reality, a few dishonest souls trying to multiply their importance by their frequent posting of themes. Many of them are being paid to do so.

So far, despite the dozens of emails and letters from real people, giving their home addresses or names and email addresses, confirming that faith has been supported and aided by what I wrote, I have *nothing* from anyone saying anyone left the church. A handful of have disagreed, but none of them claim to have lost their testimony or left the church. Therefore, I am left thinking this "collateral damage" theory is just a mirage intended to inhibit my honesty and not a real phenomena, but if it is a reality, I'd like to know.

Second, I do not believe it is appropriate to judge anyone (leadership or myself) on the basis of alleged "collateral damage" from actions undertaken in good faith to help others. It is a false standard which will only lead to condemning people by an unjust standard. If this is the standard to be applied to me by a fellow-Mormon, then I would ask them to see what happens if you adopt that standard for the church. As soon as they do, they will condemn those leaders who adopted the "Raising the Bar" program which left thousands of young men feeling dismissed and rejected by the church. Many of these young men are no longer active in the church. They are resentful of the way they were "judged" and told they were not worthy and *could not* become worthy through the atonement of Jesus Christ as far as the "church" was concerned. Jesus Christ paid the price for these young men and women willing to repent. Satan tells you you are unworthy. The total numbers on the "collateral damage" are shocking.

Add to the list of the "collateral damage" all those who are not ministered to because of policies in the *Church Handbook of Instructions*. The mischief that has actually resulted from strict enforcement has caused several people to leave or stay away from the church.

General relief society president Julie Beck aroused a firestorm of controversy and alienated some church members a few years ago in a general conference talk.[1995] Is she "guilty" of causing "collateral damage" by that talk? Can we apply that standard to her? I would hope not.

There are returned missionaries drifting into inactivity by the thousands (roughly 50% within two years of returning), because the experiences on the mission have been unsatisfactory for a host of reasons. Mission presidents have verbally abused some of these young men and women. Some have been told to baptize the unworthy and unconverted to create statistical proof of the success of the mission. One young missionary who served in England was told by his mission president to baptize a drunk man (he actually showed up to be baptized inebriated). He did, but it left a scar on the conscience of the young Elder. Indeed, if "collateral damage" is a good standard, there are many who we know have left the church as a consequence of policies and procedures implemented through the good faith decisions of leadership. Not fictional, but calculable numbers of actual injured young men and their families, or inactive and disassociated members now disaffected. These are real stories. We all know people affected. Yet I am confident the leaders were acting in good faith in all they have done. They were doing the best they knew how. Therefore, I reject the idea this measure is fair or appropriate. It should not be used against you, or the leaders, or me. It is a fake standard, adopted to find an excuse to condemn me, and not a sincere concern by any legitimate fellow-Mormon.

Third, I would caution those who want to adopt this standard that they risk condemning themselves. I do not apply it against others because I do not want that to be the standard used against me. I prefer to measure the missteps made by the church on the basis of my belief and trust that they want to help others. When they inadvertently cause harm or injury, I forgive them and do not measure "collateral damage" as accountable against them. If that standard is adopted by them against me, I worry the Lord will use it in the Day of Judgment against those now applying it. He said in the Sermon on the Mount that this was the standard.[1996] I do not ask this for my sake, but for the sake of my fellow-Mormon accusers. I want them to avoid condemnation by the application of a standard no man can meet.

Fourth, I would suggest there are so many who have been helped that there should be some consideration given to the fact that something good has come from something you call evil. That is, if faith has been restored in some demonstrable group (and I've furnished proof of that), then such good cannot come from something bad. It is impossible. The true intention, and the actual result of what I've done is to create and affirm faith, not to destroy it. It has actually produced faith. I would suggest you take the provable results of increased faith as the appropriate measure, not the theory of "collateral damage."

Fifth, the phrase "proud descendants of Nauvoo" is a phrase intended to be memorable. It is used to capture an idea that suggests there is an almost impossible task asked of those who are so personally involved in the history of our church. How can someone look objectively at the past, when these are people's grandfathers and grandmothers? They can only do so if they are first reminded of the inherent bias associated with their status. It is altogether reasonable, perhaps inevitable, for them to be proud. It is a fact that their families have endured much for the faith. However, when it comes to measuring our past, these personal and prideful feelings, although

---

[1996] Matthew 7:2 "For with what judgment ye judge, ye shall be judged: and with what measure ye mete, it shall be measured to you again."

natural and justified, *cannot* allow us to discard the tools of scripture and history to reveal what has been underway in God's dealings with us. The phrase is a shorthand way to alert the reader to this inherit bias. The reader can then decide for themselves if this shorthand and very pregnant phrase is useful to them in reading the account. I can tell you that there have been many "proud descendants of Nauvoo" (and they identify themselves as that in emails to me) have been pricked in their hearts and persuaded by the information presented in the last book I wrote, and who have thanked me for awakening them to their unique challenges. The phrase is a plea for dispassionate review of facts, not a deliberate insult. I did not write it as such, and it should not be taken as such.

I will continue to defend and assert my faithfulness to this religion which I accept, believe and defend. It is peculiar that I find myself accused by fellow-Mormons of being less than they, because there is no such standard permitted in my religion. We are told not to judge one another, but to endeavor to use pure knowledge, gentleness and love to persuade. We simply can't demand someone change their view. That is not permitted.

I am a Mormon and I have no intention of trying to supplant leaders, or to acquire a following. I submit and defer to them. I have no right to lead, but I do have, as all Mormons have, the right and obligation to express and defend my beliefs and bear my testimony. If you study what I've written, there is almost nothing of myself in them. A good deal of Latter-day Saint leaders, writers and speakers have themselves in the "starring role" of whatever they say, teach or write. That is not true for me. I am absent, or when present I show my weakness, foolishness and failure. The only time I appear in a positive light is when I bear testimony of the Lord, whom I have met and is a friend of mine. Even there, however, the contrast between Him and His glory and me and my weakness causes me to use words like "crushes" and "unworthy" to describe my position. In stark contrast, some of the most popular LDS personalities are constantly holding themselves up as an example, as the center of their stories, as the hero of their tales, and as the ones to admire. I'm not like that. I am disgusted by anyone who puts me on a pedestal. I don't belong there. If you cast about and do a little looking, you can find many who want to move attention from the Lord onto themselves. I'm not one of them. For me, the Lord is and ought to remain the focus of devotion for us all.

I am a Mormon; through and through, and converted to this religion. I believe it originated with God, and that God will watch over it. The measure of its success, however, cannot be gauged in statistics, convert rates, or tithing dollars. It can only be measured in whether it results in reconnecting man to God. For me it has succeeded in that. That alone makes Mormonism the "pearl of great price" Christ spoke of purchasing, even if it required all a man has to obtain it. (Matthew 13:46.) Now I try to offer that same great prize to anyone else who is searching to reconnect with God. Not through me, but through the Lord's invitation, teachings and guidance.

Answers to Last Week's Questions

There are some more questions asked this week that I'll try to answer.

On blog traffic: Approximately 750,000 total visits to the blog.

The traffic comes predominately from the following in the order of the top ten countries: United States, Canada, United Kingdom, Australia, Germany, Russia, Finland, Spain, Thailand, Ukraine. The traffic is worldwide, including Brazil, Belarus, Japan, even Mongolia.

In response to my request, I received an email from a woman who explained that her husband was very troubled by reading *Passing the Heavenly Gift*. Though they had not left the church, they had become suddenly discontent. In response to her I want to express my thanks for responding. She was not just the first, but is the only one who has spoken up saying anything like this to me. In response to her inquiry about my feelings toward the church:

The church remains important, even central to progressing toward God. In *The Second Comforter: Conversing With the Lord Through the Veil*, I remark that "the truth will scratch your eyes out, and then scratch them in again." That is a reference to how seeing the weaknesses and failures of all those around you *can* be quite discouraging, but it is necessary. It is when we see clearly how limited and failure-prone mankind is that we turn in desperation to the Lord and call on Him for mercy. We must be uncomfortable before we seek the only source of comfort. The Lord is the answer. The church is not the answer. It is pointing, or should point to Him. The church is only a means. The Lord is the journey's end. The church is the wonderful home where we get to render service to one another. It is where the Lord has asked we serve. The service is for Him, as an act of devotion to Him, and to comply with what He has asked. It is not for our own recognition or advancement. It is because we want to come to know Him. In the quiet service for others, when our minds finally come to rest on the only one who can save us, we can find that peace where the Lord comes to us and speaks words of comfort. He is real. He exists, and He comforts those who come to Him offering a broken heart and contrite spirit, and to none other.

If the book has scratched your eyes out, then let the truth scratch them in again. Do not go away blinded. Let the truth that lies beyond the despair now come to you as well.

The question about poverty and giving raises the intractable question of how to deal with the poor. Our system is broken. The answer to the problem ultimately lies in changing the entire system, but that requires people to be of one mind, and one heart, and to have Christ as their center. We are far from that. The best economic solution is a theological one. We can't have "utopia" separate from Zion. We can't have Zion while we are filled with envy, jealousy and lack conversion to Christ. We can't be converted to Christ and lose our envy and jealousy until we are brought to awaken to our awful situation. We can't be awakened until we are willing to recognize we are no different than the "Lord's people" who have failed every time He has chosen a people (other than in past Zions). We can't come to that recognition until we take much more seriously the Book of Mormon and Doctrine and Covenants. We are not prepared to do so until we are buffeted a bit more by the winds of failure and humiliation to bring down our pride. So in a very real sense it will be poverty and struggle which holds the best hope of starting us down the process that will unite us and then end poverty. So we're not going to solve poverty until the Lord first gives us the necessary experience to acquire broken hearts and contrite spirits.

On why I continually say "I'm nothing and nobody" there are doctrinal reasons. Those who are religious, and follow a converted disciple of Christ, are still damned if they substitute a man in the place that belongs only to Christ. Sincere, but deluded people who claim they are disciples of Paul, Apollos, Peter, Moses, Isaiah, even Thomas Monson, but who do not receive a testimony of Christ, are damned. They suffer the vengeance of eternal fire.[1997] They are con-

---

[1997] D&C 76:99–106 "For these are they who are of Paul, and of Apollos, and of Cephas. These are they who say they are some of one and some of another—some of Christ and some of John, and some of Moses, and some of Elias, and some of Esaias, and some of Isaiah, and some of Enoch; But received not the gospel, neither the testimony of Jesus, neither the prophets, neither the everlasting covenant. Last of all, these all are they who will not be gathered with the saints, to be caught up unto the church of the Firstborn, and received into the cloud. These are they who are liars, and sorcerers, and adulterers, and whoremongers, and whosoever loves and makes a lie. These are they who suffer the wrath of God on earth. These are they who suffer the vengeance of eternal fire. These are they who are cast down to hell and suffer the wrath of Almighty God, until the fulness of times, when Christ shall have subdued all enemies under his feet, and shall have perfected his work;"

signed to hell, and are resurrected as Telestial beings. This is because they followed a man. It is a grave mistake and salvation is lost when that mistake is made. Those who invite people to follow them, and deliberately seek devotees are anti-Christ and bringing souls to destruction. These religious Pied Pipers will incur the greater damnation. If someone is going to make that mistake by claiming they are following me, they will not do so without being told by me unequivocally and with some frequency that they are mistaken. I am nothing, and I have not ever attempted to become an anti-Christ. I point to Christ, for He alone can rescue you from the pains of hell and eternal torment. Those who put themselves up for adoration and worship are mistaken, are practicing priestcraft, are anti-Christ, and in the employ of the enemy to our souls.

In response to the question regarding good books about history, there is another book I quite liked. The new LDS Church Historian, Elder Steve Snow, recently recommended the employees of the Church History Department read the book *David O. McKay and the Rise of Modern Mormonism*, by G. Prince and R. Wright. I've quoted from that book and have also cited it in bibliographies. I agree it is worth reading by anyone interested in church history. David O. McKay's daily activities were kept in a record written by his secretary, Sister Clare Middlemiss, from 1935 until his death in 1970. She was the aunt of Robert Wright, who obtained access. Ultimately, the journals were donated to the University of Utah and are presently housed in the J. Willard Marriott Library, where the public can have access to them. The *Modern Mormonism* book is the first history written that is taken from these extensive journals. The journals are no doubt going to become a source for many other works of history. This volume was well done and introduces a host of behind-the-scenes views of the events during President McKay's presidency.

I Am a Mormon, Part 4

I am a Mormon. The church I belong to, support, and believe in has intentionally kept a good deal of its history concealed. The archives are not completely open, and have never been available to the public. One of the reasons Assistant LDS Church Historian Davis Bitton "did not have a testimony of church history" was because our history has yet to be fully written. It is a work yet to be discovered and revealed. Right now we have only glimpses and excerpts, not the full panoply of material to draw from in order for any of us to reach fully informed conclusions.

The church could remove this impediment by opening its archives. However, it is apparent they aren't going to do this. Therefore, we all live (and I'm talking about *all* of us, including the ones defending this faith among our peers and friends) with the justified concern the church has something it thinks it must hide. Although I can use the materials that were released, or information that has leaked out, to show there are believers who can tolerate the foibles and weaknesses of humanity and still retain strong faith in the religion and confidence in the church, I can never advance a good enough argument to overcome the perception that there is embarrassing material that won't see the light of day. In *Passing the Heavenly Gift* I show that, to the extent the history can be reconstructed from what is now available, even the moments of profound human failure are not a good enough reason to abandon belief in the faith. That is a *defense* of the faith, not an attack on it. I reject the idea the book was intended as an attack. It wasn't. So, from the scattered comments I've heard let me continue to address concerns about that book as I understand them:

I did not criticize President Harold B. Lee about his development of Correlation. That was President David O. McKay and his counselor President Moyle. I quoted them. They were opposed to the

Correlation program that Elder Lee was advancing. They thought it would lead to the apostasy of the church from abuse by future hierarchies using their position to control and dominate other, equally deserving branches of the church. They thought it was improper for the central priesthood to claim the right to control everything instead of the separate branches having independence. I only quoted these former members of the First Presidency. (It was President Harold B. Lee who presided over the church when I joined.) Therefore, if you think that is an inappropriate idea, your quarrel is with a church president and his counselor, not me.

I did not characterize President Grant as being more interested in money than religion. That was his mother. I quoted her. Or, to be even more exact, it was President Grant quoting his mother in his own diary that I quoted. I made no independent accusation. I reported what he said about himself (and what his mother accused him of in her communication with him). Then I defended his candor and integrity because he made this self-revelation of his weakness. If you think that is an inappropriate assessment of President Grant, your quarrel is with him and his mother, not me.

It was President J. Reuben Clark who compared the modern church president to the Pope. I merely quoted him. It was LDS Church Historian Marlin Jensen who called the First Presidency and Quorum of the Twelve "the fifteen men." I only quoted him. I do not think either President Clark or Elder Jensen meant any offense. Nor do I think offense should be taken. But most of all, if offense is to be taken, then place it where it belongs: with the LDS leaders I quote, and not me. I am trying to make sense of the things they have said and done from a faithful perspective. Be careful who you damn, because you are actually turning on the very leaders you think you are defending. What I have done in *Passing the Heavenly Gift* is to defend the faith I believe in and accept, despite human weaknesses and failings. I am realistic about the shortcomings of mere men. This is why our faith must be centered in Christ, rather than foolish and weak mankind.

Is it really impermissible for a faithful member, who wants those who are worried about history, to quote from the diaries and letters of former First Presidency members? Have only the critics the right to tell more accurate history of our faith? Do those who believe have no permission to also be candid with the public while defending the faith? How, exactly, is that supposed to work out in our favor? I'm willing to be enlightened about that approach, and if you can persuade me the truth must be avoided then I will fall in line with what I'm required to do; but with all due respect the problem is not me. The problem is that from top to bottom our faith *must* be more truthful in this Internet age or we risk being mere characters and not real functioning adults with bona fide and defensible beliefs. We risk putting "fiction and fairy tales" above a sound defense of the faith. We begin to look as foolish and as immature as our critics want to paint us. Is that the goal? If not, then how should we deal with problems in history? Are we only allowed to ignore them? Or to tell versions of events that can be easily disproven? Does not the current collapse in faith among adult members who have been previously lifelong active members raise the concern that we *must* be more truthful? How much more damage are you willing to inflict on the religion before you reach the conclusion we must be truthful, even when the truth is unflattering?

All of the "problems" are already before us on the Internet. If you only study what is Correlated and sanitized, your children won't. If you have no answers, then you will find you are unequal to the challenges that lie ahead of you and your family. Whether you are ready for it or not, the waves of challenges are breaking upon us. Our missionaries return with more questions than answers because there is an organized opposition working to challenge all of our teachings, doctrines and history. We MUST be better prepared. Not from composing more limited fiction, but from facing what is known to be true.

I am not worried about the faith collapsing under the weight of truth. It will instead be vindicated by the truth. It is far more handicapped by the fiction we presently serve as the defense of our faith than by a rigorous application of truth in examining the failures of men. Even when men fail, the faith is unaffected.

It is my belief that the recent assertion by the church in the Professor Bott matter did more damage to the interests of the church than anything I've ever done. The official statement was:

"The origins of priesthood availability are not entirely clear. Some explanations with respect to this matter were made in the absence of direct revelation and references to these explanations are sometimes cited in publications. These previous personal statements do not represent Church doctrine."

In my view, this is no defense of the faith or our history. It is a worse condemnation of previous leaders than anything I've ever written. How does this kind of statement get approved as a public statement by the church? Can a "revelator" speak (as did Brigham Young, John Taylor, Wilford Woodruff, and many others in the first presidency and twelve) about this crucial matter for over a hundred years "in the absence of revelation?" How, if this critical issue involving the personal lives of so many faithful church members for generations was wrong and did not represent church doctrine, can we now trust that anything that is said by anyone on any topic represent church doctrine? There were faithful Saints kept out of the temple because of this doctrine. There were heart-wrenching discoveries of genealogy issues for people who were previously ordained who were told they could no longer use their ordination to serve in the church. They were turned down because these men at the highest levels were acting "in the absence of revelation?" Why? This is not a defense of Mormonism by the church, it is an abdication of responsibility. It makes the church look far worse than quoting President McKay's concern that Correlation will lead to apostasy.

Again, I am not worried about the faith collapsing under the weight of truth. It will instead be vindicated. It is far more handicapped by efforts to appear consistent when we are completely inconsistent than by admitting we made a mistake. We are human. We fail. That is one of the great features of humanity. We tend to let ourselves make sometimes terrible mistakes and wish we could do them over. Christ died to make that possible. He is the champion of forgiveness. Why can't we acknowledge that from time to time the church itself needs to ask for forgiveness? It would be given. Members at the lowest level of this organization are rooting for you, supporting you, and upholding you with our prayers. We want you to do your best, and know that sometimes that won't be good enough. We know you're going to fail us. I am perfectly willing to forgive you when you do. It is alright. I do not expect perfection, but I do hope for honesty. Lying to cover up a mistake is not easily forgiven. That inspires contempt, not forgiveness or respect. We forgive readily your mistakes because we all make them, but not everyone is going to lie to spare themselves embarrassment. Those who do, break trust with the public and with membership of the church. The first step in repentance is confession, and we know you forsake sins when you first confess them.[1998]

This is why in all I've written I've tried to tell it as truthfully and honestly as I am able. I know that the Lord will forgive me when I fall short. I hope the church is willing to allow itself, and me, to fall

---

[1998] D&C 58:43 "By this ye may know if a man repenteth of his sins—behold, he will confess them and forsake them."

short and still be friends mutually supporting one another in a greater cause. That greater cause is where God is involved. Our mutual mistakes are our creation, not God's. So we shouldn't pretend we are better, or more inspired, or less flawed than we all are. I am certain I will disappoint you, because I have not been and never will be free from sin and error in this mortal estate. But my heart is in the right place. I'm not trying to cover anything of myself up. I'm not pretending I am better than I am. I have repeatedly acknowledged I am flawed, and not worth following. I point to the Lord, because He is worth following. I readily admit I think the church and its members oftentimes pretend to be better than we are. I still defend her and hope for her best interests. My weakness does not limit God's grace and forgiveness. The weaknesses and mistakes of the church are able to be overcome, too, through God's grace and forgiveness.

I am a Mormon. Devoutly and actively. I intend to die as a faithful Mormon. You should never think my form of faith is too insubordinate, too candid and too open to be endured. In my view that is not a problem at my end. Exactly what is it about the truth of human failure you find so threatening? I can associate without condemning, with fellow Mormons who advocate a very shallow view of the faith I hold as true. I can let them alone and never foist my views on them. However, in the exchange of ideas among those who are actively searching the Internet and bookstores to find truth, I should be allowed to explain how I have maintained faith and active support of the church in the face of troubling history. No one is required to read what I've written. You don't have to come to this blog and let me interrupt your view of Mormonism. Go your way, believe as you like. Let those who struggle, for whom I provide some aid in coping with the difficult things they've learned about our past and our doctrine, be permitted to peaceably consider how I've come to reconcile the Gospel with these many challenges.

I think those who condemn it, rather than offer a reasonable explanation and defense of their beliefs, do not understand Mormonism. They do not understand our scriptures. They do not understand what Joseph Smith said of the religion he gave his life to restore. I've studied for years, hours a day, to gain through hard effort and prayer the things I have learned. Then I have spent decades sincerely applying those things I learned. I am most certainly a Mormon. My faith is only gained by the kind of diligence and heed I've given to it. If you don't understand or sympathize with my practice of Mormonism, that does not make me less a Mormon nor you more one. It just makes us different in how we accept this great latter-day gift from God.

The fellow-Mormons who condemn me without reading what I've written employ means that are brutal, unkind, coercive, and intimidating. They should be trying to reclaim me from the error they think I have made. I have tried through persuasion and knowledge to bring about understanding. I cannot be intimidated by what others say or do. I know He whom I serve. And therefore I must speak boldly about this faith I hold so dear.

I Am a Mormon, Part 5

The purpose of the faith restored through Joseph Smith was not to enshrine mere men as idols. It was to proclaim that all men, every one of us, can know God. The whole of Joseph's message can be summed up in the proclamation that God is no respecter of persons, but will give to all men liberally who ask of Him. It is James 1:5—God does answer prayer.[1999]

This message came to me from the Mormon elders who taught me about the Restoration of the Gospel. These young men were not

---

[1999] James 1:5 "If any of you lack wisdom, let him ask of God, that giveth to all *men* liberally, and upbraideth not; and it shall be given him."

"slick," but quite homespun. They used flannel boards and paper cut-outs. One of them was from Nephi, Utah. He was inarticulate, butchered grammar, and spoke with an odd accent. For several lessons, I literally thought he was saying "p-r-i-e-s-t-e-d." A few weeks into investigating, I was a bit chagrined when I realized he was actually trying to say "priesthood." Later, Elder Black (who baptized me) presented a better image. Some 39 years after baptizing me he is still a friend.

I did not join the church because it was powerful, rich, or slickly marketed. It appeared to me to be homely, rough and extremely unpopular when I joined. As I recall, there were less than 350,000 total priesthood holders and only a minority of them were active. What the church offered was information from, and a connection to God. I tested the process. I received an answer to my prayer about Mormonism from God.

When I joined the church I gave up everything. I lost my friends and family. I was alienated from the life I had known and lived. It required all of it to be put on the altar and set on fire. But, having heard from God in answer to prayer, there was no hesitation. Though I was realistic about my own flaws, and thought I could never be a good enough Mormon, I intended to try. I had the courage to do so because God had spoken to me in answer to prayer and I believed He wanted me to become a member.

Now, I find a nameless, distant committee in the Church Office Building questioning my faithfulness (based on Internet leaks from the COB). Though the local authorities have shown nothing but acceptance for me, and I have served honorably and without controversy in my ward and stake, these distant Strengthening the Members Committee, who know nothing of me and have never talked to me, think it their prerogative to meddle.

I left all I knew to become a member of the church because I was following God. I still follow God. I began this journey to follow God. I did not begin this journey to follow men, elders, bishops or presidents. I gave up friends and family to follow *God*. I will not hesitate to make that trade again. I can be cut off from fellowship with the church, but you have no power that can cut me off from God. It is His company that brought me to you, and will be His company I keep whether you stay in fellowship with me or not.

I would prefer to stay in fellowship with both God and the church. But the church is a poor trade to make in a bargain that would cost me association with God. I do not measure my standing before God by how many people think well of me. I could not care less. It is absolutely fine if you think I'm unworthy, misinformed and even a crank. The things I have written can, have and will help some come to Christ. Some of the things I have written can, have and will help some who are struggling with the church's doctrine and history. The Gospel originates from God, is to save mankind, and cannot be safely ignored.

I took Joseph's teachings to heart. I also asked God. He has given liberally to me. Therefore, I testify of this process and invite others to have faith and to seek Him. Not me. Not men. Not some intermediary. Seek for God. There is none who can save you but God. If the Strengthening the Members Committee determines to pressure the local authorities to make a decision they would never have made on their own, then you are casting away a friend, not an enemy. To my knowledge this would be the first time you decide to impose discipline from inside the Church Office Building against someone who:

- Does not challenge your right to preside.
- Sustains the leaders.
- Has written about the scriptures and doctrine from a faithful view.

- Has defended the restoration and Joseph Smith.
- Has attempted to conform our history to the scriptures.
- And who will be weighed against your vanity and injured pride rather than the tenants of the underlying religion.

For my fellow Latter-day Saint (and the Central Command) who choose to condemn me, there is something about this moment you ought to pause to consider. This intersection is not one you want to be in, really. What if I am telling the truth? What if I'm right? In the final analysis, I am a Mormon. I am converted to this faith and will remain converted to it whether you decide to withdraw fellowship or not. My religion will remain whether you let me remain a member of this church or not. Were I in your shoes, I'd welcome someone as committed to the faith as I am, and never adopt the role of an accuser of any Saint. I claim to belong to God, not to you. If you decide to pressure local authorities to cast me off, there is another law decreed before the foundation of the world you will perhaps inadvertently invoke against yourself. This is not the intersection you want to be in, and I mean that in all seriousness and with all my heart; for your sake, not for mine. I know my standing before God, and nothing you can do will alter or affect that, but how you treat me may alter *your* standing before Him. For your own sake, I would ask you not to do something you will later very much regret.

The Gospel of Jesus Christ is true, authentic, and holds the means for redeeming mankind. Whether the church's history is an unmitigated series of correct choices and flawless performance by leaders and members alike, it does not change one whit the obligation each of us has to come to Christ for redemption. Whether the church has everything it claims or not, doesn't change our obligation to God. So where does any of this matter? We all still must repent and obtain hope in Christ. I focus and write to further that. I have no other agenda.

I Am a Mormon, Part 6

The presentation by the missionary Elders that convinced me to "ask God" was weak. Just like the scriptures commend us to become when we tear down the false things of this world.[2000] The young men had little appeal, and were not well equipped to advance the religion. They had come to me with nothing of any value, apart from the religion being true and the Spirit bearing witness to me of that fact.

So when the church invests millions in the infrastructure to test, market, gather focus-group insights, and then opinion poll to improve the marketing of Mormonism, I am very skeptical it has any value at all. You see, I came through the conversion process. None of the marketing I saw was professional. It was amateur and simple. For the most part, the leaders of the church inherit this religion and the church from their parents, grandparents, and great-grandparents. I did not. I endured the rejection of my parents and sibling when I joined the faith. I lost family and friends because of the faith. I know *why* someone joins an inconvenient, challenging faith because I went through the process. It has nothing to do with the church being physically impressive.

The success of the church is not dependent upon, nor guaranteed by, a multi-billion-dollar downtown complex of religious and commercial buildings. If that is what motivates someone to join, they do not have the right reasons or focus, and will not contribute anything to the faith. We do not need to gather into the net those who find a slick marketing approach convincing enough to become Mormon. We only need to gather those who are pricked in their hearts, humble and who prayed to know if this is God's work or not. Those who get an answer are going to join *because* they got an answer. Such people

---

[2000] D&C 1:19 "The weak things of the world shall come forth and break down the mighty and strong ones, that man should not counsel his fellow man, neither trust in the arm of flesh—"

will have an inner strength that flows from having spoken with God. They will remain and grow in their knowledge of godliness—as long as we feed them. They will perish, however, if we feed them nothing but myth and superficial portions of the Gospel. The truth is exciting, and we risk killing their faith when we make it dull, incomplete, and mingled with misrepresentations. They will die, even if they are active in the church.

People who will listen with their hearts are going to join us. We do not need to be using Wall Street consulting firms to put together a new, improved marketing campaign. The Lord will vindicate His messengers. The expensive infrastructure detracts from the message delivered by a simple carpenter from Galilee who went about doing good. I love the Latter-day Saints. They are delightful people. When I joined, they were among the most humble people I'd ever encountered. However, as the church has grown in population and prosperity it has lost some of its humility and kindness. There is a hard edge creeping into the community of saints from the top down. The leadership knows that. They can see what the Correlation process has done and how it afflicts everything it touches. It is blighted with that hardness, and it is beginning to permeate the structure.

As committees impose central rule, they impersonalize a deeply personal faith. That impersonalization has unintended consequences. In cases we are all familiar with, it occasionally results in local leaders trying to attract favorable attention from the central command. These aspiring men do not feel the required attachment to their sheep. We have *all* seen them, lived with them, and know they are seeking upward mobility in the church organization. Their loyalty has shifted toward a distant hierarchy they seek to impress, then join. They want a "red chair."

I have been fortunate to have encountered some wonderful local leaders. The last two bishops of my current ward were/are examples of faithfulness and humility. My stake president who was just released was an extraordinary leader and disciple of Christ. My stake has been blessed with great leaders, but that is not always the case in the stakes I have been in before. A former bishop from another stake would only bear his testimony about how great a man *he* was. His wife, likewise, only bore her testimony telling us how great a man her husband was. He's now a pretty respected LDS personality. I'm puzzled by that. When those called to serve are converted to the Lord, they minister with His commands in mind. When men who are not converted to the Lord, but who want to rise in the church are called to preside, we suffer.

Like all who join the church in response to an answer to prayer, I am not a Mormon because of *you*. I support you, but my testimony was and is based on the Lord. I do not think the Strengthening the Members Committee is any better an idea than the Inquisition pursued by the Dominicans. They thought they were doing something of value to preserve the faith. That is not how it turned out. Instead it led to the breakup of Catholicism and the enduring historic conviction that the Roman Church was absolutely wrong. We should learn from that, not repeat it.

God lives. He is real. Joseph knew Him. Joseph stood in His presence. This church was instituted to bring people to the Lord. And this church has brought me to the knowledge of, and then the companionship with Him. Therefore this church has my loyalty and my gratitude. I am indebted to the church for that, but I will never change allegiance from God to men or man. It just won't happen. If that is your goal and you insist on the choice, I've already made it. As for me and my house, we will follow God. Now and always.

I Am a Mormon, Conclusion

The Church of Jesus Christ of Latter-day Saints introduced to me the idea that God would speak to mankind again today, if we asked in faith and listened for an answer. It was a very difficult idea to accept at first. It seemed God was a distant being whose involvement was ancient, and who concluded His work with man in the Bible.

When the missionary Elders "bore their testimony" and said they knew their religion was true, it puzzled me at first. I wasn't sure what that meant. They approached the subject of religion and their knowledge of their belief system with a sort of confidence I hadn't seen before. When they said Joseph Smith had seen and spoken with God the Father and Jesus Christ, it was almost too much to take in at first.

The religion they offered did not come quickly or easily to me. It was very hard for me to accept. But their sincerity affected mine, and ultimately I did "ask God" and got an answer from Him. It was so subtle, and so small an answer that at first I wondered if it was an answer from God at all. I trusted in it, acted on it, and the light grew.

From small means to greater and greater light, I have been converted to the restored Gospel of Jesus Christ. And now, after the many testimonies which have been given of Him, this is my own testimony, last of all, which I give of Him: That He lives; for I have seen Him. He has ministered to me. I adopt the words of others and confirm they, too, have seen Him:

I can say, like Nephi:

"And now I, Nephi, write more of the words of Isaiah, for my soul delighteth in his words. For I will liken his words unto my people, and I will send them forth unto all my children, for he verily saw my Redeemer, even as I have seen him. And my brother, Jacob, also has seen him as I have seen him; wherefore, I will send their words forth unto my children to prove unto them that my words are true. Wherefore, by the words of three, God hath said, I will establish my word. Nevertheless, God sendeth more witnesses, and he proveth all his words." (2 Nephi 11:2–3)

I can say, like Moroni:

"And then shall ye know that I have seen Jesus, and that he hath talked with me face to face, and that he told me in plain humility, even as a man telleth another in mine own language, concerning these things; And only a few have I written, because of my weakness in writing. And now, I would commend you to seek this Jesus of whom the prophets and apostles have written, that the grace of God the Father, and also the Lord Jesus Christ, and the Holy Ghost, which beareth record of them, may be and abide in you forever. Amen." (Ether 12:39–41)

I can say, like Alma:

"And now, behold, I say unto you, and I would that ye should remember, that God is merciful unto all who believe on his name; therefore he desireth, in the first place, that ye should believe, yea, even on his word. And now, he imparteth his word by angels unto men, yea, not only men but women also. Now this is not all; little children do have words given unto them many times, which confound the wise and the learned." (Alma 32:22–23)

I am a faithful Mormon, who, like the missionaries who first told me of Joseph Smith and God's answer to his prayer, also affirms that God does still answer prayer. He is accessible and willing to make Himself known to anyone who follows the path to get that knowledge.

"Verily, thus saith the Lord: It shall come to pass that every soul who forsaketh his sins and cometh unto me, and calleth on my name, and obeyeth my voice, and keepeth my com-

mandments, shall see my face and know that I am . . ." (D&C
93:1)

If there is a problem with Mormonism today, it is that it doesn't
believe and practice the original faith restored through Joseph Smith.
Leaders have inadvertently put themselves between the members and
God. They don't belong there. I have written eight books (at great
personal cost) showing respect to the church, gratitude for all it has
done and is doing to preserve the faith restored through Joseph, but
also reminding all who read that it is ultimately about connecting
with Jesus Christ. You will be damned if you are a successful Mormon with a good relationship with the brethren, but neglect your
relationship with Christ.

Those in the Strengthening the Membership Committee are in the
gall of bitterness when they suggest my writings are threatening to
them. To promote faith in Christ threatens their fiefdom? To testify
of Christ somehow diminishes the men who claim to represent
Him? The idea is so patently off kilter that it reveals a dark motive to
place respect for men above faith in Christ. I make no apologies for
my testimony of Christ. Nor for my healthy skepticism of men. We
are given free agency and we are required to use it. We must have the
choice. Everyone has to choose. No matter how good the man is,
men are all prone to mistakes, to vanity and pride, and to self-interests
above the interests of others.

I am and will always remain a Mormon. I have more than faith in
the religion, I have knowledge from Christ about my standing before
Him. Therefore, I state with confidence what I believe, knowing that
the Lord has made things known to me which He has kept hidden
from others simply because they will not ask Him and let Him inform them also. My confidence in the religion is not the same as my
confidence in the church, and this misbehavior by the Strengthening
the Members Committee only reduces confidence in these mere men.

Despite the fact that the church has changed dramatically in the four decades since I joined, I have not changed all that much. Because of the increasing changes and the pace at which those changes are now taking place, I began to look into church history. What I concluded is shared in *Passing The Heavenly Gift*. It is my effort to help all those fellow believers who are disoriented by the increasingly rapid changes made by the church. If it isn't "true" then disprove it. However, if it is, then why persecute me for telling the truth?

The truth will prevail. No matter who fights against it, it will prevail. I will stand with truth, and against all who oppose it; either high or low, inside or outside the church. The truth matters. Men and institutions do not.

POWER IN THE
PRIESTHOOD

Here is a quote from the *Journal of Discourses* recently brought to my attention:

"This failure to realize all the blessings and powers of the Priesthood does not apply to the elders and lesser Priesthood only; but it applies to the higher quorums, and comes home to ourselves, who are Apostles of Jesus Christ. We are presented before the Church, and sustained as prophets, seers and revelators, and we have received oftentimes the gift of prophecy and revelation, and have received many great and glorious gifts. But have we received the fullness of the blessings to which we are entitled? No, we have not. Who, among the Apostles have become seers, and enjoy all the gifts and powers pertaining to that calling? And those who are called to perform special missions in opening up dispensations of the Gospel to the children of men, as Joseph and others were called of the Lord, He endows more fully with these gifts; but this does not hinder others from enjoying similar gifts according to His promises, and according to our faithfulness. And I have thought the reason why we have not enjoyed these gifts more fully is, because we have not sought for them as diligently as we ought. I speak for one, I have not sought as diligently as I might have done. More than forty years have passed away since these promises were made. I have been blessed with some revelations and prophecies, and with dreams of things that have come to pass; but as to seeing things as a seer, and beholding heavenly things in open vision, I have not attained to these things. And who is to blame for this? Not the Lord; not brother Joseph—they are not to blame. And so it is with the promises made to you in your confirmations and endowments, and by the patriarchs, in your patriarchal blessings; we do not live up to our privileges as saints of God and elders of Israel; for though we receive many blessings that are promised to us, we do not receive them in their fullness, because we do not seek for them as diligently and faithfully as we should." (Orson Pratt, *JD* 25:145–146)

This candid statement of Elder Orson Pratt is a beautiful and faith promoting statement from an earnest and faithful Apostle. He was called by the Lord, through revelation to Joseph Smith, and held the office given him. His lament of failing to attain, because of a lack of diligence, should summon to each of us a renewed resolve to be faithful and true to the Lord. When so many have fallen short, the Lord deserves to have someone succeed. Why is that not you? Why do you not summon the faith and diligence to become His friend? This is an open invitation to everyone.[2001] Therefore it is an invitation to you.

I think the best way to view all priesthood assignments in the church as entirely probationary. That is, ordination is an invitation to come and receive. It is up to each individual whether they will come and will receive. Ordination is invitation. Acceptance is through living the principles and ordinances of the Gospel.

The Lord often spoke to "the elders of my church" as one category, in contrast to "priesthood" which is another category. We con-

---

[2001] D&C 93:1 "VERILY, thus saith the Lord: It shall come to pass that every soul who forsaketh his sins and cometh unto me, and calleth on my name, and obeyeth my voice, and keepeth my commandments, shall see my face and know that I am;"

flate the two. An elder is invited to become an actual priesthood holder, but that is dependent upon heaven, alone. It may be conferred on us, but heaven must ratify.[2002] Therefore, there are a lot of elders in the church who have no priesthood. Yet they have an authoritative invitation to connect with heaven and rise up and receive it.

We conflate so many things because we tend to be lazy. We want to be able to acquire priestly authority as easily as we acquire a merit badge. It just does not, cannot work that way. Heaven controls that end of our faith. We conform to the conditions or we do not receive. The test is measured in our hearts, not just in our outward conduct. I suspect Elder Orson Pratt was never closer to attaining what he sought than when he humbly confessed his failure and sincere desire. His heart seems broken, his confession sincere, his desire authentic.

When someone has the fullness of the priesthood, they have the ability to ask and get an answer. When Joseph received it by the voice of God in the early 1830's, the Lord confirmed "I restore all things, and make known unto you all things in due time".[2003] When the voice of God declared that it was also to be upon Hyrum Smith, it was declared by revelation that he would have the keys "whereby he may ask and receive".[2004] When Nephi, son of Helaman received it, the Lord declared:

[2002] D&C 121:36–37 "That the rights of the priesthood are inseparably connected with the powers of heaven, and that the powers of heaven cannot be controlled nor handled only upon the principles of righteousness. That they may be conferred upon us, it is true; but when we undertake to cover our sins, or to gratify our pride, our vain ambition, or to exercise control or dominion or compulsion upon the souls of the children of men, in any degree of unrighteousness, behold, the heavens withdraw themselves; the Spirit of the Lord is grieved; and when it is withdrawn, Amen to the priesthood or the authority of that man."

[2003] D&C 132:45 "For I have conferred upon you the keys and power of the priesthood, wherein I restore all things, and make known unto you all things in due time."

[2004] D&C 124:95 "That he may act in concert also with my servant Joseph; and that he shall receive counsel from my servant Joseph, who shall show unto him the keys whereby he may ask and receive, and be crowned with the same blessing, and glory, and honor, and priesthood, and gifts of the priesthood, that once were put upon him that was my servant Oliver Cowdery;"

"all things shall be done unto thee according to thy word, for thou shalt not ask that which is contrary to my will" (Helaman 10:5).

Joseph Smith explained this relationship when referring to Noah conversing with the Lord preliminary to destroying the wicked. Noah was told by the Lord how he (Noah) could save himself and his family. Joseph explained,

> "thus we behold the Keys of this priesthood consisted in obtaining the voice of Jehovah that he talked with him in a familiar and friendly manner, that he continued to him the Keys, the Covenants, the power and the glory with which he blessed Adam at the beginning and the offering of Sacrifice which also shall be continued at the last time, for all the ordinances and duties that ever have been required by the priesthood under the direction and commandments of the Almighty." (*Words of Joseph Smith*, 5 October 1840, Monday morning, Robert B. Thompson's account; spellings corrected.)

One of the reasons we know Joseph Smith had the fullness was his ability to always get an answer to his inquiries. During his life, the Lord called the church a "true and living" church because it was in constant communication with the Lord.[2005] While Joseph was at the head, the church could always ask and get an answer from the Lord through him. There was never any reason for the church or its leaders to speak in the absence of revelation. The Lord hearkened to Joseph. Joseph held "the keys of the mysteries and the revelations".[2006]

[2005] D&C 1:30 "And also those to whom these commandments were given, might have power to lay the foundation of this church, and to bring it forth out of obscurity and out of darkness, the only true and living church upon the face of the whole earth, with which I, the Lord, am well pleased, speaking unto the church collectively and not individually—"

[2006] D&C 28:7 "For I have given him the keys of the mysteries, and the revelations which are sealed, until I shall appoint unto them another in his stead."

He had the "keys of the mysteries of the kingdom".[2007] He held the "keys of the kingdom".[2008] Joseph had "this greater priesthood [which] administereth the gospel and holdeth the key of the mysteries of the kingdom, even the key of the knowledge of God".[2009] For Joseph, the fullness was getting answers, solving mysteries and always using revelation to do so.

When the Lord designated Hyrum to receive this same authority, then the Lord was bound to also heed Hyrum's inquiries and answer him. Joseph could be removed, but the church still had someone at the head who would be able to ask and get an answer, just as with Joseph.

It is a great thing when the church is "true and living" and has, at its head, someone like Joseph or Hyrum who could ask and get an answer. That is why it is so puzzling and offensive for the church's press spokesman to recently claim the church's leaders for generations spoke "in the absence of revelation" about a matter of critical importance for salvation of an entire race of people. When they said:

> "The origins of the priesthood availability are not entirely clear. Some explanations with respect to this matter were made in the absence of direct revelation and references to these explanations are sometimes cited in publications. These personal statements do not represent Church doctrine."[2010]

[2007] D&C 64:5 "And the keys of the mysteries of the kingdom shall not be taken from my servant Joseph Smith, Jun., through the means I have appointed, while he liveth, inasmuch as he obeyeth mine ordinances."

[2008] D&C 81:2 "Unto whom I have given the keys of the kingdom, which belong always unto the Presidency of the High Priesthood:"

[2009] D&C 84:19 "And this greater priesthood administereth the gospel and holdeth the key of the mysteries of the kingdom, even the key of the knowledge of God."

[2010] LDS Church Newsroom, Official Statement, "Race and the Church: All are Alike unto God", located at http://www.mormonnewsroom.org/article/race-church

The church has repeatedly claimed to have the fullness of the priesthood, therefore it is a terrible indictment of Brigham Young, John Taylor, Wilford Woodruff, Lorenzo Snow, Joseph F. Smith, Heber J. Grant, J. Reuben Clark, David O. McKay, among many others, that they spoke "in the absence of direct revelation." This surprising claim by the press spokesman contradicts the established order, recognized authority, and most importantly the church's claims. I have taken some criticism for suggesting an alternative view of our history in my last book, but I've never made such an attack as this. This is a serious accusation, and one which the spokesman ought to provide us with an explanation. Did the leadership proceed on a matter of such importance "in the absence of revelation?" That seems heartless and unkind. Perhaps it was, but I would hope we would have some follow up explanation, because the assertion is troubling.

I wanted to respond to some of last week's comments:

There is a difference between calling and election and Second Comforter. I've written about the Second Comforter, but haven't ever commented on calling and election other than what is said in *Beloved Enos*. It isn't useful, in my view, to spend time discussing or studying a topic that is between the individual and the Lord, because if they are brought to the Lord, they will receive what He intends for them to receive.

In a quote from Joseph Smith (on page 3 of *The Second Comforter*) the order he puts these events in is the calling and election first, and Second Comforter second. However, as I pointed out in Beloved Enos, it did not happen in that order for Joseph.

These are important concepts to understand. But knowing the concept and then undertaking the process are quite separate things. I have friends who know a good deal more about the literature of deep Mormon doctrine than they have the capacity to practice in their lives. I think you draw closer to the Lord when you faithfully serve in primary, or as a home teacher, or as a young women's counselor than when you are amassing knowledge of trivia about our history or doctrine. It is in the *doing* that the learning occurs. We must do what the Lord asks to understand Him. The four part Power in the Priesthood series will address that issue.

The idea of "evil speaking" has never been clearly defined by anyone, including the scriptures. Implicit in the idea is that you are trying to falsely make someone hated or reviled. You are, in essence, seeking to make a good man, or an innocent act to appear evil or corrupt when it is not. In essence you are calling good evil and evil good. The measure for that is best taken from inside the person. That is, they intend to call someone or something which is good or innocent as "evil" when they know or should know better. It reflects a malignant or at least indifferent heart.

I have suggested "the Lord's anointed" should be interpreted to be anyone who has been through the temple, which is the broadest meaning. I've never thought it is safe to narrowly define obligations. If we are wrong by narrowly defining the term, then we miss the mark. Whereas, if we are wrong in broadly defining the term, we proceed cautiously and safely.

I understand "sustaining" or "supporting" the Brethren to be doing what we are asked when asked. We get assignments or callings, and we ought to do them. When, we are asked to obey the word of wisdom, or we are asked to attend a conference, or to undertake some kind of conduct, then we do it.

On following the Prophet: I think that is quite easy. What, exactly, do you find hard about this? It is not at all difficult to attend sacrament meetings, pay tithing, do our home teaching, attend the temple, etc. They really do not ask much of us. What they do ask is by and large simple. What is the problem? The scriptures ask of us a *lot* more. It is not incompatible for you to do everything the church asks, and still pursue the things you understand the scriptures instruct you to do. They are not mutually exclusive. They are complimentary. Or, at least they ought to be. In my experience they are complimentary and the one (what the Prophet asks of us) is by far the easier of the two. I wish the scriptures (and the Lord) only wanted what we are asked to do as active members of the church. Full, faithful, diligent service in the church is a small thing. Each of us should willingly submit to it, and find joy in service there. Faithful Latter-day Saints are among the best people on earth, and are actually seeking to find God.

On detailed knowledge of church history: For faithful, active and satisfied Latter-day Saints: It certainly isn't necessary, no. But everything needs perspective. Ultimately you are alone in your test, in being proven, in finding God. The church is a profound help and a great hindrance. It is a help in all it has preserved: ordinances, scriptures, organization, libraries of material and the venue for performing ordinances and meetings. It is a hindrance when it becomes a substitute for God, and refocuses your attention away from the Lord. If you can receive its help without becoming idolatrous, then detailed study of church history is not useful or necessary. For disaffected, alienated and inactive Latter-day Saints: It is necessary, yes. It puts into perspective the things which have alienated them. When the weaknesses of men are apparent, they are easier to forgive and for you to move on to finding God. When you can see the hand of God moving in spite of the weaknesses and failing of men, you can resort the things which alienated you, put into categories the mistakes and errors, find what is good and retain faithfulness to that goodness.

On my schedule: It isn't important.

On evil spirits: I've never felt it important to discuss the topic. They exist. One of the side-effects of an inordinate preoccupation with the topic is the misunderstanding that you can relate to them. You can't. They are your enemy. Their tool in trade is deception and lying. Summary dismissal is what is taught in the scriptures and in the temple and should be the approach when dealing with them.

Internal committees of the church are all presided over by a general authority. When the committee works, they work as a group of men assigned to the task, and churn out their product. The assigned general authority will meet on occasion with them, some weekly, some monthly, some less often, to "preside" and give face time to the committee. The committee produces a product or a project and whatever that is is said to belong to the general authority because it is "his" committee. In truth, however, the work goes on among the faceless, nameless members with little more than thin oversight by the assigned general authority. This gives the Correlation process its power because the committee uses the general authority's name to shield themselves from criticism or accountability. It is "Elder Holland" or "Elder Ballard" who takes the assigned credit for "his" committee's product. This insures that even though he has but very little to do with it, the work-product is regarded as his. Almost anyone would question a bureaucratic process and decision if they knew how it worked. However, almost no active church member would dare to question "Elder Oaks." Speaking of Elder Oaks, he gets credit for the Sunday School Manual because that's his committee.

Interestingly, in one of the Mormon Stories Podcasts, a member of the BYU Religion Department who helped write the manual told an amusing story. (I think it was Peterson, but I'm not sure.) In a New Testament manual book of Acts, there is the incident where Paul spoke till midnight. He put a young man to sleep who fell from the window and died.[2011] One of the discussion questions he put into the draft manual was something to the effect, "Have you ever killed anyone in a Sacrament Meeting talk?" Of course this was tongue-in-cheek. To his surprise, the question made it through to the print proof stage before he removed it. The story shows just how "tightly" the manual committee actually scrutinizes their work. A good many of those involved are more interested in the "face time" with the presiding general authority, hoping that will give them opportunity for advancement in the structure. I believe you can be critical of a committee without having anything in mind for the general authority who has the unfortunate assignment of being "over" the committee. The purpose of Correlation is to conflate the two. Correlation relies on that conflation to work their disastrous mischief presently underway. There are a significant number of general authorities who would undo Correlation, and that number is growing.

At some point I will contrast the Light of Christ, Spirit of Christ, Holy Ghost, and gift of the Holy Ghost. But that's not appropriate in a quick response here.

Fasting in the form of abstaining from all food and drink may not be practical for the elderly, those who are diabetic or ill. For some, refraining from food and drink is possible without any danger to their health, but if they choose to do so for more than a day, then eating once in the evening allows the fast to continue the next day. For someone unable to fast, but who can surrender some part of

---

[2011] Acts 20:7–12 "And upon the first *day* of the week, when the disciples came together to break bread, Paul preached unto them, ready to depart on the morrow; and continued his speech until midnight. And there were many lights in the upper chamber, where they were gathered together. And there sat in a window a certain young man named Eutychus, being fallen into a deep sleep: and as Paul was long preaching, he sunk down with sleep, and fell down from the third loft, and was taken up dead. And Paul went down, and fell on him, and embracing *him* said, Trouble not yourselves; for his life is in him. When he therefore was come up again, and had broken bread, and eaten, and talked a long while, even till break of day, so he departed. And they brought the young man alive, and were not a little comforted."

their diet—abstaining from all sweets, for example—it can serve the purpose. Underlying the idea of the fast are two things. First, submission to God. Second, aiding the poor.[2012] You can accomplish those purposes even if the "fast" you choose has nothing to do with food. However, our appetite for food is one of the most direct ways to discipline the will of the body. Remember though, it is your thoughts, not your belly, where the real battle is fought.

Christ sanctifies us, we don't sanctify ourselves. Our "righteousness" is borrowed from Him. It can be symbolized in this way. He provides a white robe, we put it on, and then He looks upon the whiteness and purity of the robe we received from Him and treats us as if the borrowed robe is our condition. We owe Him for that. He is willing to proceed with us as if we merited the robe.[2013]

Colors all have symbolic meaning. Blue is the color of priesthood. Red is the color of judgment. Gold is the color of heavenly royalty. Green is the color of healing. There are colors we can't see. All you have to do to make something veiled from our view is to put that color on what you want to conceal. It is rather like our own practice of wearing camouflage when hunting.

Power in the Priesthood, Part 2

When Joseph Smith was confined to Liberty Jail, suffering personal abuse and abuse for his people at the hands of government, he received a revelation regarding abuse of authority. However, it was not about the power or authority of government, but instead about abusing the power of God. Sitting in a Missouri dungeon, Joseph

---

[2012] Isaiah 58:6 "*Is* not this the fast that I have chosen? to loose the bands of wickedness, to undo the heavy burdens, and to let the oppressed go free, and that ye break every yoke?"

[2013] 2 Nephi 9:14 "Wherefore, we shall have a perfect knowledge of all our guilt, and our uncleanness, and our nakedness; and the righteous shall have a perfect knowledge of their enjoyment, and their righteousness, being clothed with purity, yea, even with the robe of righteousness."

(and all those who read this revelation) are cautioned about how to handle priesthood. Things all follow rules, or laws ordained before the foundation of the world.[2014] They cannot be violated and are invoked whenever men make choices. Choices lead to consequences, and these are ordained by God. We are free to choose. But we are not free to change the consequences.

The power of priesthood is connected with heaven. If any of us sever that connection we sever the priesthood.[2015] If or when we abuse others by exercising unrighteous "control, dominion or compulsion" and thereby forfeit priesthood, we are left to ourselves. We no longer have a connection to heaven. This is true of husbands who "rule" over wives by claim of priesthood. This is true of any of us serving in the church.

The priesthood is to bless others. It succeeds when we elevate others, bless their lives, bring them truth, and connect them with the Lord. When we focus on ourselves, or seek our own vainglory, we are abusing the priesthood and therefore, do not possess it. It is a call to serve, to kneel and wash another's feet. It is not to claim superiority over anyone we are asked to serve.

[2014] D&C 130:20–21 "There is a law, irrevocably decreed in heaven before the foundations of this world, upon which all blessings are predicated— And when we obtain any blessing from God, it is by obedience to that law upon which it is predicated."

[2015] D&C 121:36–37 "That the rights of the priesthood are inseparably connected with the powers of heaven, and that the powers of heaven cannot be controlled nor handled only upon the principles of righteousness. That they may be conferred upon us, it is true; but when we undertake to cover our sins, or to gratify our pride, our vain ambition, or to exercise control or dominion or compulsion upon the souls of the children of men, in any degree of unrighteousness, behold, the heavens withdraw themselves; the Spirit of the Lord is grieved; and when it is withdrawn, Amen to the priesthood or the authority of that man."

When we behave like the "gentiles",[2016] we are left without authority or power.

This solitary state of being alone, without God in the world,[2017] or being "left to himself" has a natural progression. The progression that follows, once our priesthood is gone, is that we "kick against the pricks"—meaning we then oppose the will of God, and it will harm us.[2018] It is a law we are following. We cannot help ourselves. We must thereafter oppose the will of God and bring harm upon ourselves. In doing so, we also must "persecute the saints"—meaning that when this route is taken, we will look for and oppose those who have remained in contact with the Lord.[2019] It is a natural result, and it is irresistible. If this is the chosen course, anyone who follows it *must* seek out and oppose those who follow God's will, because they "fight against God" when they are in this gall of bitterness.

This an explanation about *priesthood abuse.* It cannot apply until someone has first been ordained, or in other words "called" to a priestly office. This is entirely internal to the church and its officers.

Further, the one engaging in the abuse must be in a position to actually assert "control" or "dominion" or "compulsion" over others. That would not include those who are not in positions of authority. Those who have no right to claim control, dominion or compulsion under the claim of priestly office would not be able to abuse

---

[2016] Luke 22:24–26 "And there was also a strife among them, which of them should be accounted the greatest. And he said unto them, The kings of the Gentiles exercise lordship over them; and they that exercise authority upon them are called benefactors. But ye *shall* not *be* so: but he that is greatest among you, let him be as the younger; and he that is chief, as he that doth serve."

[2017] Mormon 5:16 "For behold, the Spirit of the Lord hath already ceased to strive with their fathers; and they are without Christ and God in the world; and they are driven about as chaff before the wind."

[2018] D&C 121:38 "Behold, ere he is aware, he is left unto himself, to kick against the pricks, to persecute the saints, and to fight against God."

[2019] Ibid.

that power. In other words, this revelation to Joseph Smith about abusing priestly authority or status is a fundamental statement of how we conduct our church. It is how we are to behave while serving in church offices.

Note also, it would apply broadly in any context where someone relies on their "priesthood" as a basis for claiming priority or demanding surrender. For most men, that hits closest in their marriage. Persuasion, gentleness, meekness and love unfeigned has its greatest application within the family. Fathers should lead always with "pure knowledge" and through revelation.

The result is that while many are called (offered the chance to receive priesthood from heaven) only very few will be chosen, or receive power in their priesthood.[2020] Along the way the many who are called will refuse to submit to heaven and will instead become preoccupied with "covering their sins, gratifying their pride, and accomplishing their vain ambition."[2021] When they do this they will exercise unrighteous control over others, establish their dominion, and wield control over the souls of men. This is the order the Lord's return will crush, because it is the commerce of Babylon to trade in the "souls of men."[2022] Churches, like the Roman Catholic Church, or some of the Fundamentalist LDS sects, claim to hold keys to consign men to hell or raise them to heaven. Such purported keys and power from God let them trade in the souls of men. These are the

---

[2020] D&C 121:34, 40 "Behold, there are many called, but few are chosen. And why are they not chosen? Hence many are called, but few are chosen."

[2021] D&C 121:37 "That they may be conferred upon us, it is true; but when we undertake to cover our sins, or to gratify our pride, our vain ambition, or to exercise control or dominion or compulsion upon the souls of the children of men, in any degree of unrighteousness, behold, the heavens withdraw themselves; the Spirit of the Lord is grieved; and when it is withdrawn, Amen to the priesthood or the authority of that man."

[2022] Revelation 18:13 "And cinnamon, and odours, and ointments, and frankincense, and wine, and oil, and fine flour, and wheat, and beasts, and sheep, and horses, and chariots, and slaves, and souls of men."

only ones who could conceivably trade in the "souls of men" referred to in Revelation. They are, therefore, Babylon, and the target of the Lord's destruction at His return.

On the other hand, when you find a soul in possession of the priesthood their conduct is altogether different. Since it is impossible to compel men to salvation, the priesthood can only invite, and persuade. The priesthood acknowledges it has the burden to persuade, and to convince, and cannot simply say something is so *because* they have authority.[2023] Those who hold priesthood power can only proceed using "persuasion, long-suffering, gentleness and meekness" to enlighten those with eyes to see.[2024] When this process is followed there is another law which confers upon the practitioner "love unfeigned" for those to whom they minister.[2025] When they walk alongside their Lord and accept His yoke they find His love for others. This is the natural result of obeying the law governing priesthood. Love does not need to be feigned when the Lord bestows it as a grace, or an endowment, or a gift of His Spirit to one who follows Him.

It is a natural occurrence for those who abuse, rebel and apostatize from priestly ordination to then persecute the lowly and insignificant saints of God. It is natural for those who receive and magnify priesthood to find themselves loving the lowly and insignificant saints of God. These are natural gifts, normal graces bestowed by the power of God through laws instituted before the foundation of the world. It is part of the Lord's orderly program.

[2023] D&C 121:41 "No power or influence can or ought to be maintained by virtue of the priesthood, only by persuasion, by long-suffering, by gentleness and meekness, and by love unfeigned;"

[2024] Ibid.

[2025] Ibid.

Power in the Priesthood, Part 3

The most powerful tools in the priesthood are "kindness, and pure knowledge" because these things "greatly enlarge the soul."[2026] In this power, the priesthood holder acts utterly "without hypocrisy" because this power forbids it and cannot be used in that manner. Nor can it be done with guile, or pursuing any course other than the Lord's.[2027] If the priesthood holder does not completely conform to the will of the Lord, they cannot retain priesthood power. The law is violated, the conditions are not met, and the powers of heaven depart from that man. This is why "meekness" is so difficult to recognize. (As explained in *Beloved Enos*.) The attribute is found in the relationship between man and God, not man and man. That is, to be meek is to follow the Lord's will, even when you don't want to do so. Even when it brings you into conflict with your friends, family or community. You measure meekness as between the servant and the Lord, not as between the servant and his critics.

Loving others does not preclude the priestly man from rebuking those he loves from time to time. The rebuke must originate from God and be inspired by His Spirit, not a jealousy or ambition. When a rebuke is delivered by someone motivated by the Holy Ghost, it will not be accompanied by strong feelings, anger or hurt feelings. It will be godly. In other words, it comes from pure intelligence, designed to elevate the target of the rebuke, to reclaim them, and show them God's love. It cannot be motivated by any lower source, or it would not be the product of the Holy Ghost.[2028]

[2026] D&C 121:42 "By kindness, and pure knowledge, which shall greatly enlarge the soul without hypocrisy, and without guile—"

[2027] Ibid.

[2028] D&C 121:43–44 "Reproving betimes with sharpness, when moved upon by the Holy Ghost; and then showing forth afterwards an increase of love toward him whom thou hast reproved, lest he esteem thee to be his enemy; That he may know that thy faithfulness is stronger than the cords of death."

When this pattern is followed, and these conditions are met, then the priesthood holder finds he is able to make intercession for "all men" because he has become a vessel of charity. His "bowels [are] full of charity toward all men" including even "the household of faith" where undoubtedly will be found his persecutors.[2029] For, as the Lord taught, it will be a man's "own household" that will be his foes.[2030] It is always the case that within the community of fellow-believers, there will be many who are hypocrites, cunning deceivers, proud, vain and ambitious men. These sorts always belong to the "household of faith" but instead of following the religion they hold, they employ it as a tool to judge and condemn others. These sorts are the "foes" of the true Saint. Still in all, the priesthood holder will have charity toward them, also. At personal risk they will stay, invite and teach repentance, and work to fulfill the will of the Lord. This is a pattern you should recognize from scripture. The Lord was chief in this example, but there are many others. The Book of Mormon is filled with examples. Hence the need for those who come to possess priesthood to have charity "toward the household of faith" for it will be within that "household" the priestly work is begun.

Power in the priesthood is literally the product of knowing and following the Lord. His friends hold His authority. His friends act within the same pattern, following the same law, observing the same principles, and exciting the same opposition as He did.

Only then can a person understand the saying,

"let virtue garnish thy thoughts unceasingly; then shall thy confidence wax strong in the presence of God; and the doc-

---

[2029] D&C 121:45 "Let thy bowels also be full of charity towards all men, and to the household of faith, and let virtue garnish thy thoughts unceasingly; then shall thy confidence wax strong in the presence of God; and the doctrine of the priesthood shall distil upon thy soul as the dews from heaven."

[2030] Matthew 10:36 "And a man's foes *shall be* they of his own household."

trine of the priesthood shall distil upon thy soul as the dews from heaven." (D&C 121:45)

This is a great mystery to many. But it is an actual process to those who follow the pattern.

As I explained recently, virtue is not righteousness. Virtue is almost always passive, constraining from abrupt and improper behavior. It contains and limits. It is a strong barrier against misconduct. It has protocols and expects behavior to be mild. Righteousness will often require or impose action, sometimes action which exceeds mere virtue. Nephi was constrained to kill Laban. Elijah mocked the false priests. Christ rebuked the Scribes and Pharisees as unclean "whited sepulchers" filled with rot and decay. These kinds of righteous actions are not ungoverned or spontaneous. They are carefully controlled, and are undertaken only when the priesthood holder, whose thoughts are virtuous and disciplined, is led by the power of the Holy Ghost to rebuke sharply. These acts are constrained. They are moved. These servants are taken by God's power to become His instrument to deliver His words. Oftentimes the servant does not enjoy that aspect of serving the Lord, but meekness requires it be done.

When someone is moved to transition from virtue to righteousness there are two direct results. Their confidence in God's presence is strengthened. They know the Master whom they serve. They gain understanding which cannot be obtained in any other way. This is not the natural state for any man.[2031] It is God's power and His grace which allows this to happen. They are confident because of Him. He has comforted them.

Conforming to these principles and being in the presence of God allows such understanding of God and His ways that "the doctrine of the priesthood shall distil upon the soul as the dews from heaven."[2032] Clarity. Simplicity. Understanding. Doctrine. Priesthood. God's ways. His power. His intelligence. The mysteries of God. The knowledge of the truth.

These things are not understood unless they are done. If any one will do the Lord's will, they will know the doctrine, and if they do not do so, it remains a mystery.[2033]

Power in the Priesthood, Conclusion

All things are governed by God's will. In general conference we are taught that we cannot have the Holy Ghost as our companion unless we are obedient and faithful. In a recent example, President Eyring explained how behavior such as looking at "images which incite lust" or inappropriate Internet or media access to pornography,

---

[2031] Isaiah 6:5 "Then said I, Woe *is* me! for I am undone; because I *am* a man of unclean lips, and I dwell in the midst of a people of unclean lips: for mine eyes have seen the King, the Lord of hosts."

Mormon 9:3–5 "Then will ye longer deny the Christ, or can ye behold the Lamb of God? Do ye suppose that ye shall dwell with him under a consciousness of your guilt? Do ye suppose that ye could be happy to dwell with that holy Being, when your souls are racked with a consciousness of guilt that ye have ever abused his laws? Behold, I say unto you that ye would be more miserable to dwell with a holy and just God, under a consciousness of your filthiness before him, than ye would to dwell with the damned souls in hell. For behold, when ye shall be brought to see your nakedness before God, and also the glory of God, and the holiness of Jesus Christ, it will kindle a flame of unquenchable fire upon you."

[2032] D&C 121:45 "Let thy bowels also be full of charity towards all men, and to the household of faith, and let virtue garnish thy thoughts unceasingly; then shall thy confidence wax strong in the presence of God; and the doctrine of the priesthood shall distil upon thy soul as the dews from heaven.

[2033] John 7:17 "If any man will do his will, he shall know of the doctrine, whether it be of God, or *whether* I speak of myself."

or even immodesty or vulgarity will forfeit the companionship of the Holy Ghost.[2034] This is describing how the Holy Ghost is a temporary visitor with most people, even in the church.

The power of priesthood, however, is speaking about a higher order of things. In that order the Holy Ghost is a "constant companion."[2035]

These individuals are no longer wishing they had power in the priesthood, because they have obtained knowledge through the things they have done and the pattern they have followed. They have invoked the law ordained before the foundation of the world and have obtained the associated promised blessings.

The scriptures rarely speak about the instruments of power. In the context of priesthood, however, the Lord does use the image of "scepter"—an indication of wielding the power of God; as well as "dominion"—an image of acting with God's appointment over a charge or stewardship or message given to you by Him. But in this revelation it is used as a symbol to show a connection of the individual to the constant companionship of the Holy Ghost.[2036] The revelation ties "scepter" to "an unchanging scepter of righteousness and truth" coming once "virtue" has "garnished thy thoughts unceasingly." In other words, you have come to see the difference between "virtue" and positive, directed action undertaken on the Lord's behalf and at His insistence through the Holy Ghost.

This is how priesthood power is acquired. It is how all prophets, from Adam to the present, have been called of God and then endowed with power by Him. It is a principle of action, requiring you

---

[2034] Eyring, "God Helps the Faithful Priesthood Holder," General Conference, October 2007.

[2035] D&C 121:46 "The Holy Ghost shall be thy constant companion, and thy scepter an unchanging scepter of righteousness and truth; and thy dominion shall be an everlasting dominion, and without compulsory means it shall flow unto thee forever and ever."

[2036] Ibid.

obey the law under which this power is conferred. It connects you to Him. For He alone is the source of power.

Truth and righteousness go together, but truth requires you to see things as they really are,[2037] not through a distorted lens that tells you all is well when it isn't.[2038] No person can behold the truth unless they are willing to be righteous, and act on what they learn. If they are willing, they will have a scepter forged in the truth and righteousness, in which they see clearly, as if standing in bright daylight while all around them people wander in darkness.[2039]

Such a process gives man dominion over lusts, ambitions, pride and desire to succeed in this world or to have its praise. They follow their Lord and do as He did.[2040] They know Him because they have offered sacrifice for Him in the same pattern as He did. Having obtained dominion over their own desires, they are given that dominion everlastingly, for "[their] dominion shall be an everlasting dominion" and they have overcome the flesh.[2041] The Lord overcame the world. His followers must overcome the world.[2042] When you subdue the desire to be something in this world and lay everything on the altar other than your love of God, you have won the victory. Then the

---

[2037] D&C 93:24 "And truth is knowledge of things as they are, and as they were, and as they are to come;"

[2038] 2 Nephi 28:24 "Therefore, wo be unto him that is at ease in Zion!"

[2039] D&C 50:23–24 "And that which doth not edify is not of God, and is darkness. That which is of God is light; and he that receiveth light, and continueth in God, receiveth more light; and that light groweth brighter and brighter until the perfect day."

[2040] Matthew 26:39 "And he went a little further, and fell on his face, and prayed, saying, O my Father, if it be possible, let this cup pass from me: nevertheless not as I will, but as thou wilt."

[2041] D&C 121:46 "The Holy Ghost shall be thy constant companion, and thy scepter an unchanging scepter of righteousness and truth; and thy dominion shall be an everlasting dominion, and without compulsory means it shall flow unto thee forever and ever."

[2042] D&C 63:47 "He that is faithful and endureth shall overcome the world."

"god of this world" has no claim upon you; for you belong to another.

When the followers of the Lord have gained dominion over their ambitions and lusts, thereby overcoming the world, they receive an everlasting dominion which will allow them to go no more out into the world. They have learned the principles by which all things are governed, and by their knowledge "and without compulsory means it shall flow unto [them] forever."[2043] It is not "compulsory" because they follow the Lord, act with constraint of the Spirit, and know they cannot compel men to come to salvation. They have been taught the three grand truths by which God governs. They can invite, testify, and teach, but they cannot use compulsion. Therefore, they have arrived at the point it is possible to understand the doctrine of the priesthood. They live it, therefore they understand it. They are it, and their understanding reaches into heaven itself.

Joseph knew this. It was revealed to him, and to us through him, but to understand it we must live it like Joseph lived it. For the doctrine is understood only in the doing.[2044] To everyone else it remains only a matter of mystery, or of abuse when they pretend to things which are not given to them.

Everything is in the scriptures and before us all. So we are all accountable for knowledge we claim we possess. Therefore, since we claim to have "all truth" and to offer "salvation" to all the world, even the dead, we will be judged by the standard we claim to hold. It would be wise, therefore, to begin to give careful heed to the scriptures.

[2043] D&C 121:46 "The Holy Ghost shall be thy constant companion, and thy scepter an unchanging scepter of righteousness and truth; and thy dominion shall be an everlasting dominion, and without compulsory means it shall flow unto thee forever and ever."

[2044] John 7:17 "If any man will do his will, he shall know of the doctrine, whether it be of God, or *whether* I speak of myself."

MOSIAH

Mosiah 3:2–4

The third chapter of Mosiah is one of the most important accounts in the Book of Mormon. Like Section 76, the content is delivered by a visionary encounter through the veil with a message sent by God to King Benjamin. This was between Benjamin and the angel. This is the same pattern as Moroni's nighttime visit with Joseph Smith. In both of these encounters the message was for all mankind.

There is no mistake about the source of the message: The angel told King Benjamin to "Awake" in the same manner the Lord called to Samuel in the night, calling him by name.[2045] The "angel of the Lord" after awakening King Benjamin then "stood before him" to speak the message.[2046]

The angel reiterates a second time for King Benjamin to "Awake" —and it is not redundant.[2047] It is one thing to awaken from sleep, it

---

[2045] 1 Samuel 3:3–4 "And ere the lamp of God went out in the temple of the Lord, where the ark of God *was*, and Samuel was laid down *to sleep;* That the Lord called Samuel: and he answered, Here *am* I."

[2046] Mosiah 3:2 "And the things which I shall tell you are made known unto me by an angel from God. And he said unto me: Awake; and I awoke, and behold he stood before me."

[2047] Mosiah 3:3 "And he said unto me: Awake, and hear the words which I shall tell thee; for behold, I am come to declare unto you the glad tidings of great joy."

is another to awaken to the news given by the angel. King Benjamin needed to awaken to both.

In order to "awaken" to the second, Benjamin needed to "hear the words which I shall tell." Or, in other words, to allow the message from God to enter into his heart.[2048]

Benjamin merited the audience, and it was given. The angel was to "declare" this message, and it was the king's duty to listen, then hearken, and then declare to others. It was not a negotiation, or a discussion. It was a declaration. Through that process Benjamin will finally awaken to his own salvation. It is in doing the will of heaven that we all draw near to God.

Before delivering the content of the message, the angel characterizes the message in words similar to what Gabriel would declare to the shepherds keeping watch over the flock at night; "I am come to declare unto you the glad tidings of great joy."[2049] When angels or the Lord explain His ministry to a prophet, the universal reaction is "joy" at the great redemption provided through the suffering of the Lord.[2050] There is always a juxtaposition of the Lord's suffering and universal "joy" at the result obtained from His sacrifice.

[2048] Ibid.

[2049] Ibid.
Luke 2:10 "And the angel said unto them, Fear not: for, behold, I bring you good tidings of great joy, which shall be to all people."

[2050] Moses 7:47 "And behold, Enoch saw the day of the coming of the Son of Man, even in the flesh; and his soul rejoiced, saying: The Righteous is lifted up, and the Lamb is slain from the foundation of the world; and through faith I am in the bosom of the Father, and behold, Zion is with me."
Isaiah 53:10 "Yet it pleased the Lord to bruise him; he hath put *him* to grief: when thou shalt make his soul an offering for sin, he shall see *his* seed, he shall prolong *his* days, and the pleasure of the Lord shall prosper in his hand."

King Benjamin is told, like Zacharias would later be told, "the Lord hath heard thy prayers."[2051] Both men were seeking the welfare of others. In the case of Zacharias the prayer was for the return of the light of God's countenance to Israel. In the case of Benjamin, it was for his people. They were intercessors in similitude of the Lord who would be the Great Intercessor. Therefore, their prayer was aligned with heaven itself.

In response to Benjamin's prayer, the angel declared the Lord "hath judged of thy righteousness, and hath sent me to declare unto thee that thou mayest rejoice."[2052] When the Lord determines a man's "righteousness" is acceptable before Him, then He redeems that man by parting the veil and bringing him into the company of the redeemed.[2053]

Benjamin is not to keep the news of redemption to himself, but he is to "declare unto thy people." We are all required to bear testimony of the truth to one another.[2054] The purpose of King Benjamin bearing testimony is so that others, who receive his testimony "may also be filled with joy."[2055] Of course, if they refuse to receive and accept the testimony, then they do not share in that joy.

This pattern of the angel appearing in quiet solitude, to the lone witness, is the same as the Lord's dealing with Zacharias, Joseph

---

[2051] Mosiah 3:4 "For the Lord hath heard thy prayers, and hath judged of thy righteousness, and hath sent me to declare unto thee that thou mayest rejoice; and that thou mayest declare unto thy people, that they may also be filled with joy."
Luke 1:13 "

[2052] Mosiah 3:4 "For the Lord hath heard thy prayers, and hath judged of thy righteousness, and hath sent me to declare unto thee that thou mayest rejoice; and that thou mayest declare unto thy people, that they may also be filled with joy."

[2053] D&C 76:67 "These are they who have come to an innumerable company of angels, to the general assembly and church of Enoch, and of the Firstborn."

[2054] Mosiah 3:4 "For the Lord hath heard thy prayers, and hath judged of thy righteousness, and hath sent me to declare unto thee that thou mayest rejoice; and that thou mayest declare unto thy people, that they may also be filled with joy."

[2055] Ibid.

Smith, Nephi, Enos, Samuel, Joseph F. Smith, Paul, and Elijah; all of whom were then required to tell others of their testimony. The Lord is the same. He acts the same. We tend to impose on Him rules which have never governed His conduct.

This chapter is one of the most doctrinally rich chapters in the Book of Mormon. It is worth careful study.

Mosiah 3:5–6

The angel speaking to King Benjamin undoubtedly understood doctrine better than we do. If we proceed with that premise then we can learn some things we don't presently know. We can correct the errors we presently have. It is preferable that we allow scriptures to inform us than for us to distort the scriptures to fit our preconceived notions.

The angel declares:

Christ is "the Lord Omnipotent."

Christ is the one "who reigneth" in heaven.

Christ is "from all eternity to eternity."

Christ is the one who will "come down from heaven among the children of men."

Though He is a glorified, eternal God, reigning in heaven, and holding the power to exist from eternity to eternity, He will condescend to "dwell in a tabernacle of clay."[2056]

If you can take that in, then you can understand what Joseph Smith said about "sons of God, who exalt themselves to be gods, before they were born." (*TPJS*, 375).

[2056] Mosiah 3:5 "For behold, the time cometh, and is not far distant, that with power, the Lord Omnipotent who reigneth, who was, and is from all eternity to all eternity, shall come down from heaven among the children of men, and shall dwell in a tabernacle of clay, and shall go forth amongst men, working mighty miracles, such as healing the sick, raising the dead, causing the lame to walk, the blind to receive their sight, and the deaf to hear, and curing all manner of diseases."

To be "exalted" is to already be in possession of what we hope to acquire in mortality. That is, Christ was already exalted. He did not come here for His advancement, according to this angel, but He came and descended into a "tabernacle of clay" in order to serve us.

They (the noble and great) prove us. They (the noble and great) are not being proven. They are already proven, and have exalted themselves to be gods. This doctrine being taught by the angel to Benjamin agrees with Joseph Smith's Nauvoo era sermons and the lessons in the Book of Abraham. At the end, Joseph was beginning to appreciate the doctrine of the Book of Abraham.

The "Lord Omnipotent" was to put His great power on display by "working mighty miracles" among men. These were to include "healing the sick, raising the dead, causing the lame to walk, the blind to receive their sight, and the deaf to hear, and curing all manner of diseases."[2057] In other words, the Omnipotence of the Lord would not be diminished by the tabernacle of clay He would inhabit. He would bring power with Him, rather than needing power to be given to Him.

It is true enough that He would come with a veil of forgetfulness. He would have to endure the frailties of the tabernacle of clay. He would need to study, search, pray and submit. He would have to walk the exact same path which all of us are required to walk.

It is the great condescension of God because God left His place of glory, descended here and reversed the grip of death on mankind. Once we read the words of the angel, none of us can be mistaken about how great the God's descent was to accomplish this rescue mission. This is not merely "our older Brother" who came here. He is much more, and we are ever indebted to Him.

His power includes and has always included the commanding of devils and casting out evil spirits which men allow to dwell in their

---

[2057] Ibid.

hearts.[2058] He subdued them before and they are required to obey Him here. Though He allowed Michael to physically cast them from heaven,[2059] it was Christ who accomplished the victory there,[2060] and limited Lucifer's power here.

Notice the location of the evil spirits that Christ will cast out. It is from "the hearts of the children of men."[2061] It is in our heart that we dwell on lusts, ambition, unholy desires, anger, jealousy and resentments. It is the center of our feelings that we permit evil to dwell. Christ's victory goes directly to our hearts.

Answer to Michael

Michael: I would be baptized were I you. The church has a commission from the Lord to offer that ordinance to whoever will receive it. If you receive it in faith, you will be benefitted for having done so. The church is where I worship, fellowship, serve and raise my kids. It is a great blessing. It would be wonderful to share fellowship with you in the church.

The Lord has never told me He has abandoned the church, nor do I expect Him to do so. I pray for the church, and do what I can to benefit and advance it. I believe I have obligations I owe to her, and I intend to fulfill those obligations.

[2058] Mosiah 3:6 "And he shall cast out devils, or the evil spirits which dwell in the hearts of the children of men."

[2059] Revelation 12:7–9 "And there was war in heaven: Michael and his angels fought against the dragon; and the dragon fought and his angels, And prevailed not; neither was their place found any more in heaven. And the great dragon was cast out, that old serpent, called the Devil, and Satan, which deceiveth the whole world: he was cast out into the earth, and his angels were cast out with him."

[2060] Moses 4:3 "Wherefore, because that Satan rebelled against me, and sought to destroy the agency of man, which I, the Lord God, had given him, and also, that I should give unto him mine own power; by the power of mine Only Begotten, I caused that he should be cast down;"

[2061] Mosiah 3:6 "And he shall cast out devils, or the evil spirits which dwell in the hearts of the children of men."

Having a realistic view of the church's many failings should not make you turn from it or become bitter toward it. Rather, it should allow you to serve with a renewed dedication in doing what you can that is right. You can be a great example by your service and dedication to the church in spite of what may or may not be wrong with the organization.

On the Internet and in books I've written, I address issues which those searching for answers would be interested in reading. Inside my ward and stake, I am quite content to leave the teaching to those called to teach, the presiding to those called to preside, and the conversations undisturbed by anything negative or challenging from me. I recommend that course because you needn't do more that serve faithfully to influence others. Until they ask, you needn't say a thing.

My ward and stake are remarkable. There are many very admirable acts of service and devotion going on among these faithful members I am privileged to live among. I hope when you join, the ward you enter will be full of similarly faithful members. But if not, take what good they share, and continue your own search. It is an individual religion in any event, and you can't be hindered by others.

Mosiah 3:7

This verse is the greatest summary of what the Lord would suffer in atoning for man's sins given before His mortality. King Benjamin is given this instruction because God wants all mankind to understand the great sacrifice made by the Lord Omnipotent.

Christ suffered "even more than man can suffer, except it be unto death" as part of the burden He bore.[2062] What was the burden?

[2062] Mosiah 3:7 "And lo, he shall suffer temptations, and pain of body, hunger, thirst, and fatigue, even more than man can suffer, except it be unto death; for behold, blood cometh from every pore, so great shall be his anguish for the wickedness and the abominations of his people."

First on the angel's list is "temptations." Isaiah would call it "our griefs" and "our sorrows" and "our transgressions" and "our iniquities."[2063] Alma would call it "afflictions and temptations of every kind."[2064] Paul explained how He "who knew no sin" was made "to be sin" for our sake.[2065] In other words, though Christ was not personally responsible for any transgression, He was made accountable for every one of all our transgressions. He was made "to be sin" and to feel the loathsome filthiness of our unworthiness before God.

Mormon had been in the Lord's presence. He knew how painful it was to be before God in our fallen and guilty state. Mormon explained how terrible it is to bring the weight of your own sins into God's holy presence. He describes it as "under a consciousness of your guilt" and "a consciousness of guilt that ye have ever abused his laws" and "more miserable to dwell with a holy and just God, under a consciousness of your filthiness before him, than ye would be to dwell with the damned souls in hell."[2066] He explains that in God's presence "ye shall be brought to see your nakedness before God"

[2063] Isaiah 53:4–5 "Surely he hath borne our griefs, and carried our sorrows: yet we did esteem him stricken, smitten of God, and afflicted. But he *was* wounded for our transgressions, *he was* bruised for our iniquities: the chastisement of our peace *was* upon him; and with his stripes we are healed."

[2064] Alma 7:11 "And he shall go forth, suffering pains and afflictions and temptations of every kind; and this that the word might be fulfilled which saith he will take upon him the pains and the sicknesses of his people."

[2065] 2 Corinthians 5:21 "For he hath made him *to be* sin for us, who knew no sin; that we might be made the righteousness of God in him."

[2066] Mormon 9:3–4 "Then will ye longer deny the Christ, or can ye behold the Lamb of God? Do ye suppose that ye shall dwell with him under a consciousness of your guilt? Do ye suppose that ye could be happy to dwell with that holy Being, when your souls are racked with a consciousness of guilt that ye have ever abused his laws? Behold, I say unto you that ye would be more miserable to dwell with a holy and just God, under a consciousness of your filthiness before him, than ye would to dwell with the damned souls in hell."

and it "will kindle a flame of unquenchable fire upon you."[2067] Since Mormon had been there, and knew what it was like to behold God's holy presence, he understood the great challenge we all face **if we do not repent.**

When the prophet Isaiah was brought into God's presence he collapsed in guilt and anguish, proclaiming,

> "Woe is me! for I am undone; because I am a man of unclean lips, and I dwell in the midst of a people of unclean lips: for mine eyes have seen the King, the Lord of Hosts." (Isaiah 6:5)

Beholding God brings with it the keenest appreciation of your own unworthiness before Him so it is possible to understand He is a "just and holy Being" in whom there is no darkness.

Christ succumbed to no temptations. Yet He was made to feel the guilt and misery of all mankind's great surrender to sin. Christ explained what that involved when He declared:

> "repent, lest I smite you by the rod of my mouth, and by my wrath, and by my anger, and your sufferings be sore—how sore you know not, how exquisite you know not, yea, how hard to bear you know not. For behold, I, God, have suffered these things for all, that they might not suffer if they would repent; But if they would not repent they must suffer even as I." (D&C 19:15–17)

Christ, looking back on His atonement, called the pain of it "exquisite" and "hard to bear" from a distance of two millennia.

The scriptures tell us how His suffering was accomplished. As He knelt in prayer, He was visited by a "just and holy being" to borrow

---

[2067] Mormon 9:5 "For behold, when ye shall be brought to see your nakedness before God, and also the glory of God, and the holiness of Jesus Christ, it will kindle a flame of unquenchable fire upon you."

Mormon's words.[2068] There, in the presence of the Father, Christ struggled through all the guilt, sorrow, nakedness, consciousness of guilt, and torment of being sinful, unworthy, unclean, and having ever transgressed the law of God. It was an unquenchable fire of emotion and pain, torment of mind, and recognition of failure before God. He, like all the wicked, "trembled because of pain" and "shrank" away from God in horror at His condition.[2069]

Abraham was on the mount with the knife in his hand at the sacrifice of Isaac, and God the Father was present at the sacrifice of His Son. Indeed, Christ's sufferings required the Father to be present in order to reconcile man to the Father. It was the presence of the Father that made the suffering possible. Therefore, we know the identity of the unnamed angel in Luke.[2070] Christ could not have suffered the guilt of all mankind in the presence of a just and holy God, unless during this moment of torment His suffering was before that very Being.

The suffering of Christ in atoning for mankind was not limited to spiritual torment, but was physical as well. The angel explained He would suffer "pain of body, hunger, thirst, and fatigue" as part of His great ordeal.[2071]

[2068] Luke 22:43 "And there appeared an angel unto him from heaven, strengthening him."

[2069] D&C 19:18 "Which suffering caused myself, even God, the greatest of all, to tremble because of pain, and to bleed at every pore, and to suffer both body and spirit—and would that I might not drink the bitter cup, and shrink—"

[2070] Luke 22:43 "And there appeared an angel unto him from heaven, strengthening him."

[2071] Mosiah 3:7 "And lo, he shall suffer temptations, and pain of body, hunger, thirst, and fatigue, even more than man can suffer, except it be unto death; for behold, blood cometh from every pore, so great shall be his anguish for the wickedness and the abominations of his people."

Alma explained this would include "pains and afflictions and temptations of every kind." It would extend into "the sicknesses of his people."[2072] All disease, even death were overcome by Him.

This was so the Lord could rise again, and with healing in His wings[2073] be able to succor all our ills.[2074] Because He has felt all of our "infirmities," whether they are spiritual or physical, there is no limit to His ability to understand our plight and give to us His compassionate aid.[2075]

This does not remove our own cup of suffering. Even the Lord's most favored servants endure suffering, sometimes in perplexing magnitude that seems beyond our ability to endure.[2076] Sometimes the way He consoles the suffering servant is to remind them the Master has endured more.[2077]

[2072] Alma 7:11 "And he shall go forth, suffering pains and afflictions and temptations of every kind; and this that the word might be fulfilled which saith he will take upon him the pains and the sicknesses of his people."

[2073] 2 Nephi 25:13 "Behold, they will crucify him; and after he is laid in a sepulchre for the space of three days he shall rise from the dead, with healing in his wings; and all those who shall believe on his name shall be saved in the kingdom of God. Wherefore, my soul delighteth to prophesy concerning him, for I have seen his day, and my heart doth magnify his holy name."
Malachi 4:2 "But unto you that fear my name shall the Sun of righteousness arise with healing in his wings; and ye shall go forth, and grow up as calves of the stall."

[2074] Alma 7:12 "And he will take upon him death, that he may loose the bands of death which bind his people; and he will take upon him their infirmities, that his bowels may be filled with mercy, according to the flesh, that he may know according to the flesh how to succor his people according to their infirmities."

[2075] Ibid.

[2076] D&C 121:3–4 "Yea, O Lord, how long shall they suffer these wrongs and unlawful oppressions, before thine heart shall be softened toward them, and thy bowels be moved with compassion toward them? O Lord God Almighty, maker of heaven, earth, and seas, and of all things that in them are, and who controllest and subjectest the devil, and the dark and benighted dominion of Sheol—stretch forth thy hand; let thine eye pierce; let thy pavilion be taken up; let thy hiding place no longer be covered; let thine ear be inclined; let thine heart be softened, and thy bowels moved with compassion toward us."

[2077] D&C 121:8 "And then, if thou endure it well, God shall exalt thee on high; thou shalt triumph over all thy foes."

He knows our limits, even if we do not. He protects us by limiting what the faithful endure to only that which we can handle.[2078]

The angel was sent to inform King Benjamin of this (and in turn his people and those who read the Book of Mormon) so we may understand the Lord's purchase of us from death, hell, and torment. He wants us all to understand this so we can take advantage of it by repenting.

If we look upon His suffering and remain unrepentant, then we are left to endure the just punishment for our unrepented sins. According to Christ, who suffered those pains of sin, this is beyond our comprehension.

In pleading for us to repent and turn from our sins, the Lord could only inform us:

> "how sore you know not, how exquisite you know not, yea, how hard to bear you know not. For behold, I, God, have suffered these things for all, that they might not suffer if they would repent; But if they would not repent they must suffer even as I; Which suffering caused myself, even God, the greatest of all, to tremble because of pain, and to bleed at every pore, and to suffer both body and spirit—and would that I might not drink of the bitter cup, and shrink—" (D&C 19:16–18)

Any who have looked upon the suffering of our Lord are moved beyond words at what He endured.

In *Come, Let Us Adore Him* there is a chapter on Gethsemane. The Lord's sufferings came in waves, and included all that mankind has done to one another, all mankind did to Him. This suffering gave Him the right to claim each of us through His victory. It was a hard

---

[2078] 1 Corinthians 10:13 "There hath no temptation taken you but such as is common to man: but God *is* faithful, who will not suffer you to be tempted above that ye are able; but will with the temptation also make a way to escape, that ye may be able to bear *it.*"

won victory. It means nothing if we do not repent. How foolish it is to believe you can escape the claim of justice on your own failings. You cannot. The only way to escape is through the mercy provided by Christ through the price He paid.[2079] As explained by Alma, the redemption which comes from faith in Christ empowers our repentance, so we can take advantage of His atonement by forsaking our sins.[2080] This is a difficult process, involving constant attention to His mercy which redeems you.[2081]

The angel who visited King Benjamin taught the same truths about our Lord as Isaiah:

> "He was wounded for our transgressions, he was bruised for our iniquities: the chastisement of our peace was upon him; and with his stripes we are healed." (Isaiah 53:5)

So why would we reject the invitation to repent? Why in our pride would we talk of God's great favor and blessing of us all? Why would we claim to be chosen, royal and better than others around us? Why would we ever trust for one moment that all is well and we are Zion? Why would we refuse the mercy offered to us by Christ? Why do we prefer pride and self-sufficiency? Why would we claim some man with "keys" can relieve us of our suffering for sins when the

---

[2079] Alma 34:15 "And thus he shall bring salvation to all those who shall believe on his name; this being the intent of this last sacrifice, to bring about the bowels of mercy, which overpowereth justice, and bringeth about means unto men that they may have faith unto repentance."

[2080] Ibid.

[2081] Alma 34:18–27 "Yea, cry unto him for mercy; for he is mighty to save. Yea, humble yourselves, and continue in prayer unto him. Cry unto him when ye are in your fields, yea, over all your flocks. Cry unto him in your houses, yea, over all your household, both morning, mid-day, and evening. Yea, cry unto him against the power of your enemies. Yea, cry unto him against the devil, who is an enemy to all righteousness. Cry unto him over the crops of your fields, that ye may prosper in them. Cry over the flocks of your fields, that they may increase. But this is not all; ye must pour out your souls in your closets, and your secret places, and in your wilderness. Yea, and when you do not cry unto the Lord, let your hearts be full, drawn out in prayer unto him continually for your welfare, and also for the welfare of those who are around you."

Lord has taught us otherwise? What difference does any ordinance, or ordination, or blessing or promise make if we fail to satisfy the demands of repentance in order to lay claim upon them? The realization of all blessings depends upon your faithfulness. It is only if you are true and faithful that you may later be called up and given more than an invitation through a man. Why do you also harden your hearts so that you also cannot enter into God's presence?[2082]

The sermon from the angel to King Benjamin encompasses the fullness of the Gospel of Jesus Christ, because it seeks to teach us how to be redeemed from our sins and enter into the rest of the Lord.

Mosiah 3:8

The angel identifies the Lord by name and title: "Jesus Christ" which is the English version of the Greek form of the name Joshua, or Yesheva, the Anointed or the Messiah. In other words Joshua the Messiah, or Yesheva the Messiah. In our English language equivalent, Jesus Christ.

The name "Christ" is derived from christening, or anointing. Meaning that Christ came to us designated, foretold, sent and anointed with the calling of redeeming mankind. He was God's chosen sacrifice. He came into the world to be offered as the sacrifice that would fulfill all righteousness.

He is also "the Son of God." His entry into this world came as a consequence of the Father having been directly involved in introducing Him here. He is God's own Son. He came with godly parentage, and is capable of offering a godly sacrifice.

[2082] D&C 84:23–24 "Now this Moses plainly taught to the children of Israel in the wilderness, and sought diligently to sanctify his people that they might behold the face of God; But they hardened their hearts and could not endure his presence; therefore, the Lord in his wrath, for his anger was kindled against them, swore that they should not enter into his rest while in the wilderness, which rest is the fulness of his glory."

He is also "the Father of heaven and earth," meaning He did not come here as a novice. He has been through this, and knows and presides over it all. His is the power and glory of the Father. He laid that aside to condescend to be here, but He is in reality and truth, "the Father of heaven and earth."

He is also "the Creator of all things from the beginning." Notwithstanding anything you may have been told to the contrary, the angel knows what he is saying to King Benjamin in this chapter of Mosiah. After all, the angel lives with the very person he is describing. These are not just titles, but hard won identities belonging to the One you call your "Brother." In truth, He is much more than that. He earned His exaltation before this world was begun. Therefore, He had the power to create and organize this world as the "Father of heaven and earth."

The angel adds "and his mother shall be called Mary." The mother of Christ was not selected to become the one who bore Him carelessly. She, too, was known from the foundation of the world, chosen for the role, and trusted by God the Father to bring His Son into the world. Her name is given by this angel to King Benjamin more than a century before He would be born. Consider how important her calling was for a moment, and you will have some idea of how carefully she would have been prepared, even before birth, for this role.

From verses 7 and 8 we have some idea of how significant the Lord's role, titles, power, significance and responsibilities were even before His birth here. We can also contrast the humble, obscure circumstances He came into this world with what great glory was His before birth. The only ones who recognized His birth were His parents, the family of a cousin, a handful of shepherds, and an elderly prophet and prophetess at the Temple of Jerusalem. He came into a family of limited means. He grew up without power, wealth, social standing, control over the church or state, in a beleaguered and subjugated province of Rome These were the circumstances "the Father of heaven and earth" chose to enter mortality. *We* attach such great importance to office. Christ attached nothing to it.

To the extent Christ relied on the presence of official "office," He used it to conceal His presence, and to oppose His mission. He allowed everyone who would see nothing in Him to see just that. For those whose eyes were opened to the things of heaven, He allowed them to see "the Father of heaven and earth" and the "Creator of all things from the beginning."

How often the Lord chooses to send His messengers in exactly the same way as He came! Without rank or office, and without social significance or recognition; as with Abinadi, Samuel, Peter, Luke, Joseph Smith, Amos, and Elijah. The test remains exactly the same in every generation. We can know Alma would have received Christ, because he received Abinadi's teachings. Against the opposition of the society he lived in, Alma heard in the message something from the Lord.

How difficult would it have been to have seen in the obscure and lowly station of Christ the reality that this was the Son of God? For the most part, the "Christian" world flatters themselves into believing they would have recognized and accepted Him if they lived in His day. The only reason most people claim Him now is because of the two millennia of Christian conquest, and traditions of their fathers. If they had to choose a living, teaching Christ of obscure and un-credentialed origin, they would reject Him. They want buildings, budgets, hierarchies, and social acceptance. Today Christianity offers all that to them.

The meek and lowly Lord who came was everything the angel foretold. But He came with no credentials that we should respect Him. No office, that we should recognize Him. No wealth and influence, that we should admire Him. He was without form or the kind of regalia we respect, and therefore no reason to desire Him.[2083]

Mosiah 3:9

> And lo, he cometh unto his own, that salvation might come unto the children of men even through faith on his name; and even after all this they shall consider him a man, and say that he hath a devil, and shall scourge him, and shall crucify him. (Mosiah 3:9)

In Mosiah 3:9 the angel foretells how Christ will "come unto His own" because it will be His own people who were promised He would come.[2084] Therefore, to perform on the promise, the Lord must be sent, but it will be His own who reject Him. Indeed, only His own people would consider rejecting and killing Him, because no other people would be hard-hearted enough to kill their God.[2085] Only those who are given the truth, and harden their hearts against it, can be blinded enough by the devil to pervert the truth. It takes exposure to and rejection of the light for men to sink into rejecting the Lord.

[2083] Isaiah 53:2 "For he shall grow up before him as a tender plant, and as a root out of a dry ground: he hath no form nor comeliness; and when we shall see him, *there is* no beauty that we should desire him."

[2084] Genesis 49:10 "The sceptre shall not depart from Judah, nor a lawgiver from between his feet, until Shiloh come; and unto him *shall* the gathering of the people *be.*"

[2085] 2 Nephi 10:3 "Wherefore, as I said unto you, it must needs be expedient that Christ—for in the last night the angel spake unto me that this should be his name—should come among the Jews, among those who are the more wicked part of the world; and they shall crucify him—for thus it behooveth our God, and there is none other nation on earth that would crucify their God."

This is the pattern throughout God's dealing with His own. Whenever He sent a true messenger, the established order was offended at them. They always behave in this manner.[2086]

This is how salvation comes. There is always authentic tension between good and evil, between the true and the false. The stage is always set with conflict between established tradition that has strayed and inspired messages to clarify. We always see the temporary defeat of truth followed by persistent success of error so the Lord can try the souls of men. Truth returns, within a sea of error, and the humble followers of Christ recognize it. Therefore, through this means "salvation comes unto the children of men".[2087]

This stage is where the participants must choose between the two "through faith." Tradition and community error will not bring you to Christ. In every generation we are required recognize Him, and accept "His name" or, more correctly, His names; for they are many. The angel has been giving some of them. Isaiah gave others. Joseph Smith gave yet more. Those who come to know Him come to know His names, for they are know by His friends.

Even after all the truth represented by our Lord, men will say about Him that He is "a man, and say that he hath a devil."[2088] They call what is good, bad. They insist that what has been sent from heaven is in fact of the devil. By calling God's offering something of the devil, they clarify whose side they are on, and become the servant of the one who leads them. As servants and children of the devil, they

---

[2086] Matthew 5:10–12 "Blessed *are* they which are persecuted for righteousness' sake: for theirs is the kingdom of heaven. Blessed are ye, when *men* shall revile you, and persecute *you*, and shall say all manner of evil against you falsely, for my sake. Rejoice, and be exceeding glad: for great *is* your reward in heaven: for so persecuted they the prophets which were before you."

[2087] Mosiah 3:9 "And lo, he cometh unto his own, that salvation might come unto the children of men even through faith on his name; and even after all this they shall consider him a man, and say that he hath a devil, and shall scourge him, and shall crucify him."

[2088] Ibid.

earn their condemnation by condemning the things of God. Hence the condemnation of suffering described in D&C 76, because they have followed the devil while claiming to have followed prophets and apostles.[2089] They worship men, and traditions of men, but have not received a testimony of Jesus.

To establish the truth and the authority of His commission, the Lord left His suffering as a mark of His authenticity. It would be required for Him to endure both verbal and physical persecution for the sake of His ministry. That will operate as a seal upon His testimony, because only through enduring the opposition of this world can we know for certain the message is not from this world. Only by this world's rejection can we have the certification that the message came from above.

Ultimately, as the angel foretells, the Lord will be "crucified." This clarifies that the Lord in His death would be ceremonially cursed and unclean.[2090] King Benjamin knew the Lord God omnipotent would condescend not only to come and live here among men, but to become cursed and slain for their sake.

What manner of love does our Lord have that He should suffer so? How long suffering and patient is He that He would live a life in this manner? How great a God is it who will forsake this world's success, endure this world's curses in order to remain true and faithful to His great commission?

[2089] D&C 76:99–105 "For these are they who are of Paul, and of Apollos, and of Cephas. These are they who say they are some of one and some of another—some of Christ and some of John, and some of Moses, and some of Elias, and some of Esaias, and some of Isaiah, and some of Enoch; But received not the gospel, neither the testimony of Jesus, neither the prophets, neither the everlasting covenant. Last of all, these all are they who will not be gathered with the saints, to be caught up unto the church of the Firstborn, and received into the cloud. These are they who are liars, and sorcerers, and adulterers, and whoremongers, and whosoever loves and makes a lie. These are they who suffer the wrath of God on earth. These are they who suffer the vengeance of eternal fire."

[2090] Deuteronomy 21:22 "And if a man have committed a sin worthy of death, and he be to be put to death, and thou hang him on a tree:"

It would have been interesting to observe the angel as He explained, and King Benjamin as he heard this promise of the Lord's future life and ministry. Who would believe such a report, even though given by an angel?[2091] Even today, who can believe the Lord's dealings with men?

Mosiah 3:10

The angel's message in Mosiah 3:10 is the same as Zenos' message. Zenos prophesied more than a century before Lehi left Jerusalem. His record was on the brass plates obtained from Laban. During the three days in the tomb, Zenos added the detail that the isles of the sea (which included the Americas[2092]) would be given the sign of three days of darkness.[2093] King Benjamin knew this information from existing scripture. Once the angel declared it, however, rather than having belief in the account based on study, he would have faith of the event because the angel told it from heaven. The Book of Mormon regularly moves one from belief, to faith, to knowledge. This is an example of moving from belief based on study of scripture, to faith based on the testimony of an angel.

[2091] Isaiah 53:1 "Who hath believed our report? and to whom is the arm of the Lord revealed?"

[2092] 2 Nephi 10:20 "And now, my beloved brethren, seeing that our merciful God has given us so great knowledge concerning these things, let us remember him, and lay aside our sins, and not hang down our heads, for we are not cast off; nevertheless, we have been driven out of the land of our inheritance; but we have been led to a better land, for the Lord has made the sea our path, and we are upon an isle of the sea."

[2093] 1 Nephi 19:10 "And the God of our fathers, who were led out of Egypt, out of bondage, and also were preserved in the wilderness by him, yea, the God of Abraham, and of Isaac, and the God of Jacob, yieldeth himself, according to the words of the angel, as a man, into the hands of wicked men, to be lifted up, according to the words of Zenock, and to be crucified, according to the words of Neum, and to be buried in a sepulchre, according to the words of Zenos, which he spake concerning the three days of darkness, which should be a sign given of his death unto those who should inhabit the isles of the sea, more especially given unto those who are of the house of Israel."

Not only would the Lord rise from the dead, but He would also "stand to judge the world." That is an important reference. It identifies the Lord's status as judge, and it clarifies He would "stand" to judge the world. The word "stand" is symbolic. It implies, among many other things:

- He will endure.
- He will be in control.
- He will triumph.
- He will rise up.
- He will command respect and obedience.

However, the strongest implication is that after death He will return to life to "stand" to judge the world. He who passed through the grave, and triumphed over it, will live again as the triumphant judge of the living and dead— for He has been both.

He gains capacity as He passes through these states. He does all these things "that a righteous judgment might come upon the children of men." Or, the judge will necessarily experience all He will go through so He can understand all things required for a proper judgment.[2094]

God's mercy is extended to all who have "fallen by the transgression of Adam" or, the death that comes upon mankind will be defeated.[2095] Christ's death, or His "blood atoneth" for mankind's death. Through the infinite sacrifice of an innocent life, death is satisfied. It would be unjust to ask for more than an everlasting life, for

---

[2094] D&C 88:41 "He comprehendeth all things, and all things are before him, and all things are round about him; and he is above all things, and in all things, and is through all things, and is round about all things; and all things are by him, and of him, even God, forever and ever."

[2095] D&C 88:14–17 "Now, verily I say unto you, that through the redemption which is made for you is brought to pass the resurrection from the dead. And the spirit and the body are the soul of man. And the resurrection from the dead is the redemption of the soul. And the redemption of the soul is through him that quickeneth all things, in whose bosom it is decreed that the poor and the meek of the earth shall inherit it."

by definition that life is infinite. Christ deserved everlasting life. Instead He submitted to death.

"The sins" of Adam's descendants are paid, also. He will blot them out. However, those who refuse to repent, or turn away from their sins will remain "filthy still."[2096] They may have the power to return from the grave through Christ's grace. However, if they refuse to abandon their sins, forgiving them will accomplish nothing. Because they love their sins, they remain as if there were no redemption made.

All those who died without knowing the will of God are also benefited by His atonement. For them it will be "tolerable" in the day of resurrection.[2097] Though they may not have received a fullness because they failed to qualify,[2098] they may still be "added upon".[2099] Joseph explained it this way:

> "When you climb up a ladder, you must begin at the bottom, and ascend step by step, until you arrive at the top; and so it is with the principles of the gospel—you must begin with the first, and go on until you learn all the principles of exaltation. But it will be a great while after you have passed through the veil before you will have learned them. It is not all to be comprehended in this world; it will be a great work to learn our salvation and exaltation even beyond the grave." (King Follett Discourse, *TPJS*, 348)

[2096] D&C 88:35 "That which breaketh a law, and abideth not by law, but seeketh to become a law unto itself, and willeth to abide in sin, and altogether abideth in sin, cannot be sanctified by law, neither by mercy, justice, nor judgment. Therefore, they must remain filthy still."

[2097] D&C 45:54 "And then shall the heathen nations be redeemed, and they that knew no law shall have part in the first resurrection; and it shall be tolerable for them."

[2098] D&C 130:20–21 "There is a law, irrevocably decreed in heaven before the foundations of this world, upon which all blessings are predicated— And when we obtain any blessing from God, it is by obedience to that law upon which it is predicated."

[2099] Abraham 3:26 "And they who keep their first estate shall be added upon; and they who keep not their first estate shall not have glory in the same kingdom with those who keep their first estate; and they who keep their second estate shall have glory added upon their heads for ever and ever."

No one can arrive at the throne of God in any other way than all have taken to arrive there. Everyone develops the same way, through the successive stages of Jacob's Ladder.

Christ's atonement makes it possible for all of us to attempt that trek.

Mosiah 3:11–13

The angel informed King Benjamin that Christ's blood is intended to atone for the sins of those who sinned ignorantly, or those who died without knowing God's will.[2100] However, there is a twofold wo pronounced on those who know they rebel against God. They are cast down, and for them there will be no hope, no salvation, "except it be through repentance and faith on the Lord Jesus Christ."[2101] That of course, must happen before they die.

The angel explained the Lord has sent "his holy prophets among all the children of men."[2102] When the Lord sends someone with a message, they are by definition "holy" because they bear the message of God. Having been entrusted with His word, they are derivatively holy.[2103] It does not mean they are better than other men because everyone sins. The content of what God has given them makes them

---

[2100] Mosiah 3:11 "For behold, and also his blood atoneth for the sins of those who have fallen by the transgression of Adam, who have died not knowing the will of God concerning them, or who have ignorantly sinned."

[2101] Mosiah 3:12 "But wo, wo unto him who knoweth that he rebelleth against God! For salvation cometh to none such except it be through repentance and faith on the Lord Jesus Christ."

[2102] Mosiah 3:13 "And the Lord God hath sent his holy prophets among all the children of men, to declare these things to every kindred, nation, and tongue, that thereby whosoever should believe that Christ should come, the same might receive remission of their sins, and rejoice with exceedingly great joy, even as though he had already come among them."

[2103] Acts 9:15 "But the Lord said unto him, Go thy way: for he is a chosen vessel unto me, to bear my name before the Gentiles, and kings, and the children of Israel:"

"holy" before God. Since King Benjamin has just been entrusted with God's message for his people, King Benjamin has become "holy" also.

The messages have been sent, at one time or another, "among all the children of men." All nations have had some portion of the word of God given to them. This does not mean they have been given a fullness, for that is rarely given. It does mean the Lord has concern over all of us and will call and send prophets to everyone.

How people react to what they are offered determines how much a prophet is able to teach them. If they will not give heed, then the audience receives only a portion of what they might have received.[2104] Sometimes people can be offered a "fullness" and reject it, and then have it taken from them.[2105]

The purpose of the message is for all to have "exceedingly great joy."[2106]

This joy comes from knowing the Lord. Knowing Him comes from obeying the words given to them through the "holy prophets."

One of the greatest laments of the Lord arises from how the world reacts to His holy prophets. He makes the same offer every time, whenever He calls someone as His spokesman. The offer is by

---

[2104] Alma 12:9 "And now Alma began to expound these things unto him, saying: It is given unto many to know the mysteries of God; nevertheless they are laid under a strict command that they shall not impart only according to the portion of his word which he doth grant unto the children of men, according to the heed and diligence which they give unto him."

[2105] D&C 124:28 "For there is not a place found on earth that he may come to and restore again that which was lost unto you, or which he hath taken away, even the fulness of the priesthood."

[2106] Mosiah 3:13 "And the Lord God hath sent his holy prophets among all the children of men, to declare these things to every kindred, nation, and tongue, that thereby whosoever should believe that Christ should come, the same might receive remission of their sins, and rejoice with exceedingly great joy, even as though he had already come among them."

His word, to gather His people into one and be their shelter.[2107]
Despite the many times when this might have happened, there have
been fewer than four occasions we have a record of the Lord actually
gathering His people.

The purpose of giving His word to His people is to lead them to
Him. If they will actually come to Him, He will come and dwell with
them. We were once given that opportunity.[2108]

We are promised the Lord will return again,[2109] and there will be
people prepared to meet Him. It will happen, and will be on this
land.[2110] Any gentiles who are going to survive the coming calamities
will need to flee there.[2111]

[2107] D&C 43:24 "O, ye nations of the earth, how often would I have gathered you
together as a hen gathereth her chickens under her wings, but ye would not!"
3 Nephi 10:4–6 "O ye people of these great cities which have fallen, who are descendants of Jacob, yea, who are of the house of Israel, how oft have I gathered you as a
hen gathereth her chickens under her wings, and have nourished you. And again, how
oft would I have gathered you as a hen gathereth her chickens under her wings, yea, O
ye people of the house of Israel, who have fallen; yea, O ye people of the house of
Israel, ye that dwell at Jerusalem, as ye that have fallen; yea, how oft would I have gathered you as a hen gathereth her chickens, and ye would not. O ye house of Israel
whom I have spared, how oft will I gather you as a hen gathereth her chickens under
her wings, if ye will repent and return unto me with full purpose of heart."

[2108] D&C 104:59 "For the purpose of building up my church and kingdom on the
earth, and to prepare my people for the time when I shall dwell with them, which is
nigh at hand."

[2109] Article of Faith 10 "We believe in the literal gathering of Israel and in the restoration of the Ten Tribes; that Zion (the New Jerusalem) will be built upon the American
continent; that Christ will reign personally upon the earth; and, that the earth will be
renewed and receive its paradisiacal glory."

[2110] Ether 13:5–6 "And he spake also concerning the house of Israel, and the Jerusalem
from whence Lehi should come—after it should be destroyed it should be built up
again, a holy city unto the Lord; wherefore, it could not be a new Jerusalem for it had
been in a time of old; but it should be built up again, and become a holy city of the
Lord; and it should be built unto the house of Israel. And that a New Jerusalem should
be built up upon this land, unto the remnant of the seed of Joseph, for which things
there has been a type."

[2111] D&C 133:12 "Let them, therefore, who are among the Gentiles flee unto Zion."
D&C 42:9 "Until the time shall come when it shall be revealed unto you from on high,
when the city of the New Jerusalem shall be prepared, that ye may be gathered in one,
that ye may be my people and I will be your God."

Mosiah 3:14–15

When the Lord's people wanted religion, but were unwilling to accept the fullness, He accommodated their desire and gave to them the "law of Moses" to keep them busy.[2112] It is the nature of "stiff-necked" people that they prefer religious ceremonies, and endless repetition of rituals to coming into the Lord's presence.[2113]

King Benjamin is reminded by the angel that the purpose of the "law of Moses" was not to redeem anyone. It was merely a way to keep the people busy.

In addition to the law of Moses, the Lord gave "signs and wonders" and also many "types and shadows" to acquaint the people with the fact of "his coming."[2114] These were not ends. They were all means.

Why give the law of Moses?

Why give "signs" and "wonders?"

The people confused the symbols with the real thing. They thought through the symbols they were chosen, elect, and holy. They thought they were a kingdom of priests, a royal priesthood. Instead, what they should have thought was that they were poor because the Lord was not dwelling among them, they considered themselves rich because they had "types and shadows." They preferred the symbol to the reality. The true religion was only symbolized by the rites. By worshiping the symbols and not recognizing the truths which were their foundation, they became mere idolaters. It is one of the constant risks faced by God's people, because the devil is always looking to

---

[2112] Mosiah 3:14 "Yet the Lord God saw that his people were a stiffnecked people, and he appointed unto them a law, even the law of Moses."

[2113] Ibid.

[2114] Mosiah 3:15 "And many signs, and wonders, and types, and shadows showed he unto them, concerning his coming; and also holy prophets spake unto them concerning his coming; and yet they hardened their hearts, and understood not that the law of Moses availeth nothing except it were through the atonement of his blood."

convert the holy church of God into something perverted and evil.[2115]

They could rejoice in their laws, rites, ordinances and rituals. They could consider themselves better than the nations around them because they had God's program for salvation. All the program did was "harden their hearts" because they were proud rather than humble.

These religious and proud people did not understand that all their endless rites "availeth nothing" because it was the Lord alone who could redeem them.[2116] They took their eyes off the Lord, and put them on the religion. They did not understand the religion was nothing, if it failed to point them to the Lord.

How oft might the Lord have gathered them, indeed! It is astonishing that men would prefer religion to God; prefer pride which alienates them from God to humility which could bring them into His presence.

[2115] Mormon 8:33–38 "O ye wicked and perverse and stiffnecked people, why have ye built up churches unto yourselves to get gain? Why have ye transfigured the holy word of God, that ye might bring damnation upon your souls? Behold, look ye unto the revelations of God; for behold, the time cometh at that day when all these things must be fulfilled. Behold, the Lord hath shown unto me great and marvelous things concerning that which must shortly come, at that day when these things shall come forth among you. Behold, I speak unto you as if ye were present, and yet ye are not. But behold, Jesus Christ hath shown you unto me, and I know your doing. And I know that ye do walk in the pride of your hearts; and there are none save a few only who do not lift themselves up in the pride of their hearts, unto the wearing of very fine apparel, unto envying, and strifes, and malice, and persecutions, and all manner of iniquities; and your churches, yea, even every one, have become polluted because of the pride of your hearts. For behold, ye do love money, and your substance, and your fine apparel, and the adorning of your churches, more than ye love the poor and the needy, the sick and the afflicted. O ye pollutions, ye hypocrites, ye teachers, who sell yourselves for that which will canker, why have ye polluted the holy church of God? Why are ye ashamed to take upon you the name of Christ? Why do ye not think that greater is the value of an endless happiness than that misery which never dies—because of the praise of the world?"

[2116] Mosiah 3:15 "And many signs, and wonders, and types, and shadows showed he unto them, concerning his coming; and also holy prophets spake unto them concerning his coming; and yet they hardened their hearts, and understood not that the law of Moses availeth nothing except it were through the atonement of his blood."

Signs, wonders, types, shadows are nothing if they fail to get you to look at the underlying reasons for them. They are not the real thing. They merely point to the real thing; for that, it is left between you and the Lord.

Some few will see it as it really is. They will not be limited by the failures of the generation they live in. They can be saved in any generation because they see beyond the Lord in His types, shadows, signs and wonders.[2117]

Salvation is and always has been individual. This is why there are prophets. Some will lay hold on the promises which others refuse to see.

Mosiah 3:16–17

Half a millennium following the angel's visit to King Benjamin, Mormon wrote a letter to his son Moroni addressing the topic of child baptism. The angel condemned it.[2118] Mormon condemned it.[2119] If anything, Mormon's statements are more emphatic, and condemn those who believe in such rites for children. Mormon ex-

---

[2117] Alma 12:10 "And therefore, he that will harden his heart, the same receiveth the lesser portion of the word; and he that will not harden his heart, to him is given the greater portion of the word, until it is given unto him to know the mysteries of God until he know them in full."

[2118] Mosiah 3:16 "And even if it were possible that little children could sin they could not be saved; but I say unto you they are blessed; for behold, as in Adam, or by nature, they fall, even so the blood of Christ atoneth for their sins."

[2119] Moroni 8:11–14 "And their little children need no repentance, neither baptism. Behold, baptism is unto repentance to the fulfilling the commandments unto the remission of sins. But little children are alive in Christ, even from the foundation of the world; if not so, God is a partial God, and also a changeable God, and a respecter to persons; for how many little children have died without baptism! Wherefore, if little children could not be saved without baptism, these must have gone to an endless hell. Behold I say unto you, that he that supposeth that little children need baptism is in the gall of bitterness and in the bonds of iniquity; for he hath neither faith, hope, nor charity; wherefore, should he be cut off while in the thought, he must go down to hell."

plains that little children "cannot repent",[2120] and the angel explains it is not possible for children to sin.[2121] Little children are not accountable before God, and therefore their mistakes, offenses and errors are covered by their innocence, and the atonement of Christ on the other. Anyone who thinks otherwise does not understand God.[2122]

Mankind are all subject to sin. Over a lifetime we are all corroded by this environment. To preserve this creation, death has been introduced so that no matter how far men may fall from God's grace, their lives will end. In their place, children who are innocent before God come into this world. It is by and through children that hope returns, innocence is renewed and creation continues. Little children are where God's great renewal of mankind takes place. If not for them, this world would have ripened in iniquity long ago.

The angel draws a parallel between Adam's fall and Christ's atonement.[2123] The one brought death to all, the other brings life to all. Even those who will squander their opportunity for more are still redeemed from death through Christ.

[2120] Moroni 8:19 "Little children cannot repent; wherefore, it is awful wickedness to deny the pure mercies of God unto them, for they are all alive in him because of his mercy."

[2121] Mosiah 3:16 "And even if it were possible that little children could sin they could not be saved; but I say unto you they are blessed; for behold, as in Adam, or by nature, they fall, even so the blood of Christ atoneth for their sins."

[2122] Moroni 8:17–20 "And I am filled with charity, which is everlasting love; wherefore, all children are alike unto me; wherefore, I love little children with a perfect love; and they are all alike and partakers of salvation. For I know that God is not a partial God, neither a changeable being; but he is unchangeable from all eternity to all eternity. Little children cannot repent; wherefore, it is awful wickedness to deny the pure mercies of God unto them, for they are all alive in him because of his mercy. And he that saith that little children need baptism denieth the mercies of Christ, and setteth at naught the atonement of him and the power of his redemption."

[2123] Mosiah 3:16 "And even if it were possible that little children could sin they could not be saved; but I say unto you they are blessed; for behold, as in Adam, or by nature, they fall, even so the blood of Christ atoneth for their sins."

Then the angel declares where salvation (something more than rising from the grave) is obtained. It is completely in Christ. "[T]here shall be no other name given nor any other way nor means whereby salvation can come unto the children of men, only in and through the name of Christ, the Lord Omnipotent."[2124] It is not a church. It is not an ordinance. It is not an organization, initiation, family, relationship with, or promise from a man or men, nor any other means. It will be Christ, or it will not happen.

What, then, does it mean to be saved "in and through the name of Christ?"

What is His name? Or, more correctly, what are His names? How does one become saved through His name?

King Benjamin will later have his people take upon them the actual name of Christ.[2125] How are you "called by the name of Christ?" Do you, literally need to become "Christ?" That is, do you literally need to become a "Messiah" or a "Christ" or an "anointed one?" Because the name "Christ" is akin to the word "christened" or "christening," meaning you have become anointed.

How do you become anointed? Is it through application of physical oil to the physical skin? Is that an anointing in the sense that Christ was anointed? Or, is the physical anointing a symbol of another kind of anointing, another kind of christening? If so, what does that entail?

[2124] Mosiah 3:17 "And moreover, I say unto you, that there shall be no other name given nor any other way or means whereby salvation can come unto the children of men, only in and through the name of Christ, the Lord Omnipotent."

[2125] Mosiah 5:6–7 "And now, these are the words which king Benjamin desired of them; and therefore he said unto them: Ye have spoken the words that I desired; and the covenant which ye have made is a righteous covenant. And now, because of the covenant which ye have made ye shall be called the children of Christ, his sons, and his daughters; for behold, this day he hath spiritually begotten you; for ye say that your hearts are changed through faith on his name; therefore, ye are born of him and have become his sons and his daughters."

When the angel marks a man "in the forehead"[2126] is that literal? What kind of anointing, or christening, or seal is involved?

Did Christ set the pattern? Does it mean to "take upon you His name" that you, in like manner, are christened, anointed or sealed? Can you be His without this? Can you take His name upon you without conforming to the same pattern as Christ, who is the "prototype of the saved man."[2127]

> "It is in vain for persons to fancy to themselves that they are heirs with those, or can be heirs with them, who have offered their all in sacrifice, and by this means obtained faith in God and favor with him so as to obtain eternal life, unless they, in like manner, offer unto him the same sacrifice, and through that offering obtain the knowledge that they are accepted of him . . . But those who have not made this sacrifice to God do not know that the course which they pursue is well pleasing in his sight; for . . . where doubt and uncertainty are there faith is

---

[2126] Revelation 7:3 "Saying, Hurt not the earth, neither the sea, nor the trees, till we have sealed the servants of our God in their foreheads."
D&C 77:9 "Q. What are we to understand by the angel ascending from the east, Revelation 7th chapter and 2nd verse? A. We are to understand that the angel ascending from the east is he to whom is given the seal of the living God over the twelve tribes of Israel; wherefore, he crieth unto the four angels having the everlasting gospel, saying: Hurt not the earth, neither the sea, nor the trees, till we have sealed the servants of our God in their foreheads. And, if you will receive it, this is Elias which was to come to gather together the tribes of Israel and restore all things."

[2127] *Lectures on Faith* 7:15–16 "It is scarcely necessary here to observe what we have previously noticed: That the glory which the Father and the Son have, is because they are just and holy beings; and that if they were lacking in one attribute or perfection which they have, the glory which they have, never could be enjoyed by them; for it requires them to be precisely what they are in order to enjoy it: and if the Savior gives this glory to any others, he must do it in the very way set forth in his prayer to his Father: by making them one with him, as he and the Father are one. In so doing he would give them the glory which the Father has given him; and when his disciples are made one with the Father and the Son, as the Father and the Son are one, who cannot see the propriety of the Savior's saying, The works which I do, shall they do; and greater works than these shall they do, be cause I go to the Father? These teachings of the Savior must clearly show unto us the nature of salvation; and what he proposed unto the human family when he proposed to save them--That he proposed to make them like unto himself; and he was like the Father, the great prototype of all saved beings: And for any portion of the human family to be assimilated into their likeness is to be saved; and to be unlike them is to be destroyed: and on this hinge turns the door of salvation."

not, nor can it be. For doubt and faith do not exist in the same person at the same time; so that persons whose minds are under doubts and fears cannot have unshaken confidence; . . . and where faith is weak the persons will not be able to contend against all the opposition, tribulations, and afflictions which they will have to encounter in order to be heirs of God, and joint heirs with Christ Jesus; and they will grow weary in their minds, and the adversary will have power over them and destroy them." (*Lectures on Faith* 6:8, 12.)

How does one lay hold on the salvation that comes through the name of Christ spoken of to King Benjamin by the angel in Mosiah 3:17?[2128]

Mosiah 3:18

The angel declares unequivocally that Christ "judges." Not men, not authorities. Christ "judges." Men who fancy themselves empowered to judge others deceive themselves. Judgment of others is not permitted.[2129] Even the Lord's twelve disciples were told they were not to judge others, but would be trusted to announce Christ's judgment.[2130] Christ is the only judge. He is the only keeper of the gate.[2131] When men substitute their own judgment for Christ's, they condemn themselves and do nothing to alter the one they judge be-

---

[2128] Mosiah 3:17 "And moreover, I say unto you, that there shall be no other name given nor any other way nor means whereby salvation can come unto the children of men, only in and through the name of Christ, the Lord Omnipotent."

[2129] Matthew 7:1 "Judge not, that ye be not judged."

[2130] 3 Nephi 27:27 "And know ye that ye shall be judges of this people, according to the judgment which I shall give unto you, which shall be just. Therefore, what manner of men ought ye to be? Verily I say unto you, even as I am."

[2131] 2 Nephi 9:41 "O then, my beloved brethren, come unto the Lord, the Holy One. Remember that his paths are righteous. Behold, the way for man is narrow, but it lieth in a straight course before him, and the keeper of the gate is the Holy One of Israel; and he employeth no servant there; and there is none other way save it be by the gate; for he cannot be deceived, for the Lord God is his name."

fore Christ.[2132] When men act as if they are Christ, substituting their own judgment for His, they govern others by their own light and not the Lord's. These things are condemned.[2133]

The Lord alone is judge. Hence the angel saying to King Benjamin:

"For behold he judgeth," and adding quickly "and his judgement is just." (Mosiah 3:18)

You don't need to fear an unjust judge, nor a partial and imperious man who is looking to magnify his ego or vain ambition.[2134] Their judgments can never displace Christ "For behold He judgeth," according to the words of the angel to King Benjamin.

Because He alone can judge, those who condemn little children who He has redeemed are substituting their own judgment for His. They are calling His great work of redemption incomplete and inadequate to accomplish the redemption of children. Such men "drink damnation to their own souls" because they will be judged by the standard they have established.[2135] They must not only retract their unjust judgment, but must also become like those whom they

---

[2132] Matthew 7:2 "For with what judgment ye judge, ye shall be judged: and with what measure ye mete, it shall be measured to you again."

[2133] 2 Nephi 26:29 "He commandeth that there shall be no priestcrafts; for, behold, priestcrafts are that men preach and set themselves up for a light unto the world, that they may get gain and praise of the world; but they seek not the welfare of Zion."

[2134] D&C 121:37 "That they may be conferred upon us, it is true; but when we undertake to cover our sins, or to gratify our pride, our vain ambition, or to exercise control or dominion or compulsion upon the souls of the children of men, in any degree of unrighteousness, behold, the heavens withdraw themselves; the Spirit of the Lord is grieved; and when it is withdrawn, Amen to the priesthood or the authority of that man."

[2135] Matthew 7:2 "For with what judgment ye judge, ye shall be judged: and with what measure ye mete, it shall be measured to you again."

condemn. "Except they humble themselves and become as little children" they will be lost.[2136]

The angel reminds King Benjamin (and us) there is only one source for salvation. It "was, and is, and is to come, in and through the atoning blood of Christ, the Lord Omnipotent."[2137] If you lack salvation, it is because you looked elsewhere to find it, and if you receive it, then you necessarily have come to Christ.

All the judgments of men, all the plans and schemes of men, all the pretenses and arrogance of men will not secure salvation for any soul. Salvation comes from Christ alone.

If you or I were ever to judge another man, the standard to apply is singular: It is Christ's standard. Either He reveals His judgment to you, and you announce what His judgment, or He does not. If He does not, then the choice is to either refrain from judging (which is safe), or to show mercy and forgiveness (which is safer still), but never condemn. The Lord alone has the right to condemn. For us to condemn anyone the Lord has forgiven is a mockery of His atonement, no less than condemning little children whom the Lord also has forgiven.

This lecture by the angel to King Benjamin is filled with wisdom and light. We are so much the better for having it available for us to study.

[2136] Mosiah 3:18 "For behold he judgeth, and his judgment is just; and the infant perisheth not that dieth in his infancy; but men drink damnation to their own souls except they humble themselves and become as little children, and believe that salvation was, and is, and is to come, in and through the atoning blood of Christ, the Lord Omnipotent."

[2137] Ibid.

Mosiah 3:19

The angel asserts that "the natural man is an enemy to God."[2138] Why is that so?

What is it about the natural state of man that, when a little child he is saved and anyone who thinks otherwise is in the gall of bitterness and offending God, but when grown is "an enemy to God?" How can these two statements at the opposite ends of the spectrum come from the same angel in the same message?

How does man become, in his "natural" state an enemy to God? What is it about this environment and the natural progression into adulthood that, as man becomes tempted he also becomes alienated from God? What forces contribute to this alienation?

- Hunger?
- Fatigue?
- Boredom?
- Puberty?
- Emotional insecurities?
- Abuse by others?
- Ignorance?

Is it inevitable that all develop into a condition where they are not only distant from God, but an "enemy to God?" How does that happen? What is going on here that you fall to this state? Is it "natural" for you to go through that?

If you are going to become by nature alienated from God, then how can you be certain you are not in your "natural" state as you go

---

[2138] Mosiah 3:19 "For the natural man is an enemy to God, and has been from the fall of Adam, and will be, forever and ever, unless he yields to the enticings of the Holy Spirit, and putteth off the natural man and becometh a saint through the atonement of Christ the Lord, and becometh as a child, submissive, meek, humble, patient, full of love, willing to submit to all things which the Lord seeth fit to inflict upon him, even as a child doth submit to his father."

about practicing your religion? What is there about religion itself which appeals to the "natural" man? How does religion contribute to:

- Pride?
- Anger?
- Judgment?
- Hatred?
- Abuse of others?
- Calling that which is good evil?
- Arrogance?
- Killing the messengers, and even the Son of God?

It is inevitable that the "natural" man who is religious is no better than the "natural" man who is irreligious? Can a man be both "an enemy to God" and devoted to some religion? Are not all the prophets of the past killed by those who were religious? Even the mob that killed Joseph was led by lay ministers. How can you ever be certain your own "devotion" is not, in fact, the faith of an "enemy to God?"

How can any person avoid this catastrophe? What does the angel recommend to King Benjamin?

- *yield to the enticings of the Holy Spirit"*[2139]

The word "yield" seems weak. The force of the Spirit is to invite, to request or to petition you. You are free to reject, to resist, and to refuse.

- *"become a saint through the atonement of Christ the Lord"*[2140]

The idea of "becoming" something suggests change. And how does one go about changing "through the atonement of Christ?" What does one have to do to acquire this change? How is the Holy Spirit and taking advantage of the atonement of Christ related to one another?

[2139] Ibid.

[2140] Ibid.

- *"becometh as a little child"*

How is this done? I'll not repeat the chapter on this from *The Second Comforter*, but will only remind you that it requires something more than passivity. It requires the relentless search, as children do, for understanding and knowledge. It requires curiosity and pursuit of truth, as little children do.

- *"submissive"*

To who? Men? Your peers? Your political, social, cultural, religious, or educational leaders? Or submissive to "the Holy Spirit" which only "entices" and never controls? If you submit to the arm of flesh, even the arm of a good man, are you really "submissive" in the sense spoken of here by the angel?

- *"meek"*

In the sense explained in *Beloved Enos.*

- *"humble"*

As between you and heaven, not as between you and the world. Indeed, since conflict with the world is inevitable if you follow the Lord, then humility is reckoned from a different vantage point. You will appear to the world to be rebellious, discordant, unruly, and difficult. That is because a citizen of heaven is not well fitted to this fallen world. Humility is directed toward the Lord, not your fellow man.

- *"patient"*

Because this world has little use for the truth, and will test and try you at every turn. It will fight you long enough to prove whether you are faithful in all things. Then some few will join in the struggle and also become a fellow citizen of a higher world.

- *"full of love"*

Not because of your own capacity, but because by submitting to the Holy Spirit you are able to borrow this as a gift through the atonement of Christ. Just like the angel explained.

- *"willing to submit to all things which the Lord seeth fit to inflict upon him"*

It is the Lord's work to bring about salvation and exaltation.[2141] To refine you, the Lord will "inflict" a great deal upon you. He knows when you are ready, when you are proven. You have no idea. You submit, and in the process you learn what you are capable of. Until you submit to all He sees, in His wisdom alone to inflict upon you, you remain an unfinished son or daughter. When you cry out from agony and uncertainty and you hear nothing but the patient silence of heaven, you must endure it, just as Joseph in Liberty Jail.[2142] When your cup is filled and you think you cannot endure more, He will decide if the ordeal continues. He will remind you of His suffering.[2143] You will learn from your own suffering to appreciate His.

- *"even as a child doeth submit to his father"*

If you want to be His child, you allow Him to act the role of your Father. It is His right to punish, instruct, inflict you. It is acceptance of His Fatherhood over you to submit and not question His right to do what you cannot see any need for you to endure. He is preparing you for something so much greater than what you are now, that you cannot receive the blessings unless you are enlarged. How can He "add upon" you without stretching, even breaking you? How can you grow without pain?

[2141] Moses 1:39 "For behold, this is my work and my glory—to bring to pass the immortality and eternal life of man."

[2142] D&C 121:1–3 "O GOD, where art thou? And where is the pavilion that covereth thy hiding place? How long shall thy hand be stayed, and thine eye, yea thy pure eye, behold from the eternal heavens the wrongs of thy people and of thy servants, and thine ear be penetrated with their cries? Yea, O Lord, how long shall they suffer these wrongs and unlawful oppressions, before thine heart shall be softened toward them, and thy bowels be moved with compassion toward them?"

[2143] D&C 122:8 "The Son of Man hath descended below them all. Art thou greater than he?"

How foolish is our impatience? How small our irritations! How unequal His blessings to our gratitude! When He works with us, we resent Him. When He corrects us, we resist Him. When He tries us, we cry out: It is unfair!

The Son of Man hath descended below it all, art thou greater than He?[2144]

The "natural man is an enemy to God" and you must overcome that. You proud, arrogant, weak, insecure, devoted and pretentious "Saints." You must change. Or you remain God"s enemy . . . At least if the angel who spoke with King Benjamin knew what he was talking about.

Response to a Comment

In response to a comment, perhaps the most easily shown "mistake" is President Brigham Young's claim of Adam as our God. This teaching was opposed by Orson Pratt from the time it was introduced. After hearing the doctrine advanced by President Young as a revelation from God, the following took place on March 11, 1856:

> "A very serious conversation took place between President B. Young and Orson Pratt upon doctrine. O.P. was directly opposed to the President's views and freely expressed his entire disbelief in them after being told by the President that things were so and so in the name of the Lord. He was firm in the position that the President's word in the name of the Lord was not the word of the Lord to him." (*The Complete Discourses of Brigham Young*, 2:1061)

President Brigham Young was opposed by Orson Pratt. Brigham Young was the church president at the time, and for decades after.

[2144] Ibid.

Later his "doctrine" that he claimed God revealed to him was denounced by President Spencer Kimball in general conference.

President Kimball in October 1976 general conference stated the following:

> "We warn you against the dissemination of doctrines which are not according to the Scriptures and which are alleged to have been taught by some of the General Authorities of past generations. Such, for instance, is the Adam-God theory. We denounce that theory and hope that everyone will be cautioned against this and other kinds of false doctrine." ("Our Own Liahona", *Ensign*, November 1976)

This "doctrine" was taught by President Young, opposed when taught by one of the Twelve, and later denounced by President Kimball. This is the same as the church's teachings on priesthood being abandoned, and earlier teachings, when taught by earlier church leaders, were claimed to have been made "in the absence of revelation."

This is not a problem for me, and should not be a problem for you. The errors of men and the doctrinal mistakes which get advanced cannot, do not, and will not alter the truth. Orson Pratt was ultimately vindicated for disbelieving in "Adam-God." Anyone who today holds correct views will ultimately be vindicated. It is the prerogative of the church leaders to claim priority in teaching. When they are mistaken or wrong, that will eventually be discovered, abandoned, and their errors will be made known. In the meantime, it is your right to search for and believe in truth, even if the church does not presently recognize it. As long as you do not make it a practice of publicly opposing the church leaders, there is absolutely nothing wrong with disagreeing with them. It is your duty to study and find the truth, and that duty exists independent of faithfully supporting the leaders.

Notice that Orson Pratt did not leave the church. He disagreed, but served in the Twelve. He did not start a splinter group, nor attempt to unseat President Young. They disagreed and they worked together. This is what believers do.

You do not need to surrender your own independent search for truth, even when you disagree with others who are also Mormon. We share far more in common, even with doctrinal differences, than we will ever share with Historic Christianity. You belong in the church, even if you are not in complete agreement with some of its current teachings.

The Perfect Example

The answer yesterday was the perfect example. It was chosen because it fit the issue exactly.

The answer did not attempt to explain whether "Adam-God" was right or wrong, true or false, or to side Brigham Young, Orson Pratt or President Kimball. The point is that "doctrine" becomes "false doctrine" depending on who you listen to and when you tune into the teachings.

Which is the point of the answer. YOU must sort it out, because the church will ebb and flow, and cannot be relied upon to have stable doctrine. Indeed, the reason Bruce R. McConkie's *Mormon Doctrine* is now out of print is because of shifting positions.

Yesterday's post did not explain my view on Adam as God, nor have I ever explained what I think on the topic or why.

I appreciate the many comments. Clearly there is a lot of interest and strongly held opinion on the subject.

Mosiah 3:20–22

The angel foretells of a time when "knowledge of a Savior shall spread throughout every nation, kindred, tongue, and people."[2145] This raises a question about the word "knowledge" and its meaning in the context of this verse:

- Does it mean "awareness," or that people have heard of Christ?
- Does it mean to "know," or to have met Him?

Almost always in the Book of Mormon the term "knowledge" involving Christ involves the second meaning of having met Him. In this verse, however, the context raises the possibility it is in fact the first. That is, once people are put on notice that there is a Savior, they have a duty to investigate. The burden is on them to inquire and learn what the Savior can save them from, and on what conditions He will save.

If you are being cautious, then you would use the first meaning and assume the angel is saying that as soon as you become aware of a Savior, you need to then seek for salvation through Him.

If you are reckless and willing to take a great, eternal risk, then you will confine the angel's meaning to the second, and will assume the burden is not imposed until the Lord has appeared to you. That, however, seems self-defeating. The Lord will not appear to you until you have met the conditions. Those conditions involve obedience.

The angel explains that once one is aware of the existence of a Savior for mankind because this information has been spread throughout the world, then "none shall be found blameless."[2146] Or,

---

[2145] Mosiah 3:20 "And moreover, I say unto you, that the time shall come when the knowledge of a Savior shall spread throughout every nation, kindred, tongue, and people."

[2146] Mosiah 3:21 "And behold, when that time cometh, none shall be found blameless before God, except it be little children, only through repentance and faith on the name of the Lord God Omnipotent."

in other words, the Lord will hold every person to account for how they responded to the news of a Savior. Once they know of Him, they must pursue Him. Like the wise men who embarked on a two-year journey from the east to come and worship Him, we are also obligated to seek after Him.[2147]

This burden on man is imposed as a reasonable responsibility for anyone who has learned of a Savior. When we have that news, we have that duty.

The duty is to come before God "through repentance and faith on the Lord God Omnipotent.[2148]" Here the angel uses three titles for Christ:

- "Lord" because we are to obey Him.
- "God" because we are to worship Him.
- "Omnipotent" because we are assured He has the power to save.

And so the obligation remains for us to "repent" to be saved. This is why, of course, any true prophet will always preach repentance.

[2147] Matthew 2:1–11 "Now when Jesus was born in Bethlehem of Judaea in the days of Herod the king, behold, there came wise men from the east to Jerusalem, Saying, Where is he that is born King of the Jews? for we have seen his star in the east, and are come to worship him. When Herod the king had heard *these things,* he was troubled, and all Jerusalem with him. And when he had gathered all the chief priests and scribes of the people together, he demanded of them where Christ should be born. And they said unto him, In Bethlehem of Judaea: for thus it is written by the prophet, And thou Bethlehem, *in* the land of Juda, art not the least among the princes of Juda: for out of thee shall come a Governor, that shall rule my people Israel. Then Herod, when he had privily called the wise men, enquired of them diligently what time the star appeared. And he sent them to Bethlehem, and said, Go and search diligently for the young child; and when ye have found *him,* bring me word again, that I may come and worship him also. When they had heard the king, they departed; and, lo, the star, which they saw in the east, went before them, till it came and stood over where the young child was. When they saw the star, they rejoiced with exceeding great joy. And when they were come into the house, they saw the young child with Mary his mother, and fell down, and worshipped him: and when they had opened their treasures, they presented unto him gifts; gold, and frankincense, and myrrh."

[2148] Mosiah 3:21 "And behold, when that time cometh, none shall be found blameless before God, except it be little children, only through repentance and faith on the name of the Lord God Omnipotent."

Men can only be saved through repentance. Anything which does not alert mankind they must repent is foolish and vain. Therefore, if a prophet is saying anything other than repentance they are failing in their obligation to God and to their fellow man.

Even if we never meet a prophet of God we have the words of an angel before us. We do not need to have another person declare the conditions for our salvation to us, because we have the words warning us of the duty we bear.

The words of the angel impose upon the people of King Benjamin the duty to repent and "they [are] found no more blameless" because of the words of the angel.[2149] You also have them before you. Therefore you are no longer blameless. You must repent, or you will be cast off because you are judged on the basis of the words given you. You have the words of an angel before you.

There are conditions for salvation, and the Lord can impose those conditions immediately after sending an angel to warn people. It does not matter if you take the warning seriously. The Lord has done what is required to make you accountable. You are left without any excuse.

One of the signs of authenticity in the Book of Mormon is the existence of passages like this one. It is an authentic ancient form that goes back to the beginning. The Lord delivers the message and immediately men are accountable.

King Benjamin, alone and at night, receives instructions from an angel. We have never met King Benjamin, don't have a duty to sustain him, nor reason to respect him, but we receive a written transcript of the audience between one man and an angel sent from God. We are accountable for what is contained in the warning.

[2149] Mosiah 3:22 "And even at this time, when thou shalt have taught thy people the things which the Lord thy God hath commanded thee, even then are they found no more blameless in the sight of God, only according to the words which I have spoken unto thee."

How oft would the Lord have gathered us, but we will not see what stares us plainly in the face! The Lord does the same thing generation after generation. So few ever notice, however, even when it is as plain as words can be.[2150]

Mosiah 3:23

"And now I have spoken the words which the Lord God hath commanded me." (Mosiah 3:23)

The angel added nothing. He hid nothing. He delivered what the Lord told him to deliver.

These are not merely the words of an angel. Because the angel certifies they originated from God, they are the words of God.[2151]

When anyone, man or angel, is entrusted with a message from God, the message is God's. God makes no distinction between the messenger and Himself. The words "shall all be fulfilled."[2152]

This system of empowering a messenger with a message, and then holding mankind to account may seem too slender a thread to have power. The truth is that the power is in the words, not in who speaks them. It does not matter that they come from a frail, elderly King from another time who has no authority over us today. It does not matter that he was alone at night with an unnamed angel without a second witness to vindicate the words. It is true and binding because:

[2150] 2 Nephi 32:7–8 "And now I, Nephi, cannot say more; the Spirit stoppeth mine utterance, and I am left to mourn because of the unbelief, and the wickedness, and the ignorance, and the stiffneckedness of men; for they will not search knowledge, nor understand great knowledge, when it is given unto them in plainness, even as plain as word can be. And now, my beloved brethren, I perceive that ye ponder still in your hearts; and it grieveth me that I must speak concerning this thing. For if ye would hearken unto the Spirit which teacheth a man to pray ye would know that ye must pray; for the evil spirit teacheth not a man to pray, but teacheth him that he must not pray."

[2151] D&C 1:38 "What I the Lord have spoken, I have spoken, and I excuse not myself; and though the heavens and the earth pass away, my word shall not pass away, but shall all be fulfilled, whether by mine own voice or by the voice of my servants, it is the same."

[2152] Ibid.

1. It agrees with and does not contradict any other message from God.

2. It preaches repentance and warns us of consequences.

3. The words are independently corroborated by the Spirit, if we read with the Spirit.

4. The words have been certified to us by our own inquiry.[2153]

This is how the Lord sends His message. Through a solitary figure like John the Baptist, or Samuel the Lamanite, or Abinadi, or Jonah, or Amos, or Isaiah, or so many others. The message is the credential. It puts us to the obligation of then seeking to know if it is true or not. For that we must turn to God.

The message originates with God, and the message drives us to Him to determine if it is true.

The Lord's ways are ever the same. We get no less a challenge in our own day.

As you reflect on this you can see why Zion will be a "city" and not an intercontinental, multi-million member organization spread throughout the world. It will be small. It will be local.[2154] The Saints will be gathered from all the world into Zion.[2155] This is because once a messenger has delivered "the words which the Lord God hath commanded me," then we are responsible for how we react and

---

[2153] Moroni 10:4–5 "And when ye shall receive these things, I would exhort you that ye would ask God, the Eternal Father, in the name of Christ, if these things are not true; and if ye shall ask with a sincere heart, with real intent, having faith in Christ, he will manifest the truth of it unto you, by the power of the Holy Ghost. And by the power of the Holy Ghost ye may know the truth of all things."

[2154] D&C 133:12 "Let them, therefore, who are among the Gentiles flee unto Zion."

[2155] 1 Nephi 14:14 "And it came to pass that I, Nephi, beheld the power of the Lamb of God, that it descended upon the saints of the church of the Lamb, and upon the covenant people of the Lord, who were scattered upon all the face of the earth; and they were armed with righteousness and with the power of God in great glory."

whether or not we repent. If we repent, angels will gather us.[2156] If we do not, they will not gather us.

Mosiah 3:24

Words from God, delivered by someone who is authorized to speak them, "stand as a bright testimony against this people."[2157] It is a "bright testimony" because it illuminates the wickedness and hard hearts of the people when they reject it. Or, alternatively, it is "bright" because it opens the mind of those who will receive it, and they become enlightened by receiving truth from God. Either way, it is a "bright testimony" and will cut against all who fail to respond by repenting.

The purpose of the message is to make everyone aware of their duty to follow God. That purpose becomes most fully understood "in the judgment day" when the Lord's messengers stand beside Him.[2158] It will then be obvious who He sent and who pretended to be sent.[2159]

[2156] Ibid.

[2157] Mosiah 3:24 "And thus saith the Lord: They shall stand as a bright testimony against this people, at the judgment day; whereof they shall be judged, every man according to his works, whether they be good, or whether they be evil."

[2158] Moroni 10:34 "And now I bid unto all, farewell. I soon go to rest in the paradise of God, until my spirit and body shall again reunite, and I am brought forth triumphant through the air, to meet you before the pleasing bar of the great Jehovah, the Eternal Judge of both quick and dead. Amen."
2 Nephi 33:11 "And if they are not the words of Christ, judge ye—for Christ will show unto you, with power and great glory, that they are his words, at the last day; and you and I shall stand face to face before his bar; and ye shall know that I have been commanded of him to write these things, notwithstanding my weakness."

[2159] Deuteronomy 18:20 "But the prophet, which shall presume to speak a word in my name, which I have not commanded him to speak, or that shall speak in the name of other gods, even that prophet shall die."

The angel then says "every man shall be judged according to his works."[2160] This means what you "do" in response to the warning to repent is what determines your final fate. Your "works" matter because if you respond by repenting, then you will "work out your salvation."[2161] If not, then you have procrastinated and will be damned for your failure to work.[2162]

The symmetry and simplicity of the message is astonishing. Everyone can understand it, but that is never the challenge. The challenge is always whether or not to take it seriously enough to act on it.

Acting on it does not involve a public display. It only involves what goes on inside your heart. You repent before God, and come to Him with a broken heart and contrite spirit and beg for forgiveness. When the Lord forgives, then you change from the inside out. The only real change that matters comes from within. Outward display first is artificial. When a new heart is inside a man, then the outward behavior, and eventually even countenance, will change to reflect what lies within the man.

Given the seriousness of the message, you would think all who hear it would at least consult with God before turning away. However, it has always been the most religious who will not listen to a message of repentance.

Traditions and social reinforcement from others who think alike, all prevent the message to repent from getting through. Instead of a

---

[2160] Mosiah 3:24 "And thus saith the Lord: They shall stand as a bright testimony against this people, at the judgment day; whereof they shall be judged, every man according to his works, whether they be good, or whether they be evil."

[2161] Philippians 2:12 "Wherefore, my beloved, as ye have always obeyed, not as in my presence only, but now much more in my absence, work out your own salvation with fear and trembling."

[2162] Alma 34:33 "And now, as I said unto you before, as ye have had so many witnesses, therefore, I beseech of you that ye do not procrastinate the day of your repentance until the end; for after this day of life, which is given us to prepare for eternity, behold, if we do not improve our time while in this life, then cometh the night of darkness wherein there can be no labor performed."

message of repentance, mankind prefers a prophet who tells them they are good. They are justified. They are righteous! They are chosen! God loves them in their sins! They need only pray, pay and obey and all will be well with them! Then people do pay, so that such characters become rich and powerful.[2163]

There is perhaps no greater revelation of the plan of salvation ever composed than the Book of Mormon. Beginning with Mosiah the text is abridged by Mormon. I think, however, this chapter from Mosiah was left as in the original. What Mormon did here was keep intact the transcript of the angel's message. I can almost hear it echoing still. Can't you?

Mosiah 3:25

"And if they be evil they are consigned to an awful view of their own guilt and abominations, which doth cause them to shrink from the presence of the Lord into a state of misery and endless torment, from whence they can no more return; therefore they have drunk damnation to their own souls." (Mosiah 3:25)

The angel now transitions the message to King Benjamin forward to the time of the final judgment. In that setting he suggests a scene to the unrepentant. Before looking at the words, however, why do

---

[2163] Helaman 13:26–28 "Behold ye are worse than they; for as the Lord liveth, if a prophet come among you and declareth unto you the word of the Lord, which testifieth of your sins and iniquities, ye are angry with him, and cast him out and seek all manner of ways to destroy him; yea, you will say that he is a false prophet, and that he is a sinner, and of the devil, because he testifieth that your deeds are evil. But behold, if a man shall come among you and shall say: Do this, and there is no iniquity; do that and ye shall not suffer; yea, he will say: Walk after the pride of your own hearts; yea, walk after the pride of your eyes, and do whatsoever your heart desireth—and if a man shall come among you and say this, ye will receive him, and say that he is a prophet. Yea, ye will lift him up, and ye will give unto him of your substance; ye will give unto him of your gold, and of your silver, and ye will clothe him with costly apparel; and because he speaketh flattering words unto you, and he saith that all is well, then ye will not find fault with him."

you suppose the description is from the vantage point of the damned? Why not from the vantage point of the saved? The final three verses of the message are all viewed from failure, rather than from success. Why?

Is this "negative?"

Does this make you think the angel is offensive? He doesn't "have the Spirit" with him? That you "don't get a good feeling" when you listen to his words?

Do you think the angel should be ignored because he makes you "feel bad" by the things he speaks? Would you prefer to hear a "more positive message?" Things like this just "can't be from God" because of how they make you "feel?"

If this is an angel from God speaking, and the above questions reflect your attitude about a message warning you to repent, then perhaps it is your attitude that is wrong—not the angel or his message. Perhaps the annoyance of being awakened from your deep sleep is worth the angel telling you in unmistakable and harsh terms that you are about to be lost if you do not repent. Perhaps the angel would prefer to deliver a hopeful, even lighthearted message, but the words originate from God. God's efforts are to bring you to immortality and eternal life.[2164] Maybe God has a better view of our awful state than do we.

The angel speaks in terms of:

- *"consigned to an awful view"*

What does this suggest? What would be "awful" about failing to repent? Why is it a "view?" What will we "see" in that day?

- *"own guilt and abominations"*

[2164] Moses 1:39 "For behold, this is my work and my glory—to bring to pass the immortality and eternal life of man."

Why guilt? What "abominations" attach to every soul who does not repent? Why is religious error, pride in believing falsehoods, and failure to repent always an "abomination?"

- *"doth cause them to shrink"*

Isn't this the same agony Christ experience in Gethsemane?[2165] Why would you "shrink" from the presence of God? What does "shrink" mean?

- *"into a state of misery"*

Why would you want to withdraw into a state of misery? What is it about failing to repent that causes you to behave this way when judged by God?

- *"endless torment from which there can be no return"*

Why is this the formula to describe the reaction?[2166] What is it about this experience that will last forever in the mind of anyone who suffers it?[2167] Why would this haunt the person forevermore? Even if it came to an end at some point, why are you "unable to re-

---

[2165] D&C 19:18 "Which suffering caused myself, even God, the greatest of all, to tremble because of pain, and to bleed at every pore, and to suffer both body and spirit—and would that I might not drink the bitter cup, and shrink—"

[2166] D&C 19:6–12 "Nevertheless, it is not written that there shall be no end to this torment, but it is written *endless torment*. Again, it is written *eternal damnation;* wherefore it is more express than other scriptures, that it might work upon the hearts of the children of men, altogether for my name's glory. Wherefore, I will explain unto you this mystery, for it is meet unto you to know even as mine apostles. I speak unto you that are chosen in this thing, even as one, that you may enter into my rest. For, behold, the mystery of godliness, how great is it! For, behold, I am endless, and the punishment which is given from my hand is endless punishment, for Endless is my name. Wherefore—Eternal punishment is God's punishment. Endless punishment is God's punishment."

[2167] D&C 19:15–18 "Therefore I command you to repent—repent, lest I smite you by the rod of my mouth, and by my wrath, and by my anger, and your sufferings be sore—how sore you know not, how exquisite you know not, yea, how hard to bear you know not. For behold, I, God, have suffered these things for all, that they might not suffer if they would repent; But if they would not repent they must suffer even as I; Which suffering caused myself, even God, the greatest of all, to tremble because of pain, and to bleed at every pore, and to suffer both body and spirit—and would that I might not drink the bitter cup, and shrink—"

turn" from that experience? What trauma is caused by this that can be avoided by repenting?

- *"drunk damnation to their souls"*

Why this graphic description? What is it about this experience that makes the very soul be damned by the ordeal?

Is the angel overreacting? Is this terrible assortment of adjectives necessary? Why would God send an angel with this message to King Benjamin (and to us)?

Mosiah 3:26–27

"Therefore, they have drunk out of the cup of the wrath of God, which justice could no more deny unto them than it could deny that Adam should fall because of his partaking of the forbidden fruit; therefore, mercy could have claim on then no more forever.

"And their torment is as a lake of fire and brimstone, whose flames are unquenchable, and whose smoke ascendeth up forever and ever. Thus has the Lord commanded me. Amen." (Mosiah 3:26–27)

The strong, direful, terrible warnings continue from the angel:

Those who ignore the obligation will, in the afterlife, have *"drank out of the cup of the wrath of God . . ."*.

Notice this is phrased in almost identical language to Christ's terrible suffering in the atonement.[2168] This is so awful an experience

---

[2168] 3 Nephi 11:11 "And behold, I am the light and the life of the world; and I have drunk out of that bitter cup which the Father hath given me, and have glorified the Father in taking upon me the sins of the world, in the which I have suffered the will of the Father in all things from the beginning."

D&C 19:18 "Which suffering caused myself, even God, the greatest of all, to tremble because of pain, and to bleed at every pore, and to suffer both body and spirit—and would that I might not drink the bitter cup, and shrink—"

the Lord cannot capture adequately in revelation the words to describe it.[2169]

"mercy could have claim on them no more forever"—meaning that if they choose this path, they will suffer. There will be nothing to mitigate what they will endure. Mercy will not intervene and lessen the ordeal.

How often has the Lord used such terrible phrases to describe the damned as:

"torment as a lake of fire and brimstone"—because we all know the pain of having our skin burned. It quickly conveys the idea of torment into our minds,

"whose flames are unquenchable"—because it will burn away until nothing impure remains,

"whose smoke ascendeth up forever and ever"—because this process is eternal and will be the experience of anyone and everyone, worlds without end, who merit this purging and refining fire.

These words from the angel were delivered to a king, to be taught to his people, in a gathering in which all those who attended then covenanted with God. The audience would "have no more disposition to do evil, but to do good continually."[2170]

Why does it require *this* message from the angel to produce this result?

Could they be saved by praising them, telling them they were chosen and the elect of God?

Could they be saved by telling them they were a royal priesthood?

[2169] D&C 19:15 "Therefore I command you to repent—repent, lest I smite you by the rod of my mouth, and by my wrath, and by my anger, and your sufferings be sore—how sore you know not, how exquisite you know not, yea, how hard to bear you know not."

[2170] Mosiah 5:2 "And they all cried with one voice, saying: Yea, we believe all the words which thou hast spoken unto us; and also, we know of their surety and truth, because of the Spirit of the Lord Omnipotent, which has wrought a mighty change in us, or in our hearts, that we have no more disposition to do evil, but to do good continually."

Could they be saved by telling them that all was well with them, they prosper in the land because God is with them?

Why is it necessary to tell them of hell?

Of damnation?

Of eternal suffering and unquenchable fire?

In *The Second Comforter* I remarked "there is no veil to our feelings." That is true, but the feelings one experiences by coming into the presence of God are almost universally fear and dread. The scriptures confirm how fearful this has been to mankind:

To Abraham, it was a "horror" to draw near the Lord.[2171]

To Isaiah it was woeful, and terrible.[2172]

To Daniel and his companions, quaking fell upon them, many fled, leaving Daniel alone.[2173]

Mormon explains how men react to God's presence as being "racked with a consciousness of guilt."[2174]

When popular mythology constructs fantasies of coming before the Lord, they make it happy—not dreadful. They despise the call to repent because it disagrees with their happy myths. The angel is not

---

[2171] Genesis 15:12–13 "And when the sun was going down, a deep sleep fell upon Abram; and, lo, an horror of great darkness fell upon him. And he said unto Abram, Know of a surety that thy seed shall be a stranger in a land *that is* not theirs, and shall serve them; and they shall afflict them four hundred years;"

[2172] Isaiah 6:5 "Then said I, Woe *is* me! for I am undone; because I *am* a man of unclean lips, and I dwell in the midst of a people of unclean lips: for mine eyes have seen the King, the Lord of hosts."

[2173] Daniel 10:7–8 "And I Daniel alone saw the vision: for the men that were with me saw not the vision; but a great quaking fell upon them, so that they fled to hide themselves. Therefore I was left alone, and saw this great vision, and there remained no strength in me: for my comeliness was turned in me into corruption, and I retained no strength."

[2174] Mormon 9:3–4 "Then will ye longer deny the Christ, or can ye behold the Lamb of God? Do ye suppose that ye shall dwell with him under a consciousness of your guilt? Do ye suppose that ye could be happy to dwell with that holy Being, when your souls are racked with a consciousness of guilt that ye have ever abused his laws? Behold, I say unto you that ye would be more miserable to dwell with a holy and just God, under a consciousness of your filthiness before him, than ye would to dwell with the damned souls in hell."

overstating the case. He is explaining the great gulf that exists between fallen man and God.[2175] The unrepentant and foolish are
completely unprepared for God's presence.[2176] The words of the
angel are attempting to give some indication to the faithful of how
deeply, how completely, and how great the scope of repentance must
be to avoid the similar pains of death and hell the Lord suffered on
our behalf.

We delude ourselves when we think the angel's message was not
meant for all members of the Church of Jesus Christ of Latter-day
Saints. If the King Benjamin's audience acquired their salvation by
coming down in the depths of humility and repentance,[2177] then we
fool ourselves if we think anything less will be expected of us.

Was the angel bitter? Angry? Harsh? Unkind? Of the wrong
"spirit?" Not the kind of messenger we should expect would be sent
from God?

[2175] Moses 1:10 "And it came to pass that it was for the space of many hours before
Moses did again receive his natural strength like unto man; and he said unto himself:
Now, for this cause I know that man is nothing, which thing I never had supposed."

[2176] Mormon 9:2–6 "Behold, will ye believe in the day of your visitation—behold,
when the Lord shall come, yea, even that great day when the earth shall be rolled together as a scroll, and the elements shall melt with fervent heat, yea, in that great day
when ye shall be brought to stand before the Lamb of God—then will ye say that there
is no God? Then will ye longer deny the Christ, or can ye behold the Lamb of God?
Do ye suppose that ye shall dwell with him under a consciousness of your guilt? Do ye
suppose that ye could be happy to dwell with that holy Being, when your souls are
racked with a consciousness of guilt that ye have ever abused his laws? Behold, I say
unto you that ye would be more miserable to dwell with a holy and just God, under a
consciousness of your filthiness before him, than ye would to dwell with the damned
souls in hell. For behold, when ye shall be brought to see your nakedness before God,
and also the glory of God, and the holiness of Jesus Christ, it will kindle a flame of
unquenchable fire upon you. O then ye unbelieving, turn ye unto the Lord; cry mightily
unto the Father in the name of Jesus, that perhaps ye may be found spotless, pure, fair,
and white, having been cleansed by the blood of the Lamb, at that great and last day."

[2177] Mosiah 4:2 "And they had viewed themselves in their own carnal state, even less
than the dust of the earth. And they all cried aloud with one voice, saying: O have
mercy, and apply the atoning blood of Christ that we may receive forgiveness of our
sins, and our hearts may be purified; for we believe in Jesus Christ, the Son of God,
who created heaven and earth, and all things; who shall come down among the children
of men."

Was his message not kind enough? Not inspiring? Not faith promoting?

Can an angel or a prophet ever save anyone if they do not focus on the great burden left for mankind to repent and return to God? Will flattery ever save a man?

Samuel the Lamanite was sent to cry repentance. He put the case clearly to them and to us, but his words are no more comforting than the angel's words were to King Benjamin and his people:

> "Behold ye are worse than they; for as the Lord liveth, if a prophet come among you and declareth unto you the word of the Lord, which testifieth of your sins and iniquities, ye are angry with him, and cast him out and seek all manner of ways to destroy him; yea, you will say that he is a false prophet, and that he is a sinner, and of the devil, because he testifieth that your deeds are evil.
>
> But behold, if a man shall come among you and shall say: Do this, and there is no iniquity; do that and ye shall not suffer; yea, he will say: Walk after the pride of your own hearts; yea, walk after the pride of your eyes, and do whatsoever your heart desireth—and if a man shall come among you and say this, ye will receive him, and say that he is a prophet.
>
> Yea, ye will lift him up, and ye will give unto him of your substance; ye will give unto him of your gold, and of your silver, and ye will clothe him with costly apparel; and because he speaketh flattering words unto you, and he saith that all is well, then ye will not find fault with him.
>
> O ye wicked and ye perverse generation; ye hardened and ye stiffnecked people, how long will ye suppose that the Lord will suffer you? Yea, how long will ye suffer yourselves to be led by foolish and blind guides? Yea, how long will ye choose darkness rather than light?" (Helaman 13:26–29)

The Apostle Paul described such folks as having "itching ears."[2178] It is a fairly apt description. These folks think themselves righteous, but they are unrepentant, unforgiven, and unsaved. They follow a religion which cannot save them, because it has become nothing more than a false idol, appealing to their vanity.

[2178] 2 Timothy 4:3–4 "For the time will come when they will not endure sound doctrine; but after their own lusts shall they heap to themselves teachers, having itching ears; And they shall turn away *their* ears from the truth, and shall be turned unto fables."

TATTOOS AND PLURAL WIVES

The Trick to Apostasy

The trick to successfully pulling off an apostasy is to distract people into thinking there hasn't been one. The "believers" need to think everything remains intact.

So the issue of "apostasy" becomes a discussion about individuals and individual conformity to the expectations of the group. The subject can then be a topic that polite, fellow-believers can discuss without ever searching into the overall condition of a fallen people.

The Jews mocked efforts to tell them they were apostate. They thought it was humorous when Lehi preached the idea.[2179] Because they were so very religious, so devout, so unassailably active in following God, the idea was absolutely laughable that they were apostate.

[2179] 1 Nephi 1:19 "And it came to pass that the Jews did mock him because of the things which he testified of them; for he truly testified of their wickedness and their abominations; and he testified that the things which he saw and heard, and also the things which he read in the book, manifested plainly of the coming of a Messiah, and also the redemption of the world."

The Apostle Paul said the problem would begin at the top with the shepherds, who would teach them falsehoods as truth.[2180] These new leaders would have only a form of godliness, without any real power to save.[2181]

The Christian world adopted another, false replacement of the original church. It became so universal it was hailed as the Universal, or Catholic Church. It ruled from the rivers to the ends of the earth as the only official form of the faith established by Christ.

To pull this off Satan must be concerned with the "macro" institutional failure, not just individuals falling away. It is the small, minor spirits who follow Lucifer who engage in petty tempting of individuals to sin. Success for the Adversary is not accomplished in petty enterprises. He wants failure for the whole, so none can be saved. For that, apostasy must be universal.

He has never succeeded by admitting there has been a failure. The trick is always to have the apostasy come unnoticed, unacknowledged and from within.[2182]

The topic is worth studying. When apostasy is noticed, acknowledged and exposed, then it is possible to repent and return. Until then, it progresses apace, discarding and rejecting what might have been given. All the while being happily ignored by "believers" whose devotion will not save.

[2180] Acts 20:29–30 "For I know this, that after my departing shall grievous wolves enter in among you, not sparing the flock. Also of your own selves shall men arise, speaking perverse things, to draw away disciples after them."

[2181] 2 Timothy 3:5 "Having a form of godliness, but denying the power thereof: from such turn away."

[2182] 3 Nephi 16:10 "And thus commandeth the Father that I should say unto you: At that day when the Gentiles shall sin against my gospel, and shall reject the fulness of my gospel, and shall be lifted up in the pride of their hearts above all nations, and above all the people of the whole earth, and shall be filled with all manner of lyings, and of deceits, and of mischiefs, and all manner of hypocrisy, and murders, and priestcrafts, and whoredoms, and of secret abominations; and if they shall do all those things, and shall reject the fulness of my gospel, behold, saith the Father, I will bring the fulness of my gospel from among them."

Since Christ predicted that at some point the latter-day gentiles would reject the fullness,[2183] we probably should consider what the Book of Mormon has to say about the subject.

To finish the thought about the "trick to apostasy" the D&C has a remarkable statement. Lucifer succeeds when he manages to get us NOT to reject ordinances, but to change them. As soon as they are changed, they are broken.[2184] That is an important step. Because then religious people can continue to claim they follow a true religion, while practicing one that has been broken. These practitioners become like the ancient Jews, who mocked Lehi because they knew they were still righteous. They knew Lehi was foolish, even fraudulent. They still had the truth, the ordinances, the temple, and the priesthood. Lehi was just a mistaken crank.

The Prophetic and the Priestly

There are two approaches to preserving a belief system. Scholars refer to these as "sophic" and "mantic," but the scriptural language would be "the priestly" and "the prophetic."

Priests deal with rites, ordinances, commandments and procedures. This durable approach to preserving a belief system allows a dispensation of the Gospel to continue to have a presence, long after a founder has died. Moses, for example, established a system of rites and observances which then became the religious fare of priests who perpetuated the system from the time of Moses until the coming of Christ.

Prophets deal with God and angels. They receive new insight, promises and covenants. Their conduct can even appear to violate the traditions of the religion they follow, but that is only because they

---

[2183] Ibid.

[2184] D&C 1:15 "For they have strayed from mine ordinances, and have broken mine everlasting covenant;"

are not bound to the tradition as practiced by the priests. Instead they have penetrated into the underlying meaning, the original power, the purpose of the rites.

Dispensations are founded by those who combine both traditions. Moses was a prophet, and established priestly rites. Christ was a prophet and more, and He also established priestly rites. Similarly, Joseph Smith was an authentic Dispensation Head who was both a prophet and established priestly rites.

The reason an apostasy can be concealed from the view of religious believers is because they confuse the presence of continuing priestly tradition with both. They do not notice the prophetic presence has left. Concealing the fact that the prophetic presence is gone is possible because priests focus on authority and make that idea the central, even controlling issue for salvation.

Catholics held a monopoly for a thousand years using the idea of "keys from St. Peter" as the foundation upon which the religion was built. Not until the eastern Orthodox faith departed was there any choice to be made between "keys" in Rome and "keys" in Constantinople. It took Martin Luther to finally peel away the fraud of "keys" independent from righteousness. His expositions on the "priesthood of faith" allowed a divorce between claims of priestly "keys" and faith in God.

It took Martin Luther's revolution in thinking several hundred years to create a religious landscape where Joseph Smith and a new Dispensation of the Gospel could be introduced. These things move slowly because mankind is generally imprisoned by their traditions and are incapable of seeing the difference between the priestly and the prophetic traditions. This blindness becomes the tool through which the priestly tradition controls mankind.

Priestly tradition is stable, authoritarian, controlling, focused on outward conduct, amasses wealth, power and prestige. Priestly tradition can continue in the absence of spirit, revelation or even godliness. Priestly tradition can become the friend of government, business and empires, and can work hand-in-hand with the powers of this world.

Prophetic tradition is unruly, unpredictable, and challenges the god of this world. It cannot work with the powers of this world, but strikes at its authority. It cannot exist without the direct involvement of God and angels and it cannot be divorced from continuing revelation.

You can have both without an apostasy. You can have the prophetic without an apostasy. You can have a priestly tradition exist without an apostasy, but that is much less likely. In any complete apostasy, the presence of the priestly tradition is essential to be able to accomplish the "trick" referred to in the post yesterday.

God's People

When God begins work with people, the group becomes "chosen," and therefore the focus of His continuing efforts to save mankind. Although "chosen people" do not always remain faithful to Him, they do remain the center of His work.

A good illustration of this was during the Second Temple period in ancient Israel. Throughout this time, the people were apostate. Margaret Barker's work reconstructing the era is perhaps as good a job as any scholar has been able to accomplish to date. Israel was led by corrupt and uninspired priests. The nation descended generation by generation until, by the time the New Testament era opened, the nation's "king" was appointed by Rome from a well-connected family having only quasi-Jewish lineage and no real devotion to their faith. The High Priest was also a political appointment, based on family patronage and bribery.

Into this corrupt society, the dawn of a new Dispensation conformed to the old patterns of the fallen, idolatrous religion. The angel Gabriel came to Zacharias in the place and time that honored the ceremonies established by Moses.

Zacharias was in the Holy Place, before the veil of the Temple, burning incense and offering the morning prayer. The prayer asked for the light of God's presence to return to Israel. As the cloud of incense ascended from the altar upward, symbolizing the ascent of prayers to God, Gabriel appeared on the right side of the altar.[2185] This is the exact spot a person would stand if they emerged from the Holy of Holies of the Temple, conforming to the then existing religious pattern. The angel announced to Zacharias that "thy prayer is heard",[2186] meaning that the set prayer for God's presence to return to Israel was accepted. The religious pattern was vindicated.

Though Israel had endured hundreds of years of apostate decline, when the time to refresh and restore arrived, the work resumed inside the existing pattern. God honored the religion of His chosen people, even though the religion was at the time fallen, worldly and apostate.

Zacharias lived among this apostate people and yet was unhindered by it. His prayer was heard, the angel was sent, and God's promise to return to Israel was not only vindicated, but Zacharias was told he would have a son who would "go before [the Lord] in the spirit and power of Elias."[2187]

Similarly, the prophet Simeon and the prophetess Anna lived among a fallen and apostate people, but honored the traditions, kept the faith, and saw beyond the evil of their day. Each received by reve-

---

[2185] Luke 1:11 "And there appeared unto him an angel of the Lord standing on the right side of the altar of incense."

[2186] Luke 1:13 "But the angel said unto him, Fear not, Zacharias: for thy prayer is heard; and thy wife Elisabeth shall bear thee a son, and thou shalt call his name John."

[2187] Ibid. Also Luke 1: 17 "And he shall go before him in the spirit and power of Elias, to turn the hearts of the fathers to the children, and the disobedient to the wisdom of the just; to make ready a people prepared for the Lord."

lation a promise they would live to see their Lord come into the flesh.[2188] These faithful believers, both male and female, were not hindered by the apostasy then underway.

The Lord follows the same pattern throughout, because He is the same yesterday, today and forever.[2189] Therefore, once the work recommenced through Joseph Smith, and there was a "chosen people," the work will always continue, or if necessary begin anew among the same "chosen people." Though the gentiles will fail, as Christ prophesied would eventually occur,[2190] the work will not be abandoned.

General apostasy, therefore, cannot prevent individual participation in the fullness of God's promises. Though it may be interrupted

---

[2188] Luke 2:25–38 "And, behold, there was a man in Jerusalem, whose name *was* Simeon; and the same man *was* just and devout, waiting for the consolation of Israel: and the Holy Ghost was upon him. And it was revealed unto him by the Holy Ghost, that he should not see death, before he had seen the Lord's Christ. And he came by the Spirit into the temple: and when the parents brought in the child Jesus, to do for him after the custom of the law, Then took he him up in his arms, and blessed God, and said, Lord, now lettest thou thy servant depart in peace, according to thy word: For mine eyes have seen thy salvation, Which thou hast prepared before the face of all people; A light to lighten the Gentiles, and the glory of thy people Israel. And Joseph and his mother marvelled at those things which were spoken of him. And Simeon blessed them, and said unto Mary his mother, Behold, this *child* is set for the fall and rising again of many in Israel; and for a sign which shall be spoken against; (Yea, a sword shall pierce through thy own soul also,) that the thoughts of many hearts may be revealed. And there was one Anna, a prophetess, the daughter of Phanuel, of the tribe of Aser: she was of a great age, and had lived with an husband seven years from her virginity; And she *was* a widow of about fourscore and four years, which departed not from the temple, but served *God* with fastings and prayers night and day. And she coming in that instant gave thanks likewise unto the Lord, and spake of him to all them that looked for redemption in Jerusalem."

[2189] Moroni 10:19 "And I would exhort you, my beloved brethren, that ye remember that he is the same yesterday, today, and forever, and that all these gifts of which I have spoken, which are spiritual, never will be done away, even as long as the world shall stand, only according to the unbelief of the children of men."

[2190] 3 Nephi 16:10 "And thus commandeth the Father that I should say unto you: At that day when the Gentiles shall sin against my gospel, and shall reject the fulness of my gospel, and shall be lifted up in the pride of their hearts above all nations, and above all the people of the whole earth, and shall be filled with all manner of lyings, and of deceits, and of mischiefs, and all manner of hypocrisy, and murders, and priestcrafts, and whoredoms, and of secret abominations; and if they shall do all those things, and shall reject the fulness of my gospel, behold, saith the Father, I will bring the fulness of my gospel from among them."

for three or four generations when there is rebellion,[2191] when it resumes it will begin among the same people where it left off.

This is the pattern of the Lord. And mankind's failure does nothing to prevent eventual fulfillment of the Lord's promises.[2192]

Salvation and Signs

There are "signs" that show a person is not apostate. Mormon's teachings to his son recount the signs which show God is saving souls. These teachings are in Chapter 7 of Moroni's book. The whole text is worth careful study.

Moroni records that God will let all mankind know with power and great glory at the last day that "the day of miracles" has never ceased.[2193] Nor have angels ceased to appear and teach those who are in need of instruction.[2194] Nor has the "power" of the Holy Ghost receded.[2195] This is because these things are required for "one man upon the face [of the earth] to be saved."[2196]

[2191] Exodus 20:5 "Thou shalt not bow down thyself to them, nor serve them: for I the Lord thy God *am* a jealous God, visiting the iniquity of the fathers upon the children unto the third and fourth *generation* of them that hate me;"

[2192] D&C 1:38 "What I the Lord have spoken, I have spoken, and I excuse not myself; and though the heavens and the earth pass away, my word shall not pass away, but shall all be fulfilled, whether by mine own voice or by the voice of my servants, it is the same."

[2193] Moroni 7:35 "And now, my beloved brethren, if this be the case that these things are true which I have spoken unto you, and God will show unto you, with power and great glory at the last day, that they are true, and if they are true has the day of miracles ceased?"

[2194] Moroni 7:36 "Or have angels ceased to appear unto the children of men? Or has he withheld the power of the Holy Ghost from them? Or will he, so long as time shall last, or the earth shall stand, or there shall be one man upon the face thereof to be saved?"

[2195] Ibid.

[2196] Ibid.

When there is faith, there are miracles.[2197] When there is faith, then angels minister to the faithful.[2198]

If the time comes when there are no more miracles and there are no more angels ministering to mankind, then it is because of "unbelief, and all is lost."[2199]

Moroni explains in simplicity and clarity:

> "For no man can be saved, according to the words of Christ, save they shall have faith in his name; wherefore, if these things have ceased, then has faith ceased also; and awful is the state of man, for they are as though there had been no redemption made." (Moroni 7:38)

The priestly tradition mentioned in the "Prophetic and Priestly" section above can provide the rites, teach the doctrine and preserve the truth, but the underlying reality must be pursued for salvation. Moroni explains how we must push beyond the mere symbol to the reality.

Rites may teach us about conversing with the Lord through the veil. However, when the rite is over it leaves you with only the idea, the outline, the admonition of how the Gospel operates. Then it is up to you to pursue the practice of the rites by your life, your faithfulness, and calling upon God to know Him.

Signs do not produce faith and never have. Signs do, always, and will forever, follow faith.[2200] Moroni taught sound doctrine.

[2197] Moroni 7:37 "Behold I say unto you, Nay; for it is by faith that miracles are wrought; and it is by faith that angels appear and minister unto men; wherefore, if these things have ceased wo be unto the children of men, for it is because of unbelief, and all is vain."

[2198] Ibid.

[2199] Ibid.

[2200] D&C 63:9 "But, behold, faith cometh not by signs, but signs follow those that believe."

For each of us, the priestly tradition is never enough. Ancient Israel had their rites, observances, feasts and rituals. They could acquire ceremonial cleanliness by following the rules for purification. But, as the Lord observed, outward cleanliness can belie the inward filth if they failed to connect with God.[2201] *It is always easier to be ritually clean and religiously pure than it is to be approved of God. It is much easier to rise inside an organization than it is to part the veil.*

However, for those who seek God, no amount of praise in this world can tempt them to ignore the path of faith where they encounter the Holy Ghost, angels, the Lord, and the Father.[2202]

The Trick to Avoiding Apostasy

We began this week with the topic of apostasy. That is where we will end. It is easy to distract and fool people. It is also easy to keep in mind what is essential and will save, and what is distracting and cannot save. Here are a few thoughts that can prevent apostasy:

Never confuse the symbol for the reality.

Never accept a man as your Lord, but reserve worship for Christ alone. Everything and everyone else is idolatry.

Always bear in mind that Christ alone is the keeper of the gate, and He cannot be misled.

[2201] Matthew 23:25–28 "Woe unto you, scribes and Pharisees, hypocrites! for ye make clean the outside of the cup and of the platter, but within they are full of extortion and excess. *Thou* blind Pharisee, cleanse first that *which is* within the cup and platter, that the outside of them may be clean also. Woe unto you, scribes and Pharisees, hypocrites! for ye are like unto whited sepulchres, which indeed appear beautiful outward, but are within full of dead *men's* bones, and of all uncleanness. Even so ye also outwardly appear righteous unto men, but within ye are full of hypocrisy and iniquity."

[2202] John 14:23 "Jesus answered and said unto him, If a man love me, he will keep my words: and my Father will love him, and we will come unto him, and make our abode with him."
D&C 130:3 "John 14:23—The appearing of the Father and the Son, in that verse, is a personal appearance; and the idea that the Father and the Son dwell in a man's heart is an old sectarian notion, and is false."

Always participate fully in the rites given to you as a gift from God, performed by the priests, and be worthy before God when you do so.

Take every gift from God in gratitude, and recognize His hand in what you receive.

Be grateful for what you are given, and never think yourself better than another because you think you understand more. You are measured against perfection, not your fellow man.

Forgive if you want to be forgiven.

Leaders deserve your best efforts to support them in the heavy burdens they carry. Uphold, rather than criticize them.

Most errors deserve your pity and forgiveness—not your judgment.

It is not criticism to search for truth, even if the truth exposes mistakes and errors of men. Be gracious with failure, and not distracted or preoccupied by it.

Nobody's failure can prevent your success. No other organization or person can bring you along in their success. You are required to connect with God independent of all others. Life eternal is to know Him and His Son.

Love your spouse, because this is your own flesh. There was never a saved man without a woman, nor a saved woman without a man. Adam and Eve are "the image of God" for "in the image of God created He him, male and female created He them."

It is in the private, unobserved moments when you learn the most about yourself. What you think, what you do, how you act when you think you are alone reveals more about your heart than anything else. If you are distant from God, begin to return in those moments alone.

God does live. Never doubt that. Just accept it and move forward to know Him.

It is a thin veil, not a wall, that separates you from God. Do not let it become insurmountable. It was always meant to be parted.

Fear is the opposite of faith.

Do not let borrowed fears become the barrier to your faith.

Men cannot save you, but they can condemn you. You cannot respect men too much without respecting God too little.

Religion has been the source of most of mankind's cruelty, rebellion and apostasy. Never think your own religious observances can or will connect you with God. They are only habits until you reach out and speak with God directly. Ministers, priests, Rabbis, Elders, preachers, Fathers, Presidents, Apostles and even prophets are not God. Nor should any of these roles be allowed to distance you from God.

Saving belief requires you to accept the truth. Saving faith requires you to act in conformity with correct belief. Saving knowledge comes from contact with God.

Tattoos and Plural Wives

If we convert someone who has a tattoo we do not refuse to baptize them. If a person born in the church leaves and returns again covered with tattoos, we don't refuse them fellowship. Nor do we expect anyone to undergo the painful process of having them burned away using a laser.

When the church finally abandoned the practice of taking plural wives, one of the concessions the church wanted the government to make was to allow all existing plural marriages to become legal. No new ones could be contracted, but the existing ones needed to be tolerated under the law.

Heber J. Grant was the last church president with plural wives. He was church president until his death in May 1945. The church was led by a polygamist well into World War II.

Even though we abandoned the practice publicly in 1890 and privately in 1904, we were led by polygamists at the head until respectively, 55 and 41 years later.

The argument used to persuade the government was that it was absolutely cruel to deprive children born into these plural wife families of both parents. Breaking up families was unkind, unnecessary and would cause more harm than good.

Today there are many people who are in plural marriages who ought to be the target of efforts to reconvert them to the Gospel. We stay away from them because they have relationships we condemn. They are, in a sense, tattooed and we are unwilling to accept them back unless they will undergo the painful ordeal of disengaging from their unapproved relationship. We ask more of them than we were willing to allow the government to ask of us when we abandoned the practice.

If a polygamist family is willing to return, we should welcome them. We should allow them full fellowship, and admit them back to practice faith with us. They should know we condemn the practice and we will preach against it. We will encourage and teach their children to discontinue the practice, but we should accept them back into fellowship.

With Warren Jeffs' latest decree limiting all fathering of children to his fifteen chosen inner circle, I suspect there will be a great number willing to abandon his leadership and who would reconsider fellowship with the church. The conditions we have set for reentry are so cruel, so damaging to these families, that we are essentially saying they can never return.

I would like to see polygamy ended. I would like to see those who practice it reconverted. I do not think we can reasonably expect to break apart their families. We should not break up families as a condition of return.

I've written about Section 132 in my last book. This week I'm going to return to that topic and spend a few days discussing plural marriage. I hope it will be a friendly invitation to those who practice it to reconsider whether they can get closer to God by returning to faith among the Latter-day Saints. I, for one, would be willing to fellowship with them. Though I condemn the practice and believe it should never have continued, I am not unrealistic about any existing obligations.

History, Lies, Good Faith and Myths

The topic of Mormonism's past practice/teaching of taking plural wives puts you squarely in the middle of problems in church history. Deliberate deception and public statements which contradict private behavior is a fact of Mormon history. This fact complicates the difficulty of knowing what is true and right, false and wrong, and whether something is a bona fide required part of "real" Mormonism.

The authenticity of the revelation in D&C 132 is debated. This debate is possible because of these problems with Mormon history.

To understand Mormonism requires a level of tolerance for deceit which some modern Mormons refuse to acknowledge. It is a natural reaction to want to put men on a pedestal. We resist any notion that would reduce them to anything less than completely truthful, honest in their dealings, and trustworthy in every statement they made. Therefore, when you encounter deliberate dis-information campaigns designed to mislead others, it is natural to react with disbelief.

The truth matters more than our reaction to it. Whether we find it troubling or not, the truth is valuable enough to warrant study even if it causes discomfort. The practice of taking plural wives is one of those topics requiring discomfort to wade through it and reach a conclusion.

There are some major themes in the argument advanced by those who claim it is essential to salvation. These include the sometimes inconsistent arguments that:

- It is required for exaltation.
- Those who live it are living a "higher law" and those who do not are living a lower law.
- Those living a "higher law" cannot submit to authority by those who live a lower law.
- President Taylor foresaw the discontinuance of the practice, and he gave "keys" to allow it to continue, outside the church.
- The Manifesto was merely a public relations document and did not reflect a serious abandonment of the practice.
- Plural marriages were performed by the church, including the president of the church after the 1890 Manifesto.
- The church's final abandonment occurred because of the Smoot Senate Hearings, and the pressure brought through interrogating President Joseph F. Smith.
- The "second manifesto" written in 1904 was the real basis for discontinuing the practice.
- Apostles Cowley and Taylor were forced to resign because of the "second manifesto" and the church never sustained it as binding; therefore it is not binding.
- The "fundamentalists" were allowed to use church Temples, including the Salt Lake Temple, to conduct plural marriages through the administration of David O. McKay.
- Several unpublished revelations, including to John Taylor and Wilford Woodruff, show the Lord's insistence on continuing the practice.

Those who utterly reject the practice claim the sometimes inconsistent arguments that:

- Joseph Smith's public declarations are more reliable than a secret revelation.
- Joseph Smith is not responsible for Section 132.

- Brigham Young fabricated the revelation, and pawned if off as an authentic revelation from Joseph Smith, but it was never made public in Joseph's lifetime.
- The church's declaration on marriage was sustained by the church membership and precludes multiple wives.
- The Book of Mormon condemns the practice.
- Taking multiple wives is an "abomination" which the Lord condemns.
- The First Presidency and Quorum of the 12 have "keys' and they will never be lost.
- The affidavits from putative plural wives were given long after the fact, and in a time when the practice was being challenged by the RLDS movement.
- Emma Smith denies it was practiced.
- Joseph "repented" and changed his mind; claiming he had been deceived in practicing plural wives.
- There are no children proven to have been Joseph's other than those born through Emma Smith.

This is not exhaustive of the positions, but a reasonable starting point. All of the foregoing arguments have some historical basis to support them. People who make these and other arguments are not ignoring history. They are choosing sources; sometimes between what a single source said in one place and in another.

It is not possible to accept what everyone said in every instance and come out with a single version of the events. Hence the problem of history, lies, good faith and myths which cloud this topic.

I'm going to try this week to explain why the practice is, in my view, not a necessary (or advisable) part of Mormonism. Those who care intensely about this topic can find material to both support and oppose the explanation I give.

Did Joseph Receive a Revelation?

Section 132 of the Doctrine & Covenants is not universally accepted as a revelation received by Joseph Smith. When the discussion cannot proceed beyond whether this originated from Joseph Smith, by revelation, the discussion goes nowhere. Therefore, the first step must be to resolve whether the revelation came through Joseph Smith, or was a later fabrication of Brigham Young and his inner circle of polygamists.

The following information persuades me Section 132 came through Joseph Smith and was reduced to writing on July 12, 1843:

The Nauvoo Diaries of William Clayton were written chronologically and have the following entries (exactly as in original):

July 11, 1843: At noon rode out to farm with Margt. P.M. J & family rode out in the carriage.

July 12, 1843: This A.M. I wrote a Revelation consisting of 10 pages on the order of the priesthood, showing the designs in Moses, Abraham, David and Solomon having many wives & concubines. After it was wrote Prests. Joseph and Hyrum presented it and read it to E. who said she did not believe a word of it and appeared very rebellious. J told me to Deed all the unincumbered lots to E & the children. He appears much troubled about E.

July 13:1843: This A.M. J sent for me & when I arrived he called me up into his private room with E. and there stated an agreement they had mutually entered into. they both stated their feelings on many subjects & wept considerable. O may the Lord soften her heart that she may be willing to keep and abide his Holy Law.

July 15, 1843: Made Deed for 1/2 S. B. Iowa from J. to Emma. Also a Deed to E. for over 60 city lots.

July 16, 1843: A.M. at home writing bro. Kimballs lecture. P.M. went to the Grove and heard Pres. J. preach on the law of the priesthood. He stated that Hyrum held the office of prophet to the church by birthright & he was going to have a reformation and the saints must regard Hyrum for he has authority. He showed that a man must enter into an everlasting covenant with his wife in this world or he will have no claim on her in the next. He said that he could not reveal the fulness of these things untill the Temple is completed &c.

July 17, 1843: A.M. at the Temple & at Prest. J's. conversed with J. & Hyrum on the priesthood.

In addition to the foregoing, I checked surrounding public events, and the diary is consistent with other records of those days. For example, the event on July 16th is recorded as having taken place "At Stand in Grove, West of Temple" and appears in a letter of Willard Richards to Brigham Young, the Joseph Smith diary kept by Willard Richards, the Levi Richards Diary and the Willard Richards Diary. The afternoon of the 16th also records a public meeting on the "Temple Stand" in the Franklin Richards, William Clayton, and Levi Richards diaries and in the Letter of Willard Richards to Brigham Young, as well as in the Joseph Smith diary kept by Willard Richards.

Disputes after Joseph's death also confirm a disagreement between Emma and the church over ownership in the steamboat the *Maid of Iowa*.

These entries seem credible, and therefore I believe they show Section 132 was recorded on July 12, 1843 and originated from Joseph Smith. In addition, the August 12, 1843 meeting of the Nauvoo High Council records there was "teaching by Hyrum Smith" which four witnesses later confirmed included reading Section 132. These witnesses were Austin Cowles (who rejected the doctrine and left the church), David Fulmer, Thomas Grover, James Allred and Aaron

Johnson. Hosea Stout was absent when Hyrum read the document, but was later told about the revelation. When Section 132 became public, Hosea Stout confirmed it "corresponded to what" he was told about the reading in August 1843.

It is possible to believe it a fabrication of Brigham Young. It was not made public until the 1850's, and the public disclosure was on Brigham Young's watch. But the document came into existence while Joseph was church president, and came through him. As much as a person may wish the document did not originate with Joseph Smith, the evidence appears to be more than adequate to show it did. It came from Joseph and was reduced to written form in July 1843.

Jacob and Section 132

Through Joseph Smith we have two scriptural sources dealing with plural wives. Jacob 2, in the Book of Mormon condemns the practice as "an abomination," but leaves it open to be practiced if the Lord commands. The reason the Lord would command is to "raise up seed unto [Him]."

Section 132, beginning at verse 29, discusses why earlier prophets took more than one wife. It "permits" taking more than one wife under two conditions. But Section 132 should be read in light of what Jacob taught regarding the limitations and purpose of having more than one wife.

Before carefully examining the scriptures, a bit of history is necessary. Joseph first learned about the subject during the translation of Jacob sometime in 1829. Oliver was with him when the answer was first received. Therefore, at least two people knew about the subject as early as 1829.

As the earlier post on William Clayton's Journal shows, Joseph did not put the revelation into writing until July 1843. Between 1829 and 1843, any explanation by Joseph (or Oliver) would have been verbal, private, and not necessarily understood properly, recorded correctly, or practiced openly. In other words, whatever happened between 1829 and 1843 is bound to be extremely difficult to accurately recreate. Those involved were trying to cover it up, and make it difficult and hopefully impossible to know it took place. They did not want it public.

Moreover, not everyone who was taken into confidence by Joseph was trustworthy, or honorable. Some men were predisposed to exploitation of vulnerable women. John C. Bennett, for example, was a sexual predator before coming to Nauvoo. When he became the Mayor and a member of the First Presidency, he learned about these unrecorded teachings and began to behave in a contemptible manner.

John Bennett would later publish salacious details of sexual misconduct in Nauvoo, attributing to Joseph some of his (Bennett's) own conduct. Some of what Bennett wrote was true (i.e., private taking of multiple wives) and some of it was sensational, untrue, and was a reflection of his own behavior projected onto others, most notably Joseph Smith.

The Bennett expose of Nauvoo underground sexual practices acquired increased credibility years later when Brigham Young began to openly practice and advocate taking plural wives. Some people who had not believed Bennett at first, changed their minds and took him as a credible source once the public revelation of plural marriage became international news.

Section 132 was not revealed *publicly* in 1843. When it *was* finally made public, it also seemed to vindicate Bennett's accusations about Nauvoo private behavior. The revelation was attributed (I think correctly) to Joseph Smith, and therefore it established a religious basis for the Bennett accusations stemming directly from Joseph.

In addition to Bennett, others also knew of the private taking of additional wives. The most vocal parties with inside information were critics of Joseph Smith who left the church. These disaffected former Mormons had little reason to tell an accurate story. They were trying to discredit the church, not to defend it. Even if they attempted to be "fair" in retelling what they knew, their accounts are colored by:

- Disaffection for Joseph Smith.
- Hostility to the religion.
- Questions about whether or not they fully understood the matter.
- Issues about how "hidden" and "secret" practices were explained.
- Their attempts to make themselves appear more moral than their private conduct actually reflected.

All of this strongly suggests to me that the words of Jacob and Section 132 need to be carefully studied, and the history of how the practice was conducted by the few who knew what was happening must be taken with some careful skepticism about its accuracy.

When characters like John Bennett and William Law were involved in seducing women and claiming there was a secret teaching allowing "spiritual wives" because Joseph Smith had actually discussed the principle with them, it becomes apparent that whatever Section 132 permits or does not permit, the principle can be abused. It was abused by these men, and other insiders. Joseph's public statements condemning adultery, and denouncing polygamy can be reconciled with Section 132. But to reconcile it all requires some knowledge about these events. It also requires recognition that the neat, tidy history that ignores these rather messy interpersonal conflicts and betrayals of trust is inadequate.

Plural wives is as unpleasant a topic as you encounter in our religion. However, its unpleasantness does not detract from the importance of sorting it out. Given the various conflicting charges and countercharges, it is a relief to just accept a superficial account and hope it is true. That applies to BOTH sides. BOTH those who reject the practice, as well as those who welcome it, need to be willing to sort through it and reach the correct conclusion.

Just because the fundamentalists have recognized more of the truth about the history does not mean they have sorted it out aright, nor that they are living a "higher" law. It may mean they are just as wrong about their conclusions as they *think* the church is for abandoning the practice.

I've taken the topic seriously. I've accorded the advocates' arguments respect. I think they are wrong. As I continue this discussion I'm hoping some of them may be persuaded there is still some of the story they haven't yet sorted out correctly.

Cursing and Abominations

Before proceeding further, it is important to recognize that this is not an inconsequential matter. If someone guesses they can have plural wives and they are wrong, they have gone too far. They are taking a dangerous step. They risk eternity. Therefore this topic should not be approached casually, or because someone "thinks" this is proper. Either they know because God has instructed them by commandment, exclusively for the limited reasons it is allowed to be practiced, or they are involved in a serious, grievous sin.

In Section 132, words like "he hath broken his vow and hath committed adultery" are included for those who proceed absent the

Lord's command.[2203] Those who go too far can "fall from his exaltation" when these things are done in violation of God's will.[2204]

In Jacob, the improper taking of an additional wife is called "whoredoms and an abomination" by the Lord.[2205]

Those who proceed in our dispensation in the absence of the Lord's direct command to them are included among those the Lord described as gentiles filled with "whoredoms, and of secret abominations."[2206]

If you are engaged in the practice, and recognize it is an abomination, and you will "repent and return unto [God's ways], saith the Father, behold they shall be numbered among my people, O house of Israel."[2207]

None but fools will trifle with this topic.

Read Section 132 and see if the Lord commands you to either take or be a multiple wife. Don't impose it in the language. Don't force it into the revelation. Instead, read it as if the practice is for-

---

[2203] D&C 132:43 "And if her husband be with another woman, and he was under a vow, he hath broken his vow and hath committed adultery."

[2204] D&C 132:39 "David's wives and concubines were given unto him of me, by the hand of Nathan, my servant, and others of the prophets who had the keys of this power; and in none of these things did he sin against me save in the case of Uriah and his wife; and, therefore he hath fallen from his exaltation, and received his portion; and he shall not inherit them out of the world, for I gave them unto another, saith the Lord."

[2205] Jacob 2:28 "For I, the Lord God, delight in the chastity of women. And whoredoms are an abomination before me; thus saith the Lord of Hosts."

[2206] 3 Nephi 16:10 "And thus commandeth the Father that I should say unto you: At that day when the Gentiles shall sin against my gospel, and shall reject the fulness of my gospel, and shall be lifted up in the pride of their hearts above all nations, and above all the people of the whole earth, and shall be filled with all manner of lyings, and of deceits, and of mischiefs, and all manner of hypocrisy, and murders, and priestcrafts, and whoredoms, and of secret abominations; and if they shall do all those things, and shall reject the fulness of my gospel, behold, saith the Father, I will bring the fulness of my gospel from among them."

[2207] 3 Nephi 16:13 "But if the Gentiles will repent and return unto me, saith the Father, behold they shall be numbered among my people, O house of Israel."

bidden, an abomination, adultery, or whoredom. Where do you see it demands you to take or be a multiple wife?

Verses 2 through 28 explain celestial marriage without mentioning anything other than a single wife. This explanation of having a single wife sealed to the man is the law which "must be obeyed" or exaltation is impossible. And "if ye abide not that covenant, then are ye damned; for no one can reject this covenant and be permitted to enter into my glory" (D&C 132:3–4). The law, however, is for a man and woman to be sealed together for eternity and to have that sealing ratified by "the Holy Spirit of Promise."

But it is a man (singular) and a woman (singular).

For example:

- "a man" and "a woman" and "he" and "she" and "him" and "her"[2208]

- "a man" and "a wife"[2209]

[2208] D&C 132:15 "Therefore, if a man marry him a wife in the world, and he marry her not by me nor by my word, and he covenant with her so long as he is in the world and she with him, their covenant and marriage are not of force when they are dead, and when they are out of the world; therefore, they are not bound by any law when they are out of the world."

[2209] D&C 132:18 "And again, verily I say unto you, if a man marry a wife, and make a covenant with her for time and for all eternity, if that covenant is not by me or by my word, which is my law, and is not sealed by the Holy Spirit of promise, through him whom I have anointed and appointed unto this power, then it is not valid neither of force when they are out of the world, because they are not joined by me, saith the Lord, neither by my word; when they are out of the world it cannot be received there, because the angels and the gods are appointed there, by whom they cannot pass; they cannot, therefore, inherit my glory; for my house is a house of order, saith the Lord God."

- "a man" and "a wife"[2210]

- "a man" and "a wife" and "he" and "she"[2211]

These verses, from 2 through 28, speak in the singular through-out. One man. One woman. And these verses are the ones that speak of exaltation, thrones, dominions, kingdoms, principalities, all heights and depths.[2212] In fact, the very verse where these things are mentioned is in connection with "a man marry a wife by" the Lord's word.[2213]

[2210] D&C 132:19 "And again, verily I say unto you, if a man marry a wife by my word, which is my law, and by the new and everlasting covenant, and it is sealed unto them by the Holy Spirit of promise, by him who is anointed, unto whom I have appointed this power and the keys of this priesthood; and it shall be said unto them—Ye shall come forth in the first resurrection; and if it be after the first resurrection, in the next resurrection; and shall inherit thrones, kingdoms, principalities, and powers, dominions, all heights and depths—then shall it be written in the Lamb's Book of Life, that he shall commit no murder whereby to shed innocent blood, and if ye abide in my covenant, and commit no murder whereby to shed innocent blood, it shall be done unto them in all things whatsoever my servant hath put upon them, in time, and through all eternity; and shall be of full force when they are out of the world; and they shall pass by the angels, and the gods, which are set there, to their exaltation and glory in all things, as hath been sealed upon their heads, which glory shall be a fulness and a continuation of the seeds forever and ever."

[2211] D&C 132:26 "Verily, verily, I say unto you, if a man marry a wife according to my word, and they are sealed by the Holy Spirit of promise, according to mine appointment, and he or she shall commit any sin or transgression of the new and everlasting covenant whatever, and all manner of blasphemies, and if they commit no murder wherein they shed innocent blood, yet they shall come forth in the first resurrection, and enter into their exaltation; but they shall be destroyed in the flesh, and shall be delivered unto the buffetings of Satan unto the day of redemption, saith the Lord God."

[2212] D&C 132:19 "And again, verily I say unto you, if a man marry a wife by my word, which is my law, and by the new and everlasting covenant, and it is sealed unto them by the Holy Spirit of promise, by him who is anointed, unto whom I have appointed this power and the keys of this priesthood; and it shall be said unto them—Ye shall come forth in the first resurrection; and if it be after the first resurrection, in the next resurrection; and shall inherit thrones, kingdoms, principalities, and powers, dominions, all heights and depths—then shall it be written in the Lamb's Book of Life, that he shall commit no murder whereby to shed innocent blood, and if ye abide in my covenant, and commit no murder whereby to shed innocent blood, it shall be done unto them in all things whatsoever my servant hath put upon them, in time, and through all eternity; and shall be of full force when they are out of the world; and they shall pass by the angels, and the gods, which are set there, to their exaltation and glory in all things, as hath been sealed upon their heads, which glory shall be a fulness and a continuation of the seeds forever and ever."

[2213] Ibid.

Celestial marriage and the celestial law of inheriting exaltation is set out in the very revelation that mentions for the first time the eternal marriage covenant. This occurs ONLY in those verses which are describing marriage between "a man" and "a woman" and not elsewhere.

The focus of these verses is not on multiple wives. Rather the focus is on the preservation of marriage into eternity by God and by His word[2214] which is "sealed by the Holy Spirit of promise."[2215]

Therefore, the question is not whether you have multiple wives. The right questions are:

- Are you sealed by God?
- Are you sealed by God's word?
- Are you sealed by the Holy Spirit of Promise?

If you do not obtain this promise sealed to you by God, through His word, sealed by the Holy Spirit of promise, then it does not matter.

> "[I]f a man marry a wife, and make a covenant with her for time and for all eternity, if that covenant is not by me or by my word, which is my law, and is not sealed by the Holy Spirit of Promise, through him whom I have anointed and appointed unto this power, then it is not valid neither of force when they are out of the world, because they are not joined by me, saith the Lord, neither by my word." (D&C 132:18)

[2214] D&C 132:12 "I am the Lord thy God; and I give unto you this commandment—that no man shall come unto the Father but by me or by my word, which is my law, saith the Lord."

[2215] D&C 132:7 "And verily I say unto you, that the conditions of this law are these: All covenants, contracts, bonds, obligations, oaths, vows, performances, connections, associations, or expectations, that are not made and entered into and sealed by the Holy Spirit of promise, of him who is anointed, both as well for time and for all eternity, and that too most holy, by revelation and commandment through the medium of mine anointed, whom I have appointed on the earth to hold this power (and I have appointed unto my servant Joseph to hold this power in the last days, and there is never but one on the earth at a time on whom this power and the keys of this priesthood are conferred), are of no efficacy, virtue, or force in and after the resurrection from the dead; for all contracts that are not made unto this end have an end when men are dead."

Your individual hopes, wishes, aspirations and ambitions are nothing. The only thing which will endure is that which is established by God. Or, more completely, by God, through His word, which is then sealed by the Holy Spirit of Promise.

All of this discussion takes place in D&C 132:2–28 of the revelation. None of it forces you to read it as referring to multiple wives. You cannot find the multiple wives information anywhere in these verses. If you think it is there, it is because you have put it there by your own interpretation. Multiple wives is NOT included.

The explanation for multiple wives begins after the explanation of what is required for exaltation. These verses permit two exceptions to the prior, mandatory requirement that marriage is limited to a man and a woman who are sealed by God, through His word, by the Holy Spirit of Promise. These two exceptions will be considered next.

To reaffirm the point of this post: If you guess wrong by taking multiple wives, your mistake is called "whoredoms" and "an abomination" and will condemn you. Unless you repent and return to God, you forfeit your exaltation.

Plural Wives

Section 132 speaks to two issues: As to entering into an eternal marriage covenant between a man and a woman in this life, before death, and having that occur by God's will and word, sealed by the Holy Spirit of Promise, the revelation is clear: It is mandatory. As to taking multiple wives, the revelation states conditions, making it clearly NOT mandatory.

The problem with this whole sideshow is that the argument we have going on between devout people over the necessity for plural wives distracts from the real issue. Instead of seeking to have God, by His word, establish a union that will endure into eternity by sealing it through the Holy Spirit of Promise, the debate is over the non-mandatory issue of taking multiple wives.

This sideshow is, of course, a tool of the adversary designed to move focus away from what is required for exaltation onto an issue that will never save a man or woman. Stop being deceived. Stop being distracted. Stop being preoccupied by the second issue, and recognize you will fail in your desire to preserve yourself and your marriage if you neglect to fully comply with the first.

That having been said, the revelation is rather clear about the conditions for taking plural wives. The first requirement is that the Lord must command it in order to raise up seed. This requirement is not found in Section 132, but is in Jacob 2:30.[2216] This is where the underlying reason is stated for the Lord to give the command. Before you presume you understand this underlying doctrine, I would like to pose a few questions to consider:

- If the foundation for giving the command is found in the Lord wanting to "raise up seed unto Himself" then what is to "raise up seed unto the Lord"?
- Are you certain this is childbearing alone?
- Does having children ever "raise up seed unto the Lord?"
- Was Joseph Smith commanded?
- Did Joseph Smith "raise up seed to the Lord?"
- Why did Joseph Smith only father children with Emma Smith?
- Does the commandment to Joseph mean something other than breeding children with multiple women?
- Can a man "raise up seed unto the Lord" as Joseph Smith did, never fathering a child with any other woman than his wife, Emma?

[2216] Jacob 2:30 "For if I will, saith the Lord of Hosts, raise up seed unto me, I will command my people; otherwise they shall hearken unto these things."

- Who are the "seed" which Joseph "raised up unto the Lord?"
- How were they made Joseph's seed?

Section 132 gives some conditions for taking plural wives:

- If the Lord commands. (As in D&C 132:35 where Abraham was commanded.)[2217]
- If a man having the correct authority asks and obtains permission. (As in D&C 132:39 where David asked and the Lord, through Nathan, gave him these wives.)[2218]
- If additional wives are taken without the Lord wanting to "raise up seed unto Himself" thereby opening the way, and one of the two foregoing conditions being met, then taking additional wives is an abomination. (As in D&C 132:38.)[2219]

Further, in order to take an additional wife, someone (either the recipient or an officiator) must have the necessary keys to seal the marriage. This is complicated by the fact that there is never but "one man at a time" who holds this authority.[2220] So if Warren Jeffs has these keys, Thomas Monson cannot. But if Owen Allred has the keys,

---

[2217] D&C 132:35 "Was Abraham, therefore, under condemnation? Verily I say unto you, Nay; for I, the Lord, commanded it."

[2218] D&C 132:39 "David's wives and concubines were given unto him of me, by the hand of Nathan, my servant, and others of the prophets who had the keys of this power; and in none of these things did he sin against me save in the case of Uriah and his wife; and, therefore he hath fallen from his exaltation, and received his portion; and he shall not inherit them out of the world, for I gave them unto another, saith the Lord."

[2219] D&C 132:28 "I am the Lord thy God, and will give unto thee the law of my Holy Priesthood, as was ordained by me and my Father before the world was."

[2220] D&C 132:7 "And verily I say unto you, that the conditions of this law are these: All covenants, contracts, bonds, obligations, oaths, vows, performances, connections, associations, or expectations, that are not made and entered into and sealed by the Holy Spirit of promise, of him who is anointed, both as well for time and for all eternity, and that too most holy, by revelation and commandment through the medium of mine anointed, whom I have appointed on the earth to hold this power (and I have appointed unto my servant Joseph to hold this power in the last days, and there is never but one on the earth at a time on whom this power and the keys of this priesthood are conferred), are of no efficacy, virtue, or force in and after the resurrection from the dead; for all contracts that are not made unto this end have an end when men are dead."

then neither Warren Jeffs nor Thomas Monson can have them. And, of course, if Alex Joseph has them, then that deprives Allred, Jeffs, and Thomas Monson.

The problem is, that if you are wrong in guessing which of the groups actually have the keys (because there's only one, mind you), then you are guilty of an abominable practice and you are condemned. You not only will fail to preserve your marriage, you forfeit your exaltation and condemn yourself.

Though I do not often make disclosures of this sort, one of the reasons I am writing this series is because I have asked, and the Lord has told me, that Warren Jeffs does not hold these keys. Those who follow him thinking he is leading to a better condition in the afterlife have been deceived. I would advise them to abandon that group and repent. Has not his recent behavior taught you he is in error? Has not his last declaration about who can father children made plain the man does not speak for God? Have you not eaten husks long enough? Is it not yet time to return and repent?

Now, if you are of the view that you need to live polygamy, then you need to take every precaution to first know:

- The Lord has, in fact, commanded you; or
- You are in possession of the correct authority and you have asked God and been given His permission; and
- You are capable of "raising up seed unto the Lord" (which means that in the resurrection, you have the ability to take them with you in the ascent through the heavens, passing the sentinels who stand guard along the way, leading your company by the knowledge you have to endure that fiery ascent back to the Throne of God).

If there is any part of that you do not understand, then you are utterly incapable of satisfying the conditions and you should run from this idea because you are not capable of living the conditions.

If you understand and think you have authority to go forward, then I would further caution you that this is not something men take on themselves, but something which God or His ministering angels alone supervise. Do not trust some sentimental feeling, or "burning in the loins." These are serious matters, not to be trifled with by the foolish and aspiring—and NEVER an invitation to the carnal.

Reading Scripture

I received a question this morning about the first two verses of Section 132. The questioner presumes the first two verses frame everything that follows. According to his manner of reading the first two verses the language dealing with eternal marriage requires plural wives.

Here's my response:

God gives "liberally."[2221] This means something. The word "liberally" is illustrated frequently in scripture. For example, Joseph Smith inquired which church to join.[2222] The answer to the specific question was to "join none of them."[2223] But the answer was not limited to the question posed. It also explained that:

- Their creeds were an abomination.

- The professors were corrupt.

- The practitioners draw near with their lips, but

[2221] James 1:5 "If any of you lack wisdom, let him ask of God, that giveth to all *men* liberally, and upbraideth not; and it shall be given him."

[2222] JS–H 1:18 "My object in going to inquire of the Lord was to know which of all the sects was right, that I might know which to join. No sooner, therefore, did I get possession of myself, so as to be able to speak, than I asked the Personages who stood above me in the light, which of all the sects was right (for at this time it had never entered into my heart that all were wrong)—and which I should join."

[2223] Ibid.
JS–H 1:19 "I was answered that I must join none of them, for they were all wrong; and the Personage who addressed me said that all their creeds were an abomination in his sight; that those professors were all corrupt; that: "they draw near to me with their lips, but their hearts are far from me, they teach for doctrines the commandments of men, having a form of godliness, but they deny the power thereof.""

- Their hearts were far from God.

- They possess only a form of godliness.

- Their form of faith is powerless.

- Their doctrines are merely commandments from men.[2224]

Then the Lord added "many other things did he say unto [Joseph] which [he] could not write at this time."[2225]

This information, beyond which church to join is the Lord giving liberally.

When Joseph sought to know what his standing was before God four years later, he prayed to have his sins forgiven.[2226] In response to this inquiry, the angel Moroni appeared and gave him information about coming judgments, the future revelations to be poured out as promised in Joel, the restoration of priesthood, and a book buried nearby giving a history of the ancient inhabitants of the American

---

[2224] Ibid.

[2225] JS–H 1:20 "He again forbade me to join with any of them; and many other things did he say unto me, which I cannot write at this time. When I came to myself again, I found myself lying on my back, looking up into heaven. When the light had departed, I had no strength; but soon recovering in some degree, I went home. And as I leaned up to the fireplace, mother inquired what the matter was. I replied, "Never mind, all is well—I am well enough off." I then said to my mother, "I have learned for myself that Presbyterianism is not true." It seems as though the adversary was aware, at a very early period of my life, that I was destined to prove a disturber and an annoyer of his kingdom; else why should the powers of darkness combine against me? Why the opposition and persecution that arose against me, almost in my infancy?"

[2226] JS–H 1:29 "In consequence of these things, I often felt condemned for my weakness and imperfections; when, on the evening of the above-mentioned twenty-first of September, after I had retired to my bed for the night, I betook myself to prayer and supplication to Almighty God for forgiveness of all my sins and follies, and also for a manifestation to me, that I might know of my state and standing before him; for I had full confidence in obtaining a divine manifestation, as I previously had one."

continent.[2227] The answer was far beyond the scope of the inquiry. This was God giving "liberally."

When the Brother of Jared tried to solve the problem of interior lighting in eight barges, the Lord's answer had very little to do with

---

[2227] JS–H 1:33–43 "He called me by name, and said unto me that he was a messenger sent from the presence of God to me, and that his name was Moroni; that God had a work for me to do; and that my name should be had for good and evil among all nations, kindreds, and tongues, or that it should be both good and evil spoken of among all people. He said there was a book deposited, written upon gold plates, giving an account of the former inhabitants of this continent, and the source from whence they sprang. He also said that the fulness of the everlasting Gospel was contained in it, as delivered by the Savior to the ancient inhabitants; Also, that there were two stones in silver bows—and these stones, fastened to a breastplate, constituted what is called the Urim and Thummim—deposited with the plates; and the possession and use of these stones were what constituted "seers" in ancient or former times; and that God had prepared them for the purpose of translating the book. After telling me these things, he commenced quoting the prophecies of the Old Testament. He first quoted part of the third chapter of Malachi; and he quoted also the fourth or last chapter of the same prophecy, though with a little variation from the way it reads in our Bibles. Instead of quoting the first verse as it reads in our books, he quoted it thus: For behold, the day cometh that shall burn as an oven, and all the proud, yea, and all that do wickedly shall burn as stubble; for they that come shall burn them, saith the Lord of Hosts, that it shall leave them neither root nor branch. And again, he quoted the fifth verse thus: Behold, I will reveal unto you the Priesthood, by the hand of Elijah the prophet, before the coming of the great and dreadful day of the Lord. He also quoted the next verse differently: And he shall plant in the hearts of the children the promises made to the fathers, and the hearts of the children shall turn to their fathers. If it were not so, the whole earth would be utterly wasted at his coming. In addition to these, he quoted the eleventh chapter of Isaiah, saying that it was about to be fulfilled. He quoted also the third chapter of Acts, twenty-second and twenty-third verses, precisely as they stand in our New Testament. He said that that prophet was Christ; but the day had not yet come when "they who would not hear his voice should be cut off from among the people," but soon would come. He also quoted the second chapter of Joel, from the twenty-eighth verse to the last. He also said that this was not yet fulfilled, but was soon to be. And he further stated that the fulness of the Gentiles was soon to come in. He quoted many other passages of scripture, and offered many explanations which cannot be mentioned here. Again, he told me, that when I got those plates of which he had spoken—for the time that they should be obtained was not yet fulfilled—I should not show them to any person; neither the breastplate with the Urim and Thummim; only to those to whom I should be commanded to show them; if I did I should be destroyed. While he was conversing with me about the plates, the vision was opened to my mind that I could see the place where the plates were deposited, and that so clearly and distinctly that I knew the place again when I visited it. After this communication, I saw the light in the room begin to gather immediately around the person of him who had been speaking to me, and it continued to do so until the room was again left dark, except just around him; when, instantly I saw, as it were, a conduit open right up into heaven, and he ascended till he entirely disappeared, and the room was left as it had been before this heavenly light had made its appearance."

the lighting problem.[2228] The Lord's answer redeemed this prophet from the fall,[2229] included ministering to him as the Lord administered to the Nephites at a later time,[2230] and the Lord "ministered to him," which would have included a great deal more than solving lighting issues.[2231] This is what "liberally" means.

The question asked by Joseph concerned plural wives and created the circumstance where the Lord could then "give liberally" to Joseph. The question is posed in verses 1–2. The Lord gives liberally, and explains the eternal marriage covenant (*not responsive to the question asked*). Then he also answers the question, beginning at about verse 34 and going through verse 44. Moreover Joseph receives his calling and election, and is given the sealing authority in verses 45 through 50. This, once again, has nothing to do with the question in verses 1 and 2. This is the Lord "giving liberally."

Revelations from the Lord go well beyond the question asked. Oftentimes the issue which brings a prophet before God has nothing to do with the reason we later learn of the Lord's answer. The highly local question (which church to join, how to light a barge, where to hunt food, why some ancients had plural wives, what repentance is

---

[2228] Ether 3:1 "And it came to pass that the brother of Jared, (now the number of the vessels which had been prepared was eight) went forth unto the mount, which they called the mount Shelem, because of its exceeding height, and did molten out of a rock sixteen small stones; and they were white and clear, even as transparent glass; and he did carry them in his hands upon the top of the mount, and cried again unto the Lord"

[2229] Ether 3:13 "And when he had said these words, behold, the Lord showed himself unto him, and said: Because thou knowest these things ye are redeemed from the fall; therefore ye are brought back into my presence; therefore I show myself unto you."

[2230] Ether 3:17–18 "And now, as I, Moroni, said I could not make a full account of these things which are written, therefore it sufficeth me to say that Jesus showed himself unto this man in the spirit, even after the manner and in the likeness of the same body even as he showed himself unto the Nephites. And he ministered unto him even as he ministered unto the Nephites; and all this, that this man might know that he was God, because of the many great works which the Lord had showed unto him."

[2231] Ether 3:20 "Wherefore, having this perfect knowledge of God, he could not be kept from within the veil; therefore he saw Jesus; and he did minister unto him."

required, etc.) is largely irrelevant to us. The "liberally" given material addresses matters of universal concern:

- Apostasy and restoration.
- Priesthood restoration to Joseph.
- The fullness of God's revelations to mankind, including from the beginning to the end.
- Calling and election.
- Sealing authority.
- Visions of eternity.
- etc., etc.

It is the "liberally given" material which shows what the Lord really intends to bestow on mankind.

Therefore, although the question is posed in verses 1 and 2, the answer goes well beyond, giving liberally, and reveals for the first time the eternity of marriage. You can have plural wives without having an eternal marriage. That is what happens today in the various powerless cults. But the conditions for having an eternal marriage, bound by someone who has been into the Lord's presence and received from Him that authority (as Joseph did), is another matter.

Therefore I do not think verses 1 or 2 frame what follows any more than I think the ministry of Jesus to the Brother of Jared is confined exclusively to lighting interior of barges; or any more than Moroni's visit was confined exclusively to whether Joseph had good standing before the Lord.

The Lord Delights in Chastity

Jacob's sermon which touches on and condemns taking multiple wives includes this statement quoted from the Lord: "For I, the Lord God, delight in the chastity of women."[2232] In the same breath, and

---

[2232] Jacob 2:28 "For I, the Lord God, delight in the chastity of women. And whoredoms are an abomination before me; thus saith the Lord of Hosts."

in connection with the topic of multiple wives, the Lord adds: "And whoredoms are an abomination before me."[2233]

All those who think they are living a "higher law" by taking multiple wives should be extremely careful about their actions, in light of the Lord's overall caution about this subject. David fell from his exaltation as a consequence of offending this law, because it led to betraying Uriah, lying to protect against his immoral behavior, and ultimately taking life.[2234]

How often has violence been the product of polygamous groups? How many murders have happened while wicked and ambitious men struggle for control over followers who take multiple wives?

Joseph Smith, the recipient of the revelation which has led to these various claims by different pretenders also had something to say about chastity and adultery. The very same man through whom the revelation came also instructed the Relief Society with this advice:

> "Spoke of the organization of the Female Relief Society; said he was deeply interested, that is might be built up to the Most High in an acceptable manner; that its rules must be observed; that none should be received into it but those who were worthy; proposed a close examination of every candidate; that the society was growing too fast. It should grow up by degrees, should commence with a few individuals, thus have a select society of the virtuous, and those who would walk circumspectly; commended them for their zeal, but said sometimes their zeal was not according to knowledge. One principle object of the institution was to purge out iniquity; said they must be extremely careful in all their examinations, or the consequences would be serious . . . [T]he Saints should be a select

---

[2233] Ibid.

[2234] D&C 132:39 "David's wives and concubines were given unto him of me, by the hand of Nathan, my servant, and others of the prophets who had the keys of this power; and in none of these things did he sin against me save in the case of Uriah and his wife; and, therefore he hath fallen from his exaltation, and received his portion; and he shall not inherit them out of the world, for I gave them unto another, saith the Lord."

people, separate from all the evils of the world—choice, virtuous and holy." (*TPJS*, 201–202, March 30, 1842.)

Joseph also said:

"If a man commit adultery, he cannot receive the celestial kingdom of God. Even if he is saved in any kingdom, it cannot be the celestial kingdom."

"Inasmuch as the public mind has been unjustly abused through the fallacy of Dr. Bennett's letters, we make an extract on the subject of marriage, showing the rule of the church on this important matter. The extract is from the Book of Doctrine and Covenants, and is the only rule allowed by the Church. "Inasmuch as this church of Christ has been reproached with the crime of fornication, and polygamy; we declare that we believe, that one man should have one wife; and one woman, but one husband, except in case of death, when either is at liberty to marry again." (*Times & Seasons* 3:909, Sept. 1, 1842)

Whatever you may think you know about Joseph's intentions and practice involving plural wives, his public statements cannot be reconciled with promiscuity or exploitation of women for the gratification or vanity of men.

This may seem a contradiction. As if Joseph were talking out of both sides of his mouth. It is not. The careful manner in which the Lord controlled and permitted taking additional wives to "raise up seed unto Himself" was covenantal, sacral, and did not involve indiscriminate breeding of multiple women. Other than his own, Joseph only sealed one plural wife to one man. For Joseph, the multiple wives were governmental, sealed to him to construct the family of God on earth. Tying together lines of what was to be a single family, with himself as the patriarchal father of a new branch of the Family of Israel. It was not, as the quote above demonstrates, a matter of lust and physical gratification.

Joseph's practices were carefully guarded, hidden from public view, and so discrete that still today there are those who think he never had plural wives. If this were something for public display and advocacy, then Joseph would have done so. He did not. To the contrary, he also delighted in the chastity of women and condemned adultery and fornication.

In contrast to Joseph's remarks, Brigham Young made a remark at the return of Thomas Marsh to the church in 1857. This is a reflection of President Young's attitude toward women. I end this series with Brigham Young's words. They were spoken immediately after Thomas Marsh addressed the Saints, pleading to be welcomed back after his apostasy. Brigham Young introduced him, and while Brother Marsh spoke he (Marsh) mentioned that he was "an old man" now. Following his remarks, Brigham Young added the following:

> "He has told you that he is an old man. Do you think that I am an old man? I could prove to this congregation that I am young; for I could find more girls who would choose me for a husband that can any of the young men." (*The Complete Discourses of Brigham Young*, 3:1329, September 6, 1857)

Brigham Young added that the difference between his age and Brother Marsh's age was "one year and seven months to the day."[2235]

Somewhere between Joseph's Nauvoo and Brigham Young's Salt Lake City, the idea of multiple wives transitioned from a carefully guarded, privately practiced, severely limited relationship requiring God's approval, word and the Holy Spirit of Promise, into a broadly advocated, openly practiced, publicly defended, and church authorized form of marriage which was said to be required for exaltation.

[2235] Ibid.

In Brigham Young's form of the church, a man could not be saved if he didn't fetch multiple wives:

> "Now if any of you will deny the plurality of wives, and continue to do so, I promise you that you will be damned." (JD, 3:266)

> "The only men who become Gods, even the Sons of God, are those who enter into polygamy." (Brigham Young, JD 11:269)

It is my view that the question of taking plural wives arises with Joseph Smith, and was through a revelation to him when he inquired about the topic. He treated it as a limited, carefully curtailed, private matter. His implementation of the practice was limited to sealing his own plural wives, and one other man to two wives.

With Brigham Young, however, taking more women became not only public, but it also became a topic used to prove his own virility. A comparison between Joseph's and Brigham Young's advocacy is stark, at least to me.

The subject could be discussed endlessly. I would discourage anyone from thinking this is something to advocate or practice. Even if you believe you are a well-read polygamist, you still don't have enough information. If you think you have enough understanding to know what the topic includes, then instead of acting like Brigham Young and "finding more girls who would choose you for a husband" focus instead on qualifying to preserve one marriage.

Any man whose wife is unhappy, who is exploited and treated like his property, whose behavior fails to mirror Christ's in the heart of the women who knows him best, has not yet qualified for his marriage to be sealed by the Holy Spirit of Promise. That work should not be left undone, and certainly must precede any complication of life by introducing more women into a relationship. Stop this foolishness. Save yourself by approaching this with the caution required to avoid vanity, self-destruction, practicing an abomination, and reducing a relationship to whoredoms. You should never trifle with the souls of others.

Luke 1:8–9

Luke 1:8–9 refers to Zacharias (father of John the Baptist) officiating in the priest's office.

> "And it came to pass, that while he executed the priest's office before God in the order of his course, According to the custom of the priest's office, his lot was to burn incense when he went into the temple of the Lord."

Those who were outside knew how long it would take to burn incense and offer the morning prayer, therefore when too much time had passed they were troubled by the delay.[2236]

The prayer he offered was set, given each day as part of offering incense in the Holy Place, and is as follows:

> True it is that Thou art Jehovah our God, and the God of our fathers; our King of our fathers, our Saviour and the Saviour of our fathers; our Maker and the Rock of our salvation; our Help and our Deliverer. Thy name is from everlasting and there is no God beside Thee. A new song did they that were delivered sing to Thy name by the seashore; together did all praise and own Thee as King, and say, Jehovah shall reign who saveth Israel.

> Be graciously pleased, Jehovah our God, with Thy people Israel, and with their prayer. Restore the service to the oracle of Thy house; and the burnt-offerings of Israel and their prayer

---

[2236] Luke 1:21 "And the people waited for Zacharias, and marvelled that he tarried so long in the temple."

accept graciously and in love; and let the service of Thy people Israel be ever well-pleasing unto Thee.

We praise Thee, who art Jehovah our God, and the God of our fathers, the God of all flesh, our Creator, and the Creator from the beginning! Blessing and praise be unto Thy great and holy name, that Thou hast preserved us in life and kept us. So preserve us and keep us, and gather the scattered ones into Thy holy courts, to keep Thy statutes, and to do Thy good pleasure, and to serve Thee with our whole heart, as this day we confess unto Thee. Blessed be the Lord, unto who belongeth praise.

Appoint peace, goodness, and blessing; grace, mercy and compassion for us, and for all Israel Thy people. Bless us, O our Father, all of us as one, with the light of Thy countenance. For in the light of Thy countenance has Thou, Jehovah, our God, given us the law of life, and loving mercy, and righteousness, and blessing, and compassion, and life, and peace. And may it please Thee to bless Thy people Israel at times, and at every hour with Thy peace. Blessed be Thou, Jehovah, who blessest Thy people Israel with peace. (Alfred Edersheim, *The Temple, Its Ministry and Services*, 128–29)

When the angel appeared and said, "Fear not, Zacharias; for thy prayer is heard",[2237] the prayer asked for "the light of [God's] countenance" to shine again upon Israel. The promised son (to be named "John"[2238]) was to "go before *him* in the spirit and power of Elias."[2239] The One before whom John was to go was "the light of

---

[2237] Luke 1:13 "But the angel said unto him, Fear not, Zacharias: for thy prayer is heard; and thy wife Elisabeth shall bear thee a son, and thou shalt call his name John."

[2238] Ibid.

[2239] Luke 1:17 "And he shall go before him in the spirit and power of Elias, to turn the hearts of the fathers to the children, and the disobedient to the wisdom of the just; to make ready a people prepared for the Lord."

[God's] countenance" or, in other words, Jehovah. John was to be Elias to precede and prepare the way for Jehovah.

Following his birth, John was "ordained by the angel of God at the time he was eight days old unto this power, to overthrow the kingdom of the Jews, and to make straight the way of the Lord before the face of his people, to prepare them for the coming of the Lord, in whose hand is given all power."[2240] He prepared the way, was imprisoned and beheaded. Then he appeared with Moses on the Mount of Transfiguration.[2241] Moses opened, and John closed, the prior dispensation and met with Christ as the founder of the new dispensation.

John was as great a prophet as ever lived. The Lord said he was "more than a prophet."[2242] Foretold in prophecy, born to bring "the light of God's countenance" back to Israel, fulfilling an angel's promise, named by heaven, ordained at eight days, sent to close one and open another dispensation, slain for his testimony, and then called to minister as an angel to the Lord on the Mount of Transfiguration, John was "more than a prophet."

[2240] D&C 84:28 "For he was baptized while he was yet in his childhood, and was ordained by the angel of God at the time he was eight days old unto this power, to overthrow the kingdom of the Jews, and to make straight the way of the Lord before the face of his people, to prepare them for the coming of the Lord, in whose hand is given all power."

[2241] JST–Mark 9:4 "And there appeared unto them Elias with Moses, *or in other words, John the Baptist and Moses.* and they were talking with Jesus."
Matthew 17:2–3, 13 "And was transfigured before them: and his face did shine as the sun, and his raiment was white as the light. And, behold, there appeared unto them Moses and Elias talking with him. Then the disciples understood that he spake unto them of John the Baptist."

[2242] Luke 7:24–28 "And when the messengers of John were departed, he began to speak unto the people concerning John, What went ye out into the wilderness for to see? A reed shaken with the wind? But what went ye out for to see? A man clothed in soft raiment? Behold, they which are gorgeously apparelled, and live delicately, are in kings' courts. But what went ye out for to see? A prophet? Yea, I say unto you, and much more than a prophet. This is *he,* of whom it is written, Behold, I send my messenger before thy face, which shall prepare thy way before thee. For I say unto you, Among those that are born of women there is not a greater prophet than John the Baptist: but he that is least in the kingdom of God is greater than he."

RECEIVED OF
HIS FULNESS

Received of His Fullness

When the heavens opened to Joseph and Sidney Rigdon jointly in 1832, they saw and heard many things. Among the many things shown them was the Father sitting on His Throne and the Son beside Him.[2243] The Vision included not just the final state of mankind in the various kingdoms of glory, but also included an explanation of the rebellion by an angel in a position of authority before God.[2244]

[2243] D&C 76:23 "For we saw him, even on the right hand of God; and we heard the voice bearing record that he is the Only Begotten of the Father—"

[2244] D&C 76:25 "And this we saw also, and bear record, that an angel of God who was in authority in the presence of God, who rebelled against the Only Begotten Son whom the Father loved and who was in the bosom of the Father, was thrust down from the presence of God and the Son,"

They saw the heavens weep over this rebellious angel.[2245] They saw the terrible, inexpressible end to him, and all who follow him.[2246]

They saw the final state of mankind. They also beheld many things they were not permitted to write.[2247] Their knowledge exceeded what is lawful for man to know. Because of this knowledge, they were not like the others of their generation.

They entered into the Throne Room of the Father, and beheld Him in His glory. Because of this, both Joseph and Sidney "received of his fulness".[2248] This is how the fullness is received. It can be symbolized, ritualized, or conferred by an ordinance, but the fullness itself involves God the Father and His Son Jesus Christ, personally. Therefore, when we speak of "fullness" through symbol, ordinance and ritual, we are speaking of the type. When we speak of the "fullness" itself, we are speaking of the real thing. There is a custom to accept the rites and symbols in place of the real thing. This is so much so that, today, some doubt the need for the real thing.

The "fullness of the Father" includes the "fullness of the priesthood." It also includes more. Joseph and Sidney joined the holy an-

---

[2245] D&C 76:26 "And was called Perdition, for the heavens wept over him—he was Lucifer, a son of the morning."

[2246] D&C 76:44–48 "Wherefore, he saves all except them—they shall go away into everlasting punishment, which is endless punishment, which is eternal punishment, to reign with the devil and his angels in eternity, where their worm dieth not, and the fire is not quenched, which is their torment— And the end thereof, neither the place thereof, nor their torment, no man knows; Neither was it revealed, neither is, neither will be revealed unto man, except to them who are made partakers thereof; Nevertheless, I, the Lord, show it by vision unto many, but straightway shut it up again; Wherefore, the end, the width, the height, the depth, and the misery thereof, they understand not, neither any man except those who are ordained unto this condemnation."

[2247] D&C 76:114–115 "But great and marvelous are the works of the Lord, and the mysteries of his kingdom which he showed unto us, which surpass all understanding in glory, and in might, and in dominion; Which he commanded us we should not write while we were yet in the Spirit, and are not lawful for man to utter;"

[2248] D&C 76:20 "And we beheld the glory of the Son, on the right hand of the Father, and received of his fulness;"

gels who stood before God.[2249] Therefore, they would be among those who "came to an innumerable company of angels, to the general assembly and church of Enoch, and of the Firstborn."[2250]

By 1841 the fullness of the priesthood had been forfeited by the church.[2251] Christ offered, on condition of the completion of the Nauvoo Temple, to come and restore that fullness again to the church. That required Him to come.[2252] If He came, then men would be redeemed from the fall and return to God's presence.[2253]

To have Zion, God must come and dwell with His people.[2254] To have Zion is to have people who:

- are of one heart, and

- are of one mind, and

- dwell in righteousness, and

- have no poor among them.[2255]

There are many things which occupy the attention of Latter-day Saints. This short list, however, would seem to be the most important place to begin, assuming we were interested in having Zion re-

---

[2249] D&C 76:21 "And saw the holy angels, and them who are sanctified before his throne, worshiping God, and the Lamb, who worship him forever and ever."

[2250] D&C 76:67 "These are they who have come to an innumerable company of angels, to the general assembly and church of Enoch, and of the Firstborn."

[2251] D&C 124:28 "For there is not a place found on earth that he may come to and restore again that which was lost unto you, or which he hath taken away, even the fulness of the priesthood."

[2252] Ibid.

[2253] Ether 3:13 "And when he had said these words, behold, the Lord showed himself unto him, and said: Because thou knowest these things ye are redeemed from the fall; therefore ye are brought back into my presence; therefore I show myself unto you."

[2254] Moses 7:69 "And Enoch and all his people walked with God, and he dwelt in the midst of Zion; and it came to pass that Zion was not, for God received it up into his own bosom; and from thence went forth the saying, Zion is Fled."

[2255] Moses 7:18 "And the Lord called his people Zion, because they were of one heart and one mind, and dwelt in righteousness; and there was no poor among them."

turn. We are not currently unified and for the most part are fragmenting. This is the inverse of what brings Zion.

Received of His Fullness, Part 2

It will only be when the gentiles begin to have faith like the Brother of Jared that the Lord will make the fullness known again.[2256] It was the plan to withhold the fullness from the gentiles, and not confer it upon them. The Lord told Moroni "they shall not go forth unto the Gentiles until the day that they shall repent of their iniquity, and become clean before the Lord."[2257]

Joseph and Sidney "received of His fullness" in the vision.[2258] The Lord once offered it again. Joseph may or may not impress you as a valiant soul (he certainly does me), but almost no one looks at Sidney Rigdon and sees a great, valiant soul. There has been nearly two hundred years of disparaging of Sidney by those who voted to follow Brigham Young and the Twelve and their descendants. It would be well to remember that Sidney "received of His fullness" and   Brigham Young died hoping the Lord would visit him if he lived to be 85 years old.

If Sidney, despite all you have heard and read concerning him, and despite his subsequent disaffection from the church, "received of His fullness" then you should recognize this is NOT so great a thing as to be impossible for you. Take heart.

[2256] Ether 4:6–7 "For the Lord said unto me: They shall not go forth unto the Gentiles until the day that they shall repent of their iniquity, and become clean before the Lord. And in that day that they shall exercise faith in me, saith the Lord, even as the brother of Jared did, that they may become sanctified in me, then will I manifest unto them the things which the brother of Jared saw, even to the unfolding unto them all my revelations, saith Jesus Christ, the Son of God, the Father of the heavens and of the earth, and all things that in them are."

[2257] Ibid.

[2258] D&C 76:20 "And we beheld the glory of the Son, on the right hand of the Father, and received of his fulness;"

What is it that the Vision tells us about the exalted hosts?

They are the "church of the Firstborn."[2259] Meaning they are all sons and daughters of God.

The Father has given "into their hands" what is called "all things."[2260] That is, they have handled something.

They have "received of His fullness and of His glory."[2261] Both Joseph and Sidney recite this as having taken place.[2262]

Though it would not be until sometime in 1843 before Joseph began to unfurl in private the process of becoming a "king and priest" unto God, Sidney and Joseph were acquainted with this in the Vision in 1832.[2263] This is the only way such kings and priests can be made; although you can have a ceremony which symbolizes it. Joseph and Sidney's accomplishment was an invitation for others to follow. It was not intended to be the end of the restoration process, but a harbinger of what would follow.

If Joseph and Sidney were the only ones who were to "receive of His fullness" then the prophecies promising a return of Zion could never be fulfilled.

Why are we allowing the restoration to end?

Why are we not looking to see a return of Zion?

[2259] D&C 76:54 "They are they who are the church of the Firstborn."

[2260] D&C 76:55 "They are they into whose hands the Father has given all things—"

[2261] D&C 76:56 "They are they who are priests and kings, who have received of his fulness, and of his glory;"

[2262] D&C 76:19–20 "And while we meditated upon these things, the Lord touched the eyes of our understandings and they were opened, and the glory of the Lord shone round about. And we beheld the glory of the Son, on the right hand of the Father, and received of his fulness;"

[2263] D&C 76:56–57 "They are they who are priests and kings, who have received of his fulness, and of his glory; And are priests of the Most High, after the order of Melchizedek, which was after the order of Enoch, which was after the order of the Only Begotten Son."

Why are we content to trust others will bring it, when each of us has a responsibility to individually prepare to see it return?

What good does it do to study the revelations if we are unwilling to do the works required by the revelations?

Is theoretical knowledge and symbolic ritual enough?

Will Zion only return as a distant symbol in this dispensation?

Will the Lord only symbolically return?

Will the world only symbolically end?

Will the wicked only be symbolically destroyed?

What is it that you find so compelling about your current plight that you won't awake, arise and look into the matter of the fullness as set out in scripture? To receive it you only need to "love him, and purify yourself before him" and He will "grant this privilege of seeing and knowing for yourself."[2264] But this must be "while in the flesh" and not after you leave here.[2265] This is the only way you can then be able to "bear his presence in the world of glory."[2266]

Received of His Fullness, Part 3

The often quoted verses in Section 84 have an objective event that is consistently ignored. It is not merely "the ordinances" of the priesthood which are of value. The "power of godliness"[2267] is in-

---

[2264] D&C 76:116–117 "Neither is man capable to make them known, for they are only to be seen and understood by the power of the Holy Spirit, which God bestows on those who love him, and purify themselves before him; To whom he grants this privilege of seeing and knowing for themselves;"

[2265] D&C 76:118 "That through the power and manifestation of the Spirit, while in the flesh, they may be able to bear his presence in the world of glory."

[2266] Ibid.

[2267] D&C 84:20 "Therefore, in the ordinances thereof, the power of godliness is manifest."

separably connected with these ordinances.[2268] Without the "power of godliness" our rites are much like the apostate world Christ condemned in His initial visit with Joseph.[2269]

D&C 84:20–22[2270] tells us about:

-Power of Godliness

-Authority of the Priesthood

-Seeing the face of God the Father.

These verses do not vindicate ordinances as an end in themselves. Far from it. Instead, they commend us to reach upward. If the ordinances alone were enough, there would be no mention of "power of godliness" and "authority of the priesthood" and "seeing the face of God, even the Father." Therefore, how ought you to view the ordinances? If they have value, what value do they have? Why do we want or need them? What should they inspire within us?

Where and how did Joseph and Sidney "receive of His fullness?"[2271]

Why, in speaking of "the power of godliness" and "the authority of the priesthood," does it then connect with "seeing the face of God, even the Father?"[2272]

[2268] D&C 121:36 "That the rights of the priesthood are inseparably connected with the powers of heaven, and that the powers of heaven cannot be controlled nor handled only upon the principles of righteousness."

[2269] JS–H 1:19 "I was answered that I must join none of them, for they were all wrong; and the Personage who addressed me said that all their creeds were an abomination in his sight; that those professors were all corrupt; that: "they draw near to me with their lips, but their hearts are far from me, they teach for doctrines the commandments of men, having a form of godliness, but they deny the power thereof.""

[2270] D&C 84:20–22 "Therefore, in the ordinances thereof, the power of godliness is manifest. And without the ordinances thereof, and the authority of the priesthood, the power of godliness is not manifest unto men in the flesh; For without this no man can see the face of God, even the Father, and live."

[2271] D&C 76:20 "And we beheld the glory of the Son, on the right hand of the Father, and received of his fulness;"

[2272] D&C 84:22 "For without this no man can see the face of God, even the Father, and live."

Why, in the "oath and covenant of the priesthood" (as we have taken to identifying it), does it mention "*receiving* Christ?"[2273] Is this to be taken as descriptive of receiving the priesthood, or as merely some future vague promise for the afterlife? If you read it as the afterlife, where do you find support for that reading in the revelation? Is that reading consistent with mortals having priesthood? If the priesthood is gained in mortality, why then is "receiving Christ" only post-mortality? Or, does the priesthood then become post-mortal as well?

Why does the Lord say if we "receive Him" we will also "receive His Father?"[2274] How is coming into Christ's presence related to coming into the Father's presence? Are these connected? How? And how does this connect with "priesthood" since that is the topic of the revelation? Is the priesthood proprietary, meaning that it belongs like a franchise to some group, institution or individuals? Or is the priesthood instead best viewed as a relationship between God and man? If a relationship between God and man, then is it based on trust? Personal trust between God and the specific man? If that is the case, what is required to receive priesthood?

Who are His "servants" He requires you to "receive?"[2275] How would such a servant aid you in coming to God and receiving priesthood? What is the relationship between receiving a servant, then receiving Christ, then receiving the Father? How is Joseph Smith an example of this?

Does the statement given in 1835 in D&C 107:1 describe the condition of the church at that time?[2276] Or, does it describe a con-

---

[2273] D&C 84:36 "For he that receiveth my servants receiveth me;"

[2274] D&C 84:37–38 "And he that receiveth me receiveth my Father; And he that receiveth my Father receiveth my Father's kingdom; therefore all that my Father hath shall be given unto him."

[2275] D&C 84:36 "For he that receiveth my servants receiveth me;"

[2276] D&C 107:1 "THERE are, in the church, two priesthoods, namely, the Melchizedek and Aaronic, including the Levitical Priesthood."

tinuing presence of priesthood forever thereafter? Can priesthood be lost?[2277]

Do you have His fullness? Why not? How do the scriptures say you receive it?

Is this what Nephi said he did in his record? Why does he walk us through his own experience? Is he bragging, or is he instructing and inviting us to do likewise?

Are ordinances enough? Do they testify to an underlying truth? Why receive the testimony of the ordinances and ignore the underlying truth?

No matter what we have received, retained or discarded from Joseph Smith, doesn't his entire ministry come down to affirming James 1:5?[2278] Can you ask of God also? Will He not "give liberally" to you? Then it is not lack of faith in Joseph's ministry or your personal lack of keys held by those in higher priesthood offices that keeps you apart from God. Instead it is your unwillingness to do as James instructs, and your failure to ask God in faith.

[2277] D&C 121:37 "That they may be conferred upon us, it is true; but when we undertake to cover our sins, or to gratify our pride, our vain ambition, or to exercise control or dominion or compulsion upon the souls of the children of men, in any degree of unrighteousness, behold, the heavens withdraw themselves; the Spirit of the Lord is grieved; and when it is withdrawn, Amen to the priesthood or the authority of that man."

[2278] James 1:5 "If any of you lack wisdom, let him ask of God, that giveth to all *men* liberally, and upbraideth not; and it shall be given him."

Moroni told Joseph that Joel had not yet been fulfilled, but would be soon. He linked this to the "fulness of the Gentiles" which signals their end.[2279] Is that time upon us?

Is the reason so few are "chosen" even though many are "called" related to this very subject?[2280] Would you be better off trying to please God rather than getting noticed by other men?

Does it occur to you that this process in these revelations is the fullness of the Gospel in action? That the fullness of the Father, as well as the fullness of the priesthood, are part of the relationship which you are required to develop with God? Directly between you and Him, and not between you and someone else? If this is so, then what light is shed when the open vision given to Joseph and Sidney where the past rebellion of an angel in a position of authority is revealed, and the future final destiny of man is shown to them? Why is a man saved no faster than he gains knowledge? (*TPJS*, 217)

Why did Joseph comment on the vision (in Section 76) by stating:

> "I could explain a hundred fold more than I ever have of the glories of the kingdoms manifested to me in the vision, were I permitted, and were the people prepared to receive them." (*TPJS*, 304)

[2279] JS–H 1:41 "He also quoted the second chapter of Joel, from the twenty-eighth verse to the last. He also said that this was not yet fulfilled, but was soon to be. And he further stated that the fulness of the Gentiles was soon to come in. He quoted many other passages of scripture, and offered many explanations which cannot be mentioned here."

Joel 2:28–32 "And it shall come to pass afterward, *that* I will pour out my spirit upon all flesh; and your sons and your daughters shall prophesy, your old men shall dream dreams, your young men shall see visions: And also upon the servants and upon the handmaids in those days will I pour out my spirit. And I will shew wonders in the heavens and in the earth, blood, and fire, and pillars of smoke. The sun shall be turned into darkness, and the moon into blood, before the great and the terrible day of the Lord come. And it shall come to pass, *that* whosoever shall call on the name of the Lord shall be delivered: for in mount Zion and in Jerusalem shall be deliverance, as the Lord hath said, and in the remnant whom the Lord shall call."

[2280] D&C 121:34 "Behold, there are many called, but few are chosen. And why are they not chosen?"

Faithfulness to the Church

The Church of Jesus Christ of Latter-day Saints was established by the Lord through Joseph Smith to deliver more information/ revelation to mankind. The institution was authorized, or commissioned, to perform a variety of ordinances.

It was this church that baptized me. I've never belonged to another church. It was this church that delivered the Book of Mormon, the Doctrine & Covenants, and the Pearl of Great Price to me. It offered the temple rites, and other blessings which I received willingly.

For all of those who are similarly situated, it seems to me that we all have an obligation to remain faithful to the church. Jesus was faithful, even observing the rites of the Passover in Jerusalem with His disciples on the week of His atoning sacrifice. He admonished His followers to respect those who "sat in Moses' seat" even though they would ultimately crucify Him.

I believe covenants should be honored. We do not have the right to discard them. Therefore, we proceed with honor to follow what we agreed to follow.

The Lord wanted the church to remain together. The splintering began even before Joseph's death. When he died the splintering accelerated, but there was and is an obligation to remain together. No matter what you learn, how far you progress, or what great blessings you obtain from the Lord, there is an honorable obligation to remain 'gathered' with the saints.

There is still a great deal left to restore. The work is terribly incomplete and when it resumes it will be among the saints, not among the Methodists, or the Hindus. The restoration will add to the Book of Mormon, Doctrine & Covenants, and Pearl of Great Price. It will not begin over again with people unacquainted with this latest body of revelation from the Lord.

I intend to remain faithful to the church, no matter what the issues are that exist because of human failings or errors.

Because I respect the order of the church, I refuse to get out ahead. No matter what I know, I am unwilling to step outside of my narrowly confined role. This confined role allows me to elaborate on existing scripture, and still limit what I say and do. I am forced to study the existing scriptures and our history to be able to confine what I do inside the existing order, while still explaining what I may be required to explain or declare.

I do not believe I would be of any benefit to the Lord or my fellow man if I were to rebel, abandon covenants I have made, or try to become something separate and independent. The Lord requires us to be meek, to respect authority, and to submit to others. It helps us to understand Him more fully. For me, respecting the order of things inside the church is also a matter of wisdom. It keeps all of us from becoming too much or too little as we follow the Lord.

Lehi's God

When Lehi first saw the Father sitting upon His throne, the description is as follows:

> "he thought he saw God, sitting upon his throne, surrounded with numberless concourses of angels, in the attitude of singing and praising their God." (1 Nephi 1:8)

After being ministered to by Christ,[2281] the description changes as Lehi reacts to his endowment of knowledge from the Lord. The record says: "And after this manner was the language of my father in the praising of his God" (1 Nephi 1:15). God the Father has ceased

---

[2281] 1 Nephi 1:11 "And they came down and went forth upon the face of the earth; and the first came and stood before my father, and gave unto him a book, and bade him that he should read."

to be the impersonal "God" of verse 8, and has become Lehi's God by verse 15.

It is in this sense that God becomes "the God of Abraham, the God of Isaac and the God of Jacob."[2282] God established His covenant with Abraham. Then He renewed and established His covenant again with Isaac. Then He renewed it again with Jacob. He was each of their God, by covenanting with each of them. None relied on a covenant given to their father, or grandfather, but each received directly from God a covenant in their own name.

Lehi also covenanted with God. He also knew the Father as "his God." If you read what happened between verses 8 and 15, you will see how Christ ministers to a man and brings them into a relationship with the Father.

[2282] Matthew 22:32 "I am the God of Abraham, and the God of Isaac, and the God of Jacob? God is not the God of the dead, but of the living."

Compare 1 Nephi 1:11–14[2283] with Revelation 5:1–8.[2284] In both there is a book, and it is Christ who is able to access the book. In both, a prophet, (Lehi and John) are able to then get access to the information which would be otherwise hidden from the world.

Lehi, as a recipient of the covenant directly from God, joined those who could call God "his God."

It is the God of Lehi in the same way it is the God of Abraham; and the God of Isaac; and the God of Jacob; and the God of Nephi; and the God of Joseph.

Look at 2 Kings 2:14[2285] and you will see Elisha acknowledging that Elijah also knew God; and Elisha wanted to likewise come to know Him.

[2283] 1 Nephi 1:11–14 "And they came down and went forth upon the face of the earth; and the first came and stood before my father, and gave unto him a book, and bade him that he should read. And it came to pass that as he read, he was filled with the Spirit of the Lord. And he read, saying: Wo, wo, unto Jerusalem, for I have seen thine abominations! Yea, and many things did my father read concerning Jerusalem—that it should be destroyed, and the inhabitants thereof; many should perish by the sword, and many should be carried away captive into Babylon. And it came to pass that when my father had read and seen many great and marvelous things, he did exclaim many things unto the Lord; such as: Great and marvelous are thy works, O Lord God Almighty! Thy throne is high in the heavens, and thy power, and goodness, and mercy are over all the inhabitants of the earth; and, because thou art merciful, thou wilt not suffer those who come unto thee that they shall perish!"

[2284] Revelation 5:1–8 "And I saw in the right hand of him that sat on the throne a book written within and on the backside, sealed with seven seals. And I saw a strong angel proclaiming with a loud voice, Who is worthy to open the book, and to loose the seals thereof? And no man in heaven, nor in earth, neither under the earth, was able to open the book, neither to look thereon. And I wept much, because no man was found worthy to open and to read the book, neither to look thereon. And one of the elders saith unto me, Weep not: behold, the Lion of the tribe of Juda, the Root of David, hath prevailed to open the book, and to loose the seven seals thereof. And I beheld, and, lo, in the midst of the throne and of the four beasts, and in the midst of the elders, stood a Lamb as it had been slain, having seven horns and seven eyes, which are the seven Spirits of God sent forth into all the earth. And he came and took the book out of the right hand of him that sat upon the throne. And when he had taken the book, the four beasts and four *and* twenty elders fell down before the Lamb, having every one of them harps, and golden vials full of odours, which are the prayers of saints."

[2285] 2 Kings 2:14 "And he took the mantle of Elijah that fell from him, and smote the waters, and said, Where *is* the Lord God of Elijah? and when he also had smitten the waters, they parted hither and thither: and Elisha went over."

Is He also your God? If not, why will you not have Him to be your God?[2286]

Lehi's Priesthood

There is a key verse which passes by quickly. It establishes an important identity for Lehi. The verse confirms that Lehi saw God the Father sitting on His throne.[2287] In other words, Lehi beheld the face of God, the Father. This key verse identifies Lehi's authority.

Following immediately after this view of the Father, sitting on His throne, Christ descended in His glory and ministered to him. His glory was above the brightness of the sun.[2288]

After Christ ministered to him, Lehi put the Father's activities into perspective, declaring "unto the Lord: Great and marvelous are thy works, O Lord God Almighty!"[2289]

[2286] 1 Nephi 17:40 "And he loveth those who will have him to be their God. Behold, he loved our fathers, and he covenanted with them, yea, even Abraham, Isaac, and Jacob; and he remembered the covenants which he had made; wherefore, he did bring them out of the land of Egypt."

[2287] 1 Nephi 1:8 "And being thus overcome with the Spirit, he was carried away in a vision, even that he saw the heavens open, and he thought he saw God sitting upon his throne, surrounded with numberless concourses of angels in the attitude of singing and praising their God."

[2288] 1 Nephi 1:11–13 "And they came down and went forth upon the face of the earth; and the first came and stood before my father, and gave unto him a book, and bade him that he should read. And it came to pass that as he read, he was filled with the Spirit of the Lord. And he read, saying: Wo, wo, unto Jerusalem, for I have seen thine abominations! Yea, and many things did my father read concerning Jerusalem—that it should be destroyed, and the inhabitants thereof; many should perish by the sword, and many should be carried away captive into Babylon."

[2289] 1 Nephi 1:13 "And he read, saying: Wo, wo, unto Jerusalem, for I have seen thine abominations! Yea, and many things did my father read concerning Jerusalem—that it should be destroyed, and the inhabitants thereof; many should perish by the sword, and many should be carried away captive into Babylon."

He saw the face of the Father. He was ministered to by the Son. This cannot occur unless Lehi had the highest form of priesthood. This is required for a man to see the face of the Father and live.[2290]

Lehi required priesthood:

"without . . . the authority of the priesthood, and the power of godliness . . . no man can see the face of God, even the Father, and live." (D&C 84:21–22)

Lehi saw Him. Therefore part of the ministry of Christ to him necessarily included conferring priesthood.

Joseph Smith explained it like this:

"All Priesthood is Melchizedek, but there are different portions or degrees of it. That portion which brought Moses to speak with God face to face was taken away; but that which brought the ministry of angels remained. All the prophets had the Melchizedek Priesthood and were ordained by God himself." (TPJS, 180–181)

In Lehi we have an instance of an Old Testament era prophet being "ordained by God himself" in the very first chapter of the Book of Mormon.

The phrasing in verse 8 ("he thought he saw God sitting upon his throne") is an art form, or a formula. Alma would later use the same phrasing.[2291] The best way to understand this formulation is found in Paul's writings: "whether in the body, I cannot tell; or whether out of

---

[2290] D&C 84:19–22 "And this greater priesthood administereth the gospel and holdeth the key of the mysteries of the kingdom, even the key of the knowledge of God. Therefore, in the ordinances thereof, the power of godliness is manifest. And without the ordinances thereof, and the authority of the priesthood, the power of godliness is not manifest unto men in the flesh; For without this no man can see the face of God, even the Father, and live."

[2291] Alma 36:22 "Yea, methought I saw, even as our father Lehi saw, God sitting upon his throne, surrounded with numberless concourses of angels, in the attitude of singing and praising their God; yea, and my soul did long to be there."

the body, I cannot tell; God knoweth."[2292] Similarly, Joseph Smith's encounter in the First Vision was either in the body or not, and during the vision he became physically incapacitated.[2293] Daniel also physically collapsed when the Lord visited with him.[2294]

How much that book teaches us! It is only our neglect which renders it unable to teach us the fullness of the Gospel of Jesus Christ.

This is only the first chapter of the book (1 Nephi 1) and it has an example of a vision of God the Father sitting on His throne, and the Lord Jehovah ministering to and strengthening a prophet of

---

[2292] 2 Corinthians 12:2 "I knew a man in Christ above fourteen years ago, (whether in the body, I cannot tell; or whether out of the body, I cannot tell: God knoweth;) such an one caught up to the third heaven."

[2293] JS–H 1:20 "When I came to myself again, I found myself lying on my back, looking up into heaven."

[2294] Daniel 10:5–19 "Then I lifted up mine eyes, and looked, and behold a certain man clothed in linen, whose loins *were* girded with fine gold of Uphaz: His body also *was* like the beryl, and his face as the appearance of lightning, and his eyes as lamps of fire, and his arms and his feet like in colour to polished brass, and the voice of his words like the voice of a multitude. And I Daniel alone saw the vision: for the men that were with me saw not the vision; but a great quaking fell upon them, so that they fled to hide themselves. Therefore I was left alone, and saw this great vision, and there remained no strength in me: for my comeliness was turned in me into corruption, and I retained no strength. Yet heard I the voice of his words: and when I heard the voice of his words, then was I in a deep sleep on my face, and my face toward the ground. And, behold, an hand touched me, which set me upon my knees and *upon* the palms of my hands. And he said unto me, O Daniel, a man greatly beloved, understand the words that I speak unto thee, and stand upright: for unto thee am I now sent. And when he had spoken this word unto me, I stood trembling. Then said he unto me, Fear not, Daniel: for from the first day that thou didst set thine heart to understand, and to chasten thyself before thy God, thy words were heard, and I am come for thy words. But the prince of the kingdom of Persia withstood me one and twenty days: but, lo, Michael, one of the chief princes, came to help me; and I remained there with the kings of Persia. Now I am come to make thee understand what shall befall thy people in the latter days: for yet the vision *is* for *many* days. And when he had spoken such words unto me, I set my face toward the ground, and I became dumb. And, behold, *one* like the similitude of the sons of men touched my lips: then I opened my mouth, and spake, and said unto him that stood before me, O my lord, by the vision my sorrows are turned upon me, and I have retained no strength. For how can the servant of this my lord talk with this my lord? for as for me, straightway there remained no strength in me, neither is there breath left in me. Then there came again and touched me *one* like the appearance of a man, and he strengthened me, And said, O man greatly beloved, fear not: peace *be* unto thee, be strong, yea, be strong. And when he had spoken unto me, I was strengthened, and said, Let my lord speak; for thou hast strengthened me."

God! What great promise this book holds indeed if that is only the first chapter! Perhaps we should take it more seriously.[2295] No wonder President Packer can lament in General Conference about the absence of priesthood power in the church.[2296]

Lehi's Commission

When the first chapter of Nephi opens, Lehi is among those who listened to "many prophets prophesying" about the coming judgments against Jerusalem.[2297] Their message was not Lehi's. Their message was apparently upsetting to him because he responded by praying on behalf of Jerusalem.[2298] His prayer is interesting. He offers it on behalf of what he regarded as "his people."[2299]

[2295] D&C 84:54–57 "And your minds in times past have been darkened because of unbelief, and because you have treated lightly the things you have received— Which vanity and unbelief have brought the whole church under condemnation. And this condemnation resteth upon the children of Zion, even all. And they shall remain under this condemnation until they repent and remember the new covenant, even the Book of Mormon and the former commandments which I have given them, not only to say, but to do according to that which I have written—"

[2296] Packer, "The Power of the Priesthood", General Conference, April 2010.

[2297] 1 Nephi 1:4 "For it came to pass in the commencement of the first year of the reign of Zedekiah, king of Judah, (my father, Lehi, having dwelt at Jerusalem in all his days); and in that same year there came many prophets, prophesying unto the people that they must repent, or the great city Jerusalem must be destroyed."

[2298] 1 Nephi 1:5 "Wherefore it came to pass that my father, Lehi, as he went forth prayed unto the Lord, yea, even with all his heart, in behalf of his people."

[2299] Ibid.

The result of his compassionate prayer for others was a calling by God the Father, delivered by His Son, Jehovah.[2300] God takes note of those who have compassion for others and whose charity seeks the best interests of their fellow-man. Such people possess love, and it is "unfeigned."[2301] It is precisely because of their love of their fellow man that they are called to render priestly service.[2302]

Lehi was a man like Christ. Just like Christ, Lehi would intercede on behalf of "his people" and did so "with all his heart."[2303]

In response to this, Lehi's vision endowed him with knowledge about the Lord's great plan of mercy. He knew that the Lord would overrule everything for the good. Even the suffering that would be inflicted on the inhabitants of Jerusalem would be merciful, and would be predicated on the "goodness" of God.[2304] Lehi under-

---

[2300] 1 Nephi 1:8–13 "And being thus overcome with the Spirit, he was carried away in a vision, even that he saw the heavens open, and he thought he saw God sitting upon his throne, surrounded with numberless concourses of angels in the attitude of singing and praising their God. And it came to pass that he saw One descending out of the midst of heaven, and he beheld that his luster was above that of the sun at noon-day. And he also saw twelve others following him, and their brightness did exceed that of the stars in the firmament. And they came down and went forth upon the face of the earth; and the first came and stood before my father, and gave unto him a book, and bade him that he should read. And it came to pass that as he read, he was filled with the Spirit of the Lord. And he read, saying: Wo, wo, unto Jerusalem, for I have seen thine abominations! Yea, and many things did my father read concerning Jerusalem—that it should be destroyed, and the inhabitants thereof; many should perish by the sword, and many should be carried away captive into Babylon."

[2301] D&C 121:41 "No power or influence can or ought to be maintained by virtue of the priesthood, only by persuasion, by long-suffering, by gentleness and meekness, and by love unfeigned;"

[2302] Ibid.

[2303] 1 Nephi 1:15 "And after this manner was the language of my father in the praising of his God; for his soul did rejoice, and his whole heart was filled, because of the things which he had seen, yea, which the Lord had shown unto him."

[2304] 1 Nephi 1:14 "And it came to pass that when my father had read and seen many great and marvelous things, he did exclaim many things unto the Lord; such as: Great and marvelous are thy works, O Lord God Almighty! Thy throne is high in the heavens, and thy power, and goodness, and mercy are over all the inhabitants of the earth; and, because thou art merciful, thou wilt not suffer those who come unto thee that they shall perish!"

stood. Because he had this knowledge, he was able to see how God's plans were always done for the benefit and ultimate salvation of man.

Before this encounter with God, Lehi was in the audience listening to the prophets cry repentance. After this encounter with God, he joined the prophets and also "began to prophesy and to declare" a message to Jerusalem.[2305] He could not "begin" to prophesy if he had been among the prophets previously. If that were the case, he would have "resumed" or "continued" to prophesy. He "began" only after encountering God. Therefore, we can know Lehi's ministry to call others to repent did not start before encountering God and receiving his commission from the Lord.

This is what true prophets do. They do not advance their own agenda. They do not volunteer. They do not deliver a message of their own. They don't look for witty quotes, or clever stories to retell. They receive a commission from God, and the result of their work is to offer those who will listen a chance to repent and return to God.

These individuals do not take the Lord's name in vain. They cannot. They have been authorized to speak in the Lord's name, and therefore their words are His.[2306] He will vindicate the words of His servants because they do not speak an idle thing in their own behalf. They speak with His authority, and deliver His message.

So with the first chapter of the Book of Mormon we also get an example of how prophets are called: alone, in God's presence, with an endowment of knowledge of God's ways sufficient to enable them to deliver a message of repentance.

[2305] 1 Nephi 1:18 "Therefore, I would that ye should know, that after the Lord had shown so many marvelous things unto my father, Lehi, yea, concerning the destruction of Jerusalem, behold he went forth among the people, and began to prophesy and to declare unto them concerning the things which he had both seen and heard."

[2306] D&C 1:38 "What I the Lord have spoken, I have spoken, and I excuse not myself; and though the heavens and the earth pass away, my word shall not pass away, but shall all be fulfilled, whether by mine own voice or by the voice of my servants, it is the same."

And this is only the first chapter! Imagine if we took the entire book to heart what we might find!

Lehi's Message

Lehi delivered two separate messages to his generation at Jerusalem. These two messages provoked two separate reactions.

The first message was that they were wicked, and were engaged in abominations before God.[2307] In other words, these were sinful people needing to repent and return to God.

When the people heard "the things which he testified of them" their reaction was to mock and ridicule him and his message.[2308] They had the scriptures, the priesthood, the Temple, the ordinances, and they were absolutely certain they were living their religion just as God wanted them to. They were "chosen" and were holy people. This idea of being "wicked" and engaging in abominable practices while they lived devoted lives seemed ridiculous to them. Lehi could not be taken seriously. If there was anything to this message, then they would expect it would come from the established hierarchy, not some obscure trader living in Jerusalem. He wasn't even a Levite for that matter.

The second message was much more serious. He spoke "plainly of the coming of a Messiah, and also the redemption of the world." [2309]Since this was an idea the Jews of that day had rejected, Lehi's testimony of Christ was too much. He was accusing them of apostasy. This aroused anger and even fury. The idea that these holy peo-

---

[2307] 1 Nephi 1:19 "And it came to pass that the Jews did mock him because of the things which he testified of them; for he truly testified of their wickedness and their abominations; and he testified that the things which he saw and heard, and also the things which he read in the book, manifested plainly of the coming of a Messiah, and also the redemption of the world."

[2308] Ibid.

[2309] Ibid.

ple, devoted to their religion, practicing the ordinances and preserving the Temple rites could be in a state of apostasy was too much for them to brook.

In response to this second message they had a second reaction: they wanted to kill him.[2310] They knew what to do with this kind of message. They would excommunicate, or "cast out" anyone who dared to preach this message. It threatened the pretenders who presided. It threatened the order of their day. It challenged the authority of the faith. It was too much.

Lehi would be either cast out (excommunicated). Or he would be "stoned" (an officially sanctioned religious punishment). Or he would be "slain" (a mob reaction not sanctioned by the religion).[2311] The first two were to be imposed by the religious leaders. The third, however, would be popular reaction. An uncontrolled mob, showing spontaneous religious zeal, having been indoctrinated by their leaders to react in this manner. The leaders would prefer the third remedy. That would show their teaching was having the desired effect. If not, then the first two would be imposed.

Two messages, and two reactions. The popular practices of religion of Lehi's day were condemning souls. No one was being saved. No leadership existed which would lead men back to God's presence.

Lehi listened to the "many prophets, prophesying unto the people that they must repent".[2312] He learned for himself, directly from

---

[2310] 1 Nephi 1:20 "And when the Jews heard these things they were angry with him; yea, even as with the prophets of old, whom they had cast out, and stoned, and slain; and they also sought his life, that they might take it away. But behold, I, Nephi, will show unto you that the tender mercies of the Lord are over all those whom he hath chosen, because of their faith, to make them mighty even unto the power of deliverance."

[2311] Ibid.

[2312] 1 Nephi 1:4 "For it came to pass in the commencement of the first year of the reign of Zedekiah, king of Judah, (my father, Lehi, having dwelt at Jerusalem in all his days); and in that same year there came many prophets, prophesying unto the people that they must repent, or the great city Jerusalem must be destroyed."

God that this was a true message. He took up the message and he delivered his own testimony.

This was a message from God, whom He had met. This was authorized and, whether the Jews of his day would acknowledge it or not, it was binding upon them. Therefore, when they rejected his testimony against them and his message requiring them to repent, they rejected God's word.

These deeply religious peers of Lehi's were astonished at the idea an obscure merchant could speak with and for God. Once again the first chapter of the Book of Mormon introduces us to a world where God alone decides who He will call. Then, after a private audience with the Lord, the commissioned spokesman proceeds to cry repentance. These are radical ideas, and prove the Book of Mormon is no ordinary text. It is a warning from God, and its precepts will bring mankind closer to the truth than the precepts you will find in any other volume of sacred text.

A Question about "Seeds of Doubt"

This comment was a question I received this week: "You are hinting that we have 'strayed from mine ordinances' and broken the covenant as a people. Does this encourage faith in the Church of Jesus Christ of Latter Day Saints? I would argue that it does not. You appear conflicted. You appear to be trying to plant seeds of doubt because of changes to the temple ceremonies over the years."

This is a question only an idolator could ask. The question presumes the object of faith should be an institution. That is idolatry.

To the extent that the church teaches faith in the Lord Jesus Christ, it is of value. To the extent it teaches faith in itself, it will damn you.

Those who inherit the Telestial Kingdom, or the lowest condition in the afterlife apart from outer darkness, will keep company with liars, thieves and adulterers.[2313] These damned folks, who are cast down to hell and suffer the wrath of Almighty God,[2314] are the ones who worship the church, but not Christ. They prefer the institutional leaders[2315] rather than receiving the testimony of Christ.[2316]

These people are those who "love and make a lie" because the truth is not in them.[2317] They lie about the terms of salvation. They substitute the commandments of men for faith in Christ. This is the heart of lying—to deceive on matters affecting the souls of mankind.

Let me be as clear as I possibly can: I am *not* trying to "encourage faith in The Church of Jesus Christ of Latter-day Saints." That would damn anyone who would listen to me. I have tried to encourage activity in the church; to encourage payment of tithes, support of leadership, serving in callings, and living its standards. But NOT faith in the church.

I am trying to encourage faith in Jesus Christ. The Articles of Faith clarify who we are to have faith in:

"We believe that the first principles and ordinances of the Gospel are: first, Faith in the Lord Jesus Christ." (Article of Faith 4)

[2313] D&C 76:103 "These are they who are liars, and sorcerers, and adulterers, and whoremongers, and whosoever loves and makes a lie."

[2314] D&C 76:106 "These are they who are cast down to hell and suffer the wrath of Almighty God, until the fulness of times, when Christ shall have subdued all enemies under his feet, and shall have perfected his work;"

[2315] D&C 76:99–100 "For these are they who are of Paul, and of Apollos, and of Cephas. These are they who say they are some of one and some of another—some of Christ and some of John, and some of Moses, and some of Elias, and some of Esaias, and some of Isaiah, and some of Enoch;"

[2316] D&C 76:101 "But received not the gospel, neither the testimony of Jesus, neither the prophets, neither the everlasting covenant."

[2317] D&C 76:103 "These are they who are liars, and sorcerers, and adulterers, and whoremongers, and whosoever loves and makes a lie."

It is incidental to that faith that we believe in a church organization.[2318] Nowhere in the Articles of Faith, nor in the scriptures does it require anyone to have "faith in The Church of Jesus Christ of Latter-day Saints" for salvation.

The person (or committee) who posed the question should repent. They suffer from a damning form of idolatry, denounced in scripture, which will condemn them to hell unless they repent—if the revelations from Jesus Christ can be trusted. If they teach this as doctrine to others, they are leading them astray.

As to the other part of the question—that the temple ordinances have been changed, let me be clear on that also. Yes, they have been changed. Your question admits it. We all know that is true. They have been substantially reworked, deleted, portions eliminated, whole characters removed from the presentation, and even the parts that are identified as "most sacred" have been altered. They certainly have been changed. I leave it for each person to decide the extent to which these alterations are or are not important to them.

I will add, however, that when a Dispensation of the Gospel is conferred on mankind through a Dispensation head (like Enoch, Moses, Joseph Smith) then those who live in that Dispensation are obligated to honor the ordinances laid down through the Dispensation head by the Lord. For so long as the ordinances remain unchanged, the ordinances are effective. When, however, the ordinances are changed without the Lord's approval [THE critical question], they are broken. At that point, the cure is for the Lord to bestow a new Dispensation in which a new covenant is made available.

IF (and I leave it to you to answer that question) you decide the ordinances are now broken by the many changes, then you should look for the Lord to deliver them again. IF (and I leave it entirely to

---

[2318] Article of Faith 6 "We believe in the same organization that existed in the Primitive Church, namely, apostles, prophets, pastors, teachers, evangelists, and so forth."

you to decide) the many changes were authorized by the Lord and approved by Him, then you have no concerns. The covenant was not broken. Everything continues intact. It would be curious to know why He changed them. Particularly when Joseph (the Dispensation head) said that couldn't be done. But if your confidence is in The Church of Jesus Christ of Latter-day Saints as the instrument of salvation, then you should not trouble yourself with this question. If your faith is in Christ, then take the matter up with Him and let Him explain to you what your state and standing is before Him. I know what mine is. I have no fear of His judgements.

I don't know if I could be any more clear. Maybe I should add that if I were a church leader, I would never have agreed to any change ever to any of the ordinances. But I was not a church leader, and when the great changes were made in 1990 no one asked me to even sustain them. Those in charge imposed them. As a member, I wasn't even afforded the chance to give a sustaining vote on the question. I have never been required to take a position, either by the church or the leaders or common consent. The church just DID it. To the extent that anyone is accountable for this, it cannot be me. That leaves everyone the freedom to decide individually what these things mean to them.

I would also add that if I'd been asked to vote I would have voted against it. Today, if the church provided periodic sessions using the earlier form, I would make it a practice to always attend only those sessions. I wish I could provide those for my own ancestors as I attend sessions now. I attended so frequently before the changes that, even today, when attending I still recite in my own mind missing portions of the ceremonies. I cannot avoid it. They are embedded and remain, despite not being present in the temple ceremony any longer.

Have faith in Christ. He doesn't change.[2319] I concede that it's weird an unchanging God has a predilection in this Dispensation of changing His ordinances. He, at least, doesn't change. If you lose your idolatry and anchor faith in Him, you will be fine.

So, where does that leave us with the issue of "seeds of doubt?" I doubt:

- men
- institutions
- lies
- foolishness
- vanity
- error
- pomposity
- arrogance
- ignorance
- good intentions
- the value of sincerity
- the commandments of men
- the present generation
- the popular solutions to most problems
- Hollywood
- opposing attorneys
- Chief Justice Roberts' reasoning
- quantitative easing as a long term solution
- quantitative easing as a short term solution

[2319] 1 Nephi 10:18 "For he is the same yesterday, to-day, and forever; and the way is prepared for all men from the foundation of the world, if it so be that they repent and come unto him."

2 Nephi 27:23 "For behold, I am God; and I am a God of miracles; and I will show unto the world that I am the same yesterday, today, and forever; and I work not among the children of men save it be according to their faith."

Moroni 10:7 "And ye may know that he is, by the power of the Holy Ghost; wherefore I would exhort you that ye deny not the power of God; for he worketh by power, according to the faith of the children of men, the same today and tomorrow, and forever."

- the assumptions contained in the question I have answered in this post.

But I do NOT doubt Christ.

Some Pending Questions

Q: Do I consider myself "a prophet?"

The testimony of Jesus is the Spirit of Prophecy.[2320] I have the testimony of Jesus.

Q: What if someone has prayed and "still not been visited" by the Second Comforter?

The problem is in the word "still." What makes you think you control timing? What makes you think you are prepared? The Lord alone determines timing. And the Lord alone judges preparation. The Lord does not come to cause faith, but in response to existing faith. If your faith would be increased by such a visit, it will not occur. The faith necessary requires the sacrifice of all things. You must develop that. That is why I wrote *The Second Comforter*.

Q: Which version of the ordinances, 1870's, 1920's, post-1990, or current, would you prefer to see in the Temple?

Brigham Young's effort to "complete" the endowment was entrusted to him by Joseph. I have to admit, there are some things he did that were excessive, but nevertheless he completed the charge. They weren't reduced to writing until the 1870's. There are steps that needed to be taken. Joseph understood what was needed, and Brigham Young likely did not. Nevertheless, Brigham Young was tasked with

---

[2320] Revelation 19:10 "And I fell at his feet to worship him. And he said unto me, See *thou do it* not: I am thy fellowservant, and of thy brethren that have the testimony of Jesus: worship God: for the testimony of Jesus is the spirit of prophecy."

the job and therefore, he operated under Joseph's charge. Details matter. Not merely in the rites but in how the rites came into being. When the Lord allows something, then what the Lord allows (and only what He allows) is permitted. When we go beyond that mark, we lose the commission and we are on our own. I'm acquainted with all the changes. I have found them all and studied them all. I know all of the many differences. In the context of the previous post, it was not important to distinguish between the original, incomplete rites above the Red Brick Store and the later developments. Nor was it necessary to suggest there were other changes between the final version written in the 1870's and those made most recently. It is the issue of *changing*, not which changes, that I was responding to in the post. The answer did not attempt to give information beyond the narrow issue. To parse through the history of the temple is a task which I've not attempted in writing, and I have no intention of undertaking such a thankless job. Those who would be most benefitted from it resent the discussion. Others revel in the information and have no benefit from it.

Q: What can you do if you're not acquainted with the pre-1990 endowment?

I don't think that's the issue. The issue is whether you will take your present covenants seriously and live true and faithful to them. Treat them as a matter between you and God, and look to Him for the further light and knowledge which He promises to send to those who are faithful in all things. If you remain true and faithful, then you should expect to receive further light and knowledge by conversing with the Lord through the veil. He employs no servant there. He will meet you and will give you such information as you need to then enter into His presence. The rites are a symbol. Treat them as such. The confirmation of the Lord's intention to preserve you as His will come from Him, not some ordinance worker practicing altered rites. What remains is still enough to inform you of the Lord's ways. Walk in those ways.

You disagree with submitting to authority as I have suggested.

Then don't. See what your rebellion gets you. As for me, I trust the Lord was sincere when He admonished following Annas and Caiphus because "they sit in Moses' seat." But, He added, we are not expected to "do as they do." The tradition has been handed down, and we fit into that tradition. We study the Book of Mormon, the Doctrine & Covenants, the Pearl of Great Price, and we thank the institution which prints and distributes them. However, we look to the contents of those for the Lord's word and will. Even the church's authorities tell us consistently the measure of truth is found in the scriptures, and the president of the church cannot contradict them. The church doesn't require much of us. Tithing, fasting, serving, supporting leaders, etc. These are nothing compared with overcoming our hearts and minds and living as a sacrifice to God.

Q: Where do women fit into the Second Comforter?

The first person to receive the risen Lord was a woman. More women saw Him before *any* of His apostles following the resurrection. The apostles were rebuked because they didn't believe the women's testimony. The requirement for priesthood is related to the man. For women, their condition and covenant with the Lord from the time of Eve is different that the condition and covenant of Adam. Male and female relationships with the Lord are not governed by the same terms. It is the partnership of those two different roles which produces the image of God. When viewed from God's perspective, woman completes the man. Without her, his condition is "not good" because he remains incomplete.

Q: Wouldn't membership in an apostate branch of the restoration do more harm than good?

No. The Lord will gather primarily from those who already accept the restoration. Those who accept the restoration as far as it got, who honor Joseph Smith's status as a Dispensation head, who accept the Book of Mormon, D&C, Pearl of Great Price and the temple rites are far better off and more able to receive what will come before Zion is built than the rest of this world. The Lord's gathering at the last will be composed, primarily (although not exclusively) from among these people.

As to Zion:

Just because you have the idea in front of you doesn't mean you have any concept of what will be required to have the angels gather you into that company. It is like the notion that you're going to be "exalted" without any idea that the eternities are completely isolated from the unworthy. No one will or can be "exalted" who is not adequately prepared. Anyone who attains that status will be required first to suffer what is suffered, minister what is required to be ministered, to prove here their fitness. How could a selfish soul ever provide to their ungrateful and abusive offspring everything necessary for them to develop? Exalted beings sacrifice themselves, and endure punishment on behalf of the guilty. They take upon themselves burdens which they do not deserve. They forgive, they succor, they uplift the unworthy. Pride is incompatible, and selfishness utterly disqualifies a soul from "exaltation." The principles which govern there are hardly understood here. Most of the faithful Latter-day Saints imagine they will able to employ means much like Lucifer's to accomplish their expected outcome. They have no concept of the sacrifices and selflessness required to be trusted by the Lord. He is the prototype of the saved man. He lived His entire existence as a sacrifice. Read 3

Nephi 11:11[2321] and you will find in His introduction of Himself what a saved man must do. There is no other way. The prideful expectation that someone here is going to attain that status hereafter is based, for the most part, on foolishness and vanity, uninformed by the great things required to become like our Lord. Only those who are exactly like Him will be given that status in the eternities. Zion will be formed from people who are willing to endure His presence. That is no small thing.

Q: If Christ doesn't change why aren't we living the Law of Moses?

Because He fulfilled that law. It was "added" and then fulfilled. It was added because the Dispensation intended to be delivered through Moses was rejected by Israel.[2322] Much like what happened with us. The Dispensation the Lord wanted to hand us was not received.[2323] Therefore, something less was added.

[2321] 3 Nephi 11:11 "And behold, I am the light and the life of the world; and I have drunk out of that bitter cup which the Father hath given me, and have glorified the Father in taking upon me the sins of the world, in the which I have suffered the will of the Father in all things from the beginning."

[2322] D&C 84:19–24 "And this greater priesthood administereth the gospel and holdeth the key of the mysteries of the kingdom, even the key of the knowledge of God. Therefore, in the ordinances thereof, the power of godliness is manifest. And without the ordinances thereof, and the authority of the priesthood, the power of godliness is not manifest unto men in the flesh; For without this no man can see the face of God, even the Father, and live. Now this Moses plainly taught to the children of Israel in the wilderness, and sought diligently to sanctify his people that they might behold the face of God; But they hardened their hearts and could not endure his presence; therefore, the Lord in his wrath, for his anger was kindled against them, swore that they should not enter into his rest while in the wilderness, which rest is the fulness of his glory."

[2323] D&C 124:28 "For there is not a place found on earth that he may come to and restore again that which was lost unto you, or which he hath taken away, even the fulness of the priesthood."

We get to partake in what *we were* willing to receive, but we were
not willing to receive what we might have been given.[2324] Now that
about four generations have passed, at some point the Lord will
open the heavens again, and we will see His hand moving to allow
another opportunity. When that happens, things will be finished. It
will be different from what we got through Joseph. It will reflect
what might have been given anciently through Moses, and what was
offered *and rejected* through Joseph Smith. It will make possible the
establishment of a city of refuge where the Lord can come and dwell
with His people.[2325]

You should note, however, that the Law from Moses till Jesus
Christ did not change. Dispensations mark changes, like the great
dance in the sky moves from constellation to constellation. The turning shows change, the Dispensations here reflect it, the heavens testify the Lord knew the end from the beginning. This is why the stars
testify of the Lord's plan and move to bear that testimony.[2326] But
inside Dispensations, ordinances have traditionally been respected
and kept unchanged. The only notable exceptions being the one
given through Christ and the one given through Joseph Smith. In the
case of Christ, the changes marked the apostasy, not the Lord's approved course of conduct. We claim our changes have been made

---

[2324] D&C 88:33 "For what doth it profit a man if a gift is bestowed upon him, and he
receive not the gift? Behold, he rejoices not in that which is given unto him, neither
rejoices in him who is the giver of the gift."

[2325] D&C 101:16–18 "Therefore, let your hearts be comforted concerning Zion; for all
flesh is in mine hands; be still and know that I am God. Zion shall not be moved out
of her place, notwithstanding her children are scattered. They that remain, and are pure
in heart, shall return, and come to their inheritances, they and their children, with songs
of everlasting joy, to build up the waste places of Zion—"

[2326] D&C 88:45–47 "The earth rolls upon her wings, and the sun giveth his light by day,
and the moon giveth her light by night, and the stars also give their light, as they roll
upon their wings in their glory, in the midst of the power of God. Unto what shall I
liken these kingdoms, that ye may understand? Behold, all these are kingdoms, and any
man who hath seen any or the least of these hath seen God moving in his majesty and
power."

with the Lord's approval. I would note, however, that the explanation given with the changes NEVER claimed the alterations of the Temple rites were because of revelation. They were made based on the claim that the church leaders "held the keys" which allowed them to make the changes. There has never been any claim made contemporaneous with any of the changes that attributed the altered ordinances to revelation from the Lord.

A general note:

Some issues would require a book to lay out the information. They are unsuitable for a blog post. Never conclude that some brief mention is all that is required to set out a matter. I've avoided some subjects because it is misleading to give a brief comment about them. As I contemplate the subjects which require some explanation, I realize it would take another book. Don't presume a comment is more than an allusion to a subject. I try to be helpful., but there is so much more that needs to be understood. I hope the answers illustrate the need for you to devote years of study. Study and prayer are the only way to unlock the mysteries of God. I cannot substitute for that, and do not attempt to provide a shortcut for you. You must engage the Gospel yourself. If you are unwilling to do that, then you will never profit from what I offer. I only refer to the least part of these matters. I raise topics. These are important. You need to investigate them. They are vast. They are hardly understood anymore. They are no longer taught. If you want to understand God, you will have to accomplish that in the same way as all who went before. Take Enoch and Abraham as examples. They studied everything they could find before asking God to show them more. God refused to move their intelligence upward until after they had first obtained a sound understanding, by study, of what He had previously revealed to the fathers.[2327] These past saved men were not merely simpletons like us, surfing the web and looking to the blogosphere to provide them shortcuts. You will delude yourself if you are not spending hours each day studying the scriptures to see what they contain. Sometimes I think the Lord has me on a fool's errand doing more harm than good. Many of you think that this is a hobby of mine; or that my opinion is just as ill-conceived as your own; or that you can get what you need by what little I post here without the effort of approaching God yourself. I think the harm from that is enough the Lord ought to just let me withdraw from this endeavor and finish the rest of what needs doing in private. He has higher regard for your potential than I have on days like today. But, then again, there are other days when I am filled with hope for all of you. Today is just not one of them.

Q: What is the "Abrahamic test?"

The Lord adapts the test required to prove a person to their unique circumstances. The test given to Abraham was adapted perfectly to him. To understand how great the sacrifice was, the account needed to inform us of the difficulty encountered by him and Sarah to obtain this child of promise. We needed to know the promised future inheritance of a posterity as numerous as the sand or the stars was tied directly to this son's survival. It was, in the context of Abraham's life and promises from God, the sacrifice of everything. All his hopes, all his promises from God, all his joy with Sarah, all his future descendants were to be laid on the altar and sacrificed. His heart could only be proven through this means. The Abrahamic Test,

---

[2327] Abraham 1:28 "But I shall endeavor, hereafter, to delineate the chronology running back from myself to the beginning of the creation, for the records have come into my hands, which I hold unto this present time."
D&C 107:57 "These things were all written in the book of Enoch, and are to be testified of in due time."

therefore, will ask the same of you. It will be adapted to what you hope to receive, or have been promised to receive from God. It will end the work of years, and will require you to sacrifice all to God. What one person prizes is never the same as another. What would be easy for one will be nearly impossible for another. The test is adapted to each person. But it will be equally painful, equally difficult and equally proving of the person. Until the heart is tried in this manner we can never know we will submit everything to the Lord. If such a test has not been given you, then it is because the Lord knows you are not prepared to face it. As soon as you are prepared, you will encounter it. For most people they will likely be in their 50's, after having spent many years preparing to overcome themselves. There are notable examples who were much younger, namely Samuel or Joseph Smith. Those are exceptions. Abraham was between 70 and 100, depending on how you reconstruct the chronology. Moses was 80. Those are not atypical examples. Until you know your own heart is purified before God, you cannot bear Him nor have the required faith in Him. This is not an avoidable option, but an essential ingredient in knowing Him. This is why there are years of preparation generally required, and warnings given about continuing forward. The recipient must volunteer. And they must be warned beforehand.

Q: What was the difference between Korihor's claims and Lehi's?

Lehi followed Christ. Korihor did not. Lehi was a disciple of the Lord's. Korihor was an enemy of His. Lehi propounded a true message, Korihor a false one. Lehi was Christ-like. Korihor was an anti-Christ. Lehi spoke the truth. Korihor was a liar. They were polar opposites. But the question illustrates that the god of this world is imitative. The difference between truth and error does not lie in the difference between religion and irreligion, but instead between true religion which will save, and false religion which cannot save. If it were any less a test, the very elect would not be deceived in the last days. Unless there are false prophets claiming they are authorized by God to preach false and idle messages, God cannot send true ones to declare the truth. The opposition of the one is required for the other. The enemy of your soul does not create a new religion, but imitates the true one. The Lord's messenger will be mirrored by the adversary's, but the reflected image will be reversed. Those who follow the image will find themselves descending, while they think they are ascending to God. Hence the name: "the Deceiver." He deceives, and even mirrors God's angels by the claim to be an "angel of light" while spreading darkness. The Deceiver's false prophets will point you to themselves, to their great works, wonderful accomplishments, and the pride you should take in following them. The Lord's will point you to Him and preach repentance. The false prophets will speak of riches here, and suggest God's favor can be measured by success in this world. The Lord will speak only of riches in another world which are only obtained through the sacrifice of all things here.

> One comment said I don't know what I'm talking about, because all the temple ordinance changes have been through revelation. The people in charge are prophets, seers, and revelators, and therefore they invariably operate through revelation. So I'm misleading people because I'm not well informed.

When the changes were made, for at least a week, sometimes longer, a letter was read to temple patrons explaining there had been changes made. Those letters invariably referred to the "keys" held by church leaders as the source to justify the changes. I listened closely. There was never any mention made of a revelation requiring the change. Further, there are obligations imposed by Acts, the Book of Mormon, and the D&C which require church leaders to provide testimony to the church of any visit from Christ, or from an angel, or declaration from God to them. That is the role of the "prophet" and the "seer" and the "revelator." Therefore when a change is made because of an angelic visit, they should testify or witness of it.[2328] They should also testify if the Lord visited.[2329] Given the absence of that explanation in the letters read to Temple patrons, and the clear statement in the letters from the First Presidency when changes were made, that holding "keys" entitled them to make the change, it is curious to me that a revelation from God would be ignored in the statement. It seems unlikely that in a Temple setting involving changes to Temple rites the fact it was changed because God revealed the change would be something "too sacred" to be stated. Accordingly, unless you impose something which those responsible never put into their statement, they have never received a revelation requiring the changes. If they wanted me to conclude the Lord revealed the change, all they needed to do was to state that. The difference between your view and mine is that I trust these leaders are fully able to say exactly what they mean. Therefore I take them at their word. You, on the other hand, think they lie incessantly and conceal some of the most important information required for their callings. I do not think they are liars.

[2328] Moroni 7:29–32 "And because he hath done this, my beloved brethren, have miracles ceased? Behold I say unto you, Nay; neither have angels ceased to minister unto the children of men. For behold, they are subject unto him, to minister according to the word of his command, showing themselves unto them of strong faith and a firm mind in every form of godliness. And the office of their ministry is to call men unto repentance, and to fulfil and to do the work of the covenants of the Father, which he hath made unto the children of men, to prepare the way among the children of men, by declaring the word of Christ unto the chosen vessels of the Lord, that they may bear testimony of him. And by so doing, the Lord God prepareth the way that the residue of men may have faith in Christ, that the Holy Ghost may have place in their hearts, according to the power thereof; and after this manner bringeth to pass the Father, the covenants which he hath made unto the children of men."

[2329] Acts 1:22 "Beginning from the baptism of John, unto that same day that he was taken up from us, must one be ordained to be a witness with us of his resurrection." D&C 107:23 "The twelve traveling councilors are called to be the Twelve Apostles, or special witnesses of the name of Christ in all the world—thus differing from other officers in the church in the duties of their calling."

Another Inquiry about Adam-God

In response to several comments (actually complaints) about my mention of Adam-God doctrine as taught by Brigham Young. Rather than remaining silent and inviting further comment I'll add this and then leave it alone.

Brigham Young is presumed by almost everyone to have been closer to Joseph than he was. He is presumed to have understood Joseph's teachings better than he actually did. He was not with Joseph during most of the years of his Apostleship when Joseph was alive.

The question to me is *not* what Brigham Young taught. That does not clarify the matter to my understanding. The question is what is true? Whether Brigham Young understood it or not, or whether he was able to explain it or not, what is true?

The answer to that question is best solved by going to the scriptures. I've tried to address the question in the paper: *The First Three Words Spoken in the Endowment.* You can download it from the blog. In it I go through the scriptures showing that the group called "noble and great" were also called "the Gods" in Chapter 4 of the Book of Abraham. Also, that Joseph referred to this group as "sons of God, who exalted themselves to be gods, even from before the foundation of the world." (*TPJS*, 375). Joseph mentioned the word-name "Elohim" is plural. "El" is the singular, Elohim is the plural. The identities of the "Elohim" is best understood in Abraham 3 and 4.

Joseph was excited about this in the last sermons he gave in Nauvoo. That is why the paper focused on Joseph's treatment of the Book of Abraham material.

The problem is not that I haven't studied Brigham Young enough, but that I do not draw my conclusions from him. He is not consistent in his comments. Furthermore, he was trying to repeat what he *thought* Joseph was teaching. You can by-pass him and go to the scriptures and figure it out for yourself, without straining the truth through Brigham Young's effort to explain something.

There is something to the doctrine. But I'm not persuaded that Brigham Young understood the matter as well as I do. Further, I am quite confident that Brigham Young did not understand Joseph Smith as well as most Latter-day Saints presume.

The question is answered using scripture.

Also, for those who think they are better read on some questions than I am, I've spent decades studying Mormon history and doctrine. Recently, I've been studying Brigham Young's statements now available for the first time in a single comprehensive collection. This five volume collection has become the best single work on the words of Brigham Young. After reading thousands of pages of his talks, I have reached a number of conclusions about Brigham Young that I will eventually write about.

Brigham Young claimed there was only one "Father" of all mankind, both as the first man and again in the pre-existence. There is more to that story than this simple reduction. But the push by the church to be more like other "Christian" faiths, along with the criticism this doctrine has brought to Mormonism, has made it a matter the church would like to leave alone. Once President Kimball denounced the matter as a "false theory," it was over as far as the church was concerned. The greatest interest in this question exists now only among fundamentalists. They have suffered greatly because of the credibility they have given to Brigham Young.

To the extent that I have felt any need to touch on this matter, it is in that paper. As to Brigham Young, however, I intend to write more about him, but not here.

Hyrum Smith

Hyrum Smith would eventually replace Joseph Smith as the prophet of the church. However, in 1829 he was given a revelation through his younger brother, Joseph. This was given before the Book of Mormon was published, before a church was organized, and while the work of the new Dispensation was in its very first stages. The content, however, is important. Not just for Hyrum, but for all of us.

Just like others, Hyrum was reminded of what it took to be called to the work: "whosoever will thrust in his sicle and reap, the same is called of God."[2330] It wasn't an extensive application and approval process, but it was based on the willingness to do what God wanted that created "the call of God" to the laborer. Without ordination, or setting apart, the relationship was between the individual and God. It is an interesting series of revelations at the beginning of the work which uniformly leave God's calling to the individual, based on their desire.[2331]

[2330] D&C 11:3–4 "Behold, the field is white already to harvest; therefore, whoso desireth to reap let him thrust in his sickle with his might, and reap while the day lasts, that he may treasure up for his soul everlasting salvation in the kingdom of God. Yea, whosoever will thrust in his sickle and reap, the same is called of God."

[2331] D&C 4:3 "Therefore, if ye have desires to serve God ye are called to the work;" D&C 12:4 "Yea, whosoever will thrust in his sickle and reap, the same is called of God."

The first stage, however, was limited to crying repentance. Hyrum was to "say nothing but repentance unto this generation."[2332] The potential for Hyrum doing more later was certain, provided he would follow the Lord's counsel.[2333]

Hyrum was instructed on how to know he was proceeding in the right way:

"put your trust in that Spirit which leadeth to do good—yea, to do justly, to walk humbly, to judge righteously; and this is my Spirit." (D&C 11:12)

Then, despite his desire and the call, Hyrum was told to temporarily stand down. The Lord instructs him:

"Behold, I command you that you need not suppose that you are called to preach until you are called. Wait a little longer, until you shall have my word, my rock, my church, and my gospel, that you may know of a surety my doctrine." (D&C 11:15–16)

The Lord told Hyrum essentially to 'stand down' and not do anything, even if he were "called" to the work. There was more needed before he could be of use to the Lord. He needed to accomplish one work:

"Behold, this is your work, to keep my commandments, yea, with all your might, mind and strength." (D&C 11:20)

Then, one of the great voices of the Restoration was told:

[2332] D&C 11:9 "Say nothing but repentance unto this generation. Keep my commandments, and assist to bring forth my work, according to my commandments, and you shall be blessed."

[2333] D&C 11:10 "Behold, thou hast a gift, or thou shalt have a gift if thou wilt desire of me in faith, with an honest heart, believing in the power of Jesus Christ, or in my power which speaketh unto thee;"

"Seek not to declare my word, but first seek to obtain my word, and they shall your tongue be loosed." (D&C 11:21)

Hyrum needed to study. He needed to fill himself with information before he began his work.

"Hold your peace; study my word which hath gone forth among the children of men, and also study my word which shall come forth among the children of men, or that which is now translating, yea, until you have obtained all which I shall grant unto the children of men in this generation, and then shall all things be added thereto." (D&C 11:22)

Hyrum had homework to do. He needed to "study" things.

Hyrum would become the church prophet and Patriarch. He would be co-president and co-testator with his younger brother, Joseph. Joseph had several other brothers, but it was Hyrum who followed the formula given him by the Lord. It was Hyrum who qualified himself to the work by his diligence and heed.

Hyrum was the designated successor to Joseph as the head of the church. But Hyrum fell first, and he and his younger brother died martyrs.

Hyrum Smith, Part 2

In order to have a meaningful discussion about Hyrum, it is necessary to provide background information that may seem strange to most modern Latter-day Saints. We have a much different story today than the story told in the beginning. To communicate across the barrier of mistaken and incomplete understanding, there are some ideas that seem strange that are required as background to begin to explain why Hyrum was so significant.

Hyrum was given the calling of "Priesthood and Patriarch" in a revelation in January, 1841.[2334] That seems a curious statement to us, since everyone is presumed to have held the "priesthood" as soon as they were "elders" in the church. In the beginning, however, it was not understood the same way it is now. The offices of "elder," like other offices, (priests, deacons, teachers) were offices in the church.[2335]

They were not coincidental to having priesthood. They were "offices . . . in the church of Christ." (This was the original name of the church.) These offices were elected, approved by common consent, and then filled by those elected. After Section 107, the two things (church office and priesthood) were conflated to mean the same thing. The office belongs to the church, and whether there is priesthood present or not, the right to preach, teach, expound, exhort, baptize, lay on hands for the Holy Ghost, bless and pass the sacrament, are all things which the Lord commissioned the church to perform. This is also why, at the time Joseph and Oliver received only the Aaronic Priesthood,[2336] they began to call one another the First and Second "elder of the church."[2337] This is also why Joseph and

---

[2334] D&C 124:91 "And again, verily I say unto you, let my servant William be appointed, ordained, and anointed, as counselor unto my servant Joseph, in the room of my servant Hyrum, that my servant Hyrum may take the office of Priesthood and Patriarch, which was appointed unto him by his father, by blessing and also by right;"

[2335] D&C 20:38 "*The duty of the elders, priests, teachers, deacons, and members of the church of Christ*—An apostle is an elder, and it is his calling to baptize;"

[2336] JS–H 1:69 "*Upon you my fellow servants, in the name of Messiah, I confer the Priesthood of Aaron, which holds the keys of the ministering of angels, and of the gospel of repentance, and of baptism by immersion for the remission of sins; and this shall never be taken again from the earth until the sons of Levi do offer again an offering unto the Lord in righteousness.*"

[2337] JS–H 1:72 "The messenger who visited us on this occasion and conferred this Priesthood upon us, said that his name was John, the same that is called John the Baptist in the New Testament, and that he acted under the direction of Peter, James and John, who held the keys of the Priesthood of Melchizedek, which Priesthood, he said, would in due time be conferred on us, and that I should be called the first Elder of the Church, and he (Oliver Cowdery) the second. It was on the fifteenth day of May, 1829, that we were ordained under the hand of this messenger, and baptized."

Oliver received the Holy Ghost when baptized[2338] even though the angel said the priesthood given did not have "the power of laying on hands for the gift of the Holy Ghost."[2339] They had the right to baptize, they were called the "First and Second elders of the church," but they did not have the "power of laying on hands" for the Holy Ghost. This is not inconsistent, but it is different from what we now overlay onto the idea of priesthood. Today we are more confused than ever even when we think ourselves in possession of the truth.

In any event, when the January 1841 revelation came, Hyrum had already proven valiant. The time arrived when the Lord wanted Hyrum to be ordained to "Priesthood" and "Patriarch" so that he might "hold the keys of the patriarchal blessings upon the heads of all my people."[2340] This same revelation appointed another "prophet, and a seer, and a revelator unto [the Lord's] church."[2341] This was the word of the Lord establishing this status and entitling Hyrum to claim this position.

[2338] JS–H 1:73 "Immediately on our coming up out of the water after we had been baptized, we experienced great and glorious blessings from our Heavenly Father. No sooner had I baptized Oliver Cowdery, than the Holy Ghost fell upon him, and he stood up and prophesied many things which should shortly come to pass. And again, so soon as I had been baptized by him, I also had the spirit of prophecy, when, standing up, I prophesied concerning the rise of this Church, and many other things connected with the Church, and this generation of the children of men. We were filled with the Holy Ghost, and rejoiced in the God of our salvation."

[2339] JS–H 1:70 "He said this Aaronic Priesthood had not the power of laying on hands for the gift of the Holy Ghost, but that this should be conferred on us hereafter; and he commanded us to go and be baptized, and gave us directions that I should baptize Oliver Cowdery, and that afterwards he should baptize me."

[2340] D&C 124:93 "That whoever he blesses shall be blessed, and whoever he curses shall be cursed; that whatsoever he shall bind on earth shall be bound in heaven; and whatsoever he shall loose on earth shall be loosed in heaven."

[2341] D&C 124:94 "And from this time forth I appoint unto him that he may be a prophet, and a seer, and a revelator unto my church, as well as my servant Joseph;"

He was then to "act in concert also with my servant Joseph" as co-president of the church.[2342] Joseph had restored to him "all things" and could ask and the Lord would "make all things known unto" him.[2343] Hyrum was likewise able to "ask and receive" answers from the Lord.[2344]

Because of this ordination by the word of the Lord, Hyrum was given the power to seal:

> "Whoever he blesses shall be blessed, and whoever he curses shall be cursed; that whatsoever he shall bind on earth shall be bound in heaven; and whatsoever he shall loose on earth shall be loosed in heaven." (D&C 124:93)

These rights made him co-equal with Joseph, though Hyrum always acted only in concert with Joseph. He was meek, like Moses[2345] and like Nephi, son of Helaman[2346]. They could be trusted by the

---

[2342] D&C 124:95 "That he may act in concert also with my servant Joseph; and that he shall receive counsel from my servant Joseph, who shall show unto him the keys whereby he may ask and receive, and be crowned with the same blessing, and glory, and honor, and priesthood, and gifts of the priesthood, that once were put upon him that was my servant Oliver Cowdery;"

[2343] D&C 132:45 "For I have conferred upon you the keys and power of the priesthood, wherein I restore all things, and make known unto you all things in due time."

[2344] D&C 124:95 "That he may act in concert also with my servant Joseph; and that he shall receive counsel from my servant Joseph, who shall show unto him the keys whereby he may ask and receive, and be crowned with the same blessing, and glory, and honor, and priesthood, and gifts of the priesthood, that once were put upon him that was my servant Oliver Cowdery;"

[2345] Numbers 12:3 "(Now the man Moses *was* very meek, above all the men which *were* upon the face of the earth.)"

[2346] Helaman 10:5 "And now, because thou hast done this with such unwearyingness, behold, I will bless thee forever; and I will make thee mighty in word and in deed, in faith and in works; yea, even that all things shall be done unto thee according to thy word, for thou shalt not ask that which is contrary to my will."

Lord because they would do what the Lord wanted, not what they wanted.[2347]

This is the kind of man Hyrum was. He was trusted by the Lord, and chose to die with his brother. Had he lived, He would have been Joseph's successor. Brigham Young said this during the debates over who should succeed Joseph as the president:

> "Did Joseph Smith ordain any man to take his place? He did. Who was it? It was Hyrum . . . " (*Times & Seasons*, October 15, 1844, 5:683)

This is an interesting fact because Hyrum was not a member of the Quorum of the Twelve at the time he was killed. However, even Brigham Young, who won the initial debate having argued that the twelve should lead, and then ultimately won an election in December 1847 to become the president of the church, acknowledged it was Hyrum's right to succeed Joseph. With Hyrum gone, and without any clear direction to follow, the church elected first the twelve, and then Brigham Young.

Brigham Young was never ordained to be church president. He was elected. The initial offices of Elder, Priest, Teacher, Deacon were elected positions. Brigham Young viewed the office of church president as similarly elected.

[2347] Alma 14:10–11 "And when Amulek saw the pains of the women and children who were consuming in the fire, he also was pained; and he said unto Alma: How can we witness this awful scene? Therefore let us stretch forth our hands, and exercise the power of God which is in us, and save them from the flames. But Alma said unto him: The Spirit constraineth me that I must not stretch forth mine hand; for behold the Lord receiveth them up unto himself, in glory; and he doth suffer that they may do this thing, or that the people may do this thing unto them, according to the hardness of their hearts, that the judgments which he shall exercise upon them in his wrath may be just; and the blood of the innocent shall stand as a witness against them, yea, and cry mightily against them at the last day."

He explained how he thought this should operate. Anyone could lead the church. All that was required was an election, then the prayers of the members. Here is the system:

> "Take any man in this kingdom, and if the people say that they will make him a President, or a Bishop, or elect him to fill any other office, and the faith of the people is concentrated to receive light through that officer or pipe laid by the power of the Priesthood from the throne of God, you might as well try to move the heavens as to receive anything wrong through that conductor. No matter whom you elect for an officer, if your faith is concentrated in him through whom to receive the things which he is appointed to administer in, light will come to you. Let a presiding officer or a Bishop turn away from righteousness, and the Lord Almighty would give him the lock-jaw, if he could not stop his mouth in any other way, or send a fit of numb palsy on him, so that he could not act, as sure as the people over whom he presided were right, that they might not be led astray." (*Complete Discourses of Brigham Young,* 3:1379, November 29, 1857; the talk can also found at *JD* 6:93)

In this system, the power of being elected coupled with the members' prayers were enough to always insure the answers you got through that leader were exactly perfect.

This was in the early days when church leaders were elected to office. Church authorities may offer names, but the congregation, stake, or church members elected them to office.

With Hyrum's death, we lost something of great value. If he had outlived Joseph, he would have been the unchallenged church president. His succession would have set the pattern for later church

presidents. They each would have chosen their own successors before they died.[2348]

By the time Brigham Young established the twelve as the seat of
power, the pattern was set. Instead of the replacement being chosen
by the sitting president through revelation, the senior apostle was
presumed to be the next in line. Today's legal structure using the
Corporation of the President of the Church of Jesus Christ of Latter-
day Saints the succession is automatic. The corporation's sole member
is the longest tenured apostle. This is in place because Hyrum did not
outlive Joseph. So we are all affected by the loss of Joseph's brother.

Hyrum Smith, Part 3

In November 1842, Hyrum Smith wrote the following letter to
the church. I reprint it in whole, without comment. Joseph was irri-
tated because the church did not seem to realize Hyrum was entitled
to lead the church. William Clayton's Journal records on July 16, 1843
that Joseph said the following: "Hyrum held the office of prophet to
the church by birthright . . . the Saints must regard Hyrum for he has
authority."

The letter (reproduced below) probably should have been included in the D&C. It tells a great deal about the kind of leader Hyrum Smith would have made had he survived Joseph's death:

> To our well beloved brother Parley P. Pratt, and to the elders
> of the Church of Jesus Christ of Latter-day Saints in Eng-

[2348] D&C 43:2–5 "For behold, verily, verily, I say unto you, that ye have received a
commandment for a law unto my church, through him whom I have appointed unto
you to receive commandments and revelations from my hand. And this ye shall know
assuredly—that there is none other appointed unto you to receive commandments and
revelations until he be taken, if he abide in me. But verily, verily, I say unto you, that
none else shall be appointed unto this gift except it be through him; for if it be taken
from him he shall not have power except to appoint another in his stead. And this shall
be a law unto you, that ye receive not the teachings of any that shall come before you
as revelations or commandments;"

land, and scattered abroad throughout all Europe, and to the Saints—Greeting:

Whereas, in times past persons have been permitted to gather with the Saints at Nauvoo, in North America—such as husbands leaving their wives and children behind; also, such as wives leaving their husbands, and such as husbands leaving their wives who have no children, and some because their companions are unbelievers. All this kind of proceedings we consider to be erroneous and for want of proper information. And the same should be taught to all the Saints, and not suffer families to be broken up on any account whatever if it be possible to avoid it. Suffer no man to leave his wife because she is an unbeliever. These things are an evil and must be forbidden by the authorities of the church or they will come under condemnation; for the gathering is not in hast nor by flight, but to prepare all things before you, and you know not but the unbeliever may be converted and the Lord heal him; but let the believers exercise faith in God, and the unbelieving husband shall be sanctified by the believing wife; and the unbelieving wife by the believing husband, and families are preserved and saved from a great evil which we have seen verified before our eyes. Behold this is a wicked generation, full of lyings, and deceit, and craftiness; and the children of the wicked are wiser than the children of light; that is, they are more crafty; and it seems that it has been the case in all ages of the world.

And the man who leaves his wife and travels to a foreign nation, has his mind overpowered with darkness, and Satan deceived him and flatters him with the graces of the harlot, and before he is aware he is disgraced forever; and greater is the danger for the woman that leaves her husband. The evils resulting from such proceedings are of such a nature as to oblige us to cut them off from the church.

And we also forbid that a woman leave her husband because he is an unbeliever. We also forbid that a man shall leave his wife because she is an unbeliever. If he be a bad man (i.e., the believer) there is a law to remedy that evil. And if the law divorce them, then they are at liberty; otherwise they are bound as long as they two shall live, and it is not our prerogative to go beyond this; if we do it, it will be at the expense of our reputation.

These things we have written in plainness and we desire that they should be publicly known, and request this to be published in the STAR.

May the Lord bestow his blessings upon all the Saints richly, and hasten the gathering, and bring about the fullness of the everlasting covenant are the prayers of your brethren.

Written by Hyrum Smith, patriarch.

Standing Offer

I have made this offer on several occasions through the church leaders, but will repeat it again here:

If there is someone who claims they have become dissatisfied with the church because of something I have written, I am willing to meet with them to discuss why they should remain faithful and active in the church. I would want to meet with them in the following setting:

First, their Bishop and Stake President would need to be present. If one or the other could not attend, then I would meet with the person and their Bishop or their Stake President, but I would prefer to meet with both present.

Second, I would want it to be in the church office of either the Bishop or the Stake President, and not in a home.

Third, I can only make this offer for those living in Utah, and I could travel within reason. (I will decide what is reasonable.)

Fourth, all arrangements need to be made by email communication through this email address dssnuffer@gmail.com.

This is a matter I mean sincerely. If there is someone you know who would benefit from this offer, talk to the Bishop and Stake President and if they want to have me come and have that discussion I would willingly do so. I can come most any evening of the week and could even meet on Sunday. These local leaders need to be present so they will know what I say, what I stand for, and that any suggestion that I want people leaving the church is exactly opposite of my intention.

The church deserves our gratitude and our faithful service. It is not perfect, but it is the best venue for coming to know God existing in any organized body on the earth today. You will only do yourself a disservice by walking away from the church.

I love my ward. Presently, I help the priests getting ready for their missions prepare for their endowment. This is the same group of priests I used to teach. The work used to be done by a member of the Draper Temple Presidency living in my ward. He and I have spoken several times about this calling. It is a wonderful opportunity. I serve in this capacity with the best efforts I can. I do my best to serve in all my callings. Church service is important and we should all render that service willingly and to the best of our abilities.

We all struggle to understand the restoration. This is a work of patience and devotion. It requires us to carefully study all the revelations, the Book of Mormon, and our history. It should be a labor of love. As we work to find truth while preserving faith, we must have the maturity and patience to allow the truth of our situation to unfold before us in humility and gratitude. The work of God is greater than we can grasp with haste. Time, and patient and ponderous thoughts are required if we are going to obtain the promises offered us. Haste and impatience will cause us only regret.

There are those who are quick to judge. They are fools. Deciding you are discouraged by some of the things men have done or failed to do makes you no better than their worst failure. Even with their shortcomings, men have rendered devoted service. If you think you see a matter more clearly, then rejoice and thank God for that clarity, but do not condemn their failure or mistakes. Studying errors should be with an eye toward avoiding them. We learn to do better, to become better, to reach higher by looking at the mistakes of the past. This should be a journey of discovery solely for the purpose of improving your own relationship with God, not to let you lose faith, become embittered, or harshly judge others.

Recognizing mistakes is only useful if it improves your understanding of, and relationship with God. If you cannot do that, then leave it alone and do something else.

Two quick asides:

First, if Hyrum's letter to the church (posted yesterday) had been followed, Parley Pratt would not have been killed. He never would have given assistance to Eleanor McLean, which motivated her husband Hector to kill Parley.

Second, don't substitute one idol for another. I'm not going to save you. Just like no other man will. That is the role of the Lord, and the Lord alone. Follow Him.

Miscellaneous Responses to Comments

The deaths of Joseph and Hyrum were necessary. The older brother as prophet-priest died first, and the younger brother as priest-king died second. The prophecies, including many of Jesus' parables about the end times, lay out two incompatible processes that were to happen.

In one, the gospel "net" extends to catch anything it can. This requires an aggressively marketed latter-day church whose sweep is non-exclusive and non-exclusionary. It must gather into itself "all manner of fish," some are good and some are bad.

In the other, the angels will pick through the "net" and gather out of it "the good" fish to be kept. It is exclusive and it is exclusionary. It comes only after the widely cast net has first gathered.

Doesn't matter if you read the parable of the Ten Virgins, or the vineyard, the theme is the same: There are two latter-day processes. If you didn't kill Joseph and Hyrum, and you left intact the process which would have created Zion, then the larger, public outreach seeking to gather anyone into the "net" would have ended. The smaller, more restrictive gathering by the angels of only "the good" would have been confined to so small a sample of humanity that the world could complain there wasn't enough of an opportunity given them.

The world was not ready for Zion. The angels were willing to begin the harvest, but then again, they would have been willing to do that in the New Testament times.[2349]

The reason for the "offer" put up yesterday is to disabuse the notion I am an enemy to the church. I am not. I am its greatest friend. But the "Sunday School" educated saints, who long ago surrendered their minds to others to be controlled, find any effort to deal with the depth, height, width and breadth of the gospel to be frightening. These insecure folks want to complain, rather than stretch or stress themselves by searching into the things required to understand our faith and our faith's history. Church leaders are very understanding— until they get alarming reports about people losing faith because of something someone has said or written.

I've thought about publishing a sample of the comments that come to me from those whose faith and church activity have been

---

[2349] Matthew 13:28 "He said unto them, An enemy hath done this. The servants said unto him, Wilt thou then that we go and gather them up?"

strengthened by what I've done, but that seems self-serving and offensive even to me; so I won't do that. Far, far more people have been helped than harmed by what I've written. But even if there is one, I'm willing to help to assist them in their crisis of faith. They deserve to be helped, and if I can help I'm willing to do so.

I got several reports about some of the "often in error but never in doubt" crowd of 'Mormon experts' who think I need to be "handled" by the church. At least one with a name you'd all recognize. The offer to meet with others was made to leave no doubt about my sincerity, faithfulness and willingness to do what I can to help keep people active, and inside the church.

The "awful situation" in Ether 8:24[2350] certainly has a political, governmental and economic component. But these are all Babylon. They will fail. Fixing them is temporary. Focusing on them can be distracting. What will endure are the souls of men. They need to be reclaimed. That happens through repentance. If they will repent, then as a natural result they will end their involvement with the many political and economic conspiracies presently underway. Attacking them without saving men's souls is an exercise in futility. This is why I do not bother spending any time writing about them.

God sees their doings. Their secrets are not hidden from Him. To the extent that they revel in their great gains and well laid plans, they are destined for disappointment. We should not be trying to join them, nor to become part of their great system of benefits. Too much of that has distracted the church and its members already.

[2350] Ether 8:24 "Wherefore, the Lord commandeth you, when ye shall see these things come among you that ye shall awake to a sense of your awful situation, because of this secret combination which shall be among you; or wo be unto it, because of the blood of them who have been slain; for they cry from the dust for vengeance upon it, and also upon those who built it up."

The cure lies in repentance. Not in politics. We aren't going to legislate or regulate salvation. The coming violence and captivity will help save men's souls.

Prophecies are not given to enable us to understand details of the Lord's plans in advance. They are not designed to allow you to parse apart God's plans and know what He plans beforehand. They are only meant to be understood after they have happened. Then, when they have happened, you will understand what God was saying and that He was in control all along.

You should be very careful about settling on a final interpretation of any prophecy because they were not given with that in mind.

Mortal man is responsible for fulfilling the Gospel. Until they rise up, everything remains unfulfilled. The "Davidic King" is not an identifiable person, nor will he be, until he has accomplished the tasks assigned to the role. Whether anyone will ever rise up to accomplish that is not a matter of destiny, but it is rather a matter of finally accepting and acting consistent with the Lord's will.

Every dispensation of the Gospel is the "last Dispensation" until it fails. Then another is sent and it is the "last" until it fails. This will continue for so long as man continues to fail. God is in no hurry. Apparently we are not either.

Responses and Response

Just because I respond to a question does not mean I associate importance with the topic. Those who were unaware of the "Davidic king" topic needn't trouble themselves to read about it. For the most part those who claim to understand the topic are not going to help you. I would leave it alone.

For the woman who has become ostracized because she has "read my books" I would suggest that reading them does not require you to talk about them. No one needs to be told what they aren't willing to hear. I stay on-topic in church meetings and discussions. I teach from the church provided materials, and participate by contributing in the context of lessons being taught by others. I do not impose my views on someone else. They either must search for it independent of the church's programs, or buy the books and read them for themselves. Until asked a question, I leave others alone. Those who want to know more are actively searching and can be assisted. Those who are completely content would not be interested in anything contrary to their understanding, and you invite arguments when you try to "convert" them.

As I said, the church IS the current program of the Lord. The broad net is spreading worldwide and gathering all manner of fish. Angels will one day sort through them. But for now, we should all work with this organization to fulfill the Lord's assignment.

The "awful situation" among us Latter-day Saints IS the primary topic I discuss.

The specifics of what one person does/did will never apply to what another must do. This is individual. There are no rules. What will break your heart is different from what broke Abraham's, which in turn was different from what broke the Lord's, and what broke Joseph's. Therefore the examples we have in scripture are all you need study.

SORTING
THINGS OUT

Sorting Things Out

We should be more interested in the truth than in just inspiring one another with stories that flatter us, or make us feel we are better than others. We cannot afford the luxury of thinking ourselves right when we believe an error. Promoting "faith" in errors is what the Book of Mormon calls "unbelief." When we prize our errors and hold them as true when they are not, we dwindle in unbelief. This is a frequent occurrence throughout the Book of Mormon, and results in the inability to understand God's word.[2351]

We cannot afford to be popular. The price is too high. We cannot turn away from truth even when it causes us painful and difficult repentance. We must not shrink away from what is required to remove the scales from our eyes.

[2351] Mosiah 26:1–3 "Now it came to pass that there were many of the rising generation that could not understand the words of king Benjamin, being little children at the time he spake unto his people; and they did not believe the tradition of their fathers. They did not believe what had been said concerning the resurrection of the dead, neither did they believe concerning the coming of Christ. And now because of their unbelief they could not understand the word of God; and their hearts were hardened."

I thought I had said all I needed on the topic of plural marriage, but a friend has loaned me a copy of the multi-volume work of Arnold Boss on the history of plural marriage. It is apparent more needs to be said to make the matter clear. Therefore, I am going to return to the subject and history to clarify some things.

As far as I can determine, Arnold Boss is an honest man. I do not question his ability to record and report what he has recorded in his account. I accept his account of the interview in 1929 of Lorin C. Woolley, meaning that I trust the interview took place and that Arnold Boss accurately reported the contents of that interview. The defect does not lie with Arnold Boss, but in the account told by Lorin C. Woolley.

Assuming they are interested in the truth, I will lay this matter out in a series of posts that I think will be helpful to the Fundamentalist community. I have been acquainted with this event for over twenty years.

Here is the account given by Woolley in the interview recorded by Arnold Boss on September 22, 1929. I leave the punctuation and spellings as in the original. The "guard" speaking in the narrative is Lorin C. Woolley. He is relating to Arnold Boss the events that took place on the night of September 26–27, 1886 involving church president John Taylor. This is what purportedly occurred during the night of September 26–27, 1886:

> That evening I was called to act as guard during the first part of the night, notwithstanding the fact that I was greatly fatigued on account of the three days trip I had just completed.

> The brethren retired to bed soon after nine o'clock. The sleeping rooms were inspected by the guard as was the custom. President Taylor's room had no outside door. The windows were heavily screened.

Sometime after the brethren retired and while I was reading the Doctrine and Covenants, I was suddenly attracted to a light appearing under the door leading to President Taylor's room, and was at once startled to hear the voices of men talking there. There were three distinct voices. I was bewildered because it was my duty to keep people out of that room and evidently some one had entered without my knowing it. I made a hasty examination and found the door leading to the room bolted as usual. I then examined the outside of the house and found all the window screens were intact. While examining the last window, and feeling greatly agitated, a voice spoke to me, saying, "Can't you feel the spirit? Why should you worry?"

At this I returned to my post and continued to hear the voices in the room. They were so audible that although I did not see the parties I could place their positions in the room from the sound of the voices. The three voices continued until about midnight, when one of them left, and the other two continued. One of them I recognized as President Taylor's voice. I called Charles Birrell and we both sat up until eight o'clock the next morning.

When President Taylor came out of his room about eight o'clock of the morning of September 27, 1886, we could scarcely look at him on account of the brightness of his appearance.

He stated, "brethren, I have had a very pleasant conversation all night with brother Joseph." (Joseph Smith) I said, "Boss, who is the man that was there until midnight?" He asked, "what do you know about it Lorin?" I told him all about my experience. He said, Brother Lorin, that was your Lord."

We had no breakfast, but assembled ourselves in a meeting. I forgot who opened the meeting. I was called to offer benediction. I think, my father John W. Woolley, offered the opening prayer. There were present at this meeting, In addition to President Taylor, George Q. Cannon, L. John Nuttal, John W. Wooley, Samuel Bateman, Charles H. Wilkins, Charles Birrell, Daniel R. Bateman, bishop Samual Sedden, George Earl, My mother Julia E. Woolley, my sister, Amy Woolley, and myself. The meeting was held from about nine o'clock in the morning until five in the afternoon without intermission, being about eight hours in all.

President Taylor called the meeting to order. He had the manifesto, that had been prepared under direction of George Q. Cannon, read again. Then he put each person under covenant that he or she would defend the principle of Celestial or Plural marriage, and that they would consecrate their lives, liberty and property to this end, and that they personally would sustain and uphold that principle.

[I skip several pages to get to the part most important to the Fundamentalist movement:]

John Taylor set five apart and gave them authority to perform marriage ceremonies, and also to set others apart to do the same thing as long as they remained on earth; and while doing so the prophet Joseph Smith stood by directing the proceedings. Two of us had not met the prophet Joseph Smith in this mortal life, and we, Charles H. Wilkins and myself, were introduce to him and shook hands with him.

Because of what I know and what the scriptures relate, this account, though I believe faithfully recorded by Arnold Boss, is riddled with errors. Lorin C. Woolley has embellished the account, and his additions reveal the fraud. We will go through some of the many errors in a series of posts to show why it is false.

There is a principle important and binding on all of us: The things given us by the Lord should never be overstated. They should be given without embellishment, additions, or interpolations. They are not ours, but the Lord's. When He entrusts us with something (or anything), then it is our duty to faithfully perform and to keep everything within the bounds the Lord set. Our additions detract from the Lord's work. Joseph constantly understated his experiences. This is one of the signs he is telling us truth.

It is in the embellishment that Lorin C. Woolley reveals this is a dishonest account. And this event is critical for those who want to claim they can still practice plural marriage, because the authority has remained in the Fundamentalist groups.

Sorting Things Out, Part 2

This incident was to have occurred on September 27th of 1886, and L. John Nuttal was in attendance. He was the Secretary to the First Presidency at the time. His journal records the following for that date:

> President Cannon still improving in his health. The rest of the party all well.

> President Taylor signed several recommends. A letter was received from Elder F. D. Richards, enclosing one from Bro. E. W. Davis of the 17th Ward, in regard to his call as a missionary and needing help.

> A letter was received from Bro. A. Miner dated Sept. 20th stating that he had perfected the reincorporation of Tooele Stake Corporation.

> A letter was received from Bro. Wm. M. Palmer at Council Bluffs September 22, 1886, giving an account of his labors to that time.

> A letter was received from Sister Ellen Norwood Billingsley of Orderville.

A letter was written to Elder Enoch Farr, President, Sandwich Islands Mission, in answer to his letter received September 7th.

A letter was also sent to Bro. Thos. G. Webber of Z.C.M.I.

A letter was written to President W. Woodruff in reply to his letter received September 25th.

President Taylor pitched quoits a while this morning, also in the afternoon.

President Cannon in the home most all day; he sat out of doors awhile in the after part of the day.

Brother S. Bateman carried in our mail matter.

The reference to "pitching quoits" means a game. The game was much like horseshoes, where you throw a ring made of rope or metal trying to ring it around a stake. In other words, the purported meeting on this day, if it happened at the times reported in the Woolley interview, would have been outdoors, and would have included both morning and afternoon games played by president Taylor. There is no real harmony between the account retold in the Woolley interview and the Nuttal record for that date. The hours' long meeting in the one and the morning and afternoon games in the other are not describing the same day.

George Q. Cannon's diary for the same day likewise makes no mention of the purported meeting which Lorin Woolley describes.

On the chance the meeting occurred the day before and was misremembered, again, the diary of L. John Nuttal is void of any reference. The meeting that day is referred to as "our usual meeting" and did not begin until 2:30 in the afternoon. Thus the dating cannot be correct. Both George Q. Cannon and L. John Nuttal were faithful reporters, and would have taken note of anything like the incident which is described by Lorin Woolley.

What that means is the account in the interview has at least one error. When relying on something for so important a matter as holding "authority" to proceed with plural marriages, these details matter a great deal. So, it appears to me the memory of Lorin Woolley is not altogether reliable, but that is a small matter. An event absent from the records of the faithful recorders (First Presidency Secretary and Councilor) does not prove that nothing happened. To be clear, I do think something happened, but what happened was far less than the event as reported by Lorin C. Woolley.

The next matter I think inaccurate in the account is the "light appearing under the door leading to president Taylor's room." This is contrary to the way these things happen.

First, from scripture, the presence of a heavenly light is not visible to unintended third-parties. An audience with one man will leave another man standing right next to him without any notice or visible exposure to the heavenly light. This is true of Daniel, who alone saw the vision and his companions did not: Daniel 10:7. It is true of the vision in Joseph Smith's childhood bedroom, where others were also sleeping when the angel Moroni appeared. See JS–H 1:30.

Second, this is not how the Vision of the Three Degrees of Glory was received. Section 76 was an open vision to Joseph and Sidney Rigdon, seen in the same room where about a dozen visitors were present. They did not see any light, or any portion of what Joseph and Sidney saw. The best account was given by Philo Dibble, reproduced in the *Juvenile Instructor* 27 (May 15, 1892), 303–04, which states in relevant part:

> The vision which is recorded in the Book of Doctrine and Covenants [D&C 76] was given at the house of "Father Johnson," in Hiram, Ohio, and during the time that Joseph and

Sidney were in the spirit and saw the heavens open, there were other men in the room, perhaps twelve, among whom I was one during a part of the time—probably two-thirds of the time,—I saw the glory and felt the power, but did not see the vision.

The events and conversation, while they were seeing what is written (and many things were seen and related that are not written,) I will relate as minutely as is necessary.

Joseph would, at intervals, say: "What do I see?" as one might say while looking out the window and beholding what all in the room could not see. Then he would relate what he had seen or what he was looking at. Then Sidney replied, "I see the same." Presently Sidney would say "what do I see?" and would repeat what he had seen or was seeing, and Joseph would reply, "I see the same."

This manner of conversation was repeated at short intervals to the end of the vision, and during the whole time not a word was spoken by any other person. Not a sound nor motion made by anyone but Joseph and Sidney, and it seemed to me that they never moved a joint or limb during the time I was there, which I think was over an hour, and to the end of the vision.

Joseph sat firmly and calmly all the time in the midst of a magnificent glory, but Sidney sat limp and pale, apparently as limber as a rag, observing which, Joseph remarked, smilingly, "Sidney is not used to it as I am."

If Woolley was not invited into the vision (and his account makes clear he was not invited to participate), then this detail of seeing the heavenly light does not belong in an authentic narrative. It is a detail that, in my view, has been added to embellish the account and make it seem more believable. However, to me it makes the account less believable.

My own experience also tells me it is not trustworthy. The Lord was with me in the Draper Temple recently, and no one present had any idea what transpired nor beheld a thing of what happened there. An interloper does not behold glory, nor participate in such things. The retelling by Woolley, however, makes the mistake of embellishing with the very kind of detail that is incorrect.

This detail, therefore, makes the account less authentic to me, not more. Whatever happened with president Taylor involving the claim he gave the power to seal plural marriages to the "five men" did not, could not, have involved an interloper beholding a heavenly light shining under a closed door. The light of heaven is not natural, coarse or physical. To behold it you must be invited in, and if not invited in you are left without any vision, or knowledge of its presence.

Be careful what tales you trust. There are more problems with Lorin Woolley's account, which we will continue to discuss . . .

Sorting Things Out, Part 3

In addition to the "light" there is the problem of the "three voices." The fact is that angels do not vibrate the air with vocal chords in order to communicate. They "speak" into the mind of the person they address. This is why there are two different quotes of the John the Baptist by Joseph and Oliver. Both of them "heard" him speak. But the "speaking" was into the mind of these two individuals. The communication "spoken" by John the Baptist was of intelligence, conveyed from the mind to the mind.

Joseph quoted John the Baptist as saying:

"Upon you my fellow servants, in the name of Messiah, I confer the Priesthood of Aaron, which holds the keys of the ministering of angels, and the gospel of repentance, and of baptism by immersion for the remission of sins; and this shall never be taken from the earth until the sons of Levi do offer again an offering unto the Lord in righteousness." (JS–H 1:69)

Oliver quoted John the Baptist as saying:

"Upon you my fellow-servants, in the name of Messiah, I confer this Priesthood and this authority, which shall remain upon the earth, that the Sons of Levi may yet offer an offering unto the Lord in righteousness." (see JS–H footnote)

For Joseph it was "the Priesthood of Aaron" and for Oliver it was "this Priesthood." The concept is identical, the words, however, are not.

For Joseph it was "which holds the keys of the ministering of angels, and the gospel of repentance, and of baptism by immersion for remission of sins" and for Oliver it was "this authority." Again, these are the words they used to convey the communication which came into their minds. Identical in substance, different in language. It is one of the evidences they were telling about an authentic event.

For Joseph it was "this shall never be taken from the earth until the sons of Levi do offer again an offering unto the Lord in righteousness" and for Oliver it was "which shall remain on the earth, that the Sons of Levi may yet offer an offering unto the Lord in righteousness."

These differences are the result of each converting into our language the thoughts or intelligence which came from the angel. Angels do not vibrate the air. They "speak" otherwise, in thought— mind to mind.

Similarly, none of those who occupied the same room, even the same bed as Joseph the night of the Angel Moroni's visit heard anything. No one was awakened during the all-night repetitious lectures to Joseph by the Angel. No one else in the room heard anything. Only silence.

So in the embellished and untrue account of Lorin Woolley he adds a detail about the "voices of three men" coming from inside the room in an attempt to add credibility to the account. It doesn't. It shows something has been added that did not happen. Details matter. From this I can say he lacks knowledge and experience in contact with angelic ministers.

Putting Joseph Smith into this setting as one of the "three voices" is additionally problematic.

It is also a questionable detail that the guard placed for the inside door would abandon his post and go outside to inspect the window screens. I assume he added this detail to insure the "credibility" of the appearance inside the room through miraculous means. Apparently the creator(s) of the account did not want to trust the lighting effect alone, but wanted to add a miraculous component to the arrival of Christ and Joseph Smith as well. Because as any skeptic would conclude, if they had broken open the exterior window screens to enter, I suppose we would not believe it was Christ or Joseph Smith.

I also note the morning-time glow of president Taylor in the account. This brightness which was difficult to look upon is akin to Moses' descent from the mount, and designed to furnish that same sense of awe and holiness to the affair. I would think if that were the case, we would have something in the George Q. Cannon or L. John Nuttal diaries about the incident.

Sorting Things Out, Part 4

The part of the account where President Taylor puts those who were present under covenant to obey the principle of plural marriage seems authentic. That was why he was in hiding, after all. He left public view and presided over the church in exile, risking arrest if found.

He sacrificed a great deal to retain the principle of plural marriage. I think that did happen, or could have happened because it is entirely consistent with the events underway at the time.

His denunciation of the "manifesto" also seems authentic to me. His motto was "the kingdom of God or nothing" and he proved himself willing to suffer for a cause he believed to be true. He refused to compromise with the Federal Government, and his refusal was known, public and held to his core. So putting people under a covenant to recommit them to resist, as he was doing by example, seems authentic. It requires no embellishment.

But there is a part of the story I left out of the account. I will mention it only in general terms, as I consider the specifics sacrilege. Those who are Fundamentalist are familiar with it. It involves President Taylor, while denouncing the manifesto, rising from the floor, levitating in the air about a foot off the ground, making certain gestures, and reciting an oath very similar in content to the first Temple covenant penalty in place in 1886.

This addition is designed to add terrible significance to the denunciation. It is to inspire awe and terror in the mind of the listener/reader, but it is entirely out of place. The idea that you needed to add a Temple sign and penalty component to the denunciation of the manifesto is too strange to attribute to President Taylor. It doesn't fit. It seems to me altogether as an embellishment put into the account in order to make the event seem more holy, more sacred and therefore more trustworthy. It does the opposite. Details like these do not belong in the account. They detract. They suggest someone is afraid they won't be believed if they tell the story the way it was. It falls apart to my mind because it takes far too much upon itself.

This leads in turn to another addition to supplement the account which also lacks scriptural support: The appearance of Joseph Smith as the slain, hand-shaking, disembodied Prophet. This detail is added, I assume, because there was concern that unless the event was tied directly to Joseph Smith some people would resist acknowledging the authority.

However, disembodied spirits do not "shake hands."[2352] Joseph's presence and hand-shaking, like the other added embellishments, are necessary to put the whole thrust of the story over. The purpose is to put into the hands of five men the ability to freelance in sealing plural marriages.

Here, then, is the nub of the whole story: "John Taylor set five apart and gave them authority to perform marriage ceremonies, and also to set others apart to do the same thing as long as they remained on the earth[.]" This is critical for what the Fundamentalists want to justify. They *must* have this in order to be able to claim post-John Taylor and post-Manifesto marriage sealings were authorized and authoritative.

First, to be clear: I think John Taylor *did* give authority to these five men to seal other plural marriages. In the time and setting, it makes absolute sense. They were sealing outside of the Temples, and this was being done by the highest church authorities. There is every reason to believe the difficulties of avoiding Federal prosecution tipped in favor of giving authority for others to move plural marriage sealings forward. Just like today there are others who seal marriages in addition to the church President.

HOWEVER,—and this is the problem in the account which nagged the telling of this tale and required its embellishment—this

---

[2352] D&C 129:6–7 "If he be the spirit of a just man made perfect he will come in his glory; for that is the only way he can appear— Ask him to shake hands with you, but he will not move, because it is contrary to the order of heaven for a just man to deceive; but he will still deliver his message."

kind of delegation won't work to perpetuate the practice indefinitely. Even if President Taylor wanted to extend his reach and allow other men to be sealers during his underground days, it won't work once President Taylor died. Their commission is entirely dependent upon the delegation by President Taylor, and cannot run independent from him. When he died, their commission needed to be renewed by President Woodruff. When it wasn't, then their commission ended.

This is because of the very revelation upon which Fundamentalist doctrine is grounded: Section 132. In Section 132 the power to seal is consolidated in but one man at a time, "and there is never but one on the earth at a time on whom this power and the keys of this priesthood are conferred" according to the revelation establishing the very doctrine they defend.[2353] If this was John Taylor when the sealing authority was given, then the one man who could authorize it was John Taylor. When he died, the one man would have been Wilford Woodruff. You can't, in any event, have "five set apart and given authority" who would later rival Wilford Woodruff's claim to the position. That alone is contrary to the order in Section 132. This has been discussed in *Beloved Enos*. The claims are unscriptural and indefensible.

This scriptural impediment to the claim is the very reason we see added the light under the door, the three voices, the levitating and sacrilegious oath pronouncing President Taylor, and the disembodied Joseph Smith shaking hands and presiding over the affair. They are

---

[2353] D&C 132:7 "And verily I say unto you, that the conditions of this law are these: All covenants, contracts, bonds, obligations, oaths, vows, performances, connections, associations, or expectations, that are not made and entered into and sealed by the Holy Spirit of promise, of him who is anointed, both as well for time and for all eternity, and that too most holy, by revelation and commandment through the medium of mine anointed, whom I have appointed on the earth to hold this power (and I have appointed unto my servant Joseph to hold this power in the last days, and there is never but one on the earth at a time on whom this power and the keys of this priesthood are conferred), are of no efficacy, virtue, or force in and after the resurrection from the dead; for all contracts that are not made unto this end have an end when men are dead."

added, though they could not possibly have happened in that way, precisely to overcome the scriptural impediment to the authority claimed by Fundamentalists to be able to continue to seal plural marriages.

I disbelieve the account, though I do not question whether President Taylor gave the ability to seal to other men in order to overcome Federal harassment at the time he was president. But that delegation ended with his death.

To now have various pretenders all claiming they can track back to John Taylor and one of these five men their "line of authority" to seal plural marriages is a deception. There is only one man at a time who can do this. Even the church now disclaims they can perform such rites.

Sorting Things Out, Part 5

The reason this whole topic of plural marriage has assumed cosmic meaning in the minds of our Fundamentalist brothers and sisters is because of Brigham Young's advocacy of this while leading the church. Brigham Young is a pretty thin reed to lean upon when it comes to doctrine, and I mean *any* doctrine. His utility to the Lord did not include his ability to teach, but his ability to lead, colonize and organize. He was a genius in these areas. Doctrinally, however, he has proven to be problematic.

Inside the church, he has been referred to as a man whose statements were "made in the absence of revelation." His position on priesthood ban for those of African blood has been denounced and abandoned. His teachings on plural marriage have been abandoned. His doctrine of Adam-God has been called a "false theory." His doctrine of annihilation of the spirits of evil beings has been renounced. However, Fundamentalists do not respect the same tradition as those who are faithful LDS members. Therefore, for those who stake their salvation on his teachings, I want to use Brigham Young's own words to help them see how thin a reed they lean on for establishing the central importance of plural marriage for exaltation.

Brigham Young's ordination to the apostleship was "not complete" according to those who ordained him, "till God has laid His hands upon [him]. We require as much to qualify us as did those who have gone before us; God is the same. If the Savior in former days laid His hands upon His disciples, why not in the latter days?" (*DHC* 2:196.) Twenty-four years later he informed the saints this had not happened. He thought that perhaps "when [he] had lived to be as old as was Moses when the Lord appeared to him, that perhaps I then may hold communion with the Lord." (*JD* 7:243.) In 1863 he reaffirmed that no such visit had taken place, but he still hoped if he lived to be eighty it might. (*JD* 10:23.) So, although he held the apostleship as an office in the church, his ordination to that office was conditioned on an event he explained had not been consummated by the Lord's confirming ordination. How much confidence should that give you when considering his teachings?

He hesitated to call himself a "prophet, seer and revelator," but allowed others to associate those titles with him:

> "[After putting the motion for himself to be sustained as 'Prophet, Seer, and Revelator,' the President remarked:] I will say that I never dictated the latter part of that sentence. I will make the remark, because those words in that connection always made feel as though I am called more than I am deserving of. I am Brigham Young, an Apostle of Joseph Smith, and also of Jesus Christ. If I have been profitable to these people, I am glad of it. The brethren call me so; and if it be so, I am glad." (*The Complete Discourses of Brigham Young,* 3:1347)

He explained he was not a visionary man:

"I am not going to interpret dreams; for I don't profess to be such a Prophet as were Joseph Smith and Daniel; but I am a Yankee guesser[.]" (*The Complete Discourses of Brigham Young*, 3:1306.)

He considered himself "called of Joseph" and not of the Lord:

"I do not want to skip Joseph, Peter, Jesus, Moses and go to my Father in Heaven. All I ask for is to be guided by the spirit of Joseph, then let others be governed by their head, or priesthood. Joseph enjoyed the privileges which I never thought I had. Joseph was called of God. I was called of Joseph." (*The Complete Discourses of Brigham Young*, 2:1108)

Is being "called of Joseph" a sufficient basis for you to trust the man with your eternal salvation?

Even when Joseph gave him the assignment to finish the Temple rites, he remained uncertain about how this would be accomplished. Ultimately, he concluded that whatever he did would be fixed by the resurrected Joseph Smith during the Millennium:

"After Joseph comes to us in his resurrected body he will more fully instruct us concerning the Baptism for the dead and the sealing ordinances. He will say be baptized for this man and that man and that man be sealed to that man and such a man to such a man, and connect the Priesthood to-gether. I tell you their [sic] will not be much of this done until Joseph comes. He is our spiritual Father. Our hearts are al-ready turned to him and his to us. This [is] the order of the Holy Priesthood and we shall continue to administer in the ordinances of the kingdom of God here on Earth." (*The Complete Discourses of Brigham Young*, 2:1034.)

Temple rites would require Joseph, not President Young, to fix the seals.

On matters affecting eternal salvation, I would not rely on a "Yankee guesser" who considered himself "called of Joseph" and not called of Christ, to give you what you need for salvation. As I have explained in *Passing the Heavenly Gift* and this blog, his insistence on plural marriage as a condition of being saved is not warranted by the language of Section 132.

Brigham Young explained how church leadership was not affected by who held office. His theory was that anyone could be elected, and as long as the followers prayed for them things would go perfectly:

> "Take any man in this kingdom, and if the people say that they will make him a President, or a Bishop, or elect him to fill any other office, and the faith of the people is concentrated to receive light through that officer or pipe laid by the power of the Priesthood from the throne of God, you might as well try to move the heavens as to receive anything wrong through that conductor. No matter whom you elect for an officer, if your faith is concentrated in him through whom to receive the things which he is appointed to administer in, light will come to you. Let a presiding officer or a Bishop turn away from righteousness, and the Lord Almighty would give him the lock-jaw, if he could not stop his mouth in any other way, or send a fit of numb palsy on him, so that he could not act, as sure as the people over whom he presided were right, that they might not be led astray." (*Complete Discourses of Brigham Young,* 3:1379, November 29, 1857; the talk can also found at *JD* 6:93)

Of course, this theory did not work. As an example, Bishop Warren Snow was elected to be Bishop in Manti, but was involved in stealing tithing. Brigham Young sent traveling Bishop A. Milton Musser, then also Orson Hyde, to review records. They found between $5,000 and $8,000 of tithing missing, a substantial sum in those times.

Though he explained this theory, I do not think Brigham Young believed it at all. Had he believed it, he would not have challenged Sidney Rigdon's claims to lead following the deaths of Joseph and Hyrum. If "any man in this kingdom" could lead, then why not Sidney? If "light will come to you" through any such man, then why not Sidney? The argument was between Sidney (who claimed revelation) and Brigham Young (who claimed to have "keys"). As a result, the debate required the church to choose between Sidney's claims based on revelation and accept Brigham Young's administrative "keys" as the source. Brigham Young's leadership theory (that anyone could lead if prayed for by the membership) would have allowed the church to have both if Sidney were sustained. But Brigham Young's insistence on having control in his quorum forced a vote by the Nauvoo Saints. The vote resulted in abandoning revelation in favor of administrative "keys"—a choice which has affected church history ever since.

This initial vote established power in the Twelve, but within three years Brigham Young found it cumbersome. He had trouble getting consensus, and John Taylor and Parley Pratt opposed him on many issues. On December 1849 he got another vote making him church president and allowing him to organize the First Presidency, an easier administrative group to control.

Once Hyrum and Joseph died, and Brigham Young succeeded in getting elected as church President, the church operated under his leadership for nearly three decades. President Taylor's entire presidency was in exile, avoiding Federal prosecution. Wilford Woodruff compromised on the plural marriage teaching for statehood, and his presidency was thereafter affected by debate about the propriety of that decision and what it meant for the church.

It was not until the 1900's that the church was not in the grip of a conflict brought about by Brigham Young's presidency and teachings.

By that time the mold had been set, and the form put into that mold had hardened. It doesn't matter whether you consider yourself "Fundamentalist" or mainstream, we are all caught inside the pattern established by the Yankee guesser and the immediate aftermath. Do you want to trust your eternal welfare to him? Do you trust that man so much that you will allow his pattern to control your belief in the restoration?

I think the church has reacted poorly to the dilemma created by this man's teachings. They have denounced his major contributions, and have cast aside many other of his teachings and practices. Those who have remained devoted to these doctrines believe what they hold dear came from a reliable source. But remember, even he rejected the idea he was a "Prophet, Seer, and Revelator" because he was only an apostle of Joseph's. The church was right to say recently that he spoke "in the absence of revelation" because that is what he did.

The mistake Fundamentalists have made is not in believing in the system, but in trusting a man. He is no more worthy of your confidence than Lorin C. Woolley. The revelation you trust is carefully composed, and defines "the eternal marriage covenant" as between one man and one wife. That is all you need for exaltation. Brigham Young's excesses on this matter are no more trustworthy than the value of another Yankee guesser. He did what he understood. But his understanding is and was flawed. This is why the church has rejected his teachings on the core of his beliefs: plural marriage, Adam-God, priesthood ban, potential annihilation of damned souls, blood atonement, kingdom of God as earthly institution, etc. There are good reasons for the doctrinal disfavor between him and the same church he led for three decades. Turning to Lorin C. Woolley to preserve Brigham Young's legacy is not improving your state. It is modeling a flawed model.

Despite this, to his credit, Brigham Young never invented visitations, claimed more for himself than that he was a "good hand to have around" and denied he was visited by the Lord. These statements reflect a great deal more credit on Brigham Young than the embellishments made by Brother Woolley reflect on him.

I do not fault Fundamentalists for these problems. They were created by the elected President successor to Joseph and Hyrum. He held the office, and he taught what he taught. But that does not make him right before God. Members of the LDS church should be the first to have charity for this circumstance. We should be willing to forgive this devotion to Brigham Young's teachings because they originated with a man who was, after all, elected to lead the church for three decades. The church refused to abandon wives when it abandoned plural marriage, and Fundamentalists who would return should not be required to tear apart their families. They should reject the doctrine, and stop teaching it to their children. But the church is so very sensitive about this issue that we don't share the same attitude.

I personally believe this problem is cured by ceasing the practice, but leaving existing families intact. I believe those who do this will be welcomed in Zion., but those who continue to advocate and insist this is fundamental to salvation itself, I don't think will be welcomed. The conditions that are required to allow it are not met, and cannot be met by the Fundamentalists. They should recognize this and repent.

Brigham Young's Telestial Kingdom

I have completed an essay about Brigham Young and his Telestial Kingdom. The paper is available for download on Scribd. You do not need a Facebook account to access Scribd, but you do need a Scribd account. They are free and easy to set up.

As always, I suggest you read the footnotes.

A Few Details

The following excerpt comes from an article by Susan Easton Black, published in *BYU Studies*:

> After the death of Emma Smith in 1879 and the demolition of the bee house that had once sheltered the graves, conjecture arose over the exact location of the martyrs' burial site. Family members could not point with confidence to where the bodies were laid. Joseph Smith III reported, "I didn't see the bodies buried. I saw them dig them up. I saw them take a knife and cut a lock of hair off of Joseph and give to Emma, but I didn't follow over and watch them bury them."

> David Hyrum Smith, youngest son of Joseph Smith Jr., composed "The Unknown Grave":

> There's an unknown grave in a green lowly spot,

> The form that it covers will ne'er be forgot.

> Where haven trees spread and the wild locusts wave

> Their fragrant white blooms over the unknown grave,

> Over the unknown grave.

> * * *

> The prophet whose life was destroyed by his foes

> Sleeps now where no hand may disturb his repose,

> Till trumpets of God drown the notes of the wave

> And we see him arise from his unknown grave,

> God bless that unknown grave.

When the waters of Lake Cooper threatened to flood the area where the graves were thought to be, leaders of the Reorganized Church of Jesus Christ of Latter Day Saints decided to locate the bodies and remove them to higher ground and to place an appropriate monument over their graves. W. O. Hands was appointed to direct a small group of surveyors and engineers to search for the missing graves. They began digging on 9 January 1928, and on 16 January they found them. The remains of Joseph Smith and his brother Hyrum, as well as those of Emma, were exhumed from their resting place. The remains were arranged in silk-lined wood boxes that were placed side-by-side seventeen feet north of where the bodies of Joseph and Hyrum had been exhumed. Then the bodies were reburied on Friday, 20 January 1928, and the graves were marked.

On 21 January 1928 Samuel O. Bennion, president of the Central States Mission, wrote to President Heber J. Grant and his counselors about the "exhuming of the bodies of the Prophet and his brother Hyrum." In his letter he reported asking Frederick M. Smith, president of the Reorganized Church of Jesus Christ of Latter Day Saints, "Why didn't you let the bodies of these men rest where they were?" In response, he was told, "[I] wanted to find out if the graves of these men were down by what was once called the Spring House." President Bennion wrote, "It is my impression brethren that he had heard reports that Brigham Young took the bodies of Joseph and Hyrum to Utah and that he wanted to prove it untrue." Bennion stated, "I could hardly keep the tears back."

In 1991, under the joint direction of leaders from the Reorganized Church of Jesus Christ of Latter Day Saints and leaders of the Church of Jesus Christ of Latter-day Saints, new tombstones marking their remains became the focus of a garden-like cemetery near the Homestead in Nauvoo. On 4 August 1991 the newly renovated cemetery was dedicated by Wallace B. Smith, great-grandson of Joseph Smith and president of the RLDS Church. Elder M. Russell Ballard, a great-great-grandson of Hyrum Smith, represented the LDS Church.

If Joseph was resurrected in 1886, his body could not have been relocated in 1928.

Lorin C. Woolley spoke throughout as an interloper. He was spying and overhearing, but wasn't invited into the events. Therefore, his statements should be viewed from that vantage point. On the Mount of Transfiguration Peter, James and John were invited by the Lord precisely so they would witness what took place. They saw and heard as invited participants, not interlopers. If Lorin C. Woolley was invited to witness the events, the description would have been otherwise and read much differently.

When Philo saw Joseph "in the midst of a magnificent glory" that was Joseph experiencing the glory, not Philo. Joseph was in the midst of this experience, seeing the Father and Son at the Throne of God. But that description is of Joseph's being in the "midst" of the experience. Others understood what Joseph was undergoing from the words being spoken.

When he states he "saw the glory and felt the power, but did not witness the vision" he is referring to the same thing any of us witness when reading Section 76. It was this section which got me serious about considering Mormonism. It is glorious. It radiated power to me the instant I first read it. But seeing the glory of that great vision as I read it, like Philo Dibble's experience hearing it dictated by Joseph, did not involve blinding light—nor seeing light from under a doorway. It was and still is a glorious document and vision. You can still feel the power of it today.

Brigham Young was a necessary preserver of the faith. Without him the church would have stumbled. Sidney Rigdon was impaired, and we would not have done as well, and may have done much worse, with him at the helm. The point is that the church was faced with a dilemma with the loss of BOTH Joseph and Hyrum. We had no good alternative. We took the one which was probably the most practical. We have to live with it.

But that does not mean we should avoid understanding the full implications of the choice. Every choice has consequences. Until we gather together our best understanding of what happened, and sort out what was going on, we can't know much of God's dealing in our day.

We should not just bury our heads and trust happy stories. WE are responsible for our own salvation or damnation.

I am the best kind of church member: I willingly accept full responsibility for the eternal outcome. As God is my witness, I will never point to Brigham Young, or Spencer W. Kimball, or Bruce R. McConkie, or Boyd K.Packer, or Thomas S. Monson in the afterlife and blame them for my own condition. I will accept sole responsibility for my eternal state. No man is my leader. No man is responsible for my understanding. I alone will blame myself for any failure, and accept no credit for what I got right. I trust only in the grace and mercy of Christ and rely utterly on His power to save me. The general authorities and local leaders ought to want every church member to be like that.

If a Fundamentalist were to return to church, they would not be welcomed by the institution. They wouldn't have membership records, nor receive callings, nor be able to pay tithing. But they could worship there, and in many wards would be fellowshipped by the members even if the institution excluded them. They would be "visitors" and not members. But that shouldn't deter them. In fact, if enough of them began this practice, the institution would not be oblivious to their presence. When a significant number of people were doing this, policies would be adapted to allow sincere people to repent and return. The leadership of the church would respond. But faithful return will have to precede that even being possible. It would require humility, to be sure.

FORGIVING AND CHARITY

Time Required to Repent

Repentance does not require a time period. Look at Alma the Younger, the sons of Mosiah, and the Apostle Paul. Now these were encounters with God, but so were the conversions of many of the Lamanites.[2354]

The Lord tells you to repent. If you do, He remembers your sins no longer. Confess and forsake them, and you will be forgiven.[2355] Or, in other words, change. Turn away from your sins and face God instead.

[2354] Alma 18:40–42 "And it came to pass that after he had said all these things, and expounded them to the king, that the king believed all his words. And he began to cry unto the Lord, saying: O Lord, have mercy; according to thy abundant mercy which thou hast had upon the people of Nephi, have upon me, and my people. And now, when he had said this, he fell unto the earth, as if he were dead."
Alma 22:18 "O God, Aaron hath told me that there is a God; and if there is a God, and if thou art God, wilt thou make thyself known unto me, and I will give away all my sins to know thee, and that I may be raised from the dead, and be saved at the last day. And now when the king had said these words, he was struck as if he were dead."

[2355] D&C 58:42–43 "Behold, he who has repented of his sins, the same is forgiven, and I, the Lord, remember them no more. By this ye may know if a man repenteth of his sins—behold, he will confess them and forsake them."

All those labors performed by Alma the Younger, the sons of Mosiah, and the Apostle Paul, after repentance, were not to obtain forgiveness. They were the "fruit" of repentance, or the result of the new direction that they were heading.[2356]

God alone forgives. His forgiveness is not dependent on your good works; your good works are proof of His forgiveness.[2357]

Freedom from Sins

The reason "confession" of sin is required, is to free the victim.[2358] Confession robs the accuser of his power to accuse.[2359]

Once the sins of Alma and Younger and the sons of Mosiah were known, confessed, and public, the sins no longer had any con-

---

[2356] Matthew 3:8 "Bring forth therefore fruits meet for repentance:"
Luke 3:8 "Bring forth therefore fruits worthy of repentance, and begin not to say within yourselves, We have Abraham to *our* father: for I say unto you, That God is able of these stones to raise up children unto Abraham."
Alma 5:62 "I speak by way of command unto you that belong to the church; and unto those who do not belong to the church I speak by way of invitation, saying: Come and be baptized unto repentance, that ye also may be partakers of the fruit of the tree of life."
Alma 13:13 "And now, my brethren, I would that ye should humble yourselves before God, and bring forth fruit meet for repentance, that ye may also enter into that rest."
Moroni 8:24–26 "Behold, my son, this thing ought not to be; for repentance is unto them that are under condemnation and under the curse of a broken law. And the first fruits of repentance is baptism; and baptism cometh by faith unto the fulfilling the commandments; and the fulfilling the commandments bringeth remission of sins; And the remission of sins bringeth meekness, and lowliness of heart; and because of meekness and lowliness of heart cometh the visitation of the Holy Ghost, which Comforter filleth with hope and perfect love, which love endureth by diligence unto prayer, until the end shall come, when all the saints shall dwell with God."

[2357] Helaman 12:24 "And may God grant, in his great fulness, that men might be brought unto repentance and good works, that they might be restored unto grace for grace, according to their works."
Galatians 5:22–25 "But the fruit of the Spirit is love, joy, peace, longsuffering, gentleness, goodness, faith, Meekness, temperance: against such there is no law. And they that are Christ's have crucified the flesh with the affections and lusts. If we live in the Spirit, let us also walk in the Spirit."

[2358] D&C 58:43 "By this ye may know if a man repenteth of his sins—behold, he will confess them and forsake them."

[2359] Revelation 12:10 "And I heard a loud voice saying in heaven, Now is come salvation, and strength, and the kingdom of our God, and the power of his Christ: for the accuser of our brethren is cast down, which accused them before our God day and night."

trol over them. They felt no shame for these sins because confessing and admitting they were sinful robbed sin of its power. Similarly, the Apostle Paul's admission of his sinful past allowed him to move on to accepting and celebrating God's grace.[2360]

There is power in confessing. It puts the confessor above his sin.[2361] We confess to celebrate God's great deliverance of us. We are all weak. It is part of worshipping Him.[2362] This is why the testimony of God's redemption by Alma the Younger included confession of his own sins.[2363]

Those who claim they are holy men, without sin, and thereby cover their weaknesses while courting the praise and admiration of others, have no truth in them.[2364] But if we confess we are sinful and weak, God is faithful to forgive us.[2365]

[2360] 1 Timothy 1:12–16 "And I thank Christ Jesus our Lord, who hath enabled me, for that he counted me faithful, putting me into the ministry; Who was before a blasphemer, and a persecutor, and injurious: but I obtained mercy, because I did *it* ignorantly in unbelief. And the grace of our Lord was exceeding abundant with faith and love which is in Christ Jesus. This *is* a faithful saying, and worthy of all acceptation, that Christ Jesus came into the world to save sinners; of whom I am chief. Howbeit for this cause I obtained mercy, that in me first Jesus Christ might shew forth all longsuffering, for a pattern to them which should hereafter believe on him to life everlasting."

[2361] James 5:16 "Confess *your* faults one to another, and pray one for another, that ye may be healed. The effectual fervent prayer of a righteous man availeth much."

[2362] D&C 59:12 "But remember that on this, the Lord's day, thou shalt offer thine oblations and thy sacraments unto the Most High, confessing thy sins unto thy brethren, and before the Lord."

[2363] Alma 36:6, 12–14 "For I went about with the sons of Mosiah, seeking to destroy the church of God; but behold, God sent his holy angel to stop us by the way. But I was racked with eternal torment, for my soul was harrowed up to the greatest degree and racked with all my sins. Yea, I did remember all my sins and iniquities, for which I was tormented with the pains of hell; yea, I saw that I had rebelled against my God, and that I had not kept his holy commandments. Yea, and I had murdered many of his children, or rather led them away unto destruction; yea, and in fine so great had been my iniquities, that the very thought of coming into the presence of my God did rack my soul with inexpressible horror."

[2364] 1 John 1:8 "If we say that we have no sin, we deceive ourselves, and the truth is not in us."

[2365] 1 John 1:9 "If we confess our sins, he is faithful and just to forgive us *our* sins, and to cleanse us from all unrighteousness."

Freedom from sin can only come through admitting your sinful nature. When we confess, He forgives.[2366]

Weakness and Repentance

We are all given weakness as part of life here in mortality. It is a gift from God.[2367] Repentance requires us to turn away from sin, and to face a new direction where God is found.

Despite our hopes, and our desires, and our best efforts, we are confined to a place and occupy circumstances where we are "weak."[2368] The Lord promises, however, that He will "make weak things strong."[2369] What does that mean? How does our "weakness" become "strong?"

It does not involve any magic. We do not get some easy and effortless cure to our weakness just because we desire to change. We must actually change. How do we change? The Lord explains that to Moroni in the same conversation:

> "I will show unto them that faith, hope and charity bringeth unto me—the fountain of righteousness" (Ether 12:28)

Or, in other words, the "strength" we hope to receive comes from "faith" in Christ. Our "hope" is found through Him. Our "charity" is a gift also.

The "strength" is entirely borrowed. We are only as strong as our dependence on Him. Our "weakness" is strength only as we depend on Him and His rescue.

[2366] D&C 64:7 "Nevertheless, he has sinned; but verily I say unto you, I, the Lord, forgive sins unto those who confess their sins before me and ask forgiveness, who have not sinned unto death."

[2367] Ether 12:27 "And if men come unto me I will show unto them their weakness. I give unto men weakness that they may be humble; and my grace is sufficient for all men that humble themselves before me; for if they humble themselves before me, and have faith in me, then will I make weak things become strong unto them."

[2368] Ibid.

[2369] Ibid.

For some of us, that "strength" will involve long-suffering and continual reminders through our failure that we have been "given weakness" for a purpose—that we may be humble. As we struggle, we find exposed to our view the weakness we despise in ourselves, long to overcome, and struggle with daily, like a thorn in our flesh tearing at us. Paul begged the Lord to remove his, and was told repeatedly this weakness would remain there to afflict him so he might be humble.[2370] Therefore, Paul took consolation in the knowledge this struggle was godly.[2371]

Why should you be spared the struggle? Why should you not be kept humble by the weakness you have within? Why should you not take up your cross and follow Him?[2372] Should your cross be anything other than a revelation to you of your own dependence on God, and need for Him?

Repentance is the start of a journey undertaken between you and your Lord. He will reveal you and Him *to you* through that journey. Hence the requirement for repentance in order to enter into His kingdom.

Forgiving to Be Forgiven

Once you begin to repent the real work commences. God forgives, but retaining forgiveness requires that we follow Him. We are

---

[2370] 2 Corinthians 12:7–9 "And lest I should be exalted above measure through the abundance of the revelations, there was given to me a thorn in the flesh, the messenger of Satan to buffet me, lest I should be exalted above measure. For this thing I besought the Lord thrice, that it might depart from me. And he said unto me, My grace is sufficient for thee: for my strength is made perfect in weakness. Most gladly therefore will I rather glory in my infirmities, that the power of Christ may rest upon me."

[2371] 2 Corinthians 12:10 "Therefore I take pleasure in infirmities, in reproaches, in necessities, in persecutions, in distresses for Christ's sake: for when I am weak, then am I strong."

[2372] Mark 10:21 "Then Jesus beholding him loved him, and said unto him, One thing thou lackest: go thy way, sell whatsoever thou hast, and give to the poor, and thou shalt have treasure in heaven: and come, take up the cross, and follow me."

not going to develop into His children until we have become acquainted with His way. He tells us what we must do to learn of Him.
We must do His work, join in His labor to save souls:

> "And as ye would that men should do to you, do ye also to
> them likewise. For if ye love them which love you, what thank
> have ye? for sinners also love those that love them. And if ye
> do good to them which do good to you, what thank have ye?
> for sinners also do even the same. And if ye lend to them of
> whom ye hope to receive, what thank have ye? for sinners also
> lend to sinners, to receive as much again. But love ye your
> enemies, and do good, and lend, hoping for nothing again;
> and your reward shall be great, and ye shall be the children of
> the Highest: for he is kind unto the unthankful and to the
> evil. Be ye therefore merciful, as your Father also is merciful.
> Judge not, and ye shall not be judged: condemn not, and ye
> shall not be condemned: forgive, and ye shall be forgiven:
> Give, and it shall be given unto you; good measure, pressed
> down, and shaken together, and running over, shall men give
> into your bosom. For with the same measure that ye mete
> withal it shall be measured to you again." (Luke 6:31–38)

Once forgiven, we forgive. We take on ourselves the role of the
intercessor by accepting the shame and abuse of this world, and both
forgive and pray for those who give offenses. Through this, we come
to understand our Lord because we are like Him.

This is what we see in Lehi. After learning of God's impending
judgments against Jerusalem, he prayed on behalf of "his people"
(those who were condemned) with "all his heart."[2373] His example
can be found mirrored in all who repent. They display His grace by
what they suffer for His cause.

Christ taught who He was, then lived the example of what a redeemed life would be. He sacrificed Himself. Similarly His followers

---

[2373] 1 Nephi 1:5 "Wherefore it came to pass that my father, Lehi, as he went forth
prayed unto the Lord, yea, even with all his heart, in behalf of his people."

sacrifice themselves. Perhaps not by dying, as He did and as Joseph did, and as Steven did, and Paul, and Peter, and Abinadi and Hyrum. But by the way they live—taking offenses and forgiving. This is how we obtain broken hearts and contrite spirits, because this world is always at war with the Saints of God. Here the Children of God are strangers and sojourners.

When

When will there ever be a generation willing to learn from the mistakes of the past? Why are the patterns and errors endlessly repeated? Will there never be people willing to let the Holy Spirit guide them rather than relying on their own conceit?

Charity

I've written about how uncharitable it is to offer truth before a person is ready for it. Choking them with information they are not ready to receive it is a technique used with some success by Mormon critics. It works. There is no need to resort to distorting things, only to tell truths before someone is prepared to receive them.

The opposite is also true. When someone needs to hear more, then to withhold it from them is equally uncharitable. We starve them, and leave them to wither and die in their faith when we tell them the longing they have to know more cannot be satisfied by the Gospel. It is unkind, uncharitable and an offense to the Lord to tell someone their endowment from God of natural curiosity should be suppressed. This longing to know more is righteous. We are supposed to hunger and thirst to know more. Some people have quenched this desire and killed the child-like attribute to search deeply and long for answers. This does not mean we all have.

No one should be left disappointed by the reply that "you don't need to know that." Joseph asserted the Gospel included "all truth." Brigham Young did as well. Joseph said,

> "Mormonism is truth; and every man who embraces it feels himself at liberty to embrace every truth: consequently the shackles of superstition, bigotry, ignorance, and priestcraft, fall at once from his neck; and his eyes are opened to see the truth, and truth greatly prevails..." (See *Teachings of the Presidents of the Church: Joseph Smith*, chapter 22)

Brigham said,

> " 'Mormonism,' so-called, embraces every principle pertaining to life and salvation, for time and eternity. No matter who has it. If the infidel has got truth it belongs to "Mormonism." The truth and sound doctrine possessed by the sectarian world, and they have a great deal, all belong to this Church. As for their morality, many of them are, morally, just as good as we are. All that is good, lovely, and praiseworthy belongs to this Church and Kingdom. 'Mormonism' includes all truth. There is no truth but what belongs to the Gospel. It is life, eternal life; it is bliss; it is the fullness of all things in the gods and in the eternities of the gods." (*Discourses of Brigham Young*, 3)

We have yet to figure out some of the things restored to us from Abraham. We have not plumbed the depths of the Doctrine and Covenants. To shut down inquiry because "we don't need to know about that" is not only bad doctrine, it is a rejection of what the Restoration was intended to bestow on us.

Of all the people on earth, Latter-day Saints ought to be the most open, most inquisitive, and most interesting people of all. We should be creative, and filled with new ideas and thought. Our church meetings were once places where exciting and interesting gospel material was openly discussed.

When our time is spent discouraging inquiries, asserting we have no business knowing about our history, and shutting minds, we run open the door for a repeat of the Dark Ages. It will be locally confined to the dogmatic and intolerant believers in the most reactionary form of Mormonism; the brand utilized by the correlating of materials. Ideas are impossible to control, but the attempt will discourage and alienate the very best minds we have among us.

Differing views are not evil. Skepticism is not vile. An honest soul struggling with our faith deserves the compassion and kindness of being allowed to express themselves without feeling like something is wrong with them. All the useful questions raised should be considered, studied and answers should be sought. We need to have the confidence to believe there are answers. Even if we haven't discovered them yet, there are still answers. And those answers can include information that requires us to rework our understanding.

Charity flows both ways: from telling too much without preparation, to hiding information from those who are ready to hear more truth. Charity also requires us to accept and fellowship with people who are scattered along a broad spectrum, from immature faith to mature understanding. How often could we benefit from hearing from others about issues which they have struggled to understand, but who remain silent because they fear our reaction?

Early Church Priorities

In 1836, Parley Pratt went to Toronto, Canada to continue his missionary work. He took a letter of introduction for John Taylor, who had been active in a religious reform movement. On May 9, 1836 Parley Pratt baptized John Taylor. That conversion was instrumental in bringing a number of others into the church who had respected John Taylor as a religious figure before his conversion.

By November, Parley Pratt was back in Kirtland and wrote a letter to his friend and recent convert. John Taylor was a new member when the letter was written, having been baptized only 6 months earlier. The content of the letter shows what was considered appropriate for even the newest of Latter-day Saints in 1836. Parley wrote:

> For my part I never can rest until my eyes have seen my Redeemer. Until I have gazed like Nephi upon the glories of the Celestial world. Until I can come into full communion and familiar converse with the angels of glory and the spirits of just men made perfect through the blood of Christ. And I testify to all, both small and great, both male and female, that if they stop short of the full enjoyment of these things they stop short of the blessings freely offered to every creature in the Gospel. (Parley Pratt letter to John Taylor, November 27, 1836; spellings and punctuation corrected.)

This was once fundamental, even basic teaching offered even to new converts. It did no damage to John Taylor.

Signs

Signs do not produce faith.[2374] Signs follow faith.[2375]

Those who "seek signs" are wicked, often adulterous.[2376] Those who want a sign before they will believe cannot develop faith.[2377]

[2374] D&C 63:9 "But, behold, faith cometh not by signs, but signs follow those that believe."

[2375] Ibid.

[2376] Matthew 12:39 "But he answered and said unto them, An evil and adulterous generation seeketh after a sign; and there shall no sign be given to it, but the sign of the prophet Jonas:"
Matthew 16:4 "A wicked and adulterous generation seeketh after a sign; and there shall no sign be given unto it, but the sign of the prophet Jonas. And he left them, and departed."

[2377] Ether 12:6 "And now, I, Moroni, would speak somewhat concerning these things; I would show unto the world that faith is things which are hoped for and not seen; wherefore, dispute not because ye see not, for ye receive no witness until after the trial of your faith."

Signs which follow faith do not come as a result of what men seek, but come as a result of what God wills.[2378]

Signs, given by God, according to His will, create mighty works by men.[2379] However, God's mighty works are often accomplished by small means. Events that are "mighty even unto the power of deliverance",[2380] can be accomplished by so little a means as God warning a family to flee.[2381]

God preserved His Son through "small means."[2382]

The Lord preserved mankind through the destruction at the time of Noah using only a small family.[2383]

There will be "signs" and "small means" and "mighty works" still, but they will seem as nothing to those who do not believe. But to people of faith, they will be the power of God unto salvation.

Nephi on Holy Spirit

[2378] D&C 63:10 "Yea, signs come by faith, not by the will of men, nor as they please, but by the will of God."

[2379] D&C 63:11 "Yea, signs come by faith, unto mighty works, for without faith no man pleaseth God; and with whom God is angry he is not well pleased; wherefore, unto such he showeth no signs, only in wrath unto their condemnation."

[2380] 1 Nephi 1:20 "And when the Jews heard these things they were angry with him; yea, even as with the prophets of old, whom they had cast out, and stoned, and slain; and they also sought his life, that they might take it away. But behold, I, Nephi, will show unto you that the tender mercies of the Lord are over all those whom he hath chosen, because of their faith, to make them mighty even unto the power of deliverance."

[2381] 1 Nephi 2:2 "For behold, it came to pass that the Lord spake unto my father, yea, even in a dream, and said unto him: Blessed art thou Lehi, because of the things which thou hast done; and because thou hast been faithful and declared unto this people the things which I commanded thee, behold, they seek to take away thy life."

[2382] Matthew 2:13–14 "And when they were departed, behold, the angel of the Lord appeareth to Joseph in a dream, saying, Arise, and take the young child and his mother, and flee into Egypt, and be thou there until I bring thee word: for Herod will seek the young child to destroy him. When he arose, he took the young child and his mother by night, and departed into Egypt:"

[2383] Genesis 7:23 "And every living substance was destroyed which was upon the face of the ground, both man, and cattle, and the creeping things, and the fowl of the heaven; and they were destroyed from the earth: and Noah only remained *alive*, and they that *were* with him in the ark."

Nephi explained that many people harden themselves against the influence of the Holy Spirit, and consequently were unable to determine what was worth keeping and what should be cast away. He wrote:

> "But behold, there are many that harden their hearts against the Holy Spirit, that it hath no place in them; wherefore, they cast many things away which are written and esteem them as things of naught." (2 Nephi 33:2)

What does it mean to "harden your heart?"

How does "hardening your heart" affect the influence of the Holy Spirit?

Why does the Holy Spirit equip you to decide whether something is to be valued or to be "cast away?"

Can you decide on your own what is of value?

Do you need to receive influence from the Holy Spirit in order to understand something is from God?

To understand something is of value?

What does it mean to "cast away" the things found in scripture?

Can you read them, even associate meaning with them, and still cast them away?

Can you support your own view using scripture and "cast them away" at the same time?

How do you turn scripture into "things of naught?"

Are distracting, inspirational stories that do not teach true doctrine capable of hardening your heart?

Are flattering words that do not call you to repent likely to harden your heart?

Can scriptures which were written under the influence of the Holy Ghost become a "thing of naught" when read by someone who has hardened their heart?

Can true doctrine become a "thing of naught" even if taught by the power of the Holy Ghost, if the listener hardens their heart?

The measure of the importance of this verse is found in a revelation given to Joseph Smith about the destruction of the wicked:

> "For they that are wise and have received the truth, and have taken the Holy Spirit for their guide, and have not been deceived—verily I say unto you, they shall not be hewn down and cast into the fire, but shall abide the day." (D&C 45:57)

What is the difference between "taking the Holy Spirit for your guide" and "hardening your heart against the Holy Spirit?"

How does the Holy Spirit guide so you cannot be deceived?

How does a person become "wise" and "receive the truth?"

What does it mean to be "hewn down and cast into the fire?"

What does it mean to "abide the day?"

How does the Holy Spirit figure into surviving the coming judgments of God?

Can you trust your own wisdom, intellect and abilities? Can any person, no matter what their IQ, be guided by the Holy Spirit? Does education, position, social status or qualifications equip you to know as much as the Holy Spirit?

Holy Ghost and Holy Spirit

Are the "Holy Ghost" and the "Holy Spirit" the same? When Nephi refers to the "Holy Ghost" in 2 Nephi 33:1, but then uses "Holy Spirit" in the next verse, does he have two different things in mind?[2384]

[2384] 2 Nephi 33:1–2 "And now I, Nephi, cannot write all the things which were taught among my people; neither am I mighty in writing, like unto speaking; for when a man speaketh by the power of the Holy Ghost the power of the Holy Ghost carrieth it unto the hearts of the children of men. But behold, there are many that harden their hearts against the Holy Spirit, that it hath no place in them; wherefore, they cast many things away which are written and esteem them as things of naught.

Joseph Smith defined the "Holy Spirit" as the "mind of the Father and Son" in the *Lectures on Faith*. Here is an excerpt:

> There are two personages who constitute the great, matchless, governing and supreme power over all things—by whom all things were created and made, that are created and made, whether visible or invisible: whether in heaven, on earth, or in the earth, under the earth, or throughout the immensity of space—They are the Father and the Son: The Father being a personage of spirit, glory and power: possessing all perfection and fulness: The Son, who was in the bosom of the Father, a personage of tabernacle, made, or fashioned like unto man, or being in the form and likeness of man, or, rather, man was formed after his likeness, and in his image;—he is also the express image and likeness of the personage of the Father: possessing all the fulness of the Father, or, the same fulness with the Father; being begotten of him, and was ordained from before the foundation of the world to be a propitiation for the sins of all those who should believe on his name, and is called the Son because of the flesh—and descended in suffering below that which man can suffer, or, in other words, suffered greater sufferings, and was exposed to more powerful contradictions than any man can be. But notwithstanding all this, he kept the law of God, and remained without sin: Showing thereby that it is in the power of man to keep the law and remain also without sin. And also, that by him a righteous judgment might come upon all flesh, and that all who walk not in the law of God, may justly be condemned by the law, and have no excuse for their sins. And he being the only begotten of the Father, full of grace and truth, and having overcome, received a fulness of the glory of the Father-possessing the same mind with the Father, which mind is the Holy Spirit, that bears record of the Father and the Son, and these three are one, or in other words, these three constitute the great, matchless, governing and supreme power over all things: by whom all things were created and made, that were created and made: and these three constitute the Godhead,

and are one: The Father and the Son possessing the same mind, the same wisdom, glory, power and fulness: Filling all in all—the Son being filled with the fulness of the Mind, glory and power, or, in other words, the Spirit, glory and power of the Father—possessing all knowledge and glory, and the same kingdom: sitting at the right hand of power, in the express image and likeness of the Father—a Mediator for man—being filled with the fulness of the Mind of the Father, or, in other words, the Spirit of the Father: which Spirit is shed forth upon all who believe on his name and keep his commandments: and all those who keep his commandments shall grow up from grace to grace, and become heirs of the heavenly kingdom, and joint heirs with Jesus Christ; possessing the same mind, being transformed into the same image or likeness, even the express image of him who fills all in all: being filled with the fulness of his glory, and become one in him, even as the Father, Son and Holy Spirit are one. (*Lectures on Faith*, Lecture 5, Paragraph 2)

The forgoing was published in 1835. In a lecture given in 1843, Joseph stated the following:

"The Father has a body of flesh and bones as tangible as man's; the Son also; but the Holy Ghost has not a body of flesh and bones, but is a personage of Spirit. Were it not so, the Holy Ghost could not dwell in us." (D&C 130:22)

If the Holy Ghost is a "personage of Spirit" and it can "dwell in us," and the Holy Spirit is "the mind of the Father and Son" then are they the same thing?

The scriptures have explained that the "Holy Ghost" which dwells in you—this personage of Spirit—has the following other descriptions, or attributes:

- the Comforter
- the record of heaven
- the truth of all things

- the peaceable things of immortal glory
- that which quickeneth all things
- that which knoweth all things
- that which has all power according to wisdom, mercy, truth, justice and judgment.

This is a description of the personage of Spirit which dwells inside you. This is the Holy Ghost.[2385] This is something that can be in contact with the Holy Spirit, or the "mind of the Father and Son."

Perhaps you should look into this topic. Perhaps there is something to be found in this review.

There are many times when the term "Ghost" and the term "Spirit" are used interchangeably. The distinction is not appreciated by some translators. Therefore, if there is a difference between these two, you will need to be careful about trusting different translator's use of the terms. They may not have any distinction in mind.

If there is a difference, then what does that say about revelation? What does that say about you? And, keeping in mind yesterday's post, what does that say about 2 Nephi 33:1–2?[2386]

Clarification about Method

For new readers, I want to clarify the methods used in this blog. Comments are for me to read. If they raise a question needing a response, they provoke a response. They are not for dialogue.

[2385] Moses 6:61 "Therefore it is given to abide in you; the record of heaven; the Comforter; the peaceable things of immortal glory; the truth of all things; that which quickeneth all things, which maketh alive all things; that which knoweth all things, and hath all power according to wisdom, mercy, truth, justice, and judgment."

[2386] 2 Nephi 33:1–2 "And now I, Nephi, cannot write all the things which were taught among my people; neither am I mighty in writing, like unto speaking; for when a man speaketh by the power of the Holy Ghost the power of the Holy Ghost carrieth it unto the hearts of the children of men. But behold, there are many that harden their hearts against the Holy Spirit, that it hath no place in them; wherefore, they cast many things away which are written and esteem them as things of naught."

New readers can go back to the beginning of the blog and read through the comments when they were posted and included. Whether critical or supportive, they were all put up. The results were distracting, and hindered my intentions. The debates and distractions ultimately proved to be too much, and comments were eliminated altogether.

We recently turned the comment feature back on, NOT to publish comments, but so readers could make comments that I would read. I do read all comments that come in, but they are never posted on the blog, and they won't ever be posted on the blog. If you are anxious to comment, debate, criticize or offer your own opinions you are welcome to do so. Use the Internet and put whatever you want up for the world to read. This is not the entire universe of opportunity to discuss. It is a small, privately written, publicly viewable blog written to explain what I think important.

Some topics are impossible to explain in this medium. They require much more. As a result there are either books or essays that deal with those topics.

I am interested in doctrine. When I write about history, it is in the context of explaining doctrine. I do not attempt to give a complete history of the restoration. I focus only on those examples taken from our history which illustrate doctrine, or the transition from one understanding of a doctrinal matter early in the restoration to how the understanding of the doctrine has changed. I provide a guideline or outline, and leave it for historians to work out the details. Almost everything I have written about history has been skeletal, and would require many more words to finish the picture. But once the outlines have been set, any historian can work to fill in the missing details. In my view, what is needed is a new outline. To me, this is for the sole purpose of understanding doctrine.

In *Brigham Young's Telestial Kingdom*, as in *Passing the Heavenly Gift*, if you read it as an exposition about doctrine you will find it more helpful than if you read it merely as history. Nephi explained his method, which was to use examples from history to preserve the truth.[2387] I focus on the doctrine, or sacred teachings in an effort to preserve the memory of the Lord's original dealings as they relate to the restoration. This will allow those who are interested in understanding the restoration to see again the missing elements.

It is not my desire to debate anyone. I've not been asked by the Lord to do that. I'm also not interested in obtaining a following, undermining the church authorities, or to create unease among faithful Latter-day Saints—which I consider myself. What I write is for the sole purpose of preserving what was restored. To do that, like Nephi, it is necessary to touch upon excerpts from our history.

There is no reason for you to read this blog if it upsets or offends you. There are many, many other blogs, books, entertainers, authors and resources where your views can be reinforced.

Next week will be spent dealing with the Holy Spirit, the Holy Ghost, and the different statements made by Joseph Smith on these topics. It was introduced in two posts last Thursday and Friday. That

---

[2387] 1 Nephi 19:3–6 "And after I had made these plates by way of commandment, I, Nephi, received a commandment that the ministry and the prophecies, the more plain and precious parts of them, should be written upon these plates; and that the things which were written should be kept for the instruction of my people, who should possess the land, and also for other wise purposes, which purposes are known unto the Lord. Wherefore, I, Nephi, did make a record upon the other plates, which gives an account, or which gives a greater account of the wars and contentions and destructions of my people. And this have I done, and commanded my people what they should do after I was gone; and that these plates should be handed down from one generation to another, or from one prophet to another, until further commandments of the Lord. And an account of my making these plates shall be given hereafter; and then, behold, I proceed according to that which I have spoken; and this I do that the more sacred things may be kept for the knowledge of my people. Nevertheless, I do not write anything upon plates save it be that I think it be sacred. And now, if I do err, even did they err of old; not that I would excuse myself because of other men, but because of the weakness which is in me, according to the flesh, I would excuse myself."

will continue next week. If it interests you, read it. If not, don't. But there will be no debate. I am not interested in contention.

Finally, my purpose is very limited. I want to discharge an obligation, not entertain. When judged by my words and works, I wish the Lord to vindicate me for having said what needed to be said, rather than to be praised by others. I appreciate contrary views, but that is all. Criticism can help me understand someone's confusion or opposition, and I read it with that in mind. But if the criticism is merely intended to say there is another way to understand our history and doctrine, then I readily concede much of what I write is different and out of sync with popular opinion in the church today. The mainstream is where I began. I have read and was persuaded by the doctrinal work of President Joseph Fielding Smith and his son-in-law Bruce R. McConkie's. I was uber-orthodox in the beginning. I continue to read what is put into print by the Brethren. I am an admirer of Boyd K. Packer. I understand the mainstream arguments and teachings, and keep myself informed by them continually. I attend church every week, read the *Ensign* and *Church News*, and speak often with people in positions of authority as well as employees inside the Church Office Building. I am as "active" as any faithful Latter-day Saint. I am as informed as you are about any recent talks, issues or concerns propounded by the church. I have an obligation to keep and that is what I work to accomplish.

Finally, I am not concerned about reputation or praise. No one need defend me. If I cared about looking good in the eyes of others, I could never have been trusted by the Lord. Long ago I left that on the altar. Therefore, if I have no need to defend myself from criticism, you need not take up that cause.

GOD'S MANY WORKS

When trying to understand how God touches us, it is better to start with His many works instead of a vocabulary. In fact, we often are misled into believing that once we know a vocabulary term we then understand what the term means. Last week the "Holy Spirit" and the "Holy Ghost" were used both in selected scriptures and in my comments. Forget for a moment what term applies to what attribute, and focus on attributes first.

God's many works are held together and organized by His power. A description of this is given in Section 88, which states the following about Christ:

> He that ascended up on high, as also he descended below all things, in that he comprehended all things, that he might be in all and through all things, the light of truth; Which truth shineth. This is the light of Christ. As also he is in the sun, and the light of the sun, and the power thereof by which it was made. As also he is in the moon, and is the light of the moon, and the power thereof by which it was made; As also the light of the stars, and the power thereof by which they were made; And the earth also, and the power thereof, even the earth upon which you stand. (D&C 88:6–10)

This describes Christ. He both ascended and descended to enable Him to be "in all and through all things." What does that mean? Why would He necessarily need to ascend above and then descend below in order to be "in all and through all things?" How is this related to being Christ? How does this activity stretching Him above and below relate to Him becoming "the light" to all?

How does this description relate to Christ's introduction of Himself (containing His definition of who He is) to the Nephites, which states:

> Behold, I am the light and the life of the world; and I have drunk out of that bitter cup which the Father hath given me, and have glorified the Father in taking upon me the sins of the world, in the which I have suffered the will of the Father in all things from the beginning. (3 Nephi 11:11)

Is there a direct relationship between ascending, descending, and becoming "the light and the life of the world?" In other words, must Christ move into all the realms to bring the truth throughout in order to become the "light and life" throughout?

Is there a connection between these requirements and Christ becoming "the power thereof by which it was made?" The things listed above in Section 88 are physical objects. The sun and its power, the moon and its power, the stars and their power and the earth upon which we stand are all physical things. These things rely on Christ's "power" to have been "made." If Christ's stewardship required Him to be above and below, and throughout all in order to become "the light" unto all, then does Christ's "power" extend beyond just redeeming them all? How does Christ's ministry also relate to the "power" to bring these things into existence? How does Christ become "the light of Christ" which spreads throughout all creation? If His power extends to make the sun, moon, stars and the earth, how far does the "light of Christ" extend? Is it merely a moral force for good? Does it also include physical creation and power? What does the "light of Christ" have to do with "the power of the sun?" How dependent is all life, including plant, animal and human, upon the power of the sun? Without sunlight, what happens to this world?

How literally should we take "the light of the sun" to be a product of Christ's light? What does it mean if Christ is "the power of the sun?"

We tend to view "the light of Christ" as a moral source. That is, the "light of Christ" is most often spoken of as a moral conscience. From these verses, however, that view is too limited for this force or power. It is something much greater.

God's Many Works, Part 2

Section 88 continues the explanation with the following:

And the light which shineth, which giveth you light, is through him who enlighteneth your eyes, which is the same light that quickeneth your understandings; (D&C 88:11)

This is not just environmental. This is now touching you. It is the "light of Christ" which "enlighteneth your eyes." What does that mean? Could you see if this were withdrawn?

What does it mean that the "light of Christ" is what "quickeneth your understandings?" Without the light of Christ would you be able to understand anything? How intimately are you connected to the "light of Christ?" How dependent are you on His light?

It continues:

Which light proceedeth forth from the presence of God to fill the immensity of space—The light which is in all things, which giveth life to all things, which is the law by which all things are governed, even the power of God who sitteth upon his throne, who is in the bosom of eternity, who is in the midst of all things. (D&C 88:12–13)

We have been reading about Christ and the "light of Christ" which empowers all of this creation. But now the source from which it proceeds is being identified. This "proceedeth forth from the presence of God." Who is this referring to? Is this Christ still?

Who "sitteth upon his throne, who is in the bosom of eternity?" Who "is in the midst of all things?" Is this still Christ?

Steven saw Christ in heaven standing beside the Throne of the Father.[2388] Joseph and Sidney saw Christ on the Father's right hand.[2389] John received the testimony of Jesus where Christ affirmed that all who overcome will be able to also sit on the Father's Throne, just as He (Christ) had overcome and could sit on the Father's Throne.[2390] If Christ had to first "overcome" and complete the descent and ascent, then whose throne (the Father's or Christ's) is referred to in D&C 88 verses 12–13 above?

Assuming it is the Father's Throne, and the Father is the one who has been sitting on it from the beginning, then what harmony is there between Christ and the Father? How can the Father's power proceed forth in all directions, but Christ be the one who is "the light and life of the world?" How complete is the harmony found in the relationship between Christ and the Father if the power originates from the Father, but is given to the Son to become "the light and life of the world?"

What does it mean that this light "giveth life to all things?" How dependent are you on this "light" for your own life? What does it mean that "Man was also in the beginning with God. Intelligence, or the light of truth, was not created or made, neither indeed can be"

[2388] Acts 7:56 "And said, Behold, I see the heavens opened, and the Son of man standing on the right hand of God."

[2389] D&C 76:21 "And saw the holy angels, and them who are sanctified before his throne, worshiping God, and the Lamb, who worship him forever and ever."

[2390] Revelation 3:21 "To him that overcometh will I grant to sit with me in my throne, even as I also overcame, and am set down with my Father in his throne."

(D&C 93:29). If "the light of truth" cannot be made or created, then what does it mean that the light "proceeds forth from the Throne of God?"

What source flows from God and proceeds throughout all creation? What is the "power" behind all creation?

If this power bestows "life" upon its recipients, then can it also bestow something else?

God's Many Works, Part 3

This brings us to King Benjamin's explanation of our relationship with God. He explained our utter dependence in these words:

> I say unto you, my brethren, that if you should render all the thanks and praise which your whole soul has power to possess, to that God who has created you, and has kept and preserved you, and has caused that ye should rejoice, and has granted that ye should live in peace one with another—I say unto you that if ye should serve him who has created you from the beginning, and is preserving you from day to day, by lending you breath, that ye may live and move and do according to your own will, and even supporting you from one moment to another—I say, if ye should serve him with all your whole souls yet ye would be unprofitable servants. (Mosiah 2:20–21)

Is God the one who "created you?" If He "created you" then what of mankind is co-eternal with God?[2391] But what is "intelligence" or the mind of man? Intelligence is co-equal with the Father because it flows from Him in His exalted state. It is His glory. "Intel-

---

[2391] D&C 93:29 "Man was also in the beginning with God. Intelligence, or the light of truth, was not created or made, neither indeed can be."
"The mind or intelligence which man possesses is co-equal with God himself." (*TPJS*, 353)

ligence, or the light of truth, was not created or made" because it exists as a part of the Father's existence.[2392]

Intelligence is God's glory or His power. "The glory of God is intelligence."[2393] This glory is also called "light and truth."[2394] Or, in other words, light and truth emanates from God the Father, and is co-extensive with Him. This light and truth is also called intelligence. This is what conscience is made from. This is the power by which man comes into existence. It is as eternal as the Father Himself because it exists as part of His glory.

According to King Benjamin, God the Father created you "from the beginning." What does it mean to have created you "from the beginning?" Whose beginning? Ours? What does it mean that He has "kept and preserved you?" What does it mean that He has "granted that ye should live?" Without the Father's power would we no longer live?

What does it mean that God is "preserving you from day to day, by lending you breath?" Could we not breathe without borrowing the power to do so from God?

What does it mean that we are able to "live" because of God's power? How dependent on God are we if we use His power to "live and move?" How utterly reliant are we on His power if it is Him who is "even supporting you from one moment to another?"

What is this relationship between God's power, which proceeds forth from Him, and sustains not only planets, stars and our sun, but also us so that we live?

This power is:

- preserving us,
- comes from the Father, and

[2392] Ibid.

[2393] D&C 93:36 "The glory of God is intelligence, or, in other words, light and truth."

[2394] Ibid.

- causes everything to exist by its power.

Therefore, the "light of Christ," which is in and through all things, is co-extensive with the Father's "glory," or "intelligence," or in other words "light and truth."[2395]

This "light of Christ" or Holy Spirit, or intelligence, or glory of God, or power, or light and truth, or mechanism is important to recognize. But until you recognize it is the power by which you exist, that sustains you from moment to moment and lends you the power to live and breathe, you haven't yet appreciated the concept you are trying to assign a word. It is only vocabulary. The underlying idea remains hidden even if you have a vocabulary for it.

Coming next is the other part of the equation.

God's Many Works, Part 4

Peter explained the means by which Old Testament prophets received messages from God:

> "For the prophecy came not in old time by the will of man: but holy men of God spake as they were moved by the Holy Ghost." (2 Peter 1:21)

This Holy Ghost has been with mankind since the time of Adam:

> "And in that day the Holy Ghost fell upon Adam, which beareth record of the Father and the Son, saying: I am the Only Begotten of the Father from the beginning, henceforth and forever, that as thou hast fallen thou mayest be redeemed, and all mankind, even as many as will." (Moses 5:9)

Adam prophesied that the same Priesthood which he received from God in the beginning of the world would again return to the

---

[2395] Ibid.

earth at the end of the world.[2396] This prophecy was given through the power of the Holy Ghost.[2397]

From Adam till Christ, the Holy Ghost was the primary voice by which revelation was delivered from God to mankind. It is active and has been active in delivering the words of prophecy to "holy men" throughout history.

Then what is this voice of truth?

Joseph Smith said,

"No man can receive the Holy Ghost without receiving revelations. The Holy Ghost is a revelator." (*TPJS*, 328)

"The Holy Ghost is a personage, and is in the form of a personage." (*TPJS*, 276.)

". . . the Holy Ghost has not a body of flesh and bones, but is a personage of Spirit. Were it not so, the Holy Ghost could not dwell in us." (D&C 130:22)

Joseph also taught,

"All sins shall be forgiven, except the sin against the Holy Ghost; for Jesus will save all except the sons of perdition. What must a man do to commit the unpardonable sin? He must receive the Holy Ghost, have the heavens opened unto him, and know God, and then sin against Him. After a man has sinned against the Holy Ghost, there is no repentance for him. He has got to say that the sun does not shine while he sees it; he has got to deny Jesus Christ when the heavens have been opened unto him, and to deny the plan of salvation with

---

[2396] Moses 6:7 "Now this same Priesthood, which was in the beginning, shall be in the end of the world also."

[2397] Moses 6:8 "Now this prophecy Adam spake, as he was moved upon by the Holy Ghost, and a genealogy was kept of the children of God. And this was the book of the generations of Adam, saying: In the day that God created man, in the likeness of God made he him;"

his eyes open to the truth of it; and from that time he begins to be an enemy." (*TPJS*, 358.)

This last quote is very helpful to understand the concept of the Holy Ghost. It equates this kind of knowledge and experience with having the heavens opened, knowing God, and seeing the sun shine with the Holy Ghost. In another place Joseph's revelation explained that heirs of Celestial glory will be sealed up to eternal life "by the Holy Spirit of Promise."[2398] These individuals who receive this "seal" are those who received from Jesus the testimony that He has saved them.[2399] They have become part of "the Church of the Firstborn" as a consequence of promises given to them by the Father and the Son.[2400] They have become "sons of God" by the decree of the Father.[2401]

These individuals have received the testimony of Jesus, and the promise of eternal life which is the Holy Spirit of Promise.[2402]

So we now have several different concepts found in scripture and Joseph's teachings:

[2398] D&C 76:53 "And who overcome by faith, and are sealed by the Holy Spirit of promise, which the Father sheds forth upon all those who are just and true."

[2399] D&C 76:51 "They are they who received the testimony of Jesus, and believed on his name and were baptized after the manner of his burial, being buried in the water in his name, and this according to the commandment which he has given—"

[2400] D&C 76:54–57 "They are they who are the church of the Firstborn. They are they into whose hands the Father has given all things— They are they who are priests and kings, who have received of his fulness, and of his glory; And are priests of the Most High, after the order of Melchizedek, which was after the order of Enoch, which was after the order of the Only Begotten Son."

[2401] D&C 76:58–59 "Wherefore, as it is written, they are gods, even the sons of God— Wherefore, all things are theirs, whether life or death, or things present, or things to come, all are theirs and they are Christ's, and Christ is God's."

[2402] D&C 88:3 "Wherefore, I now send upon you another Comforter, even upon you my friends, that it may abide in your hearts, even the Holy Spirit of promise; which other Comforter is the same that I promised unto my disciples, as is recorded in the testimony of John."

- A power which sustains all of creation.
- A "light of Christ" which is given to all mankind.
- A power which animates the sun, stars and even this earth.
- A power which lets man live, breathe and move, which sustains man from moment to moment.
- A source of revelation.
- An open vision of God the Father and His Son, which includes the promise of eternal life.
- A light or intelligence which proceeds from God's Throne.

These are two distinct beings who are responsible for these various sources affecting mankind for the good: Christ, who has descended and then ascended throughout all of creation to bring the light to everything and everyone. The Father, who is the source from whom flows the power which Christ has brought into creation.

In addition to these two distinct beings, we also have something that can be called, in Moses 6:61:

- "the record of heaven;"
- "the Comforter;"
- "the peaceable things of immortal glory;"
- "the truth of all things;"
- "that which quickeneth all things, which maketh alive all things;"
- "that which knoweth all things, and hath all power according to wisdom, mercy, truth, justice and judgment."

Therefore, it can be truly said, just as Joseph Smith taught in the *Lectures on Faith*, that the Holy Ghost represents the "mind of the Father and the Son."

I had hoped to finish this tomorrow. However comments have made it apparent I will need to take two more days to complete this. So there are two more installments left in which we will draw together some of these various truths found in scripture.

God's Many Works, Part 5

The power of God and His many methods of accomplishing His will are not conveniently reduced to a simple vocabulary. The Father and the Son are clearly able to accomplish all their works using the power which originates from the Father, in the midst of eternity, to build all creation. Not only to build, but to sustain all creation. It is the power which causes creation to exist in an organized and functioning order.

But when it comes to identifying something by the title of "the Holy Ghost" or "the Holy Spirit" or "the Holy Spirit of Promise" there are underlying concepts associated with each of these. Titles and proper nouns are inadequate.

For example, look at the following statement from Alma as he recounts the many blessings the Nephites had received in their generations:

> "Having been visited by *the Spirit of God*; having conversed with angels, and having been spoken unto by the voice of the Lord; and having the spirit of prophecy, and the spirit of revelation, and also many gifts, the gift of speaking with tongues, and the gift of preaching, and *the gift of the Holy Ghost*, and the gift of translation." (Alma 9:21)

According to Alma, these many blessings come from "the Spirit of God" and include "the gift of the Holy Ghost." What are these two different blessings? Why does Alma see them as distinct enough to mention them separately and by different names? Is the "Holy Ghost" a function or part of "the Spirit of God?" Can Alma accurately describe it in this manner? If he can, then what is the underlying truth that connects them together?

Why is the "Holy Spirit of Promise" the topic Joseph Smith had in mind as he described the sin of "denying the Holy Ghost?" Is there a relationship between the Holy Spirit of Promise and the Holy

Ghost? Are they the same? Are they different? Do they both come from the Holy Spirit of God? If so, then are they different in nature or only different in degree? Can something be different in degree and be called by a different name?

It should be clear to you that the use of the terms are in some respects inexact, even in scripture. They are referring to ideas. You need to understand the underlying concepts rather than to focus on just the words. If you are going to understand exactly what is being discussed, then relying only on vocabulary will be insufficient.

What, then, does "baptism of fire and the Holy Ghost" consist of? The effect (fire purges and removes sin) is to permit you to speak with the "tongue of angels."[2403] But Nephi also cautions that once this gift has been conferred, if you then "deny Christ" you would be better off having never known Him.[2404] This process will come to you after repentance, baptism, and comes to "show all things" and to "teach the peaceable things of the kingdom."[2405] These scriptures, baptism of "fire and the Holy Ghost" teach you and show you things, just like Joseph's remark that the Holy Ghost is

---

[2403] 2 Nephi 31:13 "Wherefore, my beloved brethren, I know that if ye shall follow the Son, with full purpose of heart, acting no hypocrisy and no deception before God, but with real intent, repenting of your sins, witnessing unto the Father that ye are willing to take upon you the name of Christ, by baptism—yea, by following your Lord and your Savior down into the water, according to his word, behold, then shall ye receive the Holy Ghost; yea, then cometh the baptism of fire and of the Holy Ghost; and then can ye speak with the tongue of angels, and shout praises unto the Holy One of Israel."

[2404] 2 Nephi 31:14 "But, behold, my beloved brethren, thus came the voice of the Son unto me, saying: After ye have repented of your sins, and witnessed unto the Father that ye are willing to keep my commandments, by the baptism of water, and have received the baptism of fire and of the Holy Ghost, and can speak with a new tongue, yea, even with the tongue of angels, and after this should deny me, it would have been better for you that ye had not known me."

[2405] D&C 39:6 "And this is my gospel—repentance and baptism by water, and then cometh the baptism of fire and the Holy Ghost, even the Comforter, which showeth all things, and teacheth the peaceable things of the kingdom."
Compare Moses 6:61 "Therefore it is given to abide in you; the record of heaven; the Comforter; the peaceable things of immortal glory; the truth of all things; that which quickeneth all things, which maketh alive all things; that which knoweth all things, and hath all power according to wisdom, mercy, truth, justice, and judgment."

a revelator and you cannot receive it without also receiving revelations. But to "speak with the tongue of angels" means you are elevated, your knowledge and your inspiration reckons from heaven itself. You have been elevated by "fire" which purges sins and purifies. In effect, you receive holiness through the sanctifying power of the Holy Spirit. This in turn makes *your own* spirit holy. Your spirit or your ghost is within you, connected to heaven to such a degree through this process that you are in possession of a "holy spirit" or a "holy ghost" within you.

Does this "baptism of fire" come from a personage, or from the "mind of God the Father and Christ," or from the "light of Christ," or the "Holy Spirit" or some source you can clearly define or describe. Or does it come from God, sitting in the midst of eternity as He sustains all His creations through His power? And if that is the source, can it be described in a specific term? What is the name of that term?

What do these terms mean:

- Holy (Who provides this to man?)
- Spirit (Whose? Yours? God's? Both?)
- Promise (What promise? Given by Whom? Who receives this promise?)

We need to consider language and terms, but more importantly we need to think about concepts that words alone can never convey adequately. Move beyond the limits of vocabulary and try to find a connection to the underlying concepts these words are attempting to convey. For in these are found connections which run from inside you back to the presence of God Himself. Or, more correctly, the Gods Themselves, for the Father and the Son are two distinct beings. They are sustaining you from moment to moment right now. You are more directly connected with Them than you can imagine. You are borrowing their power to exist at present.

God's Many Works, Conclusion

Perhaps what we have been discussing should be understood in a different context than the one we normally use. What if instead of viewing it as a description of something *outside or external*, you view it as something *internal or inside* you. Perhaps the kingdom of heaven is within us after all.[2406]

From that vantage point can it be said:

- If you ignore the presence of this Spirit you still receive the Holy Spirit, or Light of Christ because that is what allows you to live, move, breathe and exist. It is a gift from God to everyone.

- If you allow this Spirit to enter into your thoughts from time to time you "receive" the Holy Ghost within you. It has affected your thoughts. It has been "received" into your conscience.

- If you allow this Spirit to continually guide you, then you have the "gift" of the Holy Ghost. It has become your companion.

- If you open yourself to receive the visions of heaven, and behold the Father and Son, then you have received the Holy Spirit of Promise.

This last Holy Spirit of Promise is given its name because when you have received the Father and the Son you become Their child of Promise, the inheritor of all the Father has, a member of His family. To reject this, as Joseph described it, is to deny the sun at noon day. For to have been given the Holy Spirit of Promise you have seen God and received from Him a Promise. [There is always more to a subject, but for the present, I'll leave it there.]

[2406] Luke 17:21 "Neither shall they say, Lo here! or, lo there! for, behold, the kingdom of God is within you."

If God sustains everything through His Holy Spirit, which is also sometimes called the Light of Christ, then is it not already within you? If it is already within you, then you can decide to "receive" it by opening yourself up to its influence. If you decide to "receive" it by opening yourself up to its influence, then you may be able to take it into yourself as a gift from God? If that gift becomes a permanent source of influence within you, then have you received the "gift of the Holy Ghost?" If this is within you, then is it your own? If your own, then do you have the Holy Ghost as your constant companion?

When you have received this, are you in touch with God? If you are in touch with God, are you also able to become "one" with Him? Is this what Christ was teaching in John 17:20–23?[2407]

With this in mind, consider what this passage from Deuteronomy tells us:

> And the Lord thy God will make thee plenteous in every work of thine hand, in the fruit of thy body, and in the fruit of thy cattle, and in the fruit of thy land, for good: for the Lord will again rejoice over thee for good, as he rejoiced over thy fathers:

> If thou shalt hearken unto the voice of the Lord thy God, to keep his commandments and his statutes which are written in this book of the law, and if thou turn unto the Lord thy God with all thine heart, and with all thy soul.

> For this commandment which I command thee this day, it is not hidden from thee, neither is it far off. It is not in heaven, that thou shouldest say, Who shall go up for us to heaven, and

---

[2407] John 17:20–23 "Neither pray I for these alone, but for them also which shall believe on me through their word; That they all may be one; as thou, Father, *art* in me, and I in thee, that they also may be one in us: that the world may believe that thou hast sent me. And the glory which thou gavest me I have given them; that they may be one, even as we are one: I in them, and thou in me, that they may be made perfect in one; and that the world may know that thou hast sent me, and hast loved them, as thou hast loved me."

bring it unto us, that we may hear it, and do it? Neither is it beyond the sea, that thou shouldest say, Who shall go over the sea for us, and bring it unto us, that we may hear it, and do it? But the word is very nigh unto thee, in thy mouth, and in thy heart, that thou mayest do it. (Deuteronomy 30:9–14)

If your spirit has become sanctified, and you have received the presence of both the Father and the Son such that you (as Joseph described it) stand in the "noon day sun" in your understanding, then you have received the Holy Spirit of Promise. Does this mean that your own spirit reflects the promise of eternal life? Are you then a Spirit of Promise, assured of eternal life? If so, then does "denying the Holy Ghost," as Joseph described it, actually involve taking what has become sacred within you and polluting it with deliberate rejection of the God you have received and who now dwells within you?

Related to this are many questions that have come in from readers during this week. One of the greatest impediments for some people is that they rely on the explanation given by Cleon Skousen about "intelligences" and how the universe is organized using this building block. You cannot reconcile his views with scripture. Therefore, if you choose to accept Skousen's definition of "intelligences" as the building blocks of all creation, you will not understand the subject. If that is your framework, you will need to discard what the scriptures teach.

[Please understand I am not condemning Cleon Skousen. He was a good man. But I believe he erred in this subject. He confuses "intelligence*S*" in the plural with the "intelligence" in the singular, from which man was organized. The plural of the word refers to organized spirits. They, organized spirits, have been created and exist as beings.[2408] Man (or the spirit within him) was organized from "intelligence" which is singular. It is co-eternal with God. It is called "intelligence" and also "light and truth."[2409] It is also called "the glory of God."[2410] Cleon Skousen supposed that man was made from something else called "intelligences" when, in fact, once intelligence or light and truth is organized into a being and assumes a separate existence it is called "intelligences" which is plural and refers to spirits. Until then, it is only "intelligence" which is singular. Read the beginning of *Beloved Enos* where I have tried to explain this subject. I think it will help.]

The scriptures have a lot to say about this matter. I've only put together a sketch. Look at the scriptures and sort through it. I've tried to give only a skeleton. The whole picture can be hung on that skeleton. You need to do the work of finishing the search. I don't want to rob you of that wonderful experience. Let the scriptures speak to you without you bringing an interpretation with you in advance.

Christ said His words were "Spirit."[2411] What does this mean? How can Christ's words, whether spoken by Him or given to another to speak on His behalf, be "Spirit?" If you can answer that you are in possession of a great truth.

[2408] Abraham 3:22–23 "Now the Lord had shown unto me, Abraham, the intelligences that were organized before the world was; and among all these there were many of the noble and great ones; And God saw these souls that they were good, and he stood in the midst of them, and he said: These I will make my rulers; for he stood among those that were spirits, and he saw that they were good; and he said unto me: Abraham, thou art one of them; thou wast chosen before thou wast born."

[2409] D&C 93:29 "Man was also in the beginning with God. Intelligence, or the light of truth, was not created or made, neither indeed can be."

[2410] D&C 93:36 "The glory of God is intelligence, or, in other words, light and truth."

[2411] John 6:63 "It is the spirit that quickeneth; the flesh profiteth nothing: the words that I speak unto you, *they* are spirit, and *they* are life."

In response to several questions, I'll add the following to conclude this week's posts:

At one time the Father was called "a Spirit" by Joseph, and at
another time He was said to "have a body as tangible as man's." Similarly, Jesus Christ was resurrected and unquestionably had a tabernacle consisting of "flesh and bone" which could be handled.[2412] He
ate fish and broke bread with His disciples.[2413] These were physical
acts. Yet He also appeared in the upper room on the day of His resurrection without entering through the shut door.[2414] He ascended
into heaven[2415] then descended from heaven in the sight of a
multitude.[2416] These are not typical of physical bodies as we encounter them. When it comes to resurrected and glorified beings, the bod-

---

[2412] Luke 24:39–40 "Behold my hands and my feet, that it is I myself: handle me, and
see; for a spirit hath not flesh and bones, as ye see me have. And when he had thus
spoken, he shewed them *his* hands and *his* feet."

[2413] Luke 24:42–43 "And they gave him a piece of a broiled fish, and of an honeycomb.
And he took *it,* and did eat before them."
John 21:9–14 "As soon then as they were come to land, they saw a fire of coals there,
and fish laid thereon, and bread. Jesus saith unto them, Bring of the fish which ye have
now caught. Simon Peter went up, and drew the net to land full of great fishes, an
hundred and fifty and three: and for all there were so many, yet was not the net broken.
Jesus saith unto them, Come *and* dine. And none of the disciples durst ask him, Who
art thou? knowing that it was the Lord. Jesus then cometh, and taketh bread, and giveth them, and fish likewise. This is now the third time that Jesus shewed himself to his
disciples, after that he was risen from the dead."

[2414] John 20:26 "And after eight days again his disciples were within, and Thomas with
them: *then* came Jesus, the doors being shut, and stood in the midst, and said, Peace *be*
unto you."

[2415] Acts 1:9–11 "And when he had spoken these things, while they beheld, he was
taken up; and a cloud received him out of their sight. And while they looked stedfastly
toward heaven as he went up, behold, two men stood by them in white apparel; Which
also said, Ye men of Galilee, why stand ye gazing up into heaven? this same Jesus,
which is taken up from you into heaven, shall so come in like manner as ye have seen
him go into heaven."

[2416] 3 Nephi 11:8 "And it came to pass, as they understood they cast their eyes up again
towards heaven; and behold, they saw a Man descending out of heaven; and he was
clothed in a white robe; and he came down and stood in the midst of them; and the
eyes of the whole multitude were turned upon him, and they durst not open their
mouths, even one to another, and wist not what it meant, for they thought it was an
angel that had appeared unto them."

ies are not the same as our own physical, coarse constitutions. Nevertheless, God is composed of matter:

"There is no such thing as immaterial matter. All spirit is matter, but it is more fine or pure, and can only be discerned by purer eyes; We cannot see it; but when our bodies are purified we shall see it is all matter." (D&C 131:7–8)

Therefore, it is equally true that God is a Spirit, and that He also possesses a body "as tangible as man's." How "quickened" is the body when He shows Himself? Or, in this coarse environment, how great a glory has He set aside to show Himself here?

———————

God's glory exceeds man's comprehension. We can see Him in His glory only if we are transfigured.[2417] Even then we cannot behold all of His glory unless we become like Him.[2418] Therefore, to behold Him in His glory while we are mortal, we must be transfigured, but the full measure of God is not given for mortal man to behold.

Ill-Prepared Readers

It is apparent from comments there are many who have been studying their scriptures and who can benefit from this blog. Their diligence has prepared their minds and their hearts.

It is also apparent that some who read are ill-prepared for the content here. This material is more confusing than edifying. They should

———————

[2417] Moses 1:14 "For behold, I could not look upon God, except his glory should come upon me, and I were transfigured before him. But I can look upon thee in the natural man. Is it not so, surely?"

[2418] Moses 1:4–5 "And, behold, thou art my son; wherefore look, and I will show thee the workmanship of mine hands; but not all, for my works are without end, and also my words, for they never cease. Wherefore, no man can behold all my works, except he behold all my glory; and no man can behold all my glory, and afterwards remain in the flesh on the earth."

turn off their computers and take up their scriptures. They should spend their time studying the scriptures and not devote any more time to this blog. It will not do such readers any good at all.

If this edifies you, then you belong here. If you are confused, then study scripture and leave this site alone. The process of developing understanding begins with the scriptures. No matter how much you believe you understand, the scriptures will always have language that can be adapted to set out the truth. The difference between seeing what is there and being blind to the words of prophecy consists primarily in how diligent you have been in preparing your mind through study of scripture. Do that first.

For the ill-prepared, I apologize for being unclear. However, I cannot discuss some topics in any other way. Therefore, I cannot make it clear to you. You will have to search through these things yourself. But if you are sincere, the Lord will help you get there. You must take the scriptures seriously. They will tell you how to lay down your prejudices, ignorance, traditions and errors, and repent. Repenting is to turn and face God. Until you face Him, the direction you are headed will never bring you to understanding.

BAPTISM OF FIRE
AND THE
HOLY GHOST

Last week's discussion leads to this week's. For the next few days we turn to the matter of "baptism of fire and the Holy Ghost" as a doctrine. The discussion last week will help to set up the framework for understanding this topic. When I mentioned this before on this blog it was in response to a specific question, and did not attempt to lay the matter out.

The most interesting passage referring to this is in 3 Nephi 9. The Nephite destruction has happened, there is darkness covering the land, and Christ speaks to the survivors. He tells them many things, but this is the important statement:

> "And whoso cometh unto me with a broken heart and a contrite spirit, him will I baptize with fire and with the Holy Ghost, even as the Lamanites, because of their faith in me at the time of their conversion, were baptized with fire and with the Holy Ghost, and they knew it not." (3 Nephi 9:20)

This statement from the Lord clarifies that it is possible for the event to occur and those who receive it do not know what it is.

The Lamanite conversion incident referred to by the Lord is not explained. Christ's words begin in verse 2 of Chapter 9, and deal entirely with the events of that generation leading up to the destruction of the land. Among those who would have been living at the time of the destruction would have been the Lamanites who underwent a conversion to the Gospel through the missionary efforts of Lehi and Nephi. These two were put into prison for preaching,[2419] kept without food for many days,[2420] and when they came to kill them Nephi and Lehi were encircled about by fire (Helaman 5:23). There was a great earthquake, similar to 3 Nephi when Christ's voice was heard. There was a great darkness in the prison, similar to 3 Nephi when Christ's voice was heard.[2421] These events involving Lehi and Nephi are a type of the events in 3 Nephi when Christ was speaking.

With Lehi and Nephi still in the prison, the Lamanites in the prison experienced the following:

[2419] Helaman 5:21 "And it came to pass that they were taken by an army of the Lamanites and cast into prison; yea, even in that same prison in which Ammon and his brethren were cast by the servants of Limhi."

[2420] Helaman 5:22 "And after they had been cast into prison many days without food, behold, they went forth into the prison to take them that they might slay them."

[2421] Helaman 5:27–28 "And behold, when they had said these words, the earth shook exceedingly, and the walls of the prison did shake as if they were about to tumble to the earth; but behold, they did not fall. And behold, they that were in the prison were Lamanites and Nephites who were dissenters. And it came to pass that they were overshadowed with a cloud of darkness, and an awful solemn fear came upon them."

- A voice speaks to them telling them to repent.[2422]

- The voice is not thunderous, but nevertheless pierced them to their core.[2423]

- The voice repeats again a second time.[2424] (Helaman 5:32; compare with 3 Nephi 11:4.)

- The voice repeats again a third time.[2425]

- The communication includes such marvelous information man is unable to communicate it.[2426]

[2422] Helaman 5:29 "And it came to pass that there came a voice as if it were above the cloud of darkness, saying: Repent ye, repent ye, and seek no more to destroy my servants whom I have sent unto you to declare good tidings."
3 Nephi 11:3 "And it came to pass that while they were thus conversing one with another, they heard a voice as if it came out of heaven; and they cast their eyes round about, for they understood not the voice which they heard; and it was not a harsh voice, neither was it a loud voice; nevertheless, and notwithstanding it being a small voice it did pierce them that did hear to the center, insomuch that there was no part of their frame that it did not cause to quake; yea, it did pierce them to the very soul, and did cause their hearts to burn."

[2423] Helaman 5:30 "And it came to pass when they heard this voice, and beheld that it was not a voice of thunder, neither was it a voice of a great tumultuous noise, but behold, it was a still voice of perfect mildness, as if it had been a whisper, and it did pierce even to the very soul—"
See 3 Nephi 11:3 ibid.

[2424] Helaman 5:32 "And behold the voice came again, saying: Repent ye, repent ye, for the kingdom of heaven is at hand; and seek no more to destroy my servants. And it came to pass that the earth shook again, and the walls trembled."
3 Nephi 11:4 "And it came to pass that again they heard the voice, and they understood it not."

[2425] Helaman 5:33 "And also again the third time the voice came, and did speak unto them marvelous words which cannot be uttered by man; and the walls did tremble again, and the earth shook as if it were about to divide asunder."
3 Nephi 11:5–7 "And again the third time they did hear the voice, and did open their ears to hear it; and their eyes were towards the sound thereof; and they did look steadfastly towards heaven, from whence the sound came. And behold, the third time they did understand the voice which they heard; and it said unto them: Behold my Beloved Son, in whom I am well pleased, in whom I have glorified my name—hear ye him."

[2426] Ibid. Compare with 3 Nephi 17:16–17 "And after this manner do they bear record: The eye hath never seen, neither hath the ear heard, before, so great and marvelous things as we saw and heard Jesus speak unto the Father; And no tongue can speak, neither can there be written by any man, neither can the hearts of men conceive so great and marvelous things as we both saw and heard Jesus speak; and no one can conceive of the joy which filled our souls at the time we heard him pray for us unto the Father."

- The Lamanite observers saw Lehi and Nephi in a pillar of fire with angels ministering to them.[2427]

These Lamanites asked how they could be delivered from the darkness and come into the redeeming light as Lehi and Nephi[2428] and were told they must repent to be delivered.[2429] All of them cried out to the Lord, and were delivered from darkness.[2430] They then were filled with joy and found themselves likewise encircled with that same fire in which Lehi and Nephi previously stood.[2431]

After last weeks' posts, the following statement should now alert you to something:

[2427] Helaman 5:36–37 "And it came to pass that he turned him about, and behold, he saw through the cloud of darkness the faces of Nephi and Lehi; and behold, they did shine exceedingly, even as the faces of angels. And he beheld that they did lift their eyes to heaven; and they were in the attitude as if talking or lifting their voices to some being whom they beheld. And it came to pass that this man did cry unto the multitude, that they might turn and look. And behold, there was power given unto them that they did turn and look; and they did behold the faces of Nephi and Lehi."
3 Nephi 17:23–25 "And he spake unto the multitude, and said unto them: Behold your little ones. And as they looked to behold they cast their eyes towards heaven, and they saw the heavens open, and they saw angels descending out of heaven as it were in the midst of fire; and they came down and encircled those little ones about, and they were encircled about with fire; and the angels did minister unto them. And the multitude did see and hear and bear record; and they know that their record is true for they all of them did see and hear, every man for himself; and they were in number about two thousand and five hundred souls; and they did consist of men, women, and children."

[2428] Helaman 5:40 "And it came to pass that the Lamanites said unto him: What shall we do, that this cloud of darkness may be removed from overshadowing us?"

[2429] Helaman 5:41 "And Aminadab said unto them: You must repent, and cry unto the voice, even until ye shall have faith in Christ, who was taught unto you by Alma, and Amulek, and Zeezrom; and when ye shall do this, the cloud of darkness shall be removed from overshadowing you."

[2430] Helaman 5:42–43 "And it came to pass that they all did begin to cry unto the voice of him who had shaken the earth; yea, they did cry even until the cloud of darkness was dispersed. And it came to pass that when they cast their eyes about, and saw that the cloud of darkness was dispersed from overshadowing them, behold, they saw that they were encircled about, yea every soul, by a pillar of fire."

[2431] Ibid. Also Helaman 5:44–45 "And Nephi and Lehi were in the midst of them; yea, they were encircled about; yea, they were as if in the midst of a flaming fire, yet it did harm them not, neither did it take hold upon the walls of the prison; and they were filled with that joy which is unspeakable and full of glory. And behold, the Holy Spirit of God did come down from heaven, and did enter into their hearts, and they were filled as if with fire, and they could speak forth marvelous words."

"And behold, the *Holy Spirit* of God did come down from heaven, and did enter into their hearts, and they were filled as if with fire, and they could speak forth marvelous words." (Helaman 5:45)

Once again, it is the "Holy Spirit" which causes the effect. The effect upon them is called the "Holy Ghost" by Christ.[2432]

The reason these recipients "did not know" it was "the Holy Ghost" now within them was because they did not know the vocabulary, nor understand the process. But there was an experience, and the result was conversion and a new life thereafter.[2433]

This is one instance of the baptism of fire and the Holy Ghost.

Baptism of Fire and the Holy Ghost, Part 2

At the time Joseph and Oliver were baptized, they had no authority from heaven with which to confer the Holy Ghost.[2434] They had

---

[2432] 3 Nephi 9:20 "And ye shall offer for a sacrifice unto me a broken heart and a contrite spirit. And whoso cometh unto me with a broken heart and a contrite spirit, him will I baptize with fire and with the Holy Ghost, even as the Lamanites, because of their faith in me at the time of their conversion, were baptized with fire and with the Holy Ghost, and they knew it not."

[2433] Helaman 5:46–50 "And it came to pass that there came a voice unto them, yea, a pleasant voice, as if it were a whisper, saying: Peace, peace be unto you, because of your faith in my Well Beloved, who was from the foundation of the world. And now, when they heard this they cast up their eyes as if to behold from whence the voice came; and behold, they saw the heavens open; and angels came down out of heaven and ministered unto them. And there were about three hundred souls who saw and heard these things; and they were bidden to go forth and marvel not, neither should they doubt. And it came to pass that they did go forth, and did minister unto the people, declaring throughout all the regions round about all the things which they had heard and seen, insomuch that the more part of the Lamanites were convinced of them, because of the greatness of the evidences which they had received."

[2434] JS–H 1:70 "He said this Aaronic Priesthood had not the power of laying on hands for the gift of the Holy Ghost, but that this should be conferred on us hereafter; and he commanded us to go and be baptized, and gave us directions that I should baptize Oliver Cowdery, and that afterwards he should baptize me."

no ordinance available to them other than baptism.[2435] They performed the ordinance as instructed. But afterwards, without any authority to confer upon one another the Holy Ghost, they nevertheless had the gift of the Holy Ghost poured out upon them.[2436] This was not merely a temporary visit. It lingered thereafter with them so they could understand the scriptures in the manner they were intended to be understood when these scriptures were first inspired by the Holy Ghost in the minds of the prophets who wrote them.[2437]

The Holy Ghost can come and visit with a person, but not tarry with them.[2438] If it comes and visits with them, then it is said the person has "received" the Holy Ghost. This kind of visit is conditional. It is dependent upon the worthiness and desire of the recipient. If they "grieve" the spirit by misbehavior, it will depart from them. If you read general conference talks discussing this issue, you will find this is the form of Holy Ghost received by members of The Church of Jesus Christ of Latter-day Saints. For the Holy Ghost to become a constant companion which tarries, it is said to be

---

[2435] Ibid. Also JS–H 1:71 "Accordingly we went and were baptized. I baptized him first, and afterwards he baptized me—after which I laid my hands upon his head and ordained him to the Aaronic Priesthood, and afterwards he laid his hands on me and ordained me to the same Priesthood—for so we were commanded.*"
* See JS–History Footnote for Oliver Cowdery's description of events.

[2436] JS–H 1:73 "Immediately on our coming up out of the water after we had been baptized, we experienced great and glorious blessings from our Heavenly Father. No sooner had I baptized Oliver Cowdery, than the Holy Ghost fell upon him, and he stood up and prophesied many things which should shortly come to pass. And again, so soon as I had been baptized by him, I also had the spirit of prophecy, when, standing up, I prophesied concerning the rise of this Church, and many other things connected with the Church, and this generation of the children of men. We were filled with the Holy Ghost, and rejoiced in the God of our salvation."

[2437] JS–H 1:74 "Our minds being now enlightened, we began to have the scriptures laid open to our understandings, and the true meaning and intention of their more mysterious passages revealed unto us in a manner which we never could attain to previously, nor ever before had thought of. In the meantime we were forced to keep secret the circumstances of having received the Priesthood and our having been baptized, owing to a spirit of persecution which had already manifested itself in the neighborhood."

[2438] D&C 130:23 "A man may receive the Holy Ghost, and it may descend upon him and not tarry with him."

"the gift of the Holy Ghost." Because the one with this endowment has received a gift from God, and it is given to them by God to be theirs.

The ordinance given when converts are confirmed members of The Church of Jesus Christ of Latter-day Saints includes these words: "And I say unto you, receive the Holy Ghost." This is the formula given in the priesthood manuals of the church, and is included in the *General Handbook of Instructions*. It is an admonition from the church elder to the convert. The obligation to then search for and obtain a visit from the Holy Ghost is imposed on the convert.

When Christ was speaking of the Lamanites and their baptism of fire and the Holy Ghost,[2439] He was speaking not merely of the Holy Ghost descending and not tarrying with them,[2440] but of their possession of the gift which endured thereafter.[2441]

I was baptized on September 9, 1973 at Kittery Point Beach on the Atlantic coast by Elder Brian Black. The service was presided over by Brother Jim Mortenson, a counselor in the Portsmouth, New Hampshire Ward. After baptism, as I knelt on the sand, the missionaries confirmed me a member of the church and admonished me to "receive the Holy Ghost." The service was in the evening. Just prior to the laying on of hands, Elder Black spoke about the symbols in

---

[2439] 3 Nephi 9:20 "And ye shall offer for a sacrifice unto me a broken heart and a contrite spirit. And whoso cometh unto me with a broken heart and a contrite spirit, him will I baptize with fire and with the Holy Ghost, even as the Lamanites, because of their faith in me at the time of their conversion, were baptized with fire and with the Holy Ghost, and they knew it not."

[2440] D&C 130:23 "A man may receive the Holy Ghost, and it may descend upon him and not tarry with him."

[2441] Helaman 5:48–50 "And now, when they heard this they cast up their eyes as if to behold from whence the voice came; and behold, they saw the heavens open; and angels came down out of heaven and ministered unto them. And there were about three hundred souls who saw and heard these things; and they were bidden to go forth and marvel not, neither should they doubt. And it came to pass that they did go forth, and did minister unto the people, declaring throughout all the regions round about all the things which they had heard and seen, insomuch that the more part of the Lamanites were convinced of them, because of the greatness of the evidences which they had received."

the sky. The sun was setting, but still visible. The moon was also out, and the first "stars" were also faintly visible. [The "stars" we could see included Venus, hence the quotation marks.] Elder Black remarked that "all the signs of heaven were visible; the sun, symbolizing the Celestial; the moon, symbolizing the Terrestrial; and the stars, symbolizing the Telestial." His beautiful remarks affected my thinking so much I can still recall them nearly 40 years later.

As the admonition was given to me, I felt a warmth begin at the top of my head where the hands were touching me. It proceeded downward through my entire person as if something was descending and filling me. The North Atlantic water was cold, particularly at that time of year, and the sand I knelt on was also cold. But I felt a warmth which came from within that filled my entire body.

When we finished at the beach, we all went to Jim and Monte Mortenson's house for a gathering. It was dubbed a "birthday party" in reference to my baptism. When we arrived, Jim asked me to say the "opening prayer" before we ate. I was perfectly willing to say the prayer, but I hesitated for a few moments before doing so because I sensed the "spirit" wasn't quite right yet. So rather than immediately interrupt the laughter and loud voices, I tried to bring the group spirit around to something more reverent. As I hesitated, I think Jim assumed I was not yet ready to pray in public (as many new converts are), and moved on to ask another to pray. She did, and we ate.

The boisterous spirit was still there after the prayer, and as the group of us sat in the Mortenson's living room the spirit of the evening became more and more divisive. At a point there was contention between some of the group, and the evening was taking a turn downward, grieving the spirit altogether. At that moment I stood and got everyone's attention. When silence settled in, I started with one end of the gathering, and spoke in turn to each person there. I began by saying, "whatever ambition the Adversary has for tonight, I intend to resist it." I then spoke to their hearts, prophesied and let the love I felt within me pour out. The effect upon those who were there softened their demeanor, brought a spirit of friendship back into the gathering, and although none of them may remember it today, it is to me as clear as if it happened minutes ago. Jim Mortenson spoke up when I finished and said he was confident I would one day be a church patriarch—a remark that meant nothing at the time because I knew nothing about such a position.

You must remember that before conversion I was not even a likely candidate to become Mormon. When the elders were teaching me they asked that I read the Book of Mormon. I agreed. After I had read some of it, they asked me what I thought of it. I replied: "It's got to be scripture. It's every bit as boring as the Bible." I meant it. Neither the Book of Mormon or the Bible meant much to me. I couldn't sense any Spirit or depth to it. Nothing in it thrilled me or touched my heart.

After baptism, however, it all changed. Like Joseph and Oliver I could say "my mind now being enlightened, I began to have the scriptures laid open to my understanding, and the true meaning of their more mysterious passages revealed to me in a manner which I never could attain to previously, nor ever before had thought of."[2442] What I found was that the scriptures were now written *for me*. They were the means through which God could lay out His mind and His will and His voice in a way I had never dreamed possible before.

The journey back to Him begins with all He has provided and preserved of His word. It begins for each of us in the scriptures. One of the immediate effects of baptism of fire and the Holy Ghost

---

[2442] JS–H 1:74 "Our minds being now enlightened, we began to have the scriptures laid open to our understandings, and the true meaning and intention of their more mysterious passages revealed unto us in a manner which we never could attain to previously, nor ever before had thought of. In the meantime we were forced to keep secret the circumstances of having received the Priesthood and our having been baptized, owing to a spirit of persecution which had already manifested itself in the neighborhood."

is to have the scriptures come alive; to have them overwhelm you with revelation, light and truth. It is not you doing this. It is you experiencing it, but the Holy Spirit opening and lighting them so the same Spirit which gave them at first now receives them in you.

This subject (baptism of fire and the Holy Ghost) is variegated. It is important to avoid reducing it to a single, simple explanation and ignore other important features of this great gift from God.

Baptism of Fire and the Holy Ghost, Part 3

There is a balance of light and darkness. There is an opposition necessary in all things.[2443] Moses was not able to encounter the Lord without also experiencing the adversary.[2444] Joseph, likewise, felt the destructive power of our common enemy before understanding the Lord.[2445] Some days before baptism, and then about a week after, I encountered the murderous rage of the enemy who seeks to destroy us all. I do not speak or write about this, because fools are prone to give the wrong attention to such matters and thereby surrender unnecessary power to our enemies. Therefore, I leave it to others to confront this subject and only declare I know who and what my en-

---

[2443] 2 Nephi 2:11–12 "For it must needs be, that there is an opposition in all things. If not so, my first-born in the wilderness, righteousness could not be brought to pass, neither wickedness, neither holiness nor misery, neither good nor bad. Wherefore, all things must needs be a compound in one; wherefore, if it should be one body it must needs remain as dead, having no life neither death, nor corruption nor incorruption, happiness nor misery, neither sense nor insensibility. Wherefore, it must needs have been created for a thing of naught; wherefore there would have been no purpose in the end of its creation. Wherefore, this thing must needs destroy the wisdom of God and his eternal purposes, and also the power, and the mercy, and the justice of God."

[2444] Moses 1:12 "And it came to pass that when Moses had said these words, behold, Satan came tempting him, saying: Moses, son of man, worship me."

[2445] JS–H 1:16 "But, exerting all my powers to call upon God to deliver me out of the power of this enemy which had seized upon me, and at the very moment when I was ready to sink into despair and abandon myself to destruction—not to an imaginary ruin, but to the power of some actual being from the unseen world, who had such marvelous power as I had never before felt in any being—just at this moment of great alarm, I saw a pillar of light exactly over my head, above the brightness of the sun, which descended gradually until it fell upon me."

emy is. I have rarely spoken in any detail, and do not recall providing any written account of these experiences.

I make mention of this because there are some critics who suggest I may be sincere, but I have been misled. I know the difference between the Lord and the Adversary. I've met both.

These two extremes aside, the baptism of fire and the Holy Ghost, in both Helaman and 3 Nephi, include ministering by angels. The first time I beheld an angel I was caught up to an exceedingly high place. From that vantage point I could see the curvature of the earth below. It was above, high and lifted up. In an instant I understood Nephi's description of an exceeding high mountain.[2446] When I wrote *The Second Comforter: Conversing With the Lord Through the Veil*, I included a description of this. I was told by those who reviewed it before publication that the explanation seemed arrogant; as if I were comparing myself to Nephi. Therefore, it was removed from the book. There is always tension between the obligation to declare the truth of a matter on the one hand, and the mis-perception of motives on the other. The truth can be opposed either by lies or by questioning the speaker's intention or motive. Either will do, because people are so easily removed from the truth.

To explain this subject, however, the remainder of the account needs to be told. Therefore, I include here what was removed from the text of *The Second Comforter*.

As I stood before this angel I noted that he was old, as tall as I am, with a beard, a full head of hair. It was long, but not quite to his shoulders. He spoke with authority, accustomed to declaring messages with efficiency and clarity. His demeanor was somber, as if the

---

[2446] 1 Nephi 11:1 "For it came to pass after I had desired to know the things that my father had seen, and believing that the Lord was able to make them known unto me, as I sat pondering in mine heart I was caught away in the Spirit of the Lord, yea, into an exceedingly high mountain, which I never had before seen, and upon which I never had before set my foot."

weight of eternity rested upon him. Although there was nothing vocal, he spoke with the clarity of a voice which settled deep within me as he said: "On the first day of the third month in nine years, your ministry will begin. And so you must prepare." Nearly 40 years separate me from that moment, but I can close my eyes and see it still. When an angel speaks to you, you never forget. Through all that has come and gone since that day, I am still transfixed by that moment.

After he spoke to me, he stood and gazed at me saying nothing further. Thinking that was all he had for me, I began to look about. I was impressed by the blue curvature of the earth below. I noticed there were walls, but they were transparent. I wondered why walls would be built if they were transparent, because if you can see beyond them then there was no purpose. I noticed a painting on the wall and wondered why it was there. It made me curious as to why there would be any effort made to paint a portrait here in this setting. Though I had no idea why I recognized him, the painting was of Moses. I also wondered at his baldness since the High Priest could have no blemish and serve before the Lord.[2447] I assumed he would have a full head of hair. He did not.

As I stood there reflecting on the scene, I asked nothing. Eventually I was compelled to depart and I left this scene behind. It was some time before I wondered "what ministry?" "How was I to pre-

---

[2447] Leviticus 21:16–23 "And the Lord spake unto Moses, saying, Speak unto Aaron, saying, Whosoever *he be* of thy seed in their generations that hath *any* blemish, let him not approach to offer the bread of his God. For whatsoever man *he be* that hath a blemish, he shall not approach: a blind man, or a lame, or he that hath a flat nose, or any thing superfluous, Or a man that is brokenfooted, or brokenhanded, Or crookbackt, or a dwarf, or that hath a blemish in his eye, or be scurvy, or scabbed, or hath his stones broken; No man that hath a blemish of the seed of Aaron the priest shall come nigh to offer the offerings of the Lord made by fire: he hath a blemish; he shall not come nigh to offer the bread of his God. He shall eat the bread of his God, *both* of the most holy, and of the holy. Only he shall not go in unto the vail, nor come nigh unto the altar, because he hath a blemish; that he profane not my sanctuaries: for I the Lord do sanctify them."

pare?" These questions could have been asked, but I was so distracted by the circumstances that I gave them no thought at the time. When I later inquired in prayer to know these things, I received no answer. As I persisted in asking for many months, at length I was asked why I hadn't inquired of the angel at the time I was told of the ministry. It was a hard lesson, but perhaps the only way I would learn it.

It was many months later that I heard the instruction about keeping a journal. By that time I had no way of knowing the date of the visit, and therefore assumed it reckoned from the year I was baptized in 1973. I wrote it down.

I lost track of time as the years came and went. I'd finished serving in the military, had graduated from law school, and had a family. When I remembered and reconstructed the events, I renewed my anticipation early in 1982, waiting for March 1st. That day came and went and nothing happened.

I concluded I hadn't prepared for the ministry, and therefore lost the opportunity. I felt rejected and mourned at my failure. I tried to renew my devotion, and wondered what would have been given if I'd met the standard I was supposed to meet. But then again, I also thought that if the Lord had been more clear, perhaps I could have met the standard. I wanted to blame the Lord for my failure. He hadn't answered the questions about what it was I needed to do. At a minimum, I wanted the Lord to share in the blame for my failure. I also wanted to conceal it. I went to my journal and took out the pages dealing with this and destroyed them. This is why the journal now begins on page 14. But with the passage of time, I let it go and gave it no further thought. There was so much to do in life with family responsibilities that unpleasant thoughts of personal failure can be abandoned if you want.

On March 1st of the following year I was visited by President Tolman (the Sunday School President and at the time a Seminary

Teacher in the Pleasant Grove High School Seminary program) and Bishop Harris. They called me to be the Gospel Doctrine teacher. It was not until after they left that I remembered the significance of "the first day of the third month" and rehearsed it all again in my mind. I realized that the visit must have happened in 1974 and not 1973. I had the chronology wrong.

It was many years later that I remembered destroying those pages from my journal. I had to explain all these errors in a re-creation of the events. From this I have learned to leave all the failures, all the mistakes, and any hard lessons which I have had to endure and suffer complete and recorded. There can be no attempt to shield myself from criticism in these journals. The truth of matters should be left, and my pride should be abandoned. No man elevates himself by pretensions to being more than they are.

Once called as Gospel Doctrine teacher, I remained in that position in Pleasant Grove, Alpine, and Sandy, Utah for over two decades, only moving to teach Priesthood lessons when not in Gospel Doctrine. After decades of this, I was called as the Ward Mission Leader for two years, then onto the Stake High Council, then to teach the Priests' Quorum. I now do Temple Preparation for those Priests who are awaiting their mission calls.

These many years of teaching required me to study the scriptures daily, to be able to give lessons that would edify. There was not a day that went by when I did not study the scriptures for these decades.

This background is required for you to understand how I have come to my understanding on this subject. Not that *I* matter at all, but the doctrine does. It is the doctrine that will save you, not man. But you may want to understand better the background of the man who is writing about this doctrine.

If the baptism of fire and the Holy Ghost is viewed as conferring revelation and opening the scriptures to your mind (as Joseph and

Oliver recount in the JS–H), then I have received this endowment. If it is viewed as requiring ministering of angels, then I affirm I have received this endowment, also; not to make any personal claim, but to testify and affirm these things are not ancient, or distant. They are intended to continue in our own day. They are meant for all—including you.

Baptism of Fire and the Holy Ghost, Part 4

The experience of Joseph and Oliver at their baptism, months before they would receive priesthood with authority to lay on hands for the gift of the Holy Ghost, requires you to ask yourself:

- Can this experience be regarded as a form of "baptism of fire and the Holy Ghost?"
- If so, then what are the essential elements of the experience?
- If not, then what more is required?

We want to have absolute events; for the light to be either on or off. However, the scriptures use the experiences in the lives of disciples following the Lord to illustrate and teach the doctrines. Nephi in particular, is a gifted composer of experience-based doctrinal teaching. He focuses his narrative entirely on doctrine, but uses his personal experience to draw from to teach the doctrine.

Christ declared the Lamanites experienced "baptism of fire and the Holy Ghost"[2448]. This week we have compared that event with the Nephites' experience in 3 Nephi. The following is a list of what was similar between the two:

[2448] 3 Nephi 9:20 "And ye shall offer for a sacrifice unto me a broken heart and a contrite spirit. And whoso cometh unto me with a broken heart and a contrite spirit, him will I baptize with fire and with the Holy Ghost, even as the Lamanites, because of their faith in me at the time of their conversion, were baptized with fire and with the Holy Ghost, and they knew it not."

- A voice speaks to them telling them to repent.[2449]
- The voice is not thunderous, but nevertheless pierced them to their core.[2450]
- The voice repeats a second time.[2451]
- The voice repeats a third time.[2452]
- The communication includes such marvelous information man is unable to communicate it.[2453]

[2449] Helaman 5:29 "And it came to pass that there came a voice as if it were above the cloud of darkness, saying: Repent ye, repent ye, and seek no more to destroy my servants whom I have sent unto you to declare good tidings."
3 Nephi 11:3 "And it came to pass that while they were thus conversing one with another, they heard a voice as if it came out of heaven; and they cast their eyes round about, for they understood not the voice which they heard; and it was not a harsh voice, neither was it a loud voice; nevertheless, and notwithstanding it being a small voice it did pierce them that did hear to the center, insomuch that there was no part of their frame that it did not cause to quake; yea, it did pierce them to the very soul, and did cause their hearts to burn."

[2450] Helaman 5:30 "And it came to pass when they heard this voice, and beheld that it was not a voice of thunder, neither was it a voice of a great tumultuous noise, but behold, it was a still voice of perfect mildness, as if it had been a whisper, and it did pierce even to the very soul—"
Also compare 3 Nephi 11:3 (ibid).

[2451] Helaman 5:32 "And behold the voice came again, saying: Repent ye, repent ye, for the kingdom of heaven is at hand; and seek no more to destroy my servants. And it came to pass that the earth shook again, and the walls trembled."
3 Nephi 11:4 "And it came to pass that again they heard the voice, and they understood it not."

[2452] Helaman 5:33 "And also again the third time the voice came, and did speak unto them marvelous words which cannot be uttered by man; and the walls did tremble again, and the earth shook as if it were about to divide asunder."
3 Nephi 11:5–7 "And again the third time they did hear the voice, and did open their ears to hear it; and their eyes were towards the sound thereof; and they did look steadfastly towards heaven, from whence the sound came. And behold, the third time they did understand the voice which they heard; and it said unto them: Behold my Beloved Son, in whom I am well pleased, in whom I have glorified my name—hear ye him."

[2453] Ibid.

- The Lamanite observers saw Lehi and Nephi in a pillar of fire, with angels ministering to them.[2454]

As the account continued, they repented, were wrapped in fire and were able to speak inspired words.[2455] These are additional events, so you must decide:

- Do all these things need to occur *before* there has been "fire and the Holy Ghost?"
- Are they things that will unfold as a result of receiving "fire and the Holy Ghost?"
- Can you receive "fire" and have your sins purged without all of this accompanying the event?
- Can you receive the "gift of the Holy Ghost" as your companion without a visible pillar of fire?

Joseph received an audience with the Father and the Son, stood in a pillar of fire, and was commissioned to do a great work. BUT this happened *before* he was baptized, *before* any priestly authority was conferred by John the Baptist, *before* a church existed, temple rites

---

[2454] Helaman 5:36–37 "And it came to pass that he turned him about, and behold, he saw through the cloud of darkness the faces of Nephi and Lehi; and behold, they did shine exceedingly, even as the faces of angels. And he beheld that they did lift their eyes to heaven; and they were in the attitude as if talking or lifting their voices to some being whom they beheld. And it came to pass that this man did cry unto the multitude, that they might turn and look. And behold, there was power given unto them that they did turn and look; and they did behold the faces of Nephi and Lehi."
3 Nephi 17:23–25 "And he spake unto the multitude, and said unto them: Behold your little ones. And as they looked to behold they cast their eyes towards heaven, and they saw the heavens open, and they saw angels descending out of heaven as it were in the midst of fire; and they came down and encircled those little ones about, and they were encircled about with fire; and the angels did minister unto them. And the multitude did see and hear and bear record; and they know that their record is true for they all of them did see and hear, every man for himself; and they were in number about two thousand and five hundred souls; and they did consist of men, women, and children."

[2455] Helaman 5:44–45 "And Nephi and Lehi were in the midst of them; yea, they were encircled about; yea, they were as if in the midst of a flaming fire, yet it did harm them not, neither did it take hold upon the walls of the prison; and they were filled with that joy which is unspeakable and full of glory. And behold, the Holy Spirit of God did come down from heaven, and did enter into their hearts, and they were filled as if with fire, and they could speak forth marvelous words."

were restored, *before* marriage, sealing, etc. If you reflect on that for a moment you will see the order of events does not control. There is an order, and it is generally followed, but it is the fullness of this endowment that is important and not the order it is given.

In Nephi's explanation of this gift, he refers to another, much shorter list. It includes:

- Repenting of your sins.
- Witnessing your repentance by baptism in water.
- Receiving the power to "speak with the tongue of angels."[2456]

Joseph and Oliver did these things. And, as they experienced it:

"No sooner had I baptized Oliver Cowdery, than the Holy Ghost fell upon him, and he stood up and prophesied many things which should shortly come to pass. And again, so soon as I had been baptized by him, I also had the spirit of prophecy, when, standing up, I prophesied concerning the rise of this Church, and many other things." (JS–H 1:73)

The Lamanite experience in Helaman 5 does not include baptism by water before this baptism of fire and the Holy Ghost, but it did require repentance. We can know from subsequent missionary work they performed that they preached, and undoubtedly did receive baptism (or rebaptism). But the order is changed. A change in order,

---

[2456] 2 Nephi 31:13–14 "Wherefore, my beloved brethren, I know that if ye shall follow the Son, with full purpose of heart, acting no hypocrisy and no deception before God, but with real intent, repenting of your sins, witnessing unto the Father that ye are willing to take upon you the name of Christ, by baptism—yea, by following your Lord and your Savior down into the water, according to his word, behold, then shall ye receive the Holy Ghost; yea, then cometh the baptism of fire and of the Holy Ghost; and then can ye speak with the tongue of angels, and shout praises unto the Holy One of Israel. But, behold, my beloved brethren, thus came the voice of the Son unto me, saying: After ye have repented of your sins, and witnessed unto the Father that ye are willing to keep my commandments, by the baptism of water, and have received the baptism of fire and of the Holy Ghost, and can speak with a new tongue, yea, even with the tongue of angels, and after this should deny me, it would have been better for you that ye had not known me."

however, is not a change in requirement. To fully repent, they needed to witness it by baptism. Therefore, the ordinance may have followed, but it was a necessary part of the process.

The most consistent and the minimum description of this baptism of fire and the Holy Ghost includes these elements:

- repentance,
- baptism by water,
- baptism by fire and the Holy Ghost,
- evidenced by speaking with the tongue of angels.

One proof of baptism of fire is the gift of prophecy. Both Joseph and Oliver experienced the gift. So did the Lamanites, which they used to preach and declare repentance. I also experienced it after baptism in water. The gift follows as a sign to confirm baptism of fire and the Holy Ghost.[2457]

This "gift," like other signs, is designed to confirm in the one who receives it a witness to them, from God, that this baptism has occurred. It is one of the essential elements, and is present in all the accounts. It appears on Nephi's list also.

Beyond this minimum list, however, there are these other events that the Nephites and the Lamanites also experienced. There are many facets to understanding the Holy Spirit and the Holy Ghost, and there is a host of things which *can* be associated with baptism of fire and the Holy Ghost. There is a continuum.

It is in this sense that Nephi's and Joseph Smith's experiences provide us the best blueprint. The Book of Mormon accounts (with the exception of Nephi) are often sudden and compressed. Both Nephi's and Joseph's were unfolding, growing and spreading to include ultimately comprehending both God and the eternities.

[2457] D&C 63:9 "But, behold, faith cometh not by signs, but signs follow those that believe."

Baptism of Fire and the Holy Ghost, Part 5

The work of this "baptism of fire" is always sanctification. It brings the recipient into greater contact with God. The end of that increasing contact is to receive the Son, through whose blood you are sanctified.[2458] Once sanctified you are prepared for the presence of the Father.[2459] Therefore, this is how you receive "the fullness"[2460] and are able to join the "general assembly and Church of the Firstborn".[2461]

In the Lamanite experience and in the Nephite group who Christ visited in the 3 Nephi account, there came a point at which the heavens opened, a pillar of fire descended, and angels came and ministered to them all. Each were endowed with knowledge of mysteries belonging to God. There was a connection forged between them and

---

[2458] Moses 6:59–60 "That by reason of transgression cometh the fall, which fall bringeth death, and inasmuch as ye were born into the world by water, and blood, and the spirit, which I have made, and so became of dust a living soul, even so ye must be born again into the kingdom of heaven, of water, and of the Spirit, and be cleansed by blood, even the blood of mine Only Begotten; that ye might be sanctified from all sin, and enjoy the words of eternal life in this world, and eternal life in the world to come, even immortal glory; For by the water ye keep the commandment; by the Spirit ye are justified, and by the blood ye are sanctified;"

[2459] Alma 45:16 "And he said: Thus saith the Lord God—Cursed shall be the land, yea, this land, unto every nation, kindred, tongue, and people, unto destruction, which do wickedly, when they are fully ripe; and as I have said so shall it be; for this is the cursing and the blessing of God upon the land, for the Lord cannot look upon sin with the least degree of allowance."
1 Nephi 10:21 "Wherefore, if ye have sought to do wickedly in the days of your probation, then ye are found unclean before the judgment-seat of God; and no unclean thing can dwell with God; wherefore, ye must be cast off forever."

[2460] D&C 93:19–20 "I give unto you these sayings that you may understand and know how to worship, and know what you worship, that you may come unto the Father in my name, and in due time receive of his fulness. For if you keep my commandments you shall receive of his fulness, and be glorified in me as I am in the Father; therefore, I say unto you, you shall receive grace for grace."

[2461] D&C 76:66–67 "These are they who are come unto Mount Zion, and unto the city of the living God, the heavenly place, the holiest of all. These are they who have come to an innumerable company of angels, to the general assembly and church of Enoch, and of the Firstborn."

those on the other side of the veil. These others are the "general assembly and Church of the Firstborn."

There is a significant difference between the Lamanite experience and the 3 Nephi experience. The latter one *began* with Christ ministering to the recipients. This point should not be lost. Joseph Smith's experiences likewise began with the Father and Son appearing to him. As pointed out yesterday, the sequence is not important and does not control. Even with the Lord's personal ministry, you can still read in the account a similar series of events, steps and milestones. This means something. Events can and will vary in order, but do not vary in content. As explained in *Beloved Enos*, the Lord's work is consistent with all who receive redemption.

This kind of conversion is required for Zion to return[2462] because those who will be in Zion must dwell with God.[2463] The first Zion was brought through the ministry and teaching of Enoch.[2464] As a result of this the priesthood was renamed for him. When Melchizedek, by teaching righteousness brought about the City of

---

[2462] Ibid.

[2463] D&C 29:11 "For I will reveal myself from heaven with power and great glory, with all the hosts thereof, and dwell in righteousness with men on earth a thousand years, and the wicked shall not stand."
D&C 45:66–71 "And it shall be called the New Jerusalem, a land of peace, a city of refuge, a place of safety for the saints of the Most High God; And the glory of the Lord shall be there, and the terror of the Lord also shall be there, insomuch that the wicked will not come unto it, and it shall be called Zion. And it shall come to pass among the wicked, that every man that will not take his sword against his neighbor must needs flee unto Zion for safety. And there shall be gathered unto it out of every nation under heaven; and it shall be the only people that shall not be at war one with another. And it shall be said among the wicked: Let us not go up to battle against Zion, for the inhabitants of Zion are terrible; wherefore we cannot stand. And it shall come to pass that the righteous shall be gathered out from among all nations, and shall come to Zion, singing with songs of everlasting joy."

[2464] Moses 7:20 "And it came to pass that Enoch talked with the Lord; and he said unto the Lord: Surely Zion shall dwell in safety forever. But the Lord said unto Enoch: Zion have I blessed, but the residue of the people have I cursed."

Peace, the priesthood was again renamed for him.[2465] Joseph Smith could have brought again Zion, but he was betrayed by his own people, surrendered to arrest, and was killed.

When Zion returns again, the priesthood will be renamed.[2466] It will no longer be called the priesthood "after the order of Melchizedek", nor the priesthood "after the order of Enoch, but will again be called the priesthood "after the Order of the Only Begotten Son".[2467] The one whom our Lord uses to accomplish this last gathering will refuse to allow the priesthood to be called after his name; respecting instead the prophecy of Adam rather than claiming such an honor for himself.[2468] He will want it to return to the Lord. The city will likewise be the Lord's. Men must finally return to Him, and He to them.

There is a progression of blessings conferred through the fire and Holy Ghost. Even if there is a mere beginning, there is a glorious ending. As with the Lamanites, it leads to an open vision into heaven, ministering of angels, and an endowment of unspeakable learning. It brings to the initiated the knowledge of the mysteries of God.

This more distant end of the endowment also involves priestly rights. Priesthood ordination is required before entering into the ceremonial presence of God in His Temple rites. Priesthood conferral is required to enter into His actual presence. The revelations are clear in connecting baptism of fire and the Holy Ghost with knowl-

---

[2465] D&C 76:57 "And are priests of the Most High, after the order of Melchizedek, which was after the order of Enoch, which was after the order of the Only Begotten Son."

[2466] Moses 6:7 "Now this same Priesthood, which was in the beginning, shall be in the end of the world also."

[2467] D&C 76:57 "And are priests of the Most High, after the order of Melchizedek, which was after the order of Enoch, which was after the order of the Only Begotten Son."

[2468] Moses 6:7 "Now this same Priesthood, which was in the beginning, shall be in the end of the world also."

edge of God's mysteries.[2469] They are equally clear in connecting this knowledge of God with priesthood.[2470]

The fullness of the Gospel, the fullness of the Priesthood, and the baptism of fire and the Holy Ghost all have as their object to reconnect man to God and God to man. Man is unworthy to enter into God's presence, and therefore, requires a power higher than their own from which to borrow purity. This purifying agent is the Holy Ghost.[2471] Christ will administer the final rites and confer the

---

[2469] 3 Nephi 11:35–36 "Verily, verily, I say unto you, that this is my doctrine, and I bear record of it from the Father; and whoso believeth in me believeth in the Father also; and unto him will the Father bear record of me, for he will visit him with fire and with the Holy Ghost. And thus will the Father bear record of me, and the Holy Ghost will bear record unto him of the Father and me; for the Father, and I, and the Holy Ghost are one."
3 Nephi 19:13–14 "And it came to pass when they were all baptized and had come up out of the water, the Holy Ghost did fall upon them, and they were filled with the Holy Ghost and with fire. And behold, they were encircled about as if it were by fire; and it came down from heaven, and the multitude did witness it, and did bear record; and angels did come down out of heaven and did minister unto them."

[2470] D&C 84:19 "And this greater priesthood administereth the gospel and holdeth the key of the mysteries of the kingdom, even the key of the knowledge of God."
D&C 107:19 "To have the privilege of receiving the mysteries of the kingdom of heaven, to have the heavens opened unto them, to commune with the general assembly and church of the Firstborn, and to enjoy the communion and presence of God the Father, and Jesus the mediator of the new covenant."

[2471] 3 Nephi 19:22, 28 "Father, thou hast given them the Holy Ghost because they believe in me; and thou seest that they believe in me because thou hearest them, and they pray unto me; and they pray unto me because I am with them. Father, I thank thee that thou hast purified those whom I have chosen, because of their faith, and I pray for them, and also for them who shall believe on their words, that they may be purified in me, through faith on their words, even as they are purified in me."

final blessings only upon the pure.[2472] The reference to "blood" as sanctifying is a reference to the Lord.[2473] He alone sanctifies.

The Lord is directly involved in the final endowment of fire upon the Holy ones. This is what He explained in January, 1841 to the Saints when He explained to Joseph: "For there is not a place found on earth that he [meaning Christ] may come to and restore again that which was lost unto you, or which he hath taken away, even the fulness of the priesthood."[2474] The Lord can confer this upon a single man in any location. (See, e.g., D&C 132:45–50, when Joseph Smith

---

[2472] 3 Nephi 19:29–33 "Father, I pray not for the world, but for those whom thou hast given me out of the world, because of their faith, that they may be purified in me, that I may be in them as thou, Father, art in me, that we may be one, that I may be glorified in them. And when Jesus had spoken these words he came again unto his disciples; and behold they did pray steadfastly, without ceasing, unto him; and he did smile upon them again; and behold they were white, even as Jesus. And it came to pass that he went again a little way off and prayed unto the Father; And tongue cannot speak the words which he prayed, neither can be written by man the words which he prayed. And the multitude did hear and do bear record; and their hearts were open and they did understand in their hearts the words which he prayed."

[2473] Moses 6:59–60 "That by reason of transgression cometh the fall, which fall bringeth death, and inasmuch as ye were born into the world by water, and blood, and the spirit, which I have made, and so became of dust a living soul, even so ye must be born again into the kingdom of heaven, of water, and of the Spirit, and be cleansed by blood, even the blood of mine Only Begotten; that ye might be sanctified from all sin, and enjoy the words of eternal life in this world, and eternal life in the world to come, even immortal glory; For by the water ye keep the commandment; by the Spirit ye are justified, and by the blood ye are sanctified;"

[2474] D&C 124:28 "For there is not a place found on earth that he may come to and restore again that which was lost unto you, or which he hath taken away, even the fulness of the priesthood."

received it long before the first Temple was built.[2475]) But to confer it upon a group intended to become His people, He requires His House to be built for Him to meet with and confer these final rites upon them.[2476] Only there will these things take place.[2477] People can gather and build a Temple. A single man cannot.

When the Lord establishes Zion, He will come dwell with His people there and complete the process of endowing them with His knowledge and power. The power of God will protect these

---

[2475] D&C 132:45–50 "For I have conferred upon you the keys and power of the priesthood, wherein I restore all things, and make known unto you all things in due time. And verily, verily, I say unto you, that whatsoever you seal on earth shall be sealed in heaven; and whatsoever you bind on earth, in my name and by my word, saith the Lord, it shall be eternally bound in the heavens; and whosesoever sins you remit on earth shall be remitted eternally in the heavens; and whosesoever sins you retain on earth shall be retained in heaven. And again, verily I say, whomsoever you bless I will bless, and whomsoever you curse I will curse, saith the Lord; for I, the Lord, am thy God. And again, verily I say unto you, my servant Joseph, that whatsoever you give on earth, and to whomsoever you give any one on earth, by my word and according to my law, it shall be visited with blessings and not cursings, and with my power, saith the Lord, and shall be without condemnation on earth and in heaven. For I am the Lord thy God, and will be with thee even unto the end of the world, and through all eternity; for verily I seal upon you your exaltation, and prepare a throne for you in the kingdom of my Father, with Abraham your father. Behold, I have seen your sacrifices, and will forgive all your sins; I have seen your sacrifices in obedience to that which I have told you. Go, therefore, and I make a way for your escape, as I accepted the offering of Abraham of his son Isaac."

[2476] D&C 124:39 "Therefore, verily I say unto you, that your anointings, and your washings, and your baptisms for the dead, and your solemn assemblies, and your memorials for your sacrifices by the sons of Levi, and for your oracles in your most holy places wherein you receive conversations, and your statutes and judgments, for the beginning of the revelations and foundation of Zion, and for the glory, honor, and endowment of all her municipals, are ordained by the ordinance of my holy house, which my people are always commanded to build unto my holy name."

[2477] D&C 124:40–41 "And verily I say unto you, let this house be built unto my name, that I may reveal mine ordinances therein unto my people; For I deign to reveal unto my church things which have been kept hid from before the foundation of the world, things that pertain to the dispensation of the fulness of times."

people.[2478] They cannot be moved because the Lord will not permit it.[2479] While man does not have the power to do so, the laws of the Celestial Kingdom must be lived for Zion to be established.[2480] The power to do so comes from God, delivered through His Holy Spirit, making men's spirits Holy. Baptism of fire and the Holy Ghost are necessary parts of bringing mankind back to redemption and into God's presence.

Baptism of Fire and the Holy Ghost, Conclusion

The "third member of the Godhead" is still in a probationary state. "The Holy Ghost is now in a state of probation which if he should perform in righteousness he may pass through the same or a similar course of things that the Son has." (*WJS*, 27 August 1843, 245.) Perhaps you understand that now.

The Holy Ghost is "a personage of Spirit. Were it not so, the Holy Ghost could not dwell in us."[2481] It is "the testator" of the Father and the Son (*TPJS*, 190). Perhaps you understand that now.

The baptism of water is unto repentance. It is done upon the body you occupy. You no doubt should understand that.

[2478] D&C 45:66–70 "And it shall be called the New Jerusalem, a land of peace, a city of refuge, a place of safety for the saints of the Most High God; And the glory of the Lord shall be there, and the terror of the Lord also shall be there, insomuch that the wicked will not come unto it, and it shall be called Zion. And it shall come to pass among the wicked, that every man that will not take his sword against his neighbor must needs flee unto Zion for safety. And there shall be gathered unto it out of every nation under heaven; and it shall be the only people that shall not be at war one with another. And it shall be said among the wicked: Let us not go up to battle against Zion, for the inhabitants of Zion are terrible; wherefore we cannot stand."

[2479] D&C 124:45 "And if my people will hearken unto my voice, and unto the voice of my servants whom I have appointed to lead my people, behold, verily I say unto you, they shall not be moved out of their place."

[2480] D&C 105:5 "And Zion cannot be built up unless it is by the principles of the law of the celestial kingdom; otherwise I cannot receive her unto myself."

[2481] D&C 130:22 "The Father has a body of flesh and bones as tangible as man's; the Son also; but the Holy Ghost has not a body of flesh and bones, but is a personage of Spirit. Were it not so, the Holy Ghost could not dwell in us."

The baptism of fire and the Holy Ghost is unto sanctification. It is done upon the body and Spirit within you. Perhaps you understand that now.

There is "power" which sustains everything, as we have discussed over the last two weeks.[2482] That power is called the Holy Spirit. Among its many attributes is the Holy Ghost. But no matter what you think you know, there is always more to learn. The responsibility to teach what cannot be said is reserved for God. God teaches, or "reveals" to man through the Holy Ghost the deep things of God. Hence the saying by Joseph that "the Holy Ghost is a revelator" and "you cannot receive the Holy Ghost without receiving revelation." (*TPJS*, 328.)

Man was made in the image of God.[2483] Man's destiny is to be redeemed. God's work and glory is to bring to pass the eternal life and exaltation of man.[2484] That work is not completed until you sit upon the same Throne as Christ and His Father.[2485]

Nothing here is static. Things in this sphere are either growing or decaying. There is either increase or decrease. These two opposing forces bring new life into this world and then decay and destroy it. Then it is recycled as another life rises from and uses the elements of the prior, deceased plant, animal or man. The purpose of baptism of "fire and the Holy Ghost" is to preserve and to purge a living being. It is to render indestructible the organism upon which it descends. It

---

[2482] D&C 88:13 "The light which is in all things, which giveth life to all things, which is the law by which all things are governed, even the power of God who sitteth upon his throne, who is in the bosom of eternity, who is in the midst of all things."

[2483] Moses 2:27 "And I, God, created man in mine own image, in the image of mine Only Begotten created I him; male and female created I them."

[2484] Moses 1:39 "For behold, this is my work and my glory—to bring to pass the immortality and eternal life of man."

[2485] Revelation 3:21–22 "To him that overcometh will I grant to sit with me in my throne, even as I also overcame, and am set down with my Father in his throne. He that hath an ear, let him hear what the Spirit saith unto the churches."

is not to prevent earthly death, but to allow eternal life. Christ's Gospel is to bring eternal life so that those who die may live again eternally.[2486] These people never die, because they live eternally through the fire bestowed upon them.[2487] Such eternal life begins now, while still in the flesh. They live here as members of another assembly, and then pass from here to join them again.[2488] Though they are men in the flesh, they are gods, even the sons of God, and all things are given unto them.[2489]

Yet in all this man cannot glory in man, but must glory in God. The victory is His alone.[2490]

This topic cannot be adequately explained by man to another man, but it can be known to any man through God. It is intended that all should be converted and experience this, including you. Be believing. Ask. Seek. Knock. It will be opened to you, as it has for all those who are faithful and trusting of God.

The Holy Ghost is not only "the Comforter" but also:[2491]

- the record of heaven.

- the truth of all things.

- that which quickeneth all things.

[2486] John 11:25 "Jesus said unto her, I am the resurrection, and the life: he that believeth in me, though he were dead, yet shall he live:"

[2487] John 11:26 "And whosoever liveth and believeth in me shall never die. Believest thou this?"

[2488] D&C 76:67 "These are they who have come to an innumerable company of angels, to the general assembly and church of Enoch, and of the Firstborn."

[2489] D&C 76:58–60 "Wherefore, as it is written, they are gods, even the sons of God— Wherefore, all things are theirs, whether life or death, or things present, or things to come, all are theirs and they are Christ's, and Christ is God's. And they shall overcome all things."

[2490] D&C 76:61 "Wherefore, let no man glory in man, but rather let him glory in God, who shall subdue all enemies under his feet."

[2491] Moses 6:61 "Therefore it is given to abide in you; the record of heaven; the Comforter; the peaceable things of immortal glory; the truth of all things; that which quickeneth all things, which maketh alive all things; that which knoweth all things, and hath all power according to wisdom, mercy, truth, justice, and judgment."

- that which maketh alive all things.
- that which knoweth all things.
- that which has all power according to wisdom, mercy, truth, justice and judgment.

Therefore I say unto you: "receive the Holy Ghost."

Comments

There are a number of comments that come in and I only respond to them generally. In that way, I hope to cover more than just one inquiry in a single post. Here, then, are some general reminders:

How can you want so intensely what you do not yet understand?

―――――――――

The identity of who the Lord will send will be known only when that person has done the work. No one who has failed to accomplish the work can claim the identity. Vanity is no substitute for doing the works of God.

―――――――――

No man ever pleased God without repenting.

―――――――――

The greatest evidences of God's power, apart from Christ's resurrection, are yet to be. It will be the latter-day Zion:

"Therefore, behold, the days come, saith the Lord, that they shall no more say, The Lord liveth, which brought up the children of Israel out of the land of Egypt; But, The Lord liveth, which brought up and which led the seed of the house of Israel out of the north country, and from all countries whither I had driven them; and they shall dwell in their own land." (Jeremiah 23:7–8)

―――――――――

It is apparent that for many people the concept of "the Celestial Kingdom" is only an imaginary concept based upon the vaguest of understanding. But it is something they claim to "really want." Something a person claims to want ought to be the subject of a better informed investigation.

———————

There have been many questions (perhaps hundreds now) from women asking about women's issues. I've decided to spend next week addressing these questions in a very general way. However, to give you some context, here is one of the latest comments I've received. Read this and you can better understand next week's posts:

Brother Snuffer,

What happens if someone like me has concerns about some of the things the church teaches as doctrines? I always go along, never making waves. But sometimes I feel like the worst kind of hypocrite. I feel like a complete mutant when you speak of Zion and sanctification. I've had almost every calling a woman can have, and yet I feel like a stranger in the household of God. I pray, study the scriptures, fast, attend the temple, and read from good sources, such as yours. But a lot of how the church believes feels alien to my soul: the role of women chief among them. Sometimes it feels hopeless because the things you and other men in the church say just don't feel attainable to people like me. We never hear of stories of women receiving their calling and election, except through their husband. I know of no story where a woman has received the Second Comforter. No matter how it's worded, women are not valued the same as men. After all, we are given to our husbands, but they do not give themselves back. Men receive the power of God to act in his name, but women do not. We are sealed to our husbands, but they are not sealed to us. We hearken to our husbands while they hearken to God. Why can't I just hearken to God like he does? Men become the Sons of God, but women never become the Daughters of God. We are queens and priestesses to our husbands, but not to God. Everything for women is to your husband or through your husband, but not directly through God or to ourselves. Plural marriage is the greatest abomination to women that ever existed—worse than rape and prostitution—because we are expected to be happy to have our husband fall in love with and show sexual attraction to another, many other women. Yet we are selfish if this bothers us. How can this be morally clean when a man shares with another woman what he should only share with one wife? If a wife wanted to be with another husband, or many, she would immediately be called immoral, an adulteress, and kicked out. Surely a just God who is no respecter of persons would not be so favoring of His sons, and so cruel to His daughters. I have studied until I am in a deep abyss of pain. I have lost all joy for the hereafter. I have no hope to be the kind of woman the church teaches women must be. I cannot understand how women can be so blasé about such horrible positions and men can think women would want to live like this for eternity. You may think me ignorant or rebellious, but I can only say I have studied for decades and my pain is desolating to my soul. Doesn't anyone understand how inherently unfair and condescending patriarchy is? I've heard several brethren say that whatever God commands, setup, or mandates is right. Period. But would a truly loving God setup something so blatantly one-sided? Motherhood is comparable to fatherhood, not priesthood. And no, I don't lust to be a Bishop or any other position men hold. I just cannot understand how women can be relegated to such lesser status as to not hold the holy priesthood and be able to have the same responsibilities and roles as men. We are worthy, capable, and it would lift humankind to a greater level of living. It would enrich the kingdom tremendously. To be told you don't need it, you share it with your husband feels like a very patronizing stand to take. It is patronizing. Why can't we share it by both of us holding it and helping our families together? What is to become of people like me?

Thank you.

ROLE OF WOMEN

First, and foremost, the questions about the role of women arise from a misunderstanding of God's will and nature, and from mistrust of God's intentions. The first is because we teach poorly. The second is because we make the mistake of identifying God's intentions with men's behavior. The failure of men to live the ideals required by God do not alter God's intention. Therefore, you should not conflate these. You can overcome both without ever listening to anything I have to say. It is, or ought to be, between you and God. I loathe to put myself between you and Him. The understanding of these two principles is all you need to go forward and get an answer directly from Him. To overcome the second, you will need to repent of your idolatry. Do not make the church an idol, and do not judge God by that idol. Realize the church is an organization staffed by frail men trying hard, but with very difficult circumstances facing them in this fallen world. Be charitable.

With that in mind, your questions should not be viewed as a problem, but as an opportunity to learn more about (and from) God. These are wonderful concerns, and they deserve an answer. God does have answers. I cheat people when I say too much about a given subject. Particularly when the topic is so important and the answer ought to be given by God.

Ponder these questions:

- What if the "role" you occupy is not just your test, but also a test of your husband (and Mormon men generally)?

- What if the Lord has only allowed you and your husband to "suppose" he has "a little authority" when, in fact, he has nothing more than an invitation to arise and receive it from heaven?[2492]

- What if the Lord intends to judge your husband (and all Mormon men) on the basis of how the man conducts himself to see if he uses the wrong kind of "authority" to impose and control and exercise dominion?[2493]

- What if no authority can be claimed by virtue of the priesthood?[2494]

- What if to prove the heart of the man, it is necessary to put you and your husband into this probationary relationship to see if he follows the Lord or is blinded by the craftiness of men who deceive among all sects, including our own?[2495]

- What if the man chooses to ignore the Holy Spirit and proceed ahead on his own desire for patriarchal supremacy?

[2492] D&C 121:39 "We have learned by sad experience that it is the nature and disposition of almost all men, as soon as they get a little authority, as they suppose, they will immediately begin to exercise unrighteous dominion."

[2493] D&C 121:37 "That they may be conferred upon us, it is true; but when we undertake to cover our sins, or to gratify our pride, our vain ambition, or to exercise control or dominion or compulsion upon the souls of the children of men, in any degree of unrighteousness, behold, the heavens withdraw themselves; the Spirit of the Lord is grieved; and when it is withdrawn, Amen to the priesthood or the authority of that man."

[2494] D&C 121:41 "No power or influence can or ought to be maintained by virtue of the priesthood, only by persuasion, by long-suffering, by gentleness and meekness, and by love unfeigned;"

[2495] D&C 123:12 "For there are many yet on the earth among all sects, parties, and denominations, who are blinded by the subtle craftiness of men, whereby they lie in wait to deceive, and who are only kept from the truth because they know not where to find it—"

- What if the Lord intends for you to ultimately be his "judge" because you are now apparently "subject to" him and will learn best what is in his heart?

- What if, whether you want to show all the compassion of a saint toward mormon leaders (including your husband), you are nevertheless subjugated, controlled and exploited? Will they be left in such a position after this life when greater things are underway?

- What if the conditions for the salvation of man are different than the conditions for the salvation of women?

- What if the primary obligation of the man is to preserve correct doctrine, God's approval to bestow ordinances, and practice correct faith? If it is, how well have men performed this obligation throughout history? How well do men perform this today?

- What if women have a primary (not exclusive) obligation to bring children into the world, care for and nurture them, and live chaste lives? In other words, what if women will be judged primarily in their role as mothers? How well have women performed this obligation throughout history? Unlike men, has there ever been a worldwide "apostasy" by women where children were no longer born or cared for in this world?

The illusion of man's patriarchal and priesthood power allows them to put on display what is in *their* hearts.[2496] When they begin to "exercise a little authority, as they suppose" in a way which gratifies their pride, or exercises control, dominion and compulsion over the soul of another, they "prove" who and what they are. The one most immediately affected (the wife) would be the one most able to judge

---

[2496] D&C 121:35 "Because their hearts are set so much upon the things of this world, and aspire to the honors of men, that they do not learn this one lesson—"

the man's performance. Therefore a wise man will seek to elevate his wife, and a fool will abuse and dominate her. A wise woman will trust in the Lord and know that He is the judge of the living and the dead, and He will always restore only what is right, pure, merciful, just, true and worthy.[2497]

The focus of the question is wrong. It takes a topic which should be unifying and changes the it into something competitive. I do not fault anyone for having these questions. They are a product of the environment. However, marriage as intended by God should be co-operative. The relationship is intended to make of the two "one flesh."[2498] It is in becoming "one" that both the man and woman become like God. In a very real way, everything I said above, even if entirely appropriate and justified, is merely adding to the problem. The real value of the man and the woman is to be found in their unity, not in their disunity. Therefore, we must look to what the unity *should* include to know the real answer to the questions that alienate, divide spouses from one another, and make women feel subjugated.

Role of Women, Part 2

The unity of man and woman is required for either of them to be saved in the truest meaning of "saved" (meaning exalted):

[2497] Alma 41:13 "O, my son, this is not the case; but the meaning of the word restoration is to bring back again evil for evil, or carnal for carnal, or devilish for devilish—good for that which is good; righteous for that which is righteous; just for that which is just; merciful for that which is merciful."

[2498] Genesis 2:24 "Therefore shall a man leave his father and his mother, and shall cleave unto his wife: and they shall be one flesh."
Matthew 19:4–6 "And he answered and said unto them, Have ye not read, that he which made *them* at the beginning made them male and female, And said, For this cause shall a man leave father and mother, and shall cleave to his wife: and they twain shall be one flesh? Wherefore they are no more twain, but one flesh. What therefore God hath joined together, let not man put asunder."

Paul wrote: "Neither is the man without the woman, neither the woman without the man, in the Lord" (1 Corinthians 11:11). But what does that mean?

Through Joseph comes this response:

"Therefore, if a man marry him a wife in the world, and he marry her not by me nor by my word, and he covenant with her so long as he is in the world and she with him, their covenant and marriage are not of force when they are dead, and when they are out of the world; therefore, they are not bound by any law when they are out of the world. Therefore, when they are out of the world they neither marry nor are given in marriage; but are appointed angels in heaven, which angels are ministering servants, to minister for those who are worthy of a far more, and an exceeding, and an eternal weight of glory. For these angels did not abide my law; therefore, they cannot be enlarged, but remain separately and singly, without exaltation, in their saved condition, to all eternity; and from henceforth are not gods, but are angels of God forever and ever." (D&C 132:15–17)

But, even with this, how does this qualify?

- Is "sealing" enough?
- What if the couple are unworthy of being preserved because, among other things, they are not happy together?
- Why keep together what is more punishment than reward?
- If this union is required for either to be exalted, then does it matter who is sealed to who, with what language?

The unity of man and woman does not come by one dominating the other, as some view the inevitable result of patriarchy. The relationship is not worth preserving if it lacks joyful association. No relationship is unified if one party dominates the other. Godly unity comes by the man conforming to the image of God, and the woman likewise conforming to the image of God, so both reflect His image. Christ put it into these words:

> "And for their sakes I sanctify myself, that they also might be sanctified through the truth. Neither pray I for these alone, but for them also which shall believe on me through their word; That they all may be one; as thou, Father, art in me, and I in thee, that they also may be one in us: that the world may believe that thou hast sent me. And the glory which thou gavest me I have given them; that they may be one, even as we are one: I in them, and thou in me, that they may be made perfect in one; and that the world may know that thou hast sent me, and hast loved them, as thou hast loved me." (John 17:19–23)

What is this "glory" which the Lord has given to His disciples and which He offers us? How can we become "glorified" like the Father and the Son?

> "The glory of God is intelligence, or, in other words, light and truth." (D&C 93:36)

Rather than envying the authority of patriarchy or the claims to priesthood, we should all envy/seek God's glory. Why seek after something that does not exist? Why not seek after what is enduring?

Suppose you do become one with God? Suppose you do take in His glory, or light and truth, and become filled with light? And suppose further that your husband does not. What then?

- What is your responsibility?
- How can you return to God without seeking to reclaim and redeem your husband?
- Remember the counsel of Hyrum Smith when he wrote as the prophet to the church?

He said:

Whereas, in times past persons have been permitted to gather
with the Saints at Nauvoo, in North America—such as husbands leaving their wives and children behind; also, such as
wives leaving their husbands, and such as husbands leaving
their wives who have no children, and some because their
companions are unbelievers. All this kind of proceedings we
consider to be erroneous and for want of proper information.
And the same should be taught to all the Saints, and not suffer
families to be broken up on any account whatever if it be
possible to avoid it. Suffer no man to leave his wife because
she is an unbeliever. These things are an evil and must be forbidden by the authorities of the church or they will come under condemnation; for the gathering is not in hast nor by
flight, but to prepare all things before you, and you know not
but the unbeliever may be converted and the Lord heal him;
but let the believers exercise faith in God, and the unbelieving
husband shall be sanctified by the believing wife; and the unbelieving wife by the believing husband, and families are preserved and saved from a great evil which we have seen verified before our eyes. Behold this is a wicked generation, full of
lyings, and deceit, and craftiness; and the children of the
wicked are wiser than the children of light; that is, they are
more crafty; and it seems that it has been the case in all ages
of the world.

And the man who leaves his wife and travels to a foreign nation, has his mind overpowered with darkness, and Satan deceived him and flatters him with the graces of the harlot, and
before he is aware he is disgraced forever; and greater is the
danger for the woman that leaves her husband. The evils resulting from such proceedings are of such a nature as to
oblige us to cut them off from the church.

And we also forbid that a woman leave her husband because
he is an unbeliever. We also forbid that a man shall leave his
wife because she is an unbeliever. If he be a bad man (i.e., the

believer) there is a law to remedy that evil. And if the law divorce them, then they are at liberty; otherwise they are bound
as long as they two shall live, and it is not our prerogative to
go beyond this; if we do it, it will be at the expense of our
reputation. These things we have written in plainness and we
desire that they should be publicly known.[2499]

The marriage of man and woman puts into the closest and most
intimate contact two very different people. In their union it is possible to create offspring. It is this basic relationship where the two
most important things are accomplished:

1. The work of bringing new life into the world, and

2. The work of overcoming the world and becoming "one."

Yet fools seek to overcome the world while leaving their spouse
uninvolved. Or, in other words, they seek to avoid the very test that
is required and which is given to us all to help us to overcome the
world. Remember there is neither the man nor the woman without
the other in the Lord.

Assuming this is the requirement, then does the wording of church
rites matter? Does language sealing the woman to the man change
this need of unity?

Role of Women, Part 3

There are many questions about issues specific to women in the
emails I receive. They go way beyond the one email I posted on Sunday. Many express disappointment about "denying" priestly office to
women in the church. My reaction to that issue is to say: Why aspire
to be like those claiming patriarchal priority based upon an exclusive
"priesthood" when, for almost all men, their ordination will never

---

[2499] 1 Corinthians 7:13–14 "And the woman which hath an husband that believeth not,
and if he be pleased to dwell with her, let her not leave him. For the unbelieving husband is sanctified by the wife, and the unbelieving wife is sanctified by the husband:
else were your children unclean; but now are they holy."

result in heaven conferring power upon them?[2500] Why envy nothing?

There is a misapprehension about "priesthood" and authority. This can be tracked back to the failure to adequately teach in the church, and by the example we see in the management of the church. In the church the man is called to office (bishop, stake president, elder's quorum president, etc.). The man is supposed to fill that office using two counselors to help him. His wife is not one of his counselors. The positions often require confidences to be kept. Because of this, a bishop does not discuss everything about his calling with his wife. This gives the mistaken impression that the men fulfilling these roles matter more, and are trusted more by the Lord.

This model is a mirage, and to the extent the church is selected as the object of admiration and reverence, it will only fool you. Remember the church will end with death. The government of God in eternity is His Heavenly Family. These family relationships endure. The church will remain a creation of, and occupant confined to the Telestial world. It is a Telestial institution, attempting to invite you to rise up to something more, something higher, something that will endure. But the church extending that invitation is not to be envied. Service in it is not the model of Celestial glory. Your family is the critical relationship in mortality.

A man and woman would be better off if they never held any church office other than home and visiting teaching. They would be better off if they realized it is the family alone that will endure, and then devote themselves to improving that relationship. Inside the

---

[2500] D&C 121:36–37 "That the rights of the priesthood are inseparably connected with the powers of heaven, and that the powers of heaven cannot be controlled nor handled only upon the principles of righteousness. That they may be conferred upon us, it is true; but when we undertake to cover our sins, or to gratify our pride, our vain ambition, or to exercise control or dominion or compulsion upon the souls of the children of men, in any degree of unrighteousness, behold, the heavens withdraw themselves; the Spirit of the Lord is grieved; and when it is withdrawn, Amen to the priesthood or the authority of that man."

family, the woman is the natural and undeniable counselor, and she is presiding within the family alongside her husband. She should join with him in blessing their children, she should lay hands on her husband when he asks and bless him, and she should be one with him. Because inside the home it is the husband and wife, not the bishop, who presides. Even the president of the church does not call a man to office without first asking his wife to sustain him in the calling. Nor does the woman get a calling without consulting her husband. All the envy and misapprehensions notwithstanding, the fact remains that the church is inferior to the family. The church is temporary, transient and Telestial. The family can be eternal, enduring and Celestial.

To the extent that you choose the church to inform your understanding, you are setting it up as an idol. That approach does more harm than good. No institution can display what it was never intended to be. It is the unity found in marriage, not the structure of organizing the church, which should become our focus.

This week's topic has been the subject of repeated discussions between me and my wife. Each morning we spend about an hour talking about many different issues as we walk together, the role of woman being one of them. Each evening we also spend time discussing important issues, from the Gospel to family matters to finances and everything in-between. She not only edits my writing, but discusses what I write with me. She is a constant adviser and counselor to me. Her view of this subject is much more critical of women's misunderstanding than mine. She finds many complaints and complainers exasperating. Through prayer and study, she has had to come to terms with many of these same issues. On the ones she doesn't struggle with or can't get answers to, she trusts that God loves her and that "everything will be okay." We find it joyful and necessary to reason together and discuss gospel issues with one another.

If we are all the Lord's, there should be unity between us all; even more so between husband and wife. That does not come through neglect. It comes through effort. Sometimes the effort must begin by the woman bringing to the attention of the husband what he is failing to do or to be. Then it grows from there to discussion, and finally understanding and agreement. That is the work of every relationship. It cannot be avoided. Effort and time are required for any union to be obtained.

Role of Women, Part 4

You ask about women and the Second Comforter. It is apparent from the question you have not read *Come, Let Us Adore Him.* I ask people to read what I've written to understand this blog. If you had taken that advice you would already know the first person to receive the risen Lord's personal ministry was a woman. And you would likewise know there were many others who received His companionship and ministry before any of His Apostles. When He did visit with the Apostles, He rebuked them for not receiving the testimony of the women in particular. This makes clear that the Lord values His family and closest associates and companions more than an hierarchy. You should read that book if you'd like to understand Him better.

The "ambition" to have position or authority or power or "equality" is based on our mistaken understanding of patriarchy and confuses mankind's bad example with God's intention. You have also associated the idea of priesthood with the institutional positions of the church. Therefore, since women are barred from filling those institutional positions, you've reached a wrong conclusion.

Go back to what is most basic. It is the basic truths which matter most. All great truths are simple.

What is "priestly?" Whether it is done by a "priest" or by a "priest-ess" what exactly is "priestly?"

At the core, to perform a priestly act is to do something for the Lord; to act as His surrogate, or to act as His agent. The greatest of these priestly acts are rendered through service to others, and can be done by anyone, almost at any time, and in almost any circumstance.

When administering relief to others, you can act on the Lord's behalf. When you clothe the naked and needy, or visit the sick and confined, or feed the hungry, you are doing His work.[2501]

The "chief seats" don't matter. When men obtain the honors of others, sit in the chief seats, and receive public acclaim, they are not the ones to envy. Those who support themselves through the widow's tithes are damned.[2502]

The Lord has respect to the obscure, and He took greater notice of the faithful who donated her two mites than the rich who made a show.[2503] This is who He is. This is who you are to serve. He has no respect for those who consume these donations from the poor. When you serve others, you are a priestess whom the Lord will rec-

---

[2501] Matthew 25:34–46 "I was a stranger, and ye took me not in: naked, and ye clothed me not: sick, and in prison, and ye visited me not. Then shall they also answer him, saying, Lord, when saw we thee an hungred, or athirst, or a stranger, or naked, or sick, or in prison, and did not minister unto thee? Then shall he answer them, saying, Verily I say unto you, Inasmuch as ye did *it* not to one of the least of these, ye did *it* not to me. And these shall go away into everlasting punishment: but the righteous into life eternal."

[2502] Luke 20:45–47 "Then in the audience of all the people he said unto his disciples, Beware of the scribes, which desire to walk in long robes, and love greetings in the markets, and the highest seats in the synagogues, and the chief rooms at feasts; Which devour widows' houses, and for a shew make long prayers: the same shall receive greater damnation."

[2503] Luke 21:1–4 "And he looked up, and saw the rich men casting their gifts into the treasury. And he saw also a certain poor widow casting in thither two mites. And he said, Of a truth I say unto you, that this poor widow hath cast in more than they all: For all these have of their abundance cast in unto the offerings of God: but she of her penury hath cast in all the living that she had."

ognize and are the one He intends to exalt.[2504] It is not the ruler who will be honored, but the servant.[2505]

There is nothing to envy from anyone who receives public acclaim, praise, adoration and celebration.[2506] When crowds gather to proclaim your greatness, this is neither priestly nor godly, and you have your reward.[2507] But when you serve in quiet and are faithful in secret, then you are priestly and the Lord will honor you.[2508]

There is nothing preventing you from acting the part of the priestess in blessing others and serving on the Lord's behalf.[2509] If

---

[2504] Matthew 23:11–12 "But he that is greatest among you shall be your servant. And whosoever shall exalt himself shall be abased; and he that shall humble himself shall be exalted."

[2505] Matthew 23:8–12 "But be not ye called Rabbi: for one is your Master, *even* Christ; and all ye are brethren. And call no *man* your father upon the earth: for one is your Father, which is in heaven. Neither be ye called masters: for one is your Master, *even* Christ. But he that is greatest among you shall be your servant. And whosoever shall exalt himself shall be abased; and he that shall humble himself shall be exalted."

[2506] Matthew 23:5–8 "But all their works they do for to be seen of men: they make broad their phylacteries, and enlarge the borders of their garments, And love the uppermost rooms at feasts, and the chief seats in the synagogues, And greetings in the markets, and to be called of men, Rabbi, Rabbi. But be not ye called Rabbi: for one is your Master, *even* Christ; and all ye are brethren."

[2507] Matthew 6:1–4 "Take heed that ye do not your alms before men, to be seen of them: otherwise ye have no reward of your Father which is in heaven. Therefore when thou doest *thine* alms, do not sound a trumpet before thee, as the hypocrites do in the synagogues and in the streets, that they may have glory of men. Verily I say unto you, They have their reward. But when thou doest alms, let not thy left hand know what thy right hand doeth: That thine alms may be in secret: and thy Father which seeth in secret himself shall reward thee openly."

[2508] Matthew 6:5–6 "And when thou prayest, thou shalt not be as the hypocrites *are:* for they love to pray standing in the synagogues and in the corners of the streets, that they may be seen of men. Verily I say unto you, They have their reward. But thou, when thou prayest, enter into thy closet, and when thou hast shut thy door, pray to thy Father which is in secret; and thy Father which seeth in secret shall reward thee openly."

[2509] D&C 58:26–29 "For behold, it is not meet that I should command in all things; for he that is compelled in all things, the same is a slothful and not a wise servant; wherefore he receiveth no reward. Verily I say, men should be anxiously engaged in a good cause, and do many things of their own free will, and bring to pass much righteousness; For the power is in them, wherein they are agents unto themselves. And inasmuch as men do good they shall in nowise lose their reward. But he that doeth not anything until he is commanded, and receiveth a commandment with doubtful heart, and keepeth it with slothfulness, the same is damned."

you wait to act the part of a priestess until someone calls you to a priestly position, and then only want to hold office to be seen and recognized as a priestess, then you have failed to know your Lord.

You have confused priestly service for God and to your fellow man with rank, position and institutional authority. That is nothing. Worse than nothing. These institutional positions confuse both holders and observers into thinking this is what matters. Misused church position can become little different than membership in a civic club, as some leaders I have known. You probably have seen such people in your own experience. If your "service" is entirely confined there, and you do nothing to benefit the poor, the weak, the needy, the naked and you let the beggar pass by you unnoticed, then priestly service is for you only vanity and pride. It is not something to connect you with God.[2510] You can do that without any institution con-

---

[2510] Mosiah 4:12–27 "And behold, I say unto you that if ye do this ye shall always rejoice, and be filled with the love of God, and always retain a remission of your sins; and ye shall grow in the knowledge of the glory of him that created you, or in the knowledge of that which is just and true. And ye will not have a mind to injure one another, but to live peaceably, and to render to every man according to that which is his due. And ye will not suffer your children that they go hungry, or naked; neither will ye suffer that they transgress the laws of God, and fight and quarrel one with another, and serve the devil, who is the master of sin, or who is the evil spirit which hath been spoken of by our fathers, he being an enemy to all righteousness. But ye will teach them to walk in the ways of truth and soberness; ye will teach them to love one another, and to serve one another. And also, ye yourselves will succor those that stand in need of your succor; ye will administer of your substance unto him that standeth in need; and ye will not suffer that the beggar putteth up his petition to you in vain, and turn him out to perish. Perhaps thou shalt say: The man has brought upon himself his misery; therefore I will stay my hand, and will not give unto him of my food, nor impart unto him of my substance that he may not suffer, for his punishments are just— But I say unto you, O man, whosoever doeth this the same hath great cause to repent; and except he repenteth of that which he hath done he perisheth forever, and hath no interest in the kingdom of God. For behold, are we not all beggars? Do we not all depend upon the same Being, even God, for all the substance which we have, for both food and raiment, and for gold, and for silver, and for all the riches which we have of every kind? And behold, even at this time, ye have been calling on his name, and begging for a remission of your sins. And has he suffered that ye have begged in vain? Nay; he has poured out his Spirit upon you, and has caused that your hearts should be filled with joy, and has caused that your mouths should be stopped that ye could not find utterance, so exceedingly great was your joy. And now, if God, who has created you, on whom you are dependent for your lives and for all that ye have and are, doth grant unto you whatsoever ye ask that is right, in faith, believing that ye shall receive, O then, how ye ought to impart of the substance that ye have one to another. And if ye judge the man who putteth up his petition to you for your substance that he perish not, and condemn him, how much more just will be your condemnation for withholding your substance, which doth not belong to you but to God, to whom also your life belongeth; and yet ye put up no petition, nor repent of the thing which thou hast done. I say unto you, wo be unto that man, for his substance shall perish with him; and now, I say these things unto those who are rich as pertaining to the things of this world. And again, I say unto the poor, ye who have not and yet have sufficient, that ye remain from day to day; I mean all you who deny the beggar, because ye have not; I would that ye say in your hearts that: I give not because I have not, but if I had I would give. And now, if ye say this in your hearts ye remain guiltless, otherwise ye are condemned; and your condemnation is just for ye covet that which ye have not received. And now, for the sake of these things which I have spoken unto you—that is, for the sake of retaining a remission of your sins from day to day, that ye may walk guiltless before God—I would that ye should impart of your substance to the poor, every man according to that which he hath, such as feeding the hungry, clothing the naked, visiting the sick and administering to their relief, both spiritually and temporally, according to their wants. And see that all these things are done in wisdom and order; for it is not requisite that a man should run faster than he has strength. And again, it is expedient that he should be diligent, that thereby he might win the prize; therefore, all things must be done in order."

ferring upon you, like "the Great and Powerful Oz" what is in reality nothing more than a watch, a certificate and a medal.

I would advise against looking to those who are almost always damned to decide what example to follow.[2511] The ones acclaimed the most, celebrated the most, and who hold the greatest public eye generally have no authority from God anyway.[2512] Do not either envy them or take them for your model. People who make this mistake aspire to be a child of hell.[2513]

Even if we receive all the praise men can bestow upon us, we are *still* not priestly. For that, you need to serve our Lord. The honors of men are nothing. They never have been anything.[2514]

[2511] D&C 121:39–40 "We have learned by sad experience that it is the nature and disposition of almost all men, as soon as they get a little authority, as they suppose, they will immediately begin to exercise unrighteous dominion. Hence many are called, but few are chosen."

[2512] D&C 121:34–37 "Behold, there are many called, but few are chosen. And why are they not chosen? Because their hearts are set so much upon the things of this world, and aspire to the honors of men, that they do not learn this one lesson— That the rights of the priesthood are inseparably connected with the powers of heaven, and that the powers of heaven cannot be controlled nor handled only upon the principles of righteousness. That they may be conferred upon us, it is true; but when we undertake to cover our sins, or to gratify our pride, our vain ambition, or to exercise control or dominion or compulsion upon the souls of the children of men, in any degree of unrighteousness, behold, the heavens withdraw themselves; the Spirit of the Lord is grieved; and when it is withdrawn, Amen to the priesthood or the authority of that man."

[2513] Matthew 23:10–15 "Neither be ye called masters: for one is your Master, *even* Christ. But he that is greatest among you shall be your servant. And whosoever shall exalt himself shall be abased; and he that shall humble himself shall be exalted. But woe unto you, scribes and Pharisees, hypocrites! for ye shut up the kingdom of heaven against men: for ye neither go in *yourselves,* neither suffer ye them that are entering to go in. Woe unto you, scribes and Pharisees, hypocrites! for ye devour widows' houses, and for a pretence make long prayer: therefore ye shall receive the greater damnation. Woe unto you, scribes and Pharisees, hypocrites! for ye compass sea and land to make one proselyte, and when he is made, ye make him twofold more the child of hell than yourselves."

[2514] D&C 121:34–36 "Behold, there are many called, but few are chosen. And why are they not chosen? Because their hearts are set so much upon the things of this world, and aspire to the honors of men, that they do not learn this one lesson— That the rights of the priesthood are inseparably connected with the powers of heaven, and that the powers of heaven cannot be controlled nor handled only upon the principles of righteousness."

You want to be priestly? Then cry repentance. It will offend others, and will cause them to despise you, but will bring you to know your Lord. He is meek and lowly. He speaks to man in plain humility, as one man speaks to another.

His first witness of His resurrection, and therefore the first apostolic voice having authority to declare her witness that He who was dead is alive, was a woman. She was not among the church hierarchy, but the Lord rebuked the them for ignoring her authoritative and true witness. They were "fools and slow of heart" for this error.

Our Lord is no respecter of persons. You ought not be either. To the extent you allow false and exaggerated claims to inform your understanding of a meek and lowly Lord, you will always reach errant conclusions. That is part of the deception we are required to overcome here.

Role of Women, Part 5

I know more than I can or ought to say about this matter, but that has been a deeply personal journey. You should take that same journey. I do not want to rob you of discovery. Therefore, let me reiterate that this is a worthy topic and ought to be something you take to the Lord and inquire of Him. He can make it plain to you, only if you are prepared to receive it.

What is required to qualify us for the kingdom of Heaven is driven by what we each lack. In each person that is different. However, the final standard is the same for all of us.

Do not think a merciful and self-sacrificing Lord, who endured infinite suffering to redeem you, has any intention of disappointing you, much less of making you miserable. He will exalt you. But you cannot be as He is without first learning to trust Him and then to follow Him. He descended below it all. Are you greater than He?[2515]

Man is incomplete. Woman is incomplete. The "image of God" is both male and female.[2516]

There is a reason for this necessity of both the man and woman to complete the image of God. The capacity of one is different from the other. Without betraying too much, I will close by saying this, which if you were to understand you would know more about God than you do at present:

The role of the man is knowledge.

The role of the woman is wisdom.

These are eternal, and not merely found here.

Even the names of God reflect these separate roles and the scriptures associate wisdom with the feminine. Underlying this are things which we are only shown to the faithful when we have first become more like God.

There is nothing to your lamentation and complaints that God will not provide a more than adequate reward for enduring. God will not leave you comfortless on this issue any more than He will on any subject which causes you tears. They will all be wiped away.[2517] You need to develop the faith to trust Him. He will not disappoint you.

Each of us needs to find God. Then we should lead our spouse to Him likewise. There is a lifetime of effort required to do so.

[2515] D&C 122:8 "The Son of Man hath descended below them all. Art thou greater than he?"

[2516] Genesis 1:27 "So God created man in his *own* image, in the image of God created he him; male and female created he them."

[2517] Revelation 7:17 "For the Lamb which is in the midst of the throne shall feed them, and shall lead them unto living fountains of waters: and God shall wipe away all tears from their eyes."

Role of Women, Conclusion

I've addressed the issue of "plural wives" elsewhere. I do not believe it is a requirement imposed on those who are sealed by the Holy Spirit of Promise. The greatest challenge is to produce a couple who, in the image of God, are one. If a couple manage to overcome the world and become so, they do not need additional women to join them to qualify for exaltation. And if a group insists upon complicating the process by the multiplicity of wives before they are sealed by the Holy Spirit of Promise, the challenge to become one may never be overcome.

I have no doubts about the Lord's kindness and compassion for all men and women. Therefore, I have no doubt about the circumstances of the single, or the forsaken woman who is faithful to the Gospel. There will be none who are abandoned by the Lord who are faithful to His teachings.

The role of woman is more glorious than I can explain in the present circumstances. To discuss all I know would be to violate the present order, which I will not do. But I have no hesitation to say that the "many great and important things" which are "yet to be revealed" (Articles of Faith 9) will include a great deal more than presently understood about women. I do not know if that will need to wait until after the Lord's second coming, or if it will be known to the church before then. What I do know, however, is that the full picture of woman's past and future glory is presently withheld from man's view in the wisdom of the Lord.

Temple rites are not complete. I've said that before on a number of occasions. When they are, the role of women will be greatly clarified. But it is not my calling or my right to get ahead of the Lord on such matters. What I can do, however, is to testify that among the things which "eye hath not seen, nor ear heard, nor yet entered into the heart of man" is included a sound understanding of the role of women. It is only withheld at present because of our wickedness. What we have is enough to test us, and we are being tested. Will we ever be enough to pass the test to warrant the Lord giving more?

When we have more before we are ready to receive it then it only condemns us. The Lord is merciful in withholding such things.

What I also know is that if He will reveal things to any man, He will do so to all mankind. Therefore as I said at the beginning, these are legitimate and worthy questions. They deserve an answer. Ask the Lord and trust His answer.

No man has ever been elevated to a throne in eternity who was not placed upon it by his wife.

THE BATTLE IS WITHIN YOU

What We Control

We are not accountable for things we do not control. The Lord alone in His wisdom will determine what will be done about such things. For us, it is what we *do* control that will matter. Our decisions about what opportunities He offers have eternal consequences.

One of those decisions is whether we recognize the opportunities before us. We allow a great deal to blind us and let us think the opportunity was never ours, when it was really within our control all along.

Waiting on Others

The fullness of the Gospel is found in the Book of Mormon. There you will find individual after individual who have returned, through faith, back to God's presence. Once they have returned to God's presence, they have a different view of themselves and others.

In the case of Lehi and his family, he listened to the testimony of others warning of the destruction of Jerusalem, took their warning seriously, and begged God on behalf of his people.[2518] As a result of his intercession and compassion for others, he was visited by God.[2519]

Lehi's family did not believe him. They followed him into the wilderness, but only because of the respect accorded to the father in their society. None of the family could believe what he was saying.

The younger son, Nephi, prayed to be able to believe what his father Lehi was saying. Even though Nephi wanted to acquire faith, it was not easy to trust his father's message. Because of his desire to believe, Nephi reports the Lord "did visit me;" this sounds like something more than it was. The Lord's initial "visit" to Nephi consisted only in 'softening Nephi's heart so that he was able to believe his father.'[2520]

This is the beginning. This is the first step. When the Lord first takes hold of your hand, it is a faint grip, a partial contact, a weak beginning. It is the token, however, that everyone must first receive. It comes from obeying and then acting faithfully on what has been shown to you. It requires you to sacrifice your own will to the Lord's.

No one will return to the presence of God who has not received this gentle grip from the Lord. It is a true token given by the Lord; not just something ceremonial. It is the companion to faith. It is the start of the path you will walk back to the presence of God, passing the sentinels who stand along the way. They will want to know you

---

[2518] 1 Nephi 1:5 "Wherefore it came to pass that my father, Lehi, as he went forth prayed unto the Lord, yea, even with all his heart, in behalf of his people."

[2519] 1 Nephi 1:6 "And it came to pass as he prayed unto the Lord, there came a pillar of fire and dwelt upon a rock before him; and he saw and heard much; and because of the things which he saw and heard he did quake and tremble exceedingly."

[2520] 1 Nephi 2:16 "And it came to pass that I, Nephi, being exceedingly young, nevertheless being large in stature, and also having great desires to know of the mysteries of God, wherefore, I did cry unto the Lord; and behold he did visit me, and did soften my heart that I did believe all the words which had been spoken by my father; wherefore, I did not rebel against him like unto my brothers."

have learned all you need from your experiences here to be able to return to God's presence.

When the most dramatic points of struggle happen along the path, the Book of Mormon provides us with a view into the person where the struggle takes place. Nephi's record of the fullness includes his testimony of kneeling on a dark Jerusalem street where he found the person of Laban lying drunk and unconscious before him.[2521] He disarmed him. Then took the time to admire the weapon of war he had taken from his fallen uncle, noting its precious material and workmanship.[2522]

While admiring the sword, he had the urge to slay Laban.[2523] Though Nephi attributed this impulse to "the Spirit" it was nothing more than an impulse. Here is where the cosmic struggle plays out. In Nephi's heart, there is a strong urge to kill a man which, in Nephi's life, is unprecedented. It is foreign to him. It is "the Spirit" and not Nephi who has this will to kill the man.

Nephi's hesitancy is not based solely on moral scruples, but on all he believes about himself. He is not a man of war. He has "never before shed the blood of man" and does not think it appropriate to start now.[2524] This is not about self control, this is about who his identity. This is who Nephi believes himself to be. He is better than this base impulse. It is beneath him.

[2521] 1 Nephi 4:7–8 "Nevertheless I went forth, and as I came near unto the house of Laban I beheld a man, and he had fallen to the eart And when I came to him I found that it was Laban."

[2522] 1 Nephi 4:9 "And I beheld his sword, and I drew it forth from the sheath thereof; and the hilt thereof was of pure gold, and the workmanship thereof was exceedingly fine, and I saw that the blade thereof was of the most precious steel."

[2523] 1 Nephi 4:10 "And it came to pass that I was constrained by the Spirit that I should kill Laban; but I said in my heart: Never at any time have I shed the blood of man. And I shrunk and would that I might not slay him."

[2524] Ibid.

When he resists this impulse, "the Spirit" elevates the message. No longer is it "constraint" or inclination, but "the Spirit" now "speaks" to him in unmistakable words.[2525] The message not only clearly tells Nephi the Lord's will in 'delivering Laban into his hands,' but also makes enough sense to Nephi that he can immediately recognize the many reasons for the Lord accomplishing this.[2526] The proof of the Lord's hand lays before Nephi. After all, Laban is lying helpless, and "has been delivered into thy hands" as the most tangible, clear proof of God's power.[2527]

Yet all of this struggle is internal to Nephi. You could stand on the same street, at the same moment and see the same scene play out before you, and you would not be a witness to God's great work underway.

The fullness of the Gospel requires us to recognize the hand of God guiding us. The battle we join is within. No one is spared from these stages of growth and development.

The church cannot provide you with an alternative means to get there. It is between you and God, alone. The scene will be as the Book of Mormon continually portrays it. That record is the most comprehensive retelling of how to return to God's presence ever compiled. It was put together by those who made the journey along the path, passing all the sentinels who stand guard along the way. They embraced their Lord through the veil before entering again into His presence. Then, having been true and faithful, they were brought

---

[2525] 1 Nephi 4:11 "And the Spirit said unto me again: Behold the Lord hath delivered him into thy hands. Yea, and I also knew that he had sought to take away mine own life; yea, and he would not hearken unto the commandments of the Lord; and he also had taken away our property."

[2526] Ibid.

[2527] Ibid.

back into His presence and redeemed from the fall of mankind.[2528] They, like the Brother of Jared, were redeemed because of their knowledge.[2529]

Yet you insist on captivity because you have no knowledge.[2530] You take blind guides and are therefore, blinded by your own ignorance.[2531] You insist on keeping what can never inform you, while rejecting what is told you in plain words.[2532] You refuse to see and are willingly blind and therefore the greater darkness lies within you.

You can wait, as one recent and frequent, *anonymous* commentator has insisted, until there is a program offered to you by an institution and see how long it takes for you to learn of God. Or, believe in the Book of Mormon and remove yourself from condemnation.[2533] But if you seek for approval from an institution, then the Lord cannot overcome the barrier you have erected between you and Him.

[2528] Ether 3:13 "And when he had said these words, behold, the Lord showed himself unto him, and said: Because thou knowest these things ye are redeemed from the fall; therefore ye are brought back into my presence; therefore I show myself unto you."

[2529] Ether 3:19 "And because of the knowledge of this man he could not be kept from beholding within the veil; and he saw the finger of Jesus, which, when he saw, he fell with fear; for he knew that it was the finger of the Lord; and he had faith no longer, for he knew, nothing doubting."

[2530] Isaiah 5:13 "Therefore my people are gone into captivity, because *they have* no knowledge: and their honourable men *are* famished, and their multitude dried up with thirst."

[2531] Matthew 23:16 "Woe unto you, *ye* blind guides, which say, Whosoever shall swear by the temple, it is nothing; but whosoever shall swear by the gold of the temple, he is a debtor!"

[2532] 2 Nephi 32:7 "And now I, Nephi, cannot say more; the Spirit stoppeth mine utterance, and I am left to mourn because of the unbelief, and the wickedness, and the ignorance, and the stiffneckedness of men; for they will not search knowledge, nor understand great knowledge, when it is given unto them in plainness, even as plain as word can be."

[2533] D&C 84:56–57 "And this condemnation resteth upon the children of Zion, even all. And they shall remain under this condemnation until they repent and remember the new covenant, even the Book of Mormon and the former commandments which I have given them, not only to say, but to do according to that which I have written—"

The Church's Greatest Appeal

There are many disagreements among Latter-day Saints. Sitting in on a Sunday lesson in my High Priest's Group will show just how many topics divide us. We understand a great deal differently from our history, our doctrine, and our priorities. This is normal among any group of people, even when they join together as fellow believers.

The most unifying thing about the church, however, is the service we render to others. Unlike many other denominations, our church is filled with opportunities to serve. It is expected. And it is rendered. Everywhere you turn the members are giving service.

I am not particularly political. The differences between political parties is so little as to not justify enthusiasm for either. However, I watched the evening of Mitt Romney's acceptance last week. A number of speakers extolled his past service to others. There wasn't a dry eye in the house as parents spoke about the support they received from Bishop Romney for their troubles.

As I listened, it seemed to me this was a description of a typical Mormon Bishop. It can be found in thousands of wards throughout the church. It is an expected part of the calling. And that service and support is rendered willingly, week after week, throughout the church.

From Home Teachers to Visiting Teachers, Relief Society Presidents and Bishops, Elder's Quorums and Young Women Leaders, there are continual acts of service and support expected and delivered.

It is my view this is the church's greatest strength and its greatest appeal. We take it for granted. But when behavior which is "normal" for a Mormon Bishop was put on public display, it touched people to the point of tears. We get used to it. We shouldn't. It is, after all, the pure religion of Christ.[2534] It is what we do, more than what we say, that matters in practicing our faith.

This should unify us no matter what may divide us.

Proverbs 6:20–23

My son, keep thy father's commandment, and forsake not the law of thy mother: Bind them continually upon thine heart, and tie them about thy neck. When thou goest, it shall lead thee; when thou sleepest, it shall keep thee; and when thou awakest, it shall talk with thee. For the commandment is a lamp; and the law is light; and reproofs of instruction are the way of life:

We should teach with more simplicity. We should take the counsel in the scriptures to heart and bind them to us.

Faith

The scriptures say that without faith it is impossible to please God.[2535] Have you thought about what that means? From the Lectures on Faith it is clear that faith is a "principle of action." If it is a principle of action, whose action is it? Must you do something, and if so, what? What *action* must you take? What is the role you occupy in faith?

[2534] James 1:22–27 "But be ye doers of the word, and not hearers only, deceiving your own selves. For if any be a hearer of the word, and not a doer, he is like unto a man beholding his natural face in a glass: For he beholdeth himself, and goeth his way, and straightway forgetteth what manner of man he was. But whoso looketh into the perfect law of liberty, and continueth *therein,* he being not a forgetful hearer, but a doer of the work, this man shall be blessed in his deed. If any man among you seem to be religious, and bridleth not his tongue, but deceiveth his own heart, this man's religion *is* vain. Pure religion and undefiled before God and the Father is this, To visit the fatherless and widows in their affliction, *and* to keep himself unspotted from the world."

[2535] Hebrews 11:6 "But without faith *it is* impossible to please *him:* for he that cometh to God must believe that he is, and *that* he is a rewarder of them that diligently seek him."

The Lectures on Faith also say that faith is a "principle of power." What does that mean? Whose power? Is there a relationship between the action of man and the power of God?

Think of any great example of faith in scriptures and apply these questions to them. It can be as simple as David and Goliath, or as complicated as Elijah. After you have studied the example, ask yourself, "what action did the man or woman take? Why did they act in that way? What was the intention? How was God's power used? Who controlled the power? More precisely, from what source did the power come? Is this principle of power connected with priesthood?[2536] If it is, then when any person exercises faith as a principle of power, are they exercising priesthood?

Bearing Testimony vs. Presiding

When Mary Magdalene, and Joanna and Mary and other women saw the angels in the empty tomb, and then testified of what they saw and knew, were they disrespecting the proper authority?[2537] Was

---

[2536] D&C 121:36 "That the rights of the priesthood are inseparably connected with the powers of heaven, and that the powers of heaven cannot be controlled nor handled only upon the principles of righteousness."

[2537] Luke 24:1–10 "Now upon the first *day* of the week, very early in the morning, they came unto the sepulchre, bringing the spices which they had prepared, and certain *others* with them. And they found the stone rolled away from the sepulchre. And they entered in, and found not the body of the Lord Jesus. And it came to pass, as they were much perplexed thereabout, behold, two men stood by them in shining garments: And as they were afraid, and bowed down *their* faces to the earth, they said unto them, Why seek ye the living among the dead? He is not here, but is risen: remember how he spake unto you when he was yet in Galilee, Saying, The Son of man must be delivered into the hands of sinful men, and be crucified, and the third day rise again. And they remembered his words, And returned from the sepulchre, and told all these things unto the eleven, and to all the rest. It was Mary Magdalene, and Joanna, and Mary *the mother* of James, and other *women that were* with them, which told these things unto the apostles."

there something improper about them knowing something that the Lord's Apostles did not know yet?[2538]

Was there something wrong with the Lord appearing to, and speaking with Mary on the morning of His resurrection, even before He returned to His Father?[2539]

Was there something improper, too sacred, or too private in these events to prevent these witnesses from testifying of them? Isn't everyone required to bear their testimony of the Lord? If those who can read the Lord's revelation are required to testify they have "heard his voice"[2540] how much greater an obligation is imposed upon those who have seen Him?

Testimony of Christ is not co-equal with presiding. All who can do so should testify. Presiding, however, is based on the common consent given exclusively to those who are in the church's hierarchy.

[2538] Luke 24:11–12 "And their words seemed to them as idle tales, and they believed them not. Then arose Peter, and ran unto the sepulchre; and stooping down, he beheld the linen clothes laid by themselves, and departed, wondering in himself at that which was come to pass."

[2539] John 20:11–17 "But Mary stood without at the sepulchre weeping: and as she wept, she stooped down, *and looked* into the sepulchre, And seeth two angels in white sitting, the one at the head, and the other at the feet, where the body of Jesus had lain. And they say unto her, Woman, why weepest thou? She saith unto them, Because they have taken away my Lord, and I know not where they have laid him. And when she had thus said, she turned herself back, and saw Jesus standing, and knew not that it was Jesus. Jesus saith unto her, Woman, why weepest thou? whom seekest thou? She, supposing him to be the gardener, saith unto him, Sir, if thou have borne him hence, tell me where thou hast laid him, and I will take him away. Jesus saith unto her, Mary. She turned herself, and saith unto him, Rabboni; which is to say, Master. Jesus saith unto her, Touch me not; for I am not yet ascended to my Father: but go to my brethren, and say unto them, I ascend unto my Father, and your Father; and *to* my God, and your God."

[2540] D&C 18:35–36 "For it is my voice which speaketh them unto you; for they are given by my Spirit unto you, and by my power you can read them one to another; and save it were by my power you could not have them; Wherefore, you can testify that you have heard my voice, and know my words."

Unless sustained to such presiding positions, no one has the right to such office.[2541]

What Is Meant by Keys

There are many different ways in which the words "key" or "keys" are used in scripture. It is an interesting topic to research. President John Taylor was so interested in the word that he did a study he titled, "The Book of Keys" wherein he attempted to reconstruct the topic in whole. So far as I have been able to learn, that book no longer exists.

In Temple Recommend interviews you are asked to acknowledge the current church president "holds all the keys" and "is the only person authorized to exercise them" on the earth today. This is a question we all answer. But in discussions with bishops, stake presidents, religion professors, friends and mission presidents, I've never been able to determine, nor has anyone been able to explain what is included. Below is the answer given in *The Encyclopedia of Mormonism*, (entry written by Alan Perish):

> The keys of the priesthood refer to the right to exercise power in the name of Jesus Christ or to preside over a priesthood function, quorum, or organizational division of the Church. Keys are necessary to maintain order and to see that the functions of the Church are performed in the proper time, place, and manner. They are given by the laying on of hands in an ordination or setting apart by a person who presides and who holds the appropriate keys at a higher level. Many keys were restored to men on earth by heavenly messengers to the Prophet Joseph Smith and Oliver Cowdery.

[2541] D&C 26:2 "And all things shall be done by common consent in the church, by much prayer and faith, for all things you shall receive by faith. Amen."
D&C 28:13 "For all things must be done in order, and by common consent in the church, by the prayer of faith."

The keys of the kingdom of God on earth are held by the apostles. The president of the church, who is the senior apostle, holds all the keys presently on earth and presides over all the organizational and ordinance work of the Church.[2542] He delegates authority by giving the keys of specific offices to others.[2543] Only presiding priesthood officers (including General Authorities, stake presidents, mission presidents, temple presidents, bishops, branch presidents, and quorum presidents) hold keys pertaining to their respective offices. Latter-day Saints distinguish between holding the priesthood and holding keys to direct the work of the priesthood: one does not receive additional priesthood when one is given keys (Joseph F. Smith, *IE* 4 [Jan. 1901]:230).

The Prophet Joseph Smith taught that "the fundamental principles, government, and doctrine of the Church are vested in the keys of the kingdom" (*TPJS*, 21).

"The keys have to be brought from heaven whenever the Gospel is sent"; they are revealed to man under the authority of Adam, for he was the first to be given them when he was given dominion over all things. They have come down through the dispensations of the gospel to prophets, including Noah, Abraham, Moses, Elijah; to Peter, James, and John; and to Joseph Smith and the designated prophets of the latter days (*HC* 3:385–87). Keys to perform or preside over various priesthood functions were bestowed upon Joseph Smith and Oliver Cowdery by John the Baptist (see Aaronic Priesthood:

[2542] D&C 107:8–9, 91–92 "The Melchizedek Priesthood holds the right of presidency, and has power and authority over all the offices in the church in all ages of the world, to administer in spiritual things. The Presidency of the High Priesthood, after the order of Melchizedek, have a right to officiate in all the offices in the church. And again, the duty of the President of the office of the High Priesthood is to preside over the whole church, and to be like unto Moses— Behold, here is wisdom; yea, to be a seer, a revelator, and a translator, and a prophet, having all the gifts of God which he bestows upon the head of the church."

[2543] D&C 124:123 "Verily I say unto you, I now give unto you the officers belonging to my Priesthood, that ye may hold the keys thereof, even the Priesthood which is after the order of Melchizedek, which is after the order of mine Only Begotten Son."

Restoration), by Peter, James, and John (see Melchizedek Priesthood: Restoration of Melchizedek Priesthood), and by Moses, Elias, and Elijah in the Kirtland Temple (see Doctrine and Covenants: Sections 109–110).

Many types of keys are mentioned in the scriptures of the Church (see *Mormon Doctrine*, 409–413). Jesus Christ holds all the keys. Joseph Smith received the keys pertaining to the restoration of the gospel of Jesus Christ (D&C 6:25–28; 28:7; 35:18), and through him the First Presidency holds the "keys of the kingdom," including the sealing ordinances (D&C 81:1–2; 90:1–6;110:16;128:20;132:19). Specific mention of certain keys and those who hold them include the following: The Quorum of the Twelve Apostles exercises the keys "to open the door by the proclamation of the gospel of Jesus Christ" in all the world (D&C 107:35; 112:16; 124:128). Adam holds "the keys of salvation under the counsel and direction of the Holy One," and "the keys of the universe" (D&C 78:16; *TPJS*, 157); Moses, "the keys of the gathering of Israel" (D&C 110:11); Elias, the keys to bring to pass "the restoration of all things" (D&C 27:6); and Elijah, "the keys of the power of turning the hearts of the fathers to the children, and the hearts of the children to the fathers" (D&C 27:9). Holders of the Melchizedek Priesthood are said to have "the keys of the Church," "the key of knowledge," and "the keys of all the spiritual blessings of the church" (D&C 42:69; 84:19; 107:18), while belonging to the Aaronic Priesthood are "the keys of the ministering of angels, and of the gospel of repentance, and of baptism by immersion for the remission of sins" (D&C 13:1; 84:26). All these stewardships will eventually be delivered back into the hands of Jesus Christ (*TPJS*, 157).

As far as it goes, I think this is a good attempt. But when church members are asked if the church president holds "all the keys" I cannot be certain the above definition is what is meant. Here is the clearest way I think it is illustrated:

From the smallest branch to the largest ward, through all the areas, missions, stakes, wards and branches of the church, there is not a single place in the church where President Thomas Monson would not be recognized as the presiding authority in any meeting he attended. He could go anywhere, in any location, in any meeting, and he alone would be the final authority. While a bishop presides and has the keys over his ward, and in that ward can call or release anyone to any position, President Monson would preside over that bishop if he were to attend the ward. No one would doubt or question whether President Monson could release and call a replacement bishop in that, or any, ward. The same is true of any stake president, or any mission president or any area authority, or any general authority. There is simply no one other than President Monson alone who holds the keys to put the church in order. Period.

I think this is the best definition of "all the keys."

Keys of Ministering of Angels

The Aaronic Priesthood has the "keys of the ministering of angels."[2544] This raises these questions:

- Do the "keys of ministering of angels" guarantee the holder he will entertain angels?
- Does the ministry of angels depend entirely on possession of these keys?
- Does the appearance of an angel necessarily mean the one to whom the angel appears holds the Aaronic Priesthood? Even in the case of a woman, such as Mary?[2545]

[2544] D&C 84:26 "And the lesser priesthood continued, which priesthood holdeth the key of the ministering of angels and the preparatory gospel;"

[2545] Luke 1:26–27 "And in the sixth month the angel Gabriel was sent from God unto a city of Galilee, named Nazareth, To a virgin espoused to a man whose name was Joseph, of the house of David; and the virgin's name was Mary."

- If the appearance of an angel does not equate with holding of the Aaronic Priesthood, then does it equate with holding the keys of ministering of angels?

- Can the keys of ministering of angels be separated from the Aaronic Priesthood, or are they entirely confined to this priesthood?

- If the keys can be separated from the priesthood, then what is priesthood and what are "keys?"

We tend to gloss over a great deal and have too little curiosity about important questions. In *The Second Comforter,* I explained part of being "childlike" is to possess relentless curiosity about things you do not understand. We should try to get every answer to every question we can obtain from God. First through the scriptures. Then through prayer and inquiry.

What if "keys to the ministering of angels" are not coequal with the Aaronic Priesthood? Who or under what circumstances could angels minister in the absence of Aaronic Priesthood? Are there "keys" conferred whenever an angel ministers to a person, any person? If an angel appears to a woman in Tibet, does that appearance give her the "keys of ministering of angels" even if she is not Mormon? If so, what is meant by "keys of ministering of angels?"

If an angel has appeared to someone outside the church, and if, because of that, the person does hold some "keys" because of an actual appearance, what of the Mormon priest who has never had an angel appear to him? If he has never had an angelic visitor, does he still hold the "keys of the ministering of angels?"

Do "keys of the ministering of angels" guarantee angels will appear? If not, then what do the "keys" entail? What do they confer? Must an angel minister to the key holder if he demands it? Are angels subject to the keys or not? If not, then how should these "keys" be understood:

- As a right?
- As a privilege?
- As an invitation?
- As a matter to inquire into until you have understanding?

"Keys" as Challenge

What if "keys" are better viewed as a signal, or a sign post along a pathway? Instead of "I hold 'keys' and so I hold something of value."

The better view might be "I have been told one 'key' to my calling is to have angels minister to men. Therefore, I know this is a critical matter, or a key to search into."

What if "holding a key" is better viewed as being given a strong guide or route to take? It points you to something you need to obtain. You have a "key" and now need to discover what it is that must be unlocked.

A "key" is something used to open a lock. It is also something that is "important" or "central in importance." A "keystone" is the point in an arch that fits in the center, holding the arch together. Upon it all else rests.

If the word is viewed using these meanings, it suggests that holding a "key" implies using it in action. The First Presidency and Quorum of the Twelve use their key positions to manage and maintain the worldwide church organization. If not for that constant oversight, the organization of the church would lapse into disorganization. Their "keys" are indispensable to hold the entire structure together. Without them at the center, like a "keystone," the "building" would collapse. But the Gospel (and the *church*) is not a spectator sport. Even if fifteen presiding authorities waste and wear out their lives keeping the church organized, no one will be saved by observing them. It devolves upon us, each one, to obtain the keys of our own salvation by a covenant with God.

Offices belonging to others are their responsibility. For you, there are "keys" which come to us in our own sphere. We are all asked to rise up in testimony and knowledge until, at last, we arrive at "the perfect day" of understanding.[2546] We are all invited to come to know the Lord, see His face, and know that He is.[2547]

Can you imagine what a different church it would be if we were all able to say we know for ourselves, nothing doubting, our Lord? Can you imagine how all the problems we now face would evaporate overnight, if our quest was to grow from grace to grace until we too receive of the Father's fullness?[2548] Most of what now afflicts us would become trivial, left behind as we grow in light and truth.[2549]

Our temple rites symbolize the trek back to the presence of God. All of us, male and female, receive the same ceremonial blueprint to build upon. Every person within the church should obey and sacrifice (for God and not man), then learn through service, the Gospel of Christ by walking in His footsteps. You agreed to undertake obedience and sacrifice before committing to following His Gospel. This order is critical. Without it, you could err in thinking the Gospel will come to you without sacrifice.

From the *Lectures on Faith*, Lecture 6:

[2546] D&C 50:24 "That which is of God is light; and he that receiveth light, and continueth in God, receiveth more light; and that light groweth brighter and brighter until the perfect day."

[2547] D&C 93:1 "VERILY, thus saith the Lord: It shall come to pass that every soul who forsaketh his sins and cometh unto me, and calleth on my name, and obeyeth my voice, and keepeth my commandments, shall see my face and know that I am;"

[2548] D&C 93:20 "For if you keep my commandments you shall receive of his fulness, and be glorified in me as I am in the Father; therefore, I say unto you, you shall receive grace for grace."

[2549] D&C 50:23–25 "And that which doth not edify is not of God, and is darkness. That which is of God is light; and he that receiveth light, and continueth in God, receiveth more light; and that light groweth brighter and brighter until the perfect day. And again, verily I say unto you, and I say it that you may know the truth, that you may chase darkness from among you;"

7. Let us here observe, that a religion [meaning true religion, no matter what another may say or do that tempts you to depart from it] that does not require the sacrifice of all things, never has power [forget about office or position or authority to conduct a meeting, and realize this is the power to obtain eternal life] sufficient to produce the faith necessary unto life and salvation; for from the first existence of man, the faith necessary unto the enjoyment of life and salvation never could be obtained without the sacrifice of all earthly things [meaning your own reputation, your standing, and any praise you may hope to gain from others—all must be laid upon the altar even if your fellow Latter-day Saint falsely accuses you]: it was through this sacrifice, and this only, that God has ordained that men should enjoy eternal life; and it is through the medium of the sacrifice of all earthly things, that men do actually know that they are doing the things that are well pleasing in the sight of God [because God will make that known directly to you and you will know, nothing doubting]. When a man has offered in sacrifice all that he has, for the truth's sake, not even withholding his life, and believing before God that he has been called to make this sacrifice, because he seeks to do his will, he does know most assuredly, that God does and will accept his sacrifice & offering, & that he has not nor will not seek his face in vain. Under these circumstances, then, he can obtain the faith necessary for him to lay hold on eternal life.

8. It is in vain for persons to fancy to themselves that they are heirs with those, or can be heirs with them, who have offered their all in sacrifice, and by this means obtained faith in God and favor with him so as to obtain eternal life, unless they in like manner offer unto him the same sacrifice [which you learn in the temple rites and which you have covenanted to do], and through that offering obtain the knowledge that they are accepted of him.

This outlines the "keys" for your own salvation. Seek for these for they belong to each of us. Do not be jealous of church positions, they do not matter and are not necessary. One thing is necessary; therefore choose the better part.[2550]

The Equinox

This coming weekend will mark the final Equinox of the year. One in the spring, marking the change from winter to spring, and this one marking the change from summer to fall. Apart from separating our designation of the seasons, these times also represent the most colorful times of the year. New and colorful life in nature stirs with the promise of fruit, flowers and planting. In contrast, the coming event marks the harvest when nature's bounty is gathered. In an agrarian society it is a time to enjoy the fruit, work is reduced, and the brilliant colors of a season well spent in growth shows its retirement for a time.

The fall Equinox is the time when, year after year, the Angel visited with Joseph. It is also when the plates were turned over to Joseph in that final year. This may not be mere coincidence. Every Equinox marks the balance of light and dark all over the world. From the North Pole to the South Pole, every place is in harmony with the sun. Wherever man lives, they receive the light equally; twelve hours of light and twelve hours of dark.

Joseph trusted in the power of that time, and perhaps waited to inquire as to his standing before the Lord specifically trusting that

---

[2550] Luke 10:39–42 "And she had a sister called Mary, which also sat at Jesus' feet, and heard his word. But Martha was cumbered about much serving, and came to him, and said, Lord, dost thou not care that my sister hath left me to serve alone? bid her therefore that she help me. And Jesus answered and said unto her, Martha, Martha, thou art careful and troubled about many things: But one thing is needful: and Mary hath chosen that good part, which shall not be taken away from her."

day would produce an answer.[2551] I also believe the balance of light has spiritual meaning.

Days and seasons do not control angelic visitations. They happen without regard to the calendar, but according to the will of God. However our faith matters. If we have great confidence, like Joseph, then marking your submission to heaven and desire to know your standing before the Lord may well be aided by such confidence.

I must confess, although I have had a number of visits, none have been calendar related so far as I can tell. There are many scriptural records of visitations that appear to have nothing to do with the dates on the calendar. They appear to me to be based on circumstances and our needs here, or upon the will of God. Therefore, I do not believe anyone is precluded from a visit at any time of the year.

Having said all that, I do not think the Equinox should go unnoticed. And, Joseph was alone when he was visited.

An Unknown Piece of Music

Sunday night I was up late praying and thinking about many things. Sometime shortly after midnight I quieted down and began listening carefully to KBYU FM (classical 89.1) which had been playing in the background. As I listened, they played a piece that sounded to me like it was played on a french horn. Most of the piece was a solo. The piece was delicate, despite the instrument, and it soared and delivered runs of delicate notes. It was astonishing that these notes could come from such a limited instrument. Now I know that there are competent french horn players, and that with practice it is

---

[2551] JS–H 1:29 "In consequence of these things, I often felt condemned for my weakness and imperfections; when, on the evening of the above-mentioned twenty-first of September, after I had retired to my bed for the night, I betook myself to prayer and supplication to Almighty God for forgiveness of all my sins and follies, and also for a manifestation to me, that I might know of my state and standing before him; for I had full confidence in obtaining a divine manifestation, as I previously had one."

possible to acquire this kind of skill and delicacy with a somewhat cumbersome instrument.

When the piece ended, the KBYU announcer, Peter Van de Graff, informed me that this piece had been played on the tuba. This stunned me. I have never met nor heard any one who can take that heavy, cumbersome, and relatively inarticulate instrument and turn it into something that can play music which can soar into the skies and dance about like a piccolo. Here are a couple of examples: Baaddsvick and Marshall. The tuba is primarily a percussion instrument. It is like a bass guitar in a rock and roll band. They both thump out a foundation upon which the rest of the orchestra or rock band build melodies. While they exist, there are comparatively few bass guitar solos in rock music. The bass player for Primas, Les Claypool, is a rare exception, but even his amazing gift is mostly percussion. Moving them out of that role is akin to asking Andre the Giant to perform ballet.

As I pondered this, it struck me how very like the heavy, inarticulate, restricted instrument mankind is. But a skilled musician took the very same thing which in normal use gives merely a pounding back beat and brought it front and center in a solo that soared to heaven. If such skill can bring the tuba into submission, then with practice, diligence, desire and the help of God, we can likewise bring ourselves into harmony with God. All things typify Christ and the Gospel. Even that wonderful piece played on a tuba.

My vision of how high man can soar was ratified anew in the testimony of that skilled musician. I believe once we find it is possible to delicately soar in concert with heaven and enjoy the thrilling harmony in God's creation, that alone should help us rise up. May we each have the humility and the patience and undertake the long-suffering to change our clumsy efforts into a delicate symphony, even so amen.

Christ the Father

After Christ redeems the brother of Jared from the fall,[2552] He explains to the brother of Jared the doctrine of Christ's Fatherhood. The doctrine is simple. It is an elaboration on what Christ taught in the New Testament.

Here is the doctrine:

> "Behold, I am he who was prepared from the foundation of the world to redeem my people. Behold, I am Jesus Christ. I am the Father and the Son. In me shall all mankind have life, and that eternally, even they who shall believe on my name; and they shall become my sons and my daughters." (Ether 3:14)

In other words, because of our sins and the fall we have experienced, our relationship as sons and daughters of the Father cannot be restored without an intermediary who is willing to cleanse us and to accept us as His son.

This is what Jesus had reference to in John 14:6 when He declared: "I am the way, the truth, and the life: no man cometh unto the Father, but by me." If you find yourself in the circumstance that a voice from heaven declares unto you that you are a son of God because this day He has begotten you[2553] that voice will be Christ's, your Father will be Christ, and you will understand that Christ is the Father and the Son.

"Leaning" Romney

I am not particularly political. Political partisanship is generally a distraction from what our problems really are. Once you have be-

---

[2552] Ether 3:13 "And when he had said these words, behold, the Lord showed himself unto him, and said: Because thou knowest these things ye are redeemed from the fall; therefore ye are brought back into my presence; therefore I show myself unto you."

[2553] Psalm 2:7 "I will declare the decree: the Lord hath said unto me, Thou *art* my Son; this day have I begotten thee."

come partisan you tend to ignore the merits of the other side, as well as the mistakes of your own side.

We must all become converted in our hearts to Jesus Christ. If we have Christ in our hearts, all else will follow. Joseph Smith's comment that he "teaches them correct principles and they govern themselves" was not just a casual statement. It was the confidence a prophet of God in the ability of people to know the difference between good and bad, right and wrong. Even if they err, they would get closer to the correct course by considering the principles they had been taught than by assessing the argument or immediate decision before them.

When a man is converted to truth, correct principles, and true doctrine, such a man has no difficulty stating in simple, but clear terms, the truth which inhabits his heart.

Mitt Romney has been running to be the President of the United States for 5 years now. In all of that time, I find myself unconvinced that his heart is filled with sound, true, heartfelt principles and doctrines. Why can't he set forth in plainness true economic doctrine as well as I can? His background should qualify him to speak with greater plainness about the truths of economic freedom and the principles of economic growth better than I can. He does not. At times he is almost incoherent.

There are fundamental and universal God-given principles for the preservation of the freedom of mankind. Madison, Monroe, Jefferson, Washington, Mason, and the great John Adams could all state with clarity and simplicity, with the beauty that persuades you to your very core, these God-given truths. Why is Mitt Romney unable to do so?

In his first term, President Obama experimented with turning a soft hand to the Muslim world. It was something new. Although it failed, the virulent critics immediately labeled it "an apology tour." No one had any idea how the Cairo speech might move the Muslim hearts. Instead of condemning and even rooting for its failure, we should have prayed to God that our President would move the Muslim world. We should have asked God to soften the hearts of our enemies. We should asked God to embolden our friends. Instead we withheld our sustaining prayers, and in contempt, we let the matter proceed to its now complete failure.

Thinking upon the failure of that experiment, I recall how clearly Richard Nixon articulated, and Henry Kissinger elaborated, on the effective policy of projecting national strength to our enemies. Whatever terrible flaws Richard Nixon had, he was convinced to his core, and able to persuasively articulate the truth of national power in the international arena. After our national humiliation under Jimmy Carter, Ronald Reagan was elected in very large part because he could speak the principles of American power persuasively, convincingly, and from his heart.

Mitt Romney is unable to do this.

As I listen to Mitt Romney speak about any topic, principle, or true doctrine, he seems hollow. He sounds more like a spokesman for the opinions of others than a man speaking from his heart. He sounds like the chairman of a committee. He sounds like he is trying to use focus group phrases. He seems to be using the results of opinion polls to formulate his public statements. In short, he seems more like an artificial life form then a principled, true-hearted, complete convert to God given truths, proven economic doctrines, and historically successful foreign policy.

This leaves me wondering:

- It is not "who" but rather "what" am I electing?
- Is this a man with a true and converted heart and soul, or is this a weather vane prepared to be tossed to and fro with every wind of shifting opinion?
- Is he, as I suspect, double-minded and unstable as water?

If opinions shift on something which is absolutely fundamental and God-given to preserve man's freedom, will that popularity shift cause him to surrender such a principle?

Why should I regard him as something more than an empty suit espousing, without the conviction I can feel in my own heart, the results of market driven research?

I am "leaning" Romney. That is because I believe all of the quantitative easing has not worked and has hurt us all very much. This I could explain with simplicity, but that's beyond this post. I believe President Obama's soft approach foreign policy has utterly failed. I believe the stock market is over-priced, and nothing more than a politically manipulated show piece for the President's sake. I believe shutting down the pipeline was an act completely contrary to our national interest, and has resulted in increased gas prices to every American. Mitt Romney criticizes each of these things. But he sounds more like a puppet than a man of principle with a converted heart. To me, if in the end I vote for Mitt Romney, it will only be as a choice of the lesser of two evils. How I wish he were not Mormon. I think he represents the religion of conviction, devotion, and true principles (the ones which reside in my heart) in such an embarrassingly weak way that if taken as an example of our people should engender contempt and disrespect. He is like the progressively less principled Joel Osteen. As Mr. Osteen's popularity has risen, and his wealth has increased (he now lives in a $10 million dollar home) the principles he used to preach have eroded, softened, and been abandoned. He is a living example of the very problem Mitt Romney's behavior now puts on display.

May God have mercy on us all. May we all look to our Redeemer, Jesus Christ, for our salvation—both temporal and spiritual. Even so, Amen.

A Number of Clarifications

It is impossible in a short post to ever discuss any subject completely. For the most part, all posts are a abbreviated ideas to cause anyone who reads this to think. I want the reader to turn ideas over in their own minds, and reach their own conclusion, after hopefully being provoked to thought by what I say. It is a mistake to think because I have said one thing that I have then said everything.

To illustrate and hopefully clarify, and certainly cause further thought, I want to add the following comments. These are taken from input I received this week from some of you.

I pray to the Father in the name of the Son. In my mind I think of the Father. I let heaven speak to my heart concerning that name-title and I do not presume to have the right to tell anyone what comes into my mind. I also thank the Father for the sacrifice of His Son.

I would add that "El" is singular. "Elohim" is plural. In Abraham 3, there is a group identified as "the noble and great." The noble and great are the "we" who are to prove "them." This is in Abraham 3.

When the matter is settled, in chapter 4 of Abraham, that "we" or "the noble and great" commence the creation, and that group throughout Abraham 4 are continually referred to as "the Gods." The English term "the Gods" captures the same idea as the Hebrew word "Elohim."

If you have not read The First Three Words of the Endowment, you may want to do so.

It would be an astonishing, but not completely unprecedented, if one of the "sons of God" were to fall away. Were that to happen, the heavens would weep over him.

When Christ says that no man "comes unto the Father but by [Him]", this implicitly means that Christ will at some point take you to His Father.

When Christ promised not to leave us "comfortless", he added that "my Father will love him, and **we** come unto him, and make **our** abode with him" (John 14:23). Joseph Smith added "the appearing of *the Father and the Son,* in that verse is a personal appearance; and the idea that *the Father and the Son* dwell in a man's heart is an old sectarian notion, and is false" (D&C 130:3).

Joseph affirms he "saw two Personages."

It is more important that you come unto Christ and you allow Him to teach you these things. Pray to the Father in His name, ask Him, *listen to Him.* It is Christ alone who is responsible for the salvation of each of us. Read the scriptures carefully. In fact, if you will pray and study your scriptures diligently, He will open up to your mind the meaning of the more mysterious passages and use the words of the Prophets found in our scriptures to answer your questions. Do much more of that. There is *no man* who is a substitute for Jesus Christ.[2554]

I agree that the purpose of keys, and in particular priesthood keys, is to confer an authoritative invitation to the recipient from God.

I would not encourage anyone to leave the church. It was commissioned by and still authorized by God. The majority has always had a divine preference and protecting hand. Splinter groups have always dwindled or fallen into abuse and corruption. The August

---

[2554] There is nothing inconsistent in these two statements. If you can't understand it, it is because you will not ask and allow God to enlighten your mind. Remember, I am not trying to get you to understand what I understand. I am trying to get you to open your heart, your mind; look to heaven for guidance and get answers to *anything* you don't understand.

1844 vote in Nauvoo was the right of the saints under the Lord's law of "common consent." I believe the Lord did accept the vote. Whatever shortcomings that generation had, they were only like all of humanity. Our Lord suffered for all imperfect people. But He also will discipline and correct us, even if He needs to use a rod to do so.

In my thinking, a "President" or a "candidate to be the President" is a figure head. Once a man is elected to be the President of the United States, he is referred to as "the "Administration." I believe there is a great difference between a man, on the one hand, and "the President of the United States", or "the Administration", on the other.

Let me see if I can illustrate the point.

I think President Jimmy Carter was a failure. I think he was an embarrassment as an administration throughout the world. President Jimmy Carter made so many errors that in my mind I have little hesitation in thinking of him as foolish. In short, my regard for President Jimmy Carter borders on exasperation and deep disappointment.

In contrast, the man Jimmy Carter is principled, devoted, and admirable. As a man he possesses basic goodness. I think he is good-hearted.

Bear that distinction in mind. My comments concerning Mitt Romney had nothing to do with the man, and everything to do with the "the candidate", and the representative of a proposed "new Administration." Like Jimmy Carter, if I change the topic from the Candidate, to the man Mitt Romney, it's a different topic.

If you watched the GOP convention, before Mitt Romney's acceptance speech, there were many who had the opportunity to describe Mitt Romney, the man. He is a compassionate and exemplary Mormon bishop. He rendered kind, compassionate and loving support to members of his ward while he was bishop and for years afterwards. While those people were speaking, the camera panned the audience. There were many in the audience who were moved to tears as they listened to those people speak. Mitt Romney, the man, seems to me to be an example of how all bishops should be. More than that, he seems to be an example of what all of us should be.

When I said that I wish Mitt Romney did not represent my faith, I had exclusive reference to "the candidate" and not the man.

I know you cannot read my mind. So that is probably my communication failure. As to Mitt Romney the man, I am grateful he is a member of my faith.

I could write pages more. I am only offering a glimpse.

When I am in the voting booth, (and I always vote) I have never voted for evil. Therefore, I have never voted for the "lesser of two evils."

While I don't think it is anyone's business, over the years I have voted for, among other people, Jimmy Carter, Ronald Reagan, written in Lee Iacocca and former LDS church historian, Marlin Jensen. As I cast these votes, I always thought I voted for someone who would be wise and good.

That post did not represent a decision about anything. That post represented musings I thought might be helpful to others.

In addition, I hoped there would be some few who might read that post and detect some layers. For anyone who would be open to the idea, I think you could well consider those musings to be about you, me, or all of us. What ultimately turns into the "Administration" almost always reflects quite accurately a collective decision. In other words, **we** always give the power to the "Administration" that **we** deserve to have lead us.

We have made thousands of decisions, and cast millions of votes to place the Candidate Romney at the head of a political party. That is *us*.

Upcoming General Conference

I've heard from several sources that Elder Russell M. Nelson has announced to a number of Stake Presidents that President Thomas S. Monson has received a revelation that will affect every man, woman, and child in the church. This revelation is supposed to be announced in the upcoming general conference.

The last great revelatory program introduced in general conference was the Perpetual Education Fund announced by President Gordon B. Hinckley. That program is profoundly Christ-like.

During His ministry, Christ blessed lives in practical ways. He cured lepers; allowing them to return to society. He cured blindness; rescuing the blessed from darkness. He cured the lame; liberating them from physical captivity. His goodness conferred life-changing blessings, making practical changes to the lives of those he blessed.

Similarly, the Perpetual Education Fund has conferred practical, life-changing blessings. It mirrors the way Christ blessed people.

Not all beneficiaries of the Perpetual Education Fund have repaid their interest-free loans. Not all have remained active in the church. That is of no consequence. The goodness of the program is in the giving of the blessing. It does not matter whether those who are blessed are grateful. The church's (our) acts of Christ-like generosity is unchanged whether the beneficiary ever returns to thank us. Nine of the ten lepers never thanked the Lord. There is little evidence in the scriptures of the many who were healed by the Lord then becoming faithful disciples. The program is Christ-like. Its greatness consists in conferring a blessing. The Lord gives the sunshine and rain to all, the good and the bad. Very few are grateful to

Him for that. It does not stop Him from being good and continuing in sustaining us all from moment to moment.

I encourage all to listen to upcoming general conference.

Some of you were confused when I put up a reader's comments yesterday. What appears below was not written by Denver Snuffer. These words are written by a reader and unedited in any respect. It is offered only to show the kinds of comments the above post has provoked. This is a small sample and not all of the comments received:

––––––––––––

The PEF is a fantastic idea but poorly administered in practice. The money is donated freely by members, then invested by Ensign Peak, whilst very little of it is spent on those for whom it was intended at all. Those who do get it are strapped with ridiculous requirements then made to pay exorbitant interest on the loan. I expect that one reason they removed it from the tithing slips is that they already have far more money than they know what to do with, and don't want to be on the hook to give it to the PEF program.

The increase in earnings and subsequent tithing should be interest enough for the church from PEF participants, as from what the church says the loans usually triple the earnings received by the grads.

Nephi's Isaiah

Nephi states straightforwardly why he uses the Isaiah material in his own prophecy. It is in Nephi's record, but the statement comes from his brother Jacob. Nephi records what is apparently his brother's first address.

The stage is set for the sermon in 2 Nephi 5. Here we learn of the construction of a temple by the Nephites. The temple dedication ceremonies are left out of the account. It is an interesting omission. By chapter 6 the temple is in service.

Jacob's sermon could very well have been both the event marking the commissioning of the temple, and the first sermon delivered to the people in the structure. Nephi put this into his account because he obviously approved of the sermon and wanted it preserved for all time.

Jacob states this:

> "the words which I shall read are they which Isaiah spake concerning all the house of Israel; wherefore, they may be likened unto you, for ye are of the house of Israel. And there are many things which have been spoken by Isaiah which may be likened unto you, because ye are of the house of Israel." (2 Nephi 6:5)

- What does "likened unto you" mean?
- Is there a difference between something literal and being "likened?"
- Does that difference matter?
- What about the limitation Isaiah spoke about "all the house of Israel?"
- Does the Book of Mormon designation of the European bloodlines that would displace the Lamanites as "gentiles" disqualify the gentiles from "likening" the words to them?

- Does the Book of Mormon promise that the gentiles can be "numbered" with the house of Israel allow the same "likening" to apply to the converted gentiles?[2555]

Assuming the words can be "likened" to you, then what does that mean? Are the words to be taken as an analogy to guide us or as a promise given to us?

Jacob explains the analogy he wants to draw to the Nephites beginning in 2 Nephi 9. It is instructive.

Nephi 'went to school' on his younger brother's example. He fills 2 Nephi with Isaiah's words. Then, in the closing chapters of his book, he provides his own commentary. He ends his record in this manner. With all he had seen, with all he knew, and with all he was told to withhold from us, he uses Isaiah as his basis to teach, preach, exhort and expound to us. Much of it is addressed directly to the "gentiles" of our day. He applies Isaiah to the gentiles.

A great key to understanding Nephi's prophecy is that he used Isaiah's words as a tool to deliver his (Nephi's) message. Using Isaiah's intent will not help you. It is irrelevant. You must use Nephi's interpretive keys in his closing chapters to understand Nephi's intent

---

[2555] 2 Nephi 10:18 "And it came to pass that in the ending of the thirty and fourth year, behold, I will show unto you that the people of Nephi who were spared, and also those who had been called Lamanites, who had been spared, did have great favors shown unto them, and great blessings poured out upon their heads, insomuch that soon after the ascension of Christ into heaven he did truly manifest himself unto them—"
3 Nephi 16:13 "But if the Gentiles will repent and return unto me, saith the Father, behold they shall be numbered among my people, O house of Israel."
3 Nephi 21:6 "For thus it behooveth the Father that it should come forth from the Gentiles, that he may show forth his power unto the Gentiles, for this cause that the Gentiles, if they will not harden their hearts, that they may repent and come unto me and be baptized in my name and know of the true points of my doctrine, that they may be numbered among my people, O house of Israel;"
3 Nephi 30:2 "Turn, all ye Gentiles, from your wicked ways; and repent of your evil doings, of your lyings and deceivings, and of your whoredoms, and of your secret abominations, and your idolatries, and of your murders, and your priestcrafts, and your envyings, and your strifes, and from all your wickedness and abominations, and come unto me, and be baptized in my name, that ye may receive a remission of your sins, and be filled with the Holy Ghost, that ye may be numbered with my people who are of the house of Israel."

in "likening" the prophecy to his people and to the latter-day gentiles. This is why I wrote *Nephi's Isaiah*. You will be disappointed if you think it is an interpretation of Isaiah. It is not. The book is about Nephi's message, not the words he employed to "liken" unto us. If you accept this approach you don't need my book. You only need Nephi's words.

———————

As a postscript about the Perpetual Education Fund:

When President Hinckley announced it in the April 2001 General Conference he said the following:

> "they will return that which they have borrowed together with a small amount of interest designed as an incentive to repay the loan."

This was the original intent.

I've received many emails explaining the way the original program was compromised and poorly administered. I acknowledge there may be problems with how it turned out. But that is the responsibility of the employees at the Church Office Building. Those problems do not reflect the purity of intent by the church members who donated. I think there are a lot of people in the bowels of the Church Office Building who have performed poorly for the church. Since these are funds given by faithful members, there is a responsibility which hasn't been kept by some of these employees.

Answers to Questions

Q: Why do you call the PEF a revelation?

A: The church has used that description. I have accepted the church's vocabulary. Am I vile because I am willing to allow the church to control their own terminology?

Q: Doesn't a revelation require "thus sayeth the Lord" and a transcript to be presented for approval by the church?

A: That has not been the practice for a long time. If the practice of limiting a "revelation" to something preceded by "thus sayeth the Lord" then some of Joseph Smith's canonized teachings in the Doctrine & Covenants, and his personal testimony in the JS–H in the P of GP would be disqualified by the standard. Once again, I am allowing the church to control the vocabulary.

Q: Which is it, a divinely revealed program, or a poorly administered program?

A: Are the Ten Commandments a divine revelation even they have been poorly obeyed since the days of Moses? Is the Sermon on the Mount a divinely revealed elaboration on the Ten Commandments clarifying that it is what is in your heart that matters most, even though it has rarely been obeyed since the time of Christ? If God reveals a standard, as he has done many times, and men fail to reach the standard, does that mean God did not give a revelation?

Quietness

Our dispensation opened on a "beautiful, clear day" in the woods in early spring 1820.[2556]

[2556] JS–H 1:14 "So, in accordance with this, my determination to ask of God, I retired to the woods to make the attempt. It was on the morning of a beautiful, clear day, early in the spring of eighteen hundred and twenty. It was the first time in my life that I had made such an attempt, for amidst all my anxieties I had never as yet made the attempt to pray vocally."

It jumped forward again in 1823, at night, after Joseph and his family had retired to bed. It was at this time when an angel came to visit him.[2557]

These towering events happened in quiet settings. It calls to mind Isaiah's remark about quietness: "And the work of righteousness shall be peace; and the effect of righteousness quietness and assurance for ever" (Isaiah 32:17).

I think also of Paul's advice to the Thessalonians: "and that ye study to be quiet, and to do your own business, and to work with your own hands, as we commanded you" (1 Thessalonians 4:11).

Why is being quiet a virtue worth acquiring?

Why is the effect of righteousness quietness?

Was it quiet when you had your most profound spiritual experience?

Have you ever known a deeply spiritual man or woman who could not be calm or quiet?

[2557] JS–H 1:28–30 "During the space of time which intervened between the time I had the vision and the year eighteen hundred and twenty-three—having been forbidden to join any of the religious sects of the day, and being of very tender years, and persecuted by those who ought to have been my friends and to have treated me kindly, and if they supposed me to be deluded to have endeavored in a proper and affectionate manner to have reclaimed me—I was left to all kinds of temptations; and, mingling with all kinds of society, I frequently fell into many foolish errors, and displayed the weakness of youth, and the foibles of human nature; which, I am sorry to say, led me into divers temptations, offensive in the sight of God. In making this confession, no one need suppose me guilty of any great or malignant sins. A disposition to commit such was never in my nature. But I was guilty of levity, and sometimes associated with jovial company, etc., not consistent with that character which ought to be maintained by one who was called of God as I had been. But this will not seem very strange to any one who recollects my youth, and is acquainted with my native cheery temperament. In consequence of these things, I often felt condemned for my weakness and imperfections; when, on the evening of the above-mentioned twenty-first of September, after I had retired to my bed for the night, I betook myself to prayer and supplication to Almighty God for forgiveness of all my sins and follies, and also for a manifestation to me, that I might know of my state and standing before him; for I had full confidence in obtaining a divine manifestation, as I previously had one. While I was thus in the act of calling upon God, I discovered a light appearing in my room, which continued to increase until the room was lighter than at noonday, when immediately a personage appeared at my bedside, standing in the air, for his feet did not touch the floor."

Further on Quiet

Joseph Smith had been confined for months in Liberty Jail. It was a harrowing ordeal, made all the more so because of so little news about the saints. On March 24th, Joseph received letters from several friends, including his brother Don Carlos Smith, Bishop Partridge and his wife Emma.

The letters were welcomed, but sent Joseph's mind racing in all directions as he considered the plight of his family, friends and the church. He wrote:

> "[T]hose who have not been enclosed in the walls of a prison without cause or provocation, can have but little idea how sweet the voice of a friend is; one token of friendship from any source whatever awakens and calls into action every sympathetic feeling; it brings up in an instant everything that is passed; it seizes and present with the avidity of lightening; it grasps after the future with the fierceness of a tiger; it moves the mind backward and forward, from one thing to another . . . " (*TPJS*, 134)

This frenzy of thought was provoked by the letters. It set his mind whirling. He was filled with emotion and with intensity of thought about it all: past, present and future. In this state of mind he was awakened to appreciate keenly these terrible events and his own captivity.

But it was in the quietness which followed where the spirit whispered to him and we received through him revelations now contained in the D&C. He continues:

> "[U]ntil finally all enmity, malice and hatred, and past differences, misunderstandings and mismanagements are slain victorious at the feet of hope; and when the heart is sufficiently contrite, then the voice of inspiration steals along and whispers—" (*TPJS*, 134)

"My son, peace be unto thy soul; thine adversity and thine afflictions shall be but a small moment; and then if thou endure it well, God shall exalt thee on high." (D&C 121:7–8)

The voice comes so quietly Joseph uses "steals along" to tell of its arrival.

It speaks so gently Joseph uses "whispers" to describe the voice.

All earthly things?

Lectures on Faith 6:7

"Let us here observe, that a religion that does not require the sacrifice of all things never has power sufficient to produce the faith necessary unto life and salvation; for, from the first existence of man, the faith necessary unto the enjoyment of life and salvation never could be obtained without the sacrifice of all earthly things."

Is the sacrifice of all earthly things always necessary for faith unto salvation?

This kind of sacrifice is between the individual and God. You cannot fabricate a sacrifice to try and qualify. It is the Lord who sent Moses back to Egypt to confront Pharaoh. It is the Lord who asked Abraham to sacrifice Isaac. It is the Lord who sent Lehi into the wilderness. It is the Lord who allowed the brothers, Joseph and Hyrum, to fall into the peril that would take their lives.

It is only when the Lord requests the sacrifice that it becomes possible to make the sacrifice knowing you are pleasing the Lord. The result does produce saving faith.

Forty Is a Symbol

The number 40 appears in a several different places in the scriptures, almost always in the context of purging or purification. When the Lord destroyed the wicked at the time of Noah, He caused it "to rain upon the earth for forty days and forty nights" (Genesis 7:4). When Moses met with the Lord on the Mount, he was in the presence of the Lord "forty days and forty nights" (Exodus 24:18). When Israel proved unprepared to inherit the promised land, the Lord left them in the wilderness for forty years.[2558]

Elijah was fed by an angel before being sent into the wilderness. After the meal, Elijah "went in the strength of that meat forty days and forty nights unto Horeb the mount of God."[2559] In preparation for His ministry, the Lord likewise "fasted forty days and forty nights."[2560] That preparation culminated in angels ministering to the Him.[2561]

In these examples, it is not a man volunteering or choosing to afflict his soul for forty days. The period of purification is imposed by the Lord. We do not get the choose to be purified through suffering for a period of forty days, or forty years, or any other amount of time. However, if the Lord chooses to purify a soul, and that suffering does last for forty days, you can take it as a sign that the purification was given of God.

I know people have tried to voluntarily afflict themselves for forty days. I think an effort like that shows a poor understanding of how God deals with man. We wait on Him. We submit to Him. Then He alone chooses.

[2558] Deuteronomy 8:2 "And thou shalt remember all the way which the Lord thy God led thee these forty years in the wilderness, to humble thee, *and* to prove thee, to know what *was* in thine heart, whether thou wouldest keep his commandments, or no."

[2559] 1 Kings 19:8 "And he arose, and did eat and drink, and went in the strength of that meat forty days and forty nights unto Horeb the mount of God."

[2560] Matthew 4:2 "And when he had fasted forty days and forty nights, he was afterward an hungred."

[2561] Matthew 4:11 "Then the devil leaveth him, and, behold, angels came and ministered unto him."

Weightier Matters

The gospel contains practically an infinite amount of information. You can study a lifetime and not exhaust what is contained the scriptures and the ordinances.

Christ distinguished between mere physical conformity to rules, like tithing, and the "weightier matters." While acknowledging that there is a need to do the outward ordinances, Christ elevated "judgment, mercy, and faith" to the status of being "weightier."[2562]

The Apostle Paul went one step further and elevated charity (the pure love of Christ) to being so important that salvation itself depends upon a person's charity.[2563]

Paul describes charity as long-suffering, kind, without envy, humble, meek, thinking no evil, rejoicing in the truth, willing to bear all things, full of belief and hope, and willing to endure whatever is required.[2564]

Our conversion to the gospel should produce fruit. Of all the fruit that evidences our conversion, it is our charity or love toward others which most demonstrates the gospel has taken hold in our heart.

We can be proud of our knowledge. But we can never be proud of our charity. Pride and charity are incompatible. Some of the most

---

[2562] Matthew 23:23 "Woe unto you, scribes and Pharisees, hypocrites! for ye pay tithe of mint and anise and cummin, and have omitted the weightier *matters* of the law, judgment, mercy, and faith: these ought ye to have done, and not to leave the other undone."

[2563] 1 Corinthians 13:1–3 "Though I speak with the tongues of men and of angels, and have not charity, I am become *as* sounding brass, or a tinkling cymbal. And though I have *the gift of* prophecy, and understand all mysteries, and all knowledge; and though I have all faith, so that I could remove mountains, and have not charity, I am nothing. And though I bestow all my goods to feed *the poor,* and though I give my body to be burned, and have not charity, it profiteth me nothing."

[2564] 1 Corinthians 13:4–7 "Charity suffereth long, *and* is kind; charity envieth not; charity vaunteth not itself, is not puffed up, Doth not behave itself unseemly, seeketh not her own, is not easily provoked, thinketh no evil; Rejoiceth not in iniquity, but rejoiceth in the truth; Beareth all things, believeth all things, hopeth all things, endureth all things."

eager latter-day saints demonstrate by their ambition and impatience that they are unprepared for the Kingdom of God, and have not given adequate attention to the weightier matters.

Knowing the Mysteries

Despite the millions of Mormons, we live in a very small church. We cross paths with one another after years of living in different states or different parts of the world.

As a result of how small our community is, I have run into people after years of separation and often times been astonished by the difference in them. One of the increasingly frequent things I have noticed comes from a verse in Alma. Alma taught,

> "They that will harden their hearts, to them is given the lesser portion of the word until they know nothing concerning his mysteries; and then they are taken captive by the devil, and led by his will down to destruction." (Alma 12:11)

I have noticed that the vindication of this doctrine is unrelated to whether my friends have had administrative success in the church. Many of those who have lost understanding and who preach against "knowing the mysteries of God" do so because they have had local administrative positions.

Alma connects losing knowledge of God's mysteries directly to being "taken captive by the devil" and being "led by his will down to destruction." So when these friends preach to me against the mysteries and claim they have no desire to know about them, I am troubled in my heart.

The less we trust the teachings of the Book of Mormon, the more we draw distant from God.

General Conference

General Conference is now over. I listened with interest to the many talks and the few announcements. Here is what I noticed:

The word "revelation" was not used to describe the change to missionary age requirements during the conference.

Immediately following the Saturday morning session where President Monson made the announcement, there was a press conference. The press conference was conducted by Elder Holland and Elder Nelson. In the conference the words used, if my memory is correct, were "revelatory process."

The only other speaker that I recall mentioning the process was Elder Cook. The word he used was either "inspired" or "inspiration." Again, I am just going from memory.

As a result of the foregoing, the conclusion I find the most interesting is that Elder Nelson was willing to use the word "revelation" in meetings with stake presidents and mission presidents, but did not use that word in the press conference. It is interesting to me that a much stronger word would be used in private meetings.

CHURCHES
BUILT BY MEN

In our day Nephi foretells of churches that are not built to the Lord.[2565] These institutions will claim to be the Lord's though they are not.[2566]

After Nephi explains that the problem lies generally in the false teaching that men should rely on their own wisdom rather than on God,[2567] he makes this claim as the significant defect in latter-day churches:

"[B]ehold, there is no God today, for his work, and he hath given his power unto men." (2 Nephi 28:5)

The idea that the Redeemer no longer works directly with mankind is denounced. In its place we have men who pretend they have

---

[2565] 2 Nephi 28:3 "For it shall come to pass in that day that the churches which are built up, and not unto the Lord, when the one shall say unto the other: Behold, I, I am the Lord's; and the others shall say: I, I am the Lord's; and thus shall every one say that hath built up churches, and not unto the Lord—"

[2566] Ibid.

[2567] 2 Nephi 28:4 "And they shall contend one with another; and their priests shall contend one with another, and they shall teach with their learning, and deny the Holy Ghost, which giveth utterance."

authority to replace the Redeemer, and to become the new, vicarious light to which men should look for their salvation.

When men have God's power, and therefore can open or shut the doors of salvation for others, then men wielding this power command respect, power, wealth, political influence, and this world's goods. Men desiring to have salvation will give everything, even their own souls into slavery, to men who hold such power.

Nephi lists this problem as the first great lie taught by latter-day gentile churches because it is so very pernicious. It kills those who believe it. They move their love of God to a worship of men.

The Redeemer has never surrendered His role.[2568]

Only the deceived will believe the Redeemer of mankind has given His power unto men. But, based on Nephi's warnings, this false idea will control latter-day churches as one of the most successful deceptions.

Churches Built by Men, Part 2

Following hard on the idea that God has given His power to men is the necessary corollary precept that there are no longer miracles.[2569] Because the claim by men that they have been given

---

[2568] John 14:23 "Jesus answered and said unto him, If a man love me, he will keep my words: and my Father will love him, and we will come unto him, and make our abode with him."
D&C 130:3 "John 14:23 —The appearing of the Father and the Son, in that verse, is a personal appearance; and the idea that the Father and the Son dwell in a man's heart is an old sectarian notion, and is false.
2 Nephi 9:41 "O then, my beloved brethren, come unto the Lord, the Holy One. Remember that his paths are righteous. Behold, the way for man is narrow, but it lieth in a straight course before him, and the keeper of the gate is the Holy One of Israel; and he employeth no servant there; and there is none other way save it be by the gate; for he cannot be deceived, for the Lord God is his name."

[2569] 2 Nephi 28:6 "Behold, hearken ye unto my precept; if they shall say there is a miracle wrought by the hand of the Lord, believe it not; for this day he is not a God of miracles; he hath done his work."

God's power and authority *is* false, there can be no miracles. This requires the additional doctrine that miracles have ceased.

This false doctrine is also later addressed by Moroni. He bluntly informs us that "if these things have ceased [miracles, visits by angels, etc.], then has faith ceased also; and awful is the state of man, for they are as though there had been no redemption made" (Moroni 7:38). In our own day we are instructed by the Lord that "signs follow those that believe."[2570]

What then is the appeal of a religion that falsely claims to have God's power, but teaches there can't be any miracles because those have all ended? Why would this appeal to man? Nephi answers that the doctrine includes the reassuring teaching that "it shall be well with us" and we can go ahead and "eat, drink and be merry" because we are highly favored.[2571] These false religions of our day make us feel good. They assure us we are saved. We are in the right way. We can enjoy life.

These powerful and persuasive doctrines are only the beginning. Nephi's warning continues into the rest of the latter-day religious landscape.

But these initial false doctrines are sobering enough. They are a caution to all mankind about protecting ourselves against false notions that creep in and can poison any believer. They are designed to draw men away from Christ, the One who can save.

I am so grateful for the candor in Nephi's prophecy. He cares about our souls. If he didn't, his message would not be so carefully crafted, and so brutally honest about the latter-day doctrines designed to capture and captivate us.

[2570] D&C 63:9 "But, behold, faith cometh not by signs, but signs follow those that believe."

[2571] 2 Nephi 28:7 "Yea, and there shall be many which shall say: Eat, drink, and be merry, for tomorrow we die; and it shall be well with us."

Churches Built by Men, Part 3

Nephi explains these latter-day false churches accomplish the opposite of Zion. In Zion everyone is to become "one." Zion is unified in purpose and in heart. In these false churches people become competitive with one another. This leads to dishonesty between them.

"[L]ie a little, take advantage of one because of his words, dig a pit for thy neighbor" is the operating standard of conduct.[2572] This is believed to be harmless.[2573] And if you die in this fractious and competitive condition, then all will be well with you. If God is offended by it all, then you will be chastised, but "at last we shall be saved in the kingdom of God."[2574] The idea of punishment and damnation is not to be taken seriously. It is as if everyone will enjoy a position of glory, no matter their conduct. Therefore, we should enjoy our lives and not take too seriously any need to change.

Conspicuously absent from these false teachings is any need to repent. Repentance is not even part of the latter-day religious agenda. But, then again, since everyone will fare well in God's judgment, there really is no need for it under this religious system.

According to Nephi, this is the widespread doctrine of the latter-days. But these teachings are "false and vain and foolish."[2575] Nephi notes that the only effect this gives to mankind is to make us "puffed

---

[2572] 2 Nephi 28:8 "And there shall also be many which shall say: Eat, drink, and be merry; nevertheless, fear God—he will justify in committing a little sin; yea, lie a little, take the advantage of one because of his words, dig a pit for thy neighbor; there is no harm in this; and do all these things, for tomorrow we die; and if it so be that we are guilty, God will beat us with a few stripes, and at last we shall be saved in the kingdom of God."

[2573] Ibid.

[2574] Ibid.

[2575] 2 Nephi 28:9 "Yea, and there shall be many which shall teach after this manner, false and vain and foolish doctrines, and shall be puffed up in their hearts, and shall seek deep to hide their counsels from the Lord; and their works shall be in the dark."

up in [our] hearts."[2576] The vanity of it all is intoxicating. We get to wallow in our pride. After all, we are saved and highly favored.

If we are honest with ourselves, this assessment of the latter-days seems uncomfortably accurate.

Churches Built by Men, Part 4

Nephi allows for no exception to the problems facing latter-day churches. He writes they have "all gone out of the way; they have become corrupted."[2577] This presents a dilemma for me. I believe the church I belong to was established by the Lord. I also believe:

- The Lord gave my church (The Church of Jesus Christ of Latter-day Saints) a commission to baptize.
- Also a commission to lay on hands for the Gift of the Holy Ghost.
- Also a commission to bless the sacrament.
- Also a commission to preach, teach, exhort, expound and spread the Gospel of Christ to all the world.

If what I believe is true (and I think it is), then how can Nephi's all inclusive condemnation of "all" the latter-day churches be reconciled with Nephi's criticism?

It seems to me that being "chosen" by the Lord has never, in any past dispensation among any past group of believers, had the effect of removing all errors from those who were "chosen." Nor has it prevented them from falling into error. No matter the relationship between people and God, they have always remained free to choose. For the most part, that freedom has resulted in drifting from the truth, and the need to be reminded and called back. Or, in other words, the need for repentance.

[2576] Ibid.

[2577] 2 Nephi 28:11 "Yea, they have all gone out of the way; they have become corrupted."

Nephi's message is his call to us to repent. It is his reminder of the errors which will or have crept into every church, including my own. Therefore, his message is as relevant to me, as a Latter-day Saint, as it is to any other person belonging to any other faith. Perhaps it is even more relevant to me because I actually believe in the Book of Mormon, whereas other faiths do not.

Look at Nephi's explanation for why all churches have become corrupted: (And I would add, being "corrupted" is not the same thing as being utterly corrupt.)[2578]

- There is too much "pride."
- There are "false teachers" who do not teach the truth.
- There are "false doctrines" which differ from what the Lord taught to save us.
- The churches are "lifted up" and "because of pride they are puffed up."

Now Nephi can warn us all because he was shown us in vision and wrote scripture to caution and guide us. But I, on the other hand, can only take his instruction and examine myself. Am I caught up in these problems? Do I search for the doctrine of Christ? Can I detect false teachings? Am I willing to be stripped of pride? In other words, do I take Nephi seriously enough to examine my own beliefs and conduct?

The teachings of Nephi are challenging. But they have the power to rescue us if we will let them.

Churches Built by Men, Part 5

Nephi equates "robbing the poor" with misuse of wealth. Given the obligation to care for the poor, and the ultimate responsibility to

---

[2578] 2 Nephi 28:12 "Because of pride, and because of false teachers, and false doctrine, their churches have become corrupted, and their churches are lifted up; because of pride they are puffed up."

have all things in common, misuse of wealth constitutes an abuse of the poor in Nephi's warning.

I've considered the responsibility to build and maintain temples, and how the construction of temples has always meant the finest workmanship and materials as an offering to the Lord. It is His house after all. Therefore, I do not think the warning of Nephi has anything to do with construction of temples.

Nephi says we will "rob the poor because of their fine sanctuaries."[2579] If this has nothing to do with the temples, then to what is Nephi referring?

I have wondered about the City Creek project. Considering the retail portion alone, the funds used to develop the project could have funded approximately 90 temples (assuming an average cost of $30 million per temple). If you consider the office, condominium and remainder of the project, there could have been 150 temples built. The condominiums at City Creek include many priced in excess of $1 million. I "shopped" for a condo there. I found I could not afford one which would meet my needs, and if I bought what I could afford it would not be adequate. The development does indeed contain fine sanctuaries, and does bring an upscale venue to downtown Salt Lake.

Nephi does not confine his warning to us just to sanctuaries. He continues to condemn us because we "rob the poor because of their fine clothing."[2580] Meaning that if we cover ourselves with unnecessary expenses, we leave nothing to give to provide the poor with clothing. Our wealth is of value when we clothe the naked and feed

---

[2579] 2 Nephi 28:13 "They rob the poor because of their fine sanctuaries; they rob the poor because of their fine clothing; and they persecute the meek and the poor in heart, because in their pride they are puffed up."

[2580] Ibid.

the hungry, but of no value when we consume it for our own pleasure.[2581]

Nephi also draws the same conclusion from our attitudes and demeanor. We "persecute the meek and the poor in heart, because in their pride they are puffed up."[2582] Our pride alone "persecutes" the meek. Instead of fellowshipping them in meekness, we "persecute" them by our arrogance.

This standard is designed to change society. It is designed to elevate us to another level in which we are closer to God. If we heeded Nephi's warnings, we would become more unified and more equal in earthly things. If we did that, there would be abundant manifestations of the Spirit, which are presently withheld.[2583]

I think Nephi understood the doctrine better than do we.

Churches Built by Men, Part 6

Nephi makes a distinction between the institutions or churches of our day, and individuals. As to the institutions he declares:

> "They wear stiff necks and high heads; yea, and because of pride, and wickedness, and abominations, and whoredoms, they have all gone astray . . . " (2 Nephi 28:14)

I think it is possible for an institution to be different from its members. I think it is possible for a "committee" to have a different

---

[2581] Jacob 2:19 "And after ye have obtained a hope in Christ ye shall obtain riches, if ye seek them; and ye will seek them for the intent to do good—to clothe the naked, and to feed the hungry, and to liberate the captive, and administer relief to the sick and the afflicted."

[2582] 2 Nephi 28:13 "They rob the poor because of their fine sanctuaries; they rob the poor because of their fine clothing; and they persecute the meek and the poor in heart, because in their pride they are puffed up."

[2583] D&C 70:14 "Nevertheless, in your temporal things you shall be equal, and this not grudgingly, otherwise the abundance of the manifestations of the Spirit shall be withheld."

mind, or intent, or constitution from the individuals who comprise the committee. In a graduate leadership course I teach in an MBA program, we examine the difference between individual behavior and group behavior. There are a lot of studies done on this topic. My view is that it is entirely possible for a group to make a decision that no single individual in the group would make on their own. It is the "group's" decision, and does not comprise the individual thinking or mind of any of those who contributed to the outcome. Compromises, insecurities, give and take, fatigue, and conflict avoidance result in a lot of group decisions being far from what any of the participants want.

So when the institutions are condemned, I do not think that means Nephi is damning all those involved in leading. Despite this, Nephi continues:

> "they have all gone astray save it be a few, who are the humble followers of Christ . . . " (2 Nephi 28:14)

This remark makes it clear that the institutions contain humble followers of Christ. In other words, even if *things* are off track, *people* can remain on track. The challenge is always individual. It is up to each of us to focus on and be faithful to Christ. He is the Redeemer, and it is Him alone to whom we must look for our salvation.

That having been said, Nephi adds, "nevertheless, they are led, that in many instances they do err because they are taught by the precepts of men." (2 Nephi 28:14). Even humble followers of Christ are "taught by the precepts of men" in our day. This causes them to "err" "in many instances." Meaning that our doctrine is poorly and inadequately taught.

So what is the cure? The Book of Mormon, of course.[2584] This is how the "humble followers of Christ" can take in pure doctrine, uncorrupted by "the precepts of men" and find their way back to repentance. It is a lifeline extended to us by prophets who wrote for our day. They wrote as solitary individuals, not as members of a committee. They held no institutional positions, office or connections pulling them in one direction or another. They wrote as the Spirit led them and as the Lord directed them. And they wrote for us.

Nephi was one of them. And he cared deeply about us to have provided this counsel and warning to us. I think it ought to be taken very seriously. Our eternity will be affected by how we apply his writings.

Churches Built by Men, Part 7

Nephi gives a list of destructive qualities. The list is qualified by what these traits do to men: It makes them prideful. They are "puffed up in the pride of their hearts."[2585] Therefore, as you read the list keep in mind this corrosive pride as part of Nephi's warning.

The list includes:

- the wise

- the learned

- the rich.

[2584] D&C 84:54–57 "And your minds in times past have been darkened because of unbelief, and because you have treated lightly the things you have received— Which vanity and unbelief have brought the whole church under condemnation. And this condemnation resteth upon the children of Zion, even all. And they shall remain under this condemnation until they repent and remember the new covenant, even the Book of Mormon and the former commandments which I have given them, not only to say, but to do according to that which I have written—"

[2585] 2 Nephi 28:15 "O the wise, and the learned, and the rich, that are puffed up in the pride of their hearts, and all those who preach false doctrines, and all those who commit whoredoms, and pervert the right way of the Lord, wo, wo, wo be unto them, saith the Lord God Almighty, for they shall be thrust down to hell!"

It is possible to be all of these, and not be prideful. But if that is the case, then the wisdom, learning and riches of such an individual are used to elevate and serve others. They become advantages in helping the poor, the hungry, the naked and the infirm. In such cases the wisdom, learning and wealth do not become something that defines the individual. Instead, they become the tools of empathy and compassion.

In addition to the proud, Nephi adds another category, "all those who preach false doctrines."[2586] When it comes to corrupting the doctrine, pride is irrelevant. A person can be sincere, honest and devout, but if they preach false doctrine, Nephi condemns them. There is simply no excuse to justify preaching what is untrue or incomplete. Those doctrines will lead others to hell. Therefore, they are false ministers in the service of darkness.

There is a phrase that follows hard on preaching false doctrines. It is "all those who commit whoredoms."[2587] If read together, the result is this: "all those who preach false doctrines, and all those who commit whoredoms." This may be a single thought, or a single description. Because to leave the Lord and follow after another false source for salvation—a false god—is often described as "committing whoredoms." If this is Nephi's intent, then the preacher of false doctrine is condemned because they are leading others away from God.

Nephi is clear about the fate of the preachers who preach false or incomplete doctrine and lead others away from God, "wo, wo, wo be unto them." A three-fold condemnation. They could not be saved because of their false teaching. This condemnation is not Nephi's. He attributes it directly to God: "wo, wo, wo be unto them, saith the

---

[2586] Ibid.

[2587] Ibid.

Lord God Almighty."[2588] This three-part name of God mirrors the three-fold condemnation, and it is the Lord who is speaking.

"For they shall be thrust down to hell!" (2 Nephi 28:14)

Be careful what you preach. If you do not fully understand the Gospel of Christ, then you take a fearful responsibility upon yourself when you pretend to tell the truth.[2589]

Churches Built by Men, Conclusion

Nephi has a great deal more to say. You should look at the balance of what he foretells of our day.

Nephi pronounces "Wo" upon those in our day who "turn aside the just for a thing of naught, and say it is of no worth."[2590] What does this mean?

- Who are "the just" about whom he writes?
- What does it mean to be "justified" before God?
- Does this status come with an office?
- Is being justified before God a position to be called to in an organization?
- Does God determine who is "just" before Him?
- How would you know if someone is "just" or not?

[2588] Ibid.

[2589] D&C 11:21–22 "Seek not to declare my word, but first seek to obtain my word, and then shall your tongue be loosed; then, if you desire, you shall have my Spirit and my word, yea, the power of God unto the convincing of men. But now hold your peace; study my word which hath gone forth among the children of men, and also study my word which shall come forth among the children of men, or that which is now translating, yea, until you have obtained all which I shall grant unto the children of men in this generation, and then shall all things be added thereto."

[2590] 2 Nephi 28:16 "Wo unto them that turn aside the just for a thing of naught and revile against that which is good, and say that it is of no worth! For the day shall come that the Lord God will speedily visit the inhabitants of the earth; and in that day that they are fully ripe in iniquity they shall perish."

- If someone is "just" and you discard them, are you treating them as "a thing of naught?"
- What does it mean to treat the just as "naught?"
- Why is it wrong to say the "just" are "of no worth?"

-How would you change that and treat the just as having worth?

What Nephi says will ultimately provoke the Lord's wrath.

"For the day shall come that the Lord God will speedily visit the inhabitants of the earth; and in that day that they are fully ripe in iniquity they shall perish." (2 Nephi 28:16)

What is this referring to?

- What is the relationship between treating the "just" as "a thing of naught" and the Lord's wrath?
- What is the relationship between treating the "just" as having "no worth" and becoming "ripe in iniquity?"
- Why are these associated in Nephi's prophecy?
- Can I trust an organization to sort out the "just", identify and uphold them?
- Can I ignore the Spirit when it comes to these issues?
- How can you become "fully ripe" in iniquity as a result of how you react to the "just?"

Nephi does write some very provocative prophecies about us, but they don't seem to provoke us into thought or repentance. We seem content to eat, drink and be merry, trusting that the Lord will merely inflict a few stripes on us if we err; because after all, there is no hell.[2591] We have little interest in recognizing "the just" much less

---

[2591] 2 Nephi 28:8 "And there shall also be many which shall say: Eat, drink, and be merry; nevertheless, fear God—he will justify in committing a little sin; yea, lie a little, take the advantage of one because of his words, dig a pit for thy neighbor; there is no harm in this; and do all these things, for tomorrow we die; and if it so be that we are guilty, God will beat us with a few stripes, and at last we shall be saved in the kingdom of God."

becoming justified before God. And being sanctified before Him is not discussed or understood any longer.

Nephi is among the most important voices for our day.

SCRIPTURES

"[F]or ye are the temple of the living God; as God hath said, I will dwell in them, and walk in them, and I will be their God, and they shall be my people." (2 Corinthians 6:16)

"I am Jesus Christ, the Son of God; wherefore, gird up your loins and I will suddenly come to my temple." (D&C 36:8)[2592]

"Verily, thus saith the Lord: It shall come to pass that every soul who forsaketh his sins and cometh unto me, and calleth on my name, and obeyeth my voice, and keepeth my commandments, shall see my face and know that I am." (D&C 93:1)

Scriptures, Part 2

"[T]hey are only to be seen and understood by the power of the Holy Spirit, which God bestows on those who love him,

---

[2592] D&C 133:2–3 "The Lord who shall suddenly come to his temple; the Lord who shall come down upon the world with a curse to judgment; yea, upon all the nations that forget God, and upon all the ungodly among you. For he shall make bare his holy arm in the eyes of all the nations, and all the ends of the earth shall see the salvation of their God."
3 Nephi 24:1 "And it came to pass that he commanded them that they should write the words which the Father had given unto Malachi, which he should tell unto them. And it came to pass that after they were written he expounded them. And these are the words which he did tell unto them, saying: Thus said the Father unto Malachi—Behold, I will send my messenger, and he shall prepare the way before me, and the Lord whom ye seek shall suddenly come to his temple, even the messenger of the covenant, whom ye delight in; behold, he shall come, saith the Lord of Hosts."

and purify themselves before him; To whom he grants this privilege of seeing and knowing for themselves; That through the power and manifestation of the Spirit, while in the flesh, they may be able to bear his presence in the world of glory." (D&C 76:116–117)

"And it shall come to pass, that if the Gentiles shall hearken unto the Lamb of God in that day that he shall manifest himself unto them in word, and also in power, in very deed, unto the taking away of their stumbling blocks." (1 Nephi 14:1)

Scriptures, Part 3

"I will not leave you comfortless: I will come to you." (John 14:18)

"If a man love me, he will keep my words: and my Father will love him, and we will come unto him, and make our abode with him." (John 14:23)

"John 14:23—The appearing of the Father and Son, in that verse, is a personal appearance; and the idea that the Father and Son dwell in a man's heart is an old sectarian notion, and is false." (D&C 130:3)

Scriptures, Part 4

"I would that ye should be steadfast and immovable, always abounding in good works, that Christ, the Lord God Omnipotent, may seal you his, that you may be brought to heaven, that ye may have everlasting salvation and eternal life[.]" (Mosiah 5:15)

"Behold, I am the Lord God Almighty, and Endless is my name; for I am without beginning of days or end of years; and is not this endless? And, behold, thou art my son; wherefore look and I will show thee the workmanship of mine hands[.]" (Moses 1:3–4)

"And this is life eternal, that they might know thee the only true God, and Jesus Christ, whom thou has sent." (John 17:3)

"[T]he Lord showed himself unto him, and said: Because thou knowest these things ye are redeemed from the fall; therefore ye are brought back into my presence; therefore I show myself unto you." (Ether 3:13)

Parable

I saw a great mountain, and upon the top thereof was the glory of the fathers. To reach the top, all were required to enter through a narrow pass. In the pass was a great beast, cruel and pitiless.

The Lord brought people whom he had chosen to the mouth of the pass, and there He told them to wait for him, and He went away. The people did not wait for Him, but began to move forward into the narrow pass. The beast killed some and injured others, and none were able to pass through.

After great losses, many deaths, and terrible suffering, the people chosen by the Lord withdrew and departed from the mountain. After four and five generations, the Lord again brought some few back to the pass and again told them to stay at the mouth of the pass and wait on Him. But again there were those who tired of waiting, for they could see in the distance the glory of the fathers, and they desired to be there. These, being overtaken by their zeal, did not wait, but moved into the pass where again the beast killed or hurt them.

Among those who waited, however, was a man who knelt and prayed, and waited patiently for his Lord. After a great time, the Lord came to this man and took him by the hand, and led him into the pass where the great beast guarded the way. As the Lord led, however, the beast was ever occupied with attacking others, and therefore its back was turned to the Lord and the man. And so they passed by unnoticed, safely to the top. The Lord sent the man to the fathers, who when they saw the man, inquired of him, "How came you to be here and yet mortal; the last who came here were brothers who had been slain, and you are yet alive?" And the man answered: "I waited on the Lord and He brought me here safely."

D&C 90:2

I received an email asking about the meaning of D&C 90:2. Here's my response:

This verse, like most scripture, is deliberately unclear. This is why the first topic in the fireside was the Holy Ghost and its relationship to both gifts of the spirit and understanding the "mysteries" of God.[2593] The Holy Ghost inspired the text (conveying the words of Christ directly to Joseph; see D&C 90:1).[2594] Therefore, having the Holy Ghost is required to understand the meaning of the text.[2595]

The verse says:

"Therefore, thou art blessed from henceforth that bear the keys of the kingdom given unto you; which kingdom is coming forth for the last time." (D&C 90:2)

Ask yourself these questions:

- Who is "thou"? Is it Joseph Smith or some collective group or successors?

[2593] JS–H 1:74 "Our minds being now enlightened, we began to have the scriptures laid open to our understandings, and the true meaning and intention of their more mysterious passages revealed unto us in a manner which we never could attain to previously, nor ever before had thought of. In the meantime we were forced to keep secret the circumstances of having received the Priesthood and our having been baptized, owing to a spirit of persecution which had already manifested itself in the neighborhood."

[2594] D&C 90:1 "THUS saith the Lord, verily, verily I say unto you my son, thy sins are forgiven thee, according to thy petition, for thy prayers and the prayers of thy brethren have come up into my ears."

[2595] 2 Peter 1:20–21 "Knowing this first, that no prophecy of the scripture is of any private interpretation. For the prophecy came not in old time by the will of man: but holy men of God spake *as they were* moved by the Holy Ghost."

- Who "bears the keys of the kingdom" in the verse? In 1833, was that Joseph Smith? Or was it some group? Was it his successors?

- Who had the "keys of the kingdom given unto [them]"? In 1833, was that Joseph Smith, or was it someone else? Did it include a group? Successors, too?

- What does "for the last time" mean? Does it mean it will never, ever happen again? Or does it mean the "latest" or "most current"?

There are a few verses after this one that will help with some of these questions. For example, verse 3 seems to identify Joseph Smith: "Verily I say unto you, the keys of this kingdom shall never be taken from you, while thou art in the world, neither in the world to come[.]" (D&C 90:3). This seems to be singular. It is addressed to Joseph. But you must decide if it is him, or if it means anyone in the church leadership, then and now. The Holy Ghost should assist you in reaching the right conclusion.

It adds in verse 4: "Nevertheless, through you shall the oracles be given to another, yea, even unto the church." (D&C 90:4). This seems to make it clear that the "you" and the "thou" referred to earlier was Joseph Smith. But it then raises other questions:

- What are "the oracles"? Are these the revelations (i.e., sections of the D&C, parts of the Pearl of Great Price, etc.)?

- Are "the oracles" a power or gift of the Spirit?

- If some power or gift, when? To whom? Was it fulfilled in Hyrum?[2596]

[2596] D&C 124:123–124 "Verily I say unto you, I now give unto you the officers belonging to my Priesthood, that ye may hold the keys thereof, even the Priesthood which is after the order of Melchizedek, which is after the order of mine Only Begotten Son. First, I give unto you Hyrum Smith to be a patriarch unto you, to hold the sealing blessings of my church, even the Holy Spirit of promise, whereby ye are sealed up unto the day of redemption, that ye may not fall notwithstanding the hour of temptation that may come upon you."

- Was it fulfilled in the Council of Fifty when Joseph gave "the keys of the kingdom" to them, establishing the right to create a kingdom to overtake all other governments and grind all competing governments on the earth to dust in fulfillment of Daniel 2:36–44?[2597]

On the question of "the last time," verse 5 helps with the meaning:

"And all they who receive the oracles of God, let them beware how they hold them least they are accounted as a light thing, and are brought under condemnation thereby, and stumble and fall when the storms descend, and the winds blow, and the rains descend, and beat upon their house." (D&C 90:5)

If we can "stumble and fall," it suggests we can lose what we were given. If we can lose it, then it can be returned. That would mean "last time" in verse 2 is referring to the "latest," much like D&C 76:22, where "last of all" means the "most current" or the "latest" testimony.[2598] It doesn't mean that there will never be another person with a testimony of Christ.

[2597] Daniel 2:36–44 "This *is* the dream; and we will tell the interpretation thereof before the king. Thou, O king, *art* a king of kings: for the God of heaven hath given thee a kingdom, power, and strength, and glory. And wheresoever the children of men dwell, the beasts of the field and the fowls of the heaven hath he given into thine hand, and hath made thee ruler over them all. Thou *art* this head of gold. And after thee shall arise another kingdom inferior to thee, and another third kingdom of brass, which shall bear rule over all the earth. And the fourth kingdom shall be strong as iron: forasmuch as iron breaketh in pieces and subdueth all *things*: and as iron that breaketh all these, shall it break in pieces and bruise. And whereas thou sawest the feet and toes, part of potters' clay, and part of iron, the kingdom shall be divided; but there shall be in it of the strength of the iron, forasmuch as thou sawest the iron mixed with miry clay. And *as* the toes of the feet *were* part of iron, and part of clay, *so* the kingdom shall be partly strong, and partly broken. And whereas thou sawest iron mixed with miry clay, they shall mingle themselves with the seed of men: but they shall not cleave one to another, even as iron is not mixed with clay. And in the days of these kings shall the God of heaven set up a kingdom, which shall never be destroyed: and the kingdom shall not be left to other people, *but* it shall break in pieces and consume all these kingdoms, and it shall stand for ever."

[2598] D&C 76:22 "And now, after the many testimonies which have been given of him, this is the testimony, last of all, which we give of him: That he lives!"

The verse also makes it clear that everyone (including Joseph and his peers/successors) can "stumble and fall" if they treat the "oracles" lightly. To "stumble" is one thing. But to "fall" suggests departing from the way and losing what was given. This returns us to "the oracles" and the meaning of that term:

- Are they the revelations/Book of Mormon?[2599]
- Is it some ordination or gift?
- If a gift or power, and if it is possible to "fall" from it, then what does that imply?

You decide by the Holy Ghost what verse 2 means. I believe it means that Joseph Smith was blessed and he held keys which would never be taken from him, even if he died. That his possession of those keys allowed him to be regarded as a member of God's kingdom. He was the latest person, or only one living in 1833 to be regarded as a full member of that kingdom. But you should prayerfully decide what it means for yourself.

Accountability

All of us are accountable before God for our own sins.[2600] No one can escape responsibility based on their willful ignorance. If you have the scriptures, you know you cannot be saved in ignorance.[2601] You also have been warned that the scriptures have information

---

[2599] D&C 84:54–57 "And your minds in times past have been darkened because of unbelief, and because you have treated lightly the things you have received— Which vanity and unbelief have brought the whole church under condemnation. And this condemnation resteth upon the children of Zion, even all. And they shall remain under this condemnation until they repent and remember the new covenant, even the Book of Mormon and the former commandments which I have given them, not only to say, but to do according to that which I have written—"

[2600] D&C 101:78 "That every man may act in doctrine and principle pertaining to futurity, according to the moral agency which I have given unto him, that every man may be accountable for his own sins in the day of judgment."

[2601] D&C 131:6 "It is impossible for a man to be saved in ignorance."

which is able to teach you about salvation.[2602] You also have the Lord's warning to search into the scriptures if you expect eternal life.[2603] When this is before you, it is impossible to sin ignorantly, even if you are ignorant as a result of your own neglect.[2604]

[2602] 2 Timothy 3:15 "And that from a child thou hast known the holy scriptures, which are able to make thee wise unto salvation through faith which is in Christ Jesus."

[2603] John 5:39 "Search the scriptures; for in them ye think ye have eternal life: and they are they which testify of me."

[2604] 3 Nephi 6:18 "Now they did not sin ignorantly, for they knew the will of God concerning them, for it had been taught unto them; therefore they did wilfully rebel against God."

144,000

The number 144,000 appears in scriptures in a number of places.[2605] The number is associated with the last days and Christ's return. Although there are a number of myths associated with the number, the scriptures tell a specific account of these last-days people.

The number is highly symbolic. The account in Revelation makes it clear the number is associated with redeeming the Twelve Tribes of

---

[2605] D&C 133:18 "When the Lamb shall stand upon Mount Zion, and with him a hundred and forty-four thousand, having his Father's name written on their foreheads."

D&C 77:11 "Q. What are we to understand by sealing the one hundred and forty-four thousand, out of all the tribes of Israel—twelve thousand out of every tribe?
A. We are to understand that those who are sealed are high priests, ordained unto the holy order of God, to administer the everlasting gospel; for they are they who are ordained out of every nation, kindred, tongue, and people, by the angels to whom is given power over the nations of the earth, to bring as many as will come to the church of the Firstborn."

Revelation 7:4–8 "And I heard the number of them which were sealed: *and there were* sealed an hundred *and* forty *and* four thousand of all the tribes of the children of Israel. Of the tribe of Juda *were* sealed twelve thousand. Of the tribe of Reuben *were* sealed twelve thousand. Of the tribe of Gad *were* sealed twelve thousand. Of the tribe of Aser *were* sealed twelve thousand. Of the tribe of Nepthalim *were* sealed twelve thousand. Of the tribe of Manasses *were* sealed twelve thousand. Of the tribe of Simeon *were* sealed twelve thousand. Of the tribe of Levi *were* sealed twelve thousand. Of the tribe of Issachar *were* sealed twelve thousand. Of the tribe of Zabulon *were* sealed twelve thousand. Of the tribe of Joseph *were* sealed twelve thousand. Of the tribe of Benjamin *were* sealed twelve thousand."

Revelation 14:3 "And they sung as it were a new song before the throne, and before the four beasts, and the elders: and no man could learn that song but the hundred *and* forty *and* four thousand, which were redeemed from the earth."

Israel from their scattered condition. When the tribes were located in their original lands in Biblical times, they intermarried. For example, the Ten Tribes of the north had been removed by Assyria 125 years before the Book of Mormon account begins. The Southern Kingdom, or Kingdom of the Jews, was where the opening of the Book of Mormon is set. The descendants of Joseph (Ephram and Manasseh) were among the Northern Kingdom. Lehi's family were descended from Manasseh.[2606] Today, it is unlikely any individual descended from Israel is a pure descendant.

Therefore, when Revelation 7:5–8 attributes "twelve thousand" from each of Judah, Reuben, Gad, "Aser," Nepthalim, "Manasses," Simeon, Levi, Issachar, Zebulon, Joseph and Benjamin, once again the number is symbolic.[2607] The symmetry of the division between each tribe symbolizes the Lord's intention to treat all Israel alike because He is no respecter of persons.[2608]

So if the Lord intends to show respect to all the Tribes of Israel, then the language of Revelation 7:5–8 demonstrates by numerical symmetry this intent. Does it mean that literally there will be "twelve thousand" from each tribe? Does it mean of those gathered the bloodlines of each tribe will be preserved? If it means the latter, then

---

[2606] Alma 10:3 "And Aminadi was a descendant of Nephi, who was the son of Lehi, who came out of the land of Jerusalem, who was a descendant of Manasseh, who was the son of Joseph who was sold into Egypt by the hands of his brethren."

[2607] Revelation 7:5–8 "Of the tribe of Juda *were* sealed twelve thousand. Of the tribe of Reuben *were* sealed twelve thousand. Of the tribe of Gad *were* sealed twelve thousand. Of the tribe of Aser *were* sealed twelve thousand. Of the tribe of Nepthalim *were* sealed twelve thousand. Of the tribe of Manasses *were* sealed twelve thousand. Of the tribe of Simeon *were* sealed twelve thousand. Of the tribe of Levi *were* sealed twelve thousand. Of the tribe of Issachar *were* sealed twelve thousand. Of the tribe of Zabulon *were* sealed twelve thousand. Of the tribe of Joseph *were* sealed twelve thousand. Of the tribe of Benjamin *were* sealed twelve thousand."

[2608] D&C 38:26 "For what man among you having twelve sons, and is no respecter of them, and they serve him obediently, and he saith unto the one: Be thou clothed in robes and sit thou here; and to the other: Be thou clothed in rags and sit thou there—and looketh upon his sons and saith I am just?"

can one person have mixed blood within them from more than one tribe? Can one person have the blood of all the tribes within them?

In D&C 77:11, the 144,000 are explained in modern revelation.[2609] They are described as follows: "We are to understand that those who are sealed are high priests, ordained unto the holy order of God, to administer the everlasting gospel; for they are they who are ordained out of every nation, kindred, tongue, and people, by the angels to whom is given power over the nations of the earth, to bring as many as will come to the church of the Firstborn."

To understand the description it is useful to know what is meant by:

  - *"those sealed are high priests"*

Is this the office in the church?

If not, then are they going to be among the church's priesthood?

  - *"ordained unto the holy order of God"*

Is this the system in the church?

Will they hold "certificates of ordination" from a stake clerk?

Could it refer to the ordination described in JST Genesis 14?[2610]

  - *"ordained out of every nation, kindred, tongue, and people"*

Is this literal?

Does every "nation" mean the nations of the earth, or the Tribes of Israel?

[2609] D&C 77:11 "Q. What are we to understand by sealing the one hundred and forty-four thousand, out of all the tribes of Israel—twelve thousand out of every tribe? A. We are to understand that those who are sealed are high priests, ordained unto the holy order of God, to administer the everlasting gospel; for they are they who are ordained out of every nation, kindred, tongue, and people, by the angels to whom is given power over the nations of the earth, to bring as many as will come to the church of the Firstborn."

[2610] JST Genesis 14:28–30 "It being after the order of the Son of God; which order came, not by man, nor the will of man; neither by father nor mother; neither by beginning of days nor end of years; but of God; And it was delivered unto men by the calling of his own voice, according to his own will, unto as many as believed on his name. For God having sworn unto Enoch and unto his seed with an oath by himself; that every one being ordained after this order and calling should have power, by faith, to break mountains, to divide the seas, to dry up waters, to turn them out of their course;"

Does "kindred" refer to all peoples, or those who descend from Israel's scattered bloodlines?

- *"by the angels to whom is given power"*

Does this refer to "ordination?"

Do angels have to ordain these chosen ones?

If the angels are to ordain them, will they be known or recognized by the church?

- *"given power"*

Are these the angels who ordain?

Are these the "high priests" who are ordained?

What power is given?

It is interesting the 144,000 are connected to "power" and to "angels" in this description. What do these things have to do with the end times? Why would there need to be high priests, angels and power connected to these last days events?

Is 144,000 an actual total number? Is it representative? Can one person preserve within them the bloodlines of more than one tribe? Can they also preserve the bloodlines of more than one family within the tribes? Can a much smaller group represent 144,000 family lines and fulfill the Lord's intent to keep all "twelve sons" equally represented[2611] in the stock of families who begin the family of Israel again at the start of the Millennium. They, like Noah's small group, will restart the human family.[2612]

How many are really needed to fulfill the Lord's prophecies concerning the 144,000? What does the number really mean?

[2611] D&C 38:26 "For what man among you having twelve sons, and is no respecter of them, and they serve him obediently, and he saith unto the one: Be thou clothed in robes and sit thou here; and to the other: Be thou clothed in rags and sit thou there—and looketh upon his sons and saith I am just?"

[2612] Luke 17:26 "And as it was in the days of Noe, so shall it be also in the days of the Son of man."
Matthew 24:37 "But as the days of Noe *were,* so shall also the coming of the Son of man be."

144,000, Part 2

The 144,000 are "sealed" by the "four angels" in Revelation 7:1–3.[2613] They are "sealed" by "angels to whom is given power over the nations of the earth" in D&C 77:11.[2614]

In Revelation, they are sealed before "the earth, . . . the sea, . . . the trees" are "hurt" in the last days.[2615] This timing necessarily requires the "sealing" to precede great distresses which to us are still future.

- What does it mean to have an "angel to whom is given power" come and "seal the servants of our God in their foreheads?"
- Are men, or institutions, in control of this process?
- How would you expect this to happen?
- Does the "sealing" imply some kind of ordination?
- Is this connected in any way to the "oath and covenant of the priesthood?"

[2613] Revelation 7:1–3 "And after these things I saw four angels standing on the four corners of the earth, holding the four winds of the earth, that the wind should not blow on the earth, nor on the sea, nor on any tree. And I saw another angel ascending from the east, having the seal of the living God: and he cried with a loud voice to the four angels, to whom it was given to hurt the earth and the sea, Saying, Hurt not the earth, neither the sea, nor the trees, till we have sealed the servants of our God in their foreheads."

[2614] D&C 77:11 "Q. What are we to understand by sealing the one hundred and forty-four thousand, out of all the tribes of Israel—twelve thousand out of every tribe? A. We are to understand that those who are sealed are high priests, ordained unto the holy order of God, to administer the everlasting gospel; for they are they who are ordained out of every nation, kindred, tongue, and people, by the angels to whom is given power over the nations of the earth, to bring as many as will come to the church of the Firstborn."

[2615] Revelation 7:3 " Saying, Hurt not the earth, neither the sea, nor the trees, till we have sealed the servants of our God in their foreheads."

On that last question, D&C 84:33–42[2616] is often read, explained, and taught. But a context is imposed on the words that presumes a certain meaning. What if that context is incomplete, or merely a tradition, and not what the words were meant to convey? Here are the verses with another possible context inserted into them in italics and brackets as they proceed:

For whoso is faithful unto the obtaining these two priesthoods of which I have spoken, and the magnifying their calling [*notice "calling" is singular*], are sanctified by the Spirit unto the renewing of their bodies [*here? now? in the resurrection?*]. They become the sons of Moses and of Aaron [*who are "sons of Levi" and associated with the Aaronic or first priesthood*] and the seed of Abraham [who is the father of the righteous, and one of the "fathers in heaven" to whom we must connect or be "utterly wasted" at the Lord's return; and is associated with the second priesthood], and the church and kingdom, and the elect of God [*this body of chosen individuals are a "church" and that church is confined to the "elect"*]. And also all they who receive this priesthood receive me, saith the Lord [*in other words, the Lord makes Himself known to them, for that is how He is "received"*]; For he that receiveth my servants [*who are His "servants?*] receiveth me; And he that receiveth me receiveth my Father [*is this what Mosiah 5:15 is referring to when it says Christ will 'bring you to heaven, that you may have eternal life?*]; And he that receiveth my

---

[2616] D&C 84:33–42 "For whoso is faithful unto the obtaining these two priesthoods of which I have spoken, and the magnifying their calling, are sanctified by the Spirit unto the renewing of their bodies. They become the sons of Moses and of Aaron and the seed of Abraham, and the church and kingdom, and the elect of God. And also all they who receive this priesthood receive me, saith the Lord; For he that receiveth my servants receiveth me; And he that receiveth me receiveth my Father; And he that receiveth my Father receiveth my Father's kingdom; therefore all that my Father hath shall be given unto him. And this is according to the oath and covenant which belongeth to the priesthood. Therefore, all those who receive the priesthood, receive this oath and covenant of my Father, which he cannot break, neither can it be moved. But whoso breaketh this covenant after he hath received it, and altogether turneth therefrom, shall not have forgiveness of sins in this world nor in the world to come. And wo unto all those who come not unto this priesthood which ye have received, which I now confirm upon you who are present this day, by mine own voice out of the heavens; and even I have given the heavenly hosts and mine angels charge concerning you."

Father receiveth my Father's kingdom; therefore all that my Father hath shall be given unto him [*in other words, the promise of exaltation and eternal life. Therefore, obtaining these two ordinations is directly connected with the "servants" and then the ministry of the Son, and the introduction to the Father*]. And this is according to the oath and covenant which belongeth to the priesthood. Therefore, all those who receive the priesthood, receive this oath and covenant of my Father [*in other words, they have knowledge from the Father that they are His, will inherit from Him all He has, and learned this as a result of the Son's ministry with them*], which he cannot break, neither can it be moved. But whoso breaketh this covenant after he hath received it, and altogether turneth therefrom, shall not have forgiveness of sins in this world nor in the world to come [*because they have knowledge obtained from the Son, and a covenant obtained from the Father, and if they turn away they must rebel against the Godhead, whom they have come to know. They become 'sons of Perdition' because this is willful and known rebellion*]. And wo unto all those who come not unto this priesthood [*because if you do not receive this, you do not receive the fullness of the Gospel, and you do not have knowledge that will save you*] which ye have received, which I now confirm upon you who are present this day, by mine own voice out of the heavens [*because the higher priesthood is only given by the "voice of God" as described in JST Genesis 14:29: "And it was delivered unto men by the calling of his own voice".[2617] This is why the "ordination" is confirmed by God's voice here*]; and even I have given the heavenly hosts and mine angels charge concerning you [*which is how the "sealing" of the 144,000 will be connected to the "angels" who have "authority" in the verses which describe these events*].

[2617] See also JST Genesis 14:26–29 "Now Melchizedek was a man of faith, who wrought righteousness; and when a child he feared God, and stopped the mouths of lions, and quenched the violence of fire. And thus, having been approved of God, he was ordained an high priest after the order of the covenant which God made with Enoch, It being after the order of the Son of God; which order came, not by man, nor the will of man; neither by father nor mother; neither by beginning of days nor end of years; but of God; And it was delivered unto men by the calling of his own voice, according to his own will, unto as many as believed on his name."

I have inserted a possible new context into the words for you to consider. I would remind you, however, that scripture is not something for "private interpretation," but can only be unlocked through the Holy Ghost.[2618] The meaning belongs to and is controlled by God.

144,000, Part 3

One final passage of scripture seems connected to this process. A question was posed by Elias Higbee. Joseph took this question to the Lord. The question and answer is in D&C 113:7–8:

> "Questions by Elias Higbee: What is meant by the command in Isaiah, 52d chapter, 1st verse, which saith: Put on thy strength, O Zion—and what people had Isaiah reference to? He had reference to those whom God should call in the last days, who should hold the power of priesthood to bring again Zion, and the redemption of Israel; and to put on her strength is to put on the authority of the priesthood, which she, Zion, has a right to by lineage; also to return to that power which she had lost."

Although the number 144,000 is not mentioned here, this is also clearly a last-days event. The individuals involved are those who "God should call in the last days." The verses describing the 144,000

[2618] 2 Peter 1:20 "Knowing this first, that no prophecy of the scripture is of any private interpretation."

JS–H 1:74 "Our minds being now enlightened, we began to have the scriptures laid open to our understandings, and the true meaning and intention of their more mysterious passages revealed unto us in a manner which we never could attain to previously, nor ever before had thought of. In the meantime we were forced to keep secret the circumstances of having received the Priesthood and our having been baptized, owing to a spirit of persecution which had already manifested itself in the neighborhood."

make it clear they will be called of God, and will receive sealing from the angels.[2619]

The "power" of the angels "over the nations of the earth" is needed to prevent Zion from being overrun or destroyed by the nations of the earth. These other nations, if they oppose Zion, will be

---

[2619] Revelation 7:3 "Saying, Hurt not the earth, neither the sea, nor the trees, till we have sealed the servants of our God in their foreheads."

D&C 77:11 "Q. What are we to understand by sealing the one hundred and forty-four thousand, out of all the tribes of Israel—twelve thousand out of every tribe?

A. We are to understand that those who are sealed are high priests, ordained unto the holy order of God, to administer the everlasting gospel; for they are they who are ordained out of every nation, kindred, tongue, and people, by the angels to whom is given power over the nations of the earth, to bring as many as will come to the church of the Firstborn."

D&C 84:42 "And wo unto all those who come not unto this priesthood which ye have received, which I now confirm upon you who are present this day, by mine own voice out of the heavens; and even I have given the heavenly hosts and mine angels charge concerning you."

destroyed.[2620] The "powers of heaven" which will hover over Zion will discourage any army from battling her.[2621]

I put the term "powers of heaven" in quotes because this refers to the hosts of heaven. This is why the term "powers" and not "power" is used in D&C 121:36.[2622] Priesthood is always a relationship between man on earth and the "powers" or hosts of heaven.

[2620] Daniel 2:31–45 "Thou, O king, sawest, and behold a great image. This great image, whose brightness *was* excellent, stood before thee; and the form thereof *was* terrible. This image's head *was* of fine gold, his breast and his arms of silver, his belly and his thighs of brass, His legs of iron, his feet part of iron and part of clay. Thou sawest till that a stone was cut out without hands, which smote the image upon his feet *that were* of iron and clay, and brake them to pieces. Then was the iron, the clay, the brass, the silver, and the gold, broken to pieces together, and became like the chaff of the summer threshing floors; and the wind carried them away, that no place was found for them: and the stone that smote the image became a great mountain, and filled the whole earth. This *is* the dream; and we will tell the interpretation thereof before the king. Thou, O king, *art* a king of kings: for the God of heaven hath given thee a kingdom, power, and strength, and glory. And wheresoever the children of men dwell, the beasts of the field and the fowls of the heaven hath he given into thine hand, and hath made thee ruler over them all. Thou *art* this head of gold. And after thee shall arise another kingdom inferior to thee, and another third kingdom of brass, which shall bear rule over all the earth. And the fourth kingdom shall be strong as iron: forasmuch as iron breaketh in pieces and subdueth all *things:* and as iron that breaketh all these, shall it break in pieces and bruise. And whereas thou sawest the feet and toes, part of potters' clay, and part of iron, the kingdom shall be divided; but there shall be in it of the strength of the iron, forasmuch as thou sawest the iron mixed with miry clay. And *as* the toes of the feet *were* part of iron, and part of clay, *so* the kingdom shall be partly strong, and partly broken. And whereas thou sawest iron mixed with miry clay, they shall mingle themselves with the seed of men: but they shall not cleave one to another, even as iron is not mixed with clay. And in the days of these kings shall the God of heaven set up a kingdom, which shall never be destroyed: and the kingdom shall not be left to other people, *but* it shall break in pieces and consume all these kingdoms, and it shall stand for ever. Forasmuch as thou sawest that the stone was cut out of the mountain without hands, and that it brake in pieces the iron, the brass, the clay, the silver, and the gold; the great God hath made known to the king what shall come to pass hereafter: and the dream *is* certain, and the interpretation thereof sure."
D&C 87:6 "And thus, with the sword and by bloodshed the inhabitants of the earth shall mourn; and with famine, and plague, and earthquake, and the thunder of heaven, and the fierce and vivid lightning also, shall the inhabitants of the earth be made to feel the wrath, and indignation, and chastening hand of an Almighty God, until the consumption decreed hath made a full end of all nations;"

[2621] D&C 45:70 "And it shall be said among the wicked: Let us not go up to battle against Zion, for the inhabitants of Zion are terrible; wherefore we cannot stand."

[2622] D&C 121:36 "That the rights of the priesthood are inseparably connected with the powers of heaven, and that the powers of heaven cannot be controlled nor handled only upon the principles of righteousness."

These angelic or heavenly beings were those who escorted men to the first heavenly Zion,[2623] and will do so again.

It will be the relationship between those who have been "sealed . . . of our God in their foreheads"[2624] and the heavenly powers or angels which grants "the power of the priesthood to bring again Zion."[2625]

Notice the return of Zion is connected also with "lineage" in the answer above. Or, in other words, the bloodlines of Israel are required to be found in those who will be gathered. This has always been true of Zion. In the first Zion, the gathering of individuals was carefully assembled to bring together "a mixture of all the seed of Adam" so all the families were included.[2626] There was one exception, however that bloodline was likewise preserved through Noah's son's wife.[2627] The Lord, therefore, took measures to keep either in Zion or on the earth a representative descendant of "all the seed of Adam."

As the revelation explains, to "put on the authority [notice here authority is singular] of the priesthood" is necessary to "bring again

---

[2623] Moses 7:27 "And Enoch beheld angels descending out of heaven, bearing testimony of the Father and Son; and the Holy Ghost fell on many, and they were caught up by the powers of heaven into Zion."

[2624] Revelation 7:3 "Saying, Hurt not the earth, neither the sea, nor the trees, till we have sealed the servants of our God in their foreheads."

[2625] D&C 113:8 "He had reference to those whom God should call in the last days, who should hold the power of priesthood to bring again Zion, and the redemption of Israel; and to put on her strength is to put on the authority of the priesthood, which she, Zion, has a right to by lineage; also to return to that power which she had lost."

[2626] Moses 7:22 "And Enoch also beheld the residue of the people which were the sons of Adam; and they were a mixture of all the seed of Adam save it was the seed of Cain, for the seed of Cain were black, and had not place among them."

[2627] Abraham 1:21–23 "Now this king of Egypt was a descendant from the loins of Ham, and was a partaker of the blood of the Canaanites by birth. From this descent sprang all the Egyptians, and thus the blood of the Canaanites was preserved in the land. The land of Egypt being first discovered by a woman, who was the daughter of Ham, and the daughter of Egyptus, which in the Chaldean signifies Egypt, which signifies that which is forbidden;"

Zion." This is why the Lord says HE will "bring again Zion" and not men.[2628] See also the description in Moses 7:62 of the Lord's role in the final Zion.[2629]

Zion is the Lord's and His name is "the King of Zion."[2630]

In the answer found in D&C 113:8 the priesthood power has been "lost" and needs to be returned.[2631] This raises the interesting question of whether this is referring to the final calling of the 144,000, or if it means the restoration with Joseph Smith. Have/will we successfully perpetuate the authority from Joseph's time until the return of Zion?[2632] Or will it require a new connection between man and the "powers of heaven" and a new "sealing" of men in their foreheads by the angels? Revelation 7:3 implies this authority will be returned immediately prior to the plagues described in the next

---

[2628] Isaiah 52:8 "Thy watchmen shall lift up the voice; with the voice together shall they sing: for they shall see eye to eye, when the Lord shall bring again Zion."
3 Nephi 16:19 "Break forth into joy, sing together, ye waste places of Jerusalem; for the Lord hath comforted his people, he hath redeemed Jerusalem."

[2629] Moses 7:62 "And righteousness will I send down out of heaven; and truth will I send forth out of the earth, to bear testimony of mine Only Begotten; his resurrection from the dead; yea, and also the resurrection of all men; and righteousness and truth will I cause to sweep the earth as with a flood, to gather out mine elect from the four quarters of the earth, unto a place which I shall prepare, an Holy City, that my people may gird up their loins, and be looking forth for the time of my coming; for there shall be my tabernacle, and it shall be called Zion, a New Jerusalem."

[2630] Moses 7:53 "And the Lord said: Blessed is he through whose seed Messiah shall come; for he saith—I am Messiah, the King of Zion, the Rock of Heaven, which is broad as eternity; whoso cometh in at the gate and climbeth up by me shall never fall; wherefore, blessed are they of whom I have spoken, for they shall come forth with songs of everlasting joy."

[2631] D&C 113:8 "He had reference to those whom God should call in the last days, who should hold the power of priesthood to bring again Zion, and the redemption of Israel; and to put on her strength is to put on the authority of the priesthood, which she, Zion, has a right to by lineage; also to return to that power which she had lost."

[2632] D&C 86:11 "Therefore, blessed are ye if ye continue in my goodness, a light unto the Gentiles, and through this priesthood, a savior unto my people Israel. The Lord hath said it. Amen."

chapter.[2633] But it is up to the Holy Ghost to provide a correct interpretation of these verses. I leave that to you to receive.

The Lord appears in prophecy to claim a direct or immediate role in establishing Zion. And the verses we have considered appear to make it a project which will involve not only the Lord, but also angels and the Father. Indeed, the "powers of heaven" appear to all have some hand in bringing again Zion, do they not?

The most interesting thing to me is the symbolic nature of the number 144,000. If the Lord intends to preserve the blood of all Twelve Tribes, and there are perhaps as many as a thousand different families connected together in your own ancestors, could one man account for a thousand of these 144,000? Could his wife account for another thousand? How few individuals could be able to preserve the bloodlines of the twelve thousand families from each of the Twelve Tribes?

For those who are not included, they will nevertheless have part in the resurrection. The scriptures promise it will be "tolerable" for them.[2634]

A Parting Thought

I've been getting emails and comments asking if I'm alright. I'm fine. When I have something to say I'll say it. I do have one parting thought:

In the Book of Mormon a people were "destroyed" when they lost control over their government. Their ability to preserve their own values, and choose the way they were governed was taken over by others. Most often it was from a different ethnic group, though not

---

[2633] Revelation 7:3 "Saying, Hurt not the earth, neither the sea, nor the trees, till we have sealed the servants of our God in their foreheads."

[2634] D&C 45:54 "And then shall the heathen nations be redeemed, and they that knew no law shall have part in the first resurrection; and it shall be tolerable for them."

always. In the case of Amalickiah he was ethnically Nephite, but his values were Lamanite.

Once people were "destroyed" they were oppressed and suffered. Often they were oppressed with grievous taxes, and had religious liberties removed. Then they faced a choice: Either repent, in which case they came through the period of oppression with another chance. Or, if they were angry and rebellious, they would then be "swept away."

Being "destroyed" is not at all the same as being "swept away." It is possible for people to have been destroyed and not even realize it. But when swept away they face extinction, and cannot help but notice it.

I Have No Spokesman/Spokesmen

A couple of years ago I put a post up confirming that no one speaks for me.

It is still true. If I have something to say, I will say it. No one is authorized to speak on my behalf. And no one is entitled to interpret what I think, or how I view any given issue or subject. To the extent that I have a view, I will tell it.

Misunderstandings

I received the following comment, which I am putting up because it does a good job of illustrating a number of misunderstandings:

Mr. Snuffer,

I am not a follower of your blog but I love some who are. When I read your recent post, "I've been getting emails and comments asking if I'm alright. I'm fine. When I have something to say I'll say it" I thought wow. It feels so unkind? People have become dependent on your claims to know Heavenly Father's will. Many have abandoned their own voice of reasoning leaning on your daily prophesies. They no longer feel secure in their understanding of the Gospel of Jesus Christ without your input so I question how you are okay with dropping and then mocking those who you have called into your fold? I expect all is not well and pray that Heavenly Father will be able to mend His children's fearful hearts, including yours. Peace and goodwill.

This comment contains a number of misunderstandings.

It is abhorrent to me that anyone would *"become dependent"* on me. I've worked to point to the Lord, never to myself. If there are some who have *"become dependent,"* then there is every reason for me to withdraw to prevent that from happening. It is wrong for any person to be dependent upon another in matters of faith. We should all be dependent upon the Lord alone. As Moroni confirmed, citing Acts 3:22–23,[2635] the only "prophet" people must hear to avoid being "destroyed" is Christ. Those who will not hear His voice will, according to Moroni, "be cut off from among the people."[2636]

If it is true that, *"Many have abandoned their own voice of reasoning leaning on your daily prophesies. They no longer feel secure in their understanding of the Gospel of Jesus Christ without your input"* then the only proper response on my part is to withdraw. It is wrong of them to do this, and it is the more wrong for me to facilitate it. This idea is one I have rejected, repeatedly denounced, and consistently stated that I am unworthy of followers. It would be wrong of me to continue.

[2635] Acts 3:22–23 "For Moses truly said unto the fathers, A prophet shall the Lord your God raise up unto you of your brethren, like unto me; him shall ye hear in all things whatsoever he shall say unto you. And it shall come to pass, *that* every soul, which will not hear that prophet, shall be destroyed from among the people."

[2636] JS–H 1:40 "In addition to these, he quoted the eleventh chapter of Isaiah, saying that it was about to be fulfilled. He quoted also the third chapter of Acts, twenty-second and twenty-third verses, precisely as they stand in our New Testament. He said that that prophet was Christ; but the day had not yet come when "they who would not hear his voice should be cut off from among the people," but soon would come."

I have not intended to "*mock*" anyone who is seeking to know more of Christ and to understand His Gospel more clearly. I have done what I could to assist. In doing so it has been my purpose to point to Him, never to myself. I have fully recovered from the last surgery. I lift weights; I walk several miles a week, and I am in better physical condition than I have been in some time.

I have no "*fold*" and I am not a shepherd of anyone. Even my own children are asked to find Christ and His truth for themselves.

My "*heart*" is not "*fearful*" of anyone, or of anything. I am at peace with God, and I hope others will become similarly at peace with Him. I have been asked to accomplish a number of things and I have accomplished them. Until asked to do something further, I stand at the ready and await His counsel and guidance. In the meantime, I serve as asked in my ward and stake, and try not to call any undue attention to myself.

I hope that this Christmas season will be filled with remembrance of the Lord and His great condescension coming here to live among us. His birth was necessary to allow Him to die for us. He entered mortality foreordained to die for our salvation. He willingly came here, endured what was required of Him, and suffered the will of His Father in all things, even drinking out of the bitter cup given to Him when He begged to have it taken from Him. Bethlehem and Golgotha are linked together by the ministry of our Lord; the one necessary for the other. I would hope also some reflection would be given to Mary, whose soul was inevitably to be "pierced" also as the prophet Simeon foretold to her.[2637] Our Lord, His Father and His mother all paid a price both to bring Him into this world and to witness His sacrifice for us.

[2637] Luke 2:34–35 "And Simeon blessed them, and said unto Mary his mother, Behold, this *child* is set for the fall and rising again of many in Israel; and for a sign which shall be spoken against; (Yea, a sword shall pierce through thy own soul also,) that the thoughts of many hearts may be revealed."

A couple of Questions

I was asked the following:

In 1 Nephi 10:11,[2638] is this talking about a physical manifestation to the Gentiles? Does Christ show Himself to others physically by the power of the Holy Ghost? Or is this to the Gentiles' hearts and minds before the Restoration?

This is speaking about the immediate post-resurrection ministry of the Lord. At that time He visited only with the tribes of Israel in their scattered condition. He did not go among the gentiles. Nephi explained that in the last days ministry of the Lord at that time, He would appear to the gentiles "in very deed."[2639] This is why the Lord appeared to Joseph Smith[2640] and Oliver Cowdery (D&C 110), and to Sidney Rigdon (D&C 76), and to others.

[2638] 1 Nephi 10:11 "And it came to pass after my father had spoken these words he spake unto my brethren concerning the gospel which should be preached among the Jews, and also concerning the dwindling of the Jews in unbelief. And after they had slain the Messiah, who should come, and after he had been slain he should rise from the dead, and should make himself manifest, by the Holy Ghost, unto the Gentiles."

[2639] 1 Nephi 14:1 "And it shall come to pass, that if the Gentiles shall hearken unto the Lamb of God in that day that he shall manifest himself unto them in word, and also in power, in very deed, unto the taking away of their stumbling blocks—"

[2640] JS-H 1:17–19 "It no sooner appeared than I found myself delivered from the enemy which held me bound. When the light rested upon me I saw two Personages, whose brightness and glory defy all description, standing above me in the air. One of them spake unto me, calling me by name and said, pointing to the other—*This is My Beloved Son. Hear Him!* My object in going to inquire of the Lord was to know which of all the sects was right, that I might know which to join. No sooner, therefore, did I get possession of myself, so as to be able to speak, than I asked the Personages who stood above me in the light, which of all the sects was right (for at this time it had never entered into my heart that all were wrong)—and which I should join. I was answered that I must join none of them, for they were all wrong; and the Personage who addressed me said that all their creeds were an abomination in his sight; that those professors were all corrupt; that: "they draw near to me with their lips, but their hearts are far from me, they teach for doctrines the commandments of men, having a form of godliness, but they deny the power thereof.""

In Mosiah16:1[2641] and Alma 13:21,[2642] it says the phrase *"he stretched forth his hand."* What does that mean? Raising it to the square? Using the priesthood to testify of what he is about to teach? A little help here would be wonderful.

Read Mosiah 15:31[2643] to understand Mosiah 16:1. He is demonstrating the Lord's action, thereby affirming he is His messenger. He had been given the sign to testify, and used it as his sign that he was a true messenger.

In Alma 13, the prophet concludes his testimony of Melchizedek by using a sign to evidence his authority. He used this sign because he was authorized to do so, and knew what it meant as he did. Although those who were there may not have understood, it was a sign he was a true messenger.

We cannot be saved in ignorance.

Once the key of knowledge is lost, mankind is lost and cannot be saved until that key is returned. Prophets sent with messages who testify to an ignorant people use signs that the Lord recognizes and authorizes, but they may not be noticed or understood by those who hear the message. Nevertheless, the testimony becomes binding when the Lord's seal is put upon it. This often involves a required sign to be given, or in other words, for hands to be stretched forth.

[2641] Mosiah 16:1 "And now, it came to pass that after Abinadi had spoken these words he stretched forth his hand and said: The time shall come when all shall see the salvation of the Lord; when every nation, kindred, tongue, and people shall see eye to eye and shall confess before God that his judgments are just."

[2642] Alma 13:21 "And now it came to pass that when Alma had said these words unto them, he stretched forth his hand unto them and cried with a mighty voice, saying: Now is the time to repent, for the day of salvation draweth nigh;"

[2643] Mosiah 15:31 "The Lord hath made bare his holy arm in the eyes of all the nations; and all the ends of the earth shall see the salvation of our God."

The Ongoing Battle

Although I know of no one who has left the church or "lost their testimony" as a consequence of reading my book, *Passing the Heavenly Gift ("PTHG")*, there continue to be accusations that this has/does happen. Therefore, again, I want to reaffirm the purpose of *PTHG*.

Let me give some background. I joined the church while in the Air Force, stationed in New Hampshire. After joining, I was a zealous missionary, and there followed over a dozen conversions of other military young folks who would listen to me explain the restoration. I got them open to the idea, then the full-time missionaries and ward members would take over. Mormonism was an exotic religion in New England. Little was known about the faith. So we got to begin with a relatively blank slate and tell the story our way.

I was transferred to Abilene, Texas shortly after joining the church. In Texas things were very different. At the local laundromat I used, there were racks of religious tracts on the wall. Included in these were a wide assortment of anti-Mormon pamphlets intended to "prove" Mormonism was false. We went from being exotic to being the devil's workmanship. Missionary work in Texas was a good deal more difficult. Even though I served as a Stake Missionary, and took the third-Elder (who awaited his Visa to Brazil) every evening and weekend as a companion to tract and teach, the results in Texas were nothing like what had happened in New Hampshire.

The organized effort in Texas was supported by radio programs, Sunday sermons, and the occasional editorial in the local newspapers. The "Christian" churches were tired of losing their best congregants to the Mormon Elders. So the effort to oppose the church was interdenominational.

I joined the church in 1973 and finished my Air Force term in Texas in 1975. This is now long ago. Since then, the growth of the church has left no corner of the United States untouched by wards, stakes, missions, temple districts and advertising. We are no longer exotic anywhere - including New Hampshire.

The result of church growth has been the increasing awareness of Mormonism's effect on other religions. It is not a happy thing for other faiths to see our church grow at the expense of their own congregations. The original inter-denominational cooperation I saw in Texas in 1974–75 has now spread. It is now worldwide. All churches are wary of the loss of revenue and participation represented by each Mormon convert who leaves their fold to join ours.

Today there is widespread sharing of anti-Mormon material among other denominations. The best defense is an organized offense. In many areas, Elders (who are easily identified) are followed in order to discover who they are teaching. Then the investigator is contacted by volunteers who distribute anti-Mormon material to prevent conversions. Some years ago there were ministries who bragged they could not only prevent conversions, but they could take it one step further: They could convert the Mormon Elder! That led to a growth in seminars, literature and preaching about ways to "convert Mormon Elders" while they are on their missions.

I do not think there has been any significant success in actually converting active Mormon missionaries. But that isn't the point. It is the Evangelical perception of that success that has fueled two things: First, it has helped insulate converts, because if the Elders can be converted, then Mormonism must not be true (or so the reasoning goes). Second, it creates more confrontation by anti-Mormon forces aimed directly at our missionaries.

The Evangelicals have realized that the best way to practice this kind of undermining of Mormon missionary efforts is to take the soft-sale approach. Instead of Bible-bashing, just ask questions the Elders can't answer. Make the Elders do the thinking and work to solve the riddles. When they can't, then they are filled with doubts that linger.

This is not just happenstance. This is an organized and inter-denominational effort that began decades ago. It now bears so much fruit it is is alarming to Mormons. Returned missionaries are falling away. When I was in charge of missionary work in my stake, I attended regional leadership meetings at which the Mission President and a Seventy advised us of the trends underway. The inactive church members were called "low hanging fruit" who could swell our ranks just by returning to activity. One category of the "low hanging fruit" was the returned missionary population. At that time, (years ago now) it was estimated there were 40,000 returned Elders along the Wasatch Front, from Ogden to Provo, who were so inactive we didn't have a reliable address for them. The suggestion was to contact the families of the inactive, returned missionaries and locate them that way.

This background is part of why *PTHG* exists. This battle has been underway for decades, and the most successful topic being used to question our members and raise doubts is our history. The anti-Mormon forces know we are generally ignorant of our history. We don't know enough to answer hard questions. So all that needs to be done is to put the right question to the ignorant, but believing Latter-day Saint, and the doubts will eventually percolate into disbelief and abandonment. I do not think most of those who have and are leaving do so because they know the church is not true. They leave because they no longer think the church has answers to the difficult questions. Part of the reaction of the church has been to run from the hard questions, which reinforces the idea that we don't know the real answers.

So, I wrote the book to deal with anything I thought was out there being used or potentially being used against us. I assumed the audience would be those who were already in distress, already having doubts, already aware of these efforts to undermine faith and create doubts. It was intended as relief from anxiety over the battles which have raged for decades now.

Instead of this audience, there are some who have picked the book up and thought it was intended as a hostile attack on the church, its history, and its doctrine. Thankfully, such readers are already sure they belong to the "only true church" and therefore their ire is only directed at me. They aren't leaving the church. They're only interested in damning me for writing something they can't conceive of as helpful.

Well, I have literally dozens, perhaps hundreds of emails and letters from readers who were the intended audience. Person after person, young and old, male and female, returned missionaries and church leaders have thanked me. Some who left the church have returned. Some who have had their names removed from the records of the church, or were considering it, have written to tell me they were remaining in the church. At last, they say, they can find faith and answers that enables them to remain in fellowship with the church.

For those who were never intended to read the book, but are now angry at me for having addressed this problem, let me assure you:

First, I believe in the restoration of eternal truths through the prophet Joseph Smith. My testimony of this truth is rock solid. My purpose, and all that I seek to accomplish by writing, is to further this work and be a small contributor to development of God's work.

To be clear:

1.   I sustain today's church leaders as prophets, seers and revelators. The scriptures give them the right to use those titles.[2644] They preside, and it is their right to do so. They have our common consent

---

[2644] D&C 107:92 "Behold, here is wisdom; yea, to be a seer, a revelator, a translator, and a prophet, having all the gifts of God which he bestows upon the head of the church."

and ought to be upheld by our "confidence, faith and prayers".[2645] I uphold them in this way. They carry heavy burdens and have my sympathy, not my judgment, for any human frailties they display.

2.   It is utterly untrue that I have said the church is apostate. I reject the accusation. If the narrative I suggest in *PTHG* is true, then the Lord's post-Nauvoo ire is evidence the Lord is still watching over and intends to further His work with the members of this church. Those whom He loves, He chastens.[2646] Mine is not a faithless, but a faith filled history. I've reiterated this before and reiterate it again.[2647]

3.   I believe the church possesses the right to seal on earth and seal in heaven, and have agreed with President Eyring's general conference talk on the subject.[2648]

4.   I believe that all organizations, including the church, tend to characterize their history in a light most favorable to them. They

---

[2645] D&C 107:22 "Of the Melchizedek Priesthood, three Presiding High Priests, chosen by the body, appointed and ordained to that office, and upheld by the confidence, faith, and prayer of the church, form a quorum of the Presidency of the Church."

[2646] Hebrews 12:5–11 "And ye have forgotten the exhortation which speaketh unto you as unto children, My son, despise not thou the chastening of the Lord, nor faint when thou art rebuked of him: For whom the Lord loveth he chasteneth, and scourgeth every son whom he receiveth. If ye endure chastening, God dealeth with you as with sons; for what son is he whom the father chasteneth not? But if ye be without chastisement, whereof all are partakers, then are ye bastards, and not sons. Furthermore we have had fathers of our flesh which corrected *us,* and we gave *them* reverence: shall we not much rather be in subjection unto the Father of spirits, and live? For they verily for a few days chastened *us* after their own pleasure; but he for *our* profit, that *we* might be partakers of his holiness. Now no chastening for the present seemeth to be joyous, but grievous: nevertheless afterward it yieldeth the peaceable fruit of righteousness unto them which are exercised thereby."
Helaman 12:3 "And thus we see that except the Lord doth chasten his people with many afflictions, yea, except he doth visit them with death and with terror, and with famine and with all manner of pestilence, they will not remember him."
D&C 95:1 "VERILY, thus saith the Lord unto you whom I love, and whom I love I also chasten that their sins may be forgiven, for with the chastisement I prepare a way for their deliverance in all things out of temptation, and I have loved you—"

[2647] See the post titled "The Traditions of Men, Part 1".

[2648] Eyring, "Families under Covenant", General Conference, April 2012.

have that right. I take no issue with it and think it should be expected. That does not change the divine origin and mission of the church.

5.   The church provides ordinances required to see and enter into the kingdom of heaven, in addition to providing us with the necessary scriptures. Through the church, we receive the foundation of faith, repentance, baptism and enduring to the end. I hope to endure to the end myself and I seek to help others do so.

I am still in the battle to help people find and focus upon Christ. As a faithful Latter-day Saint I owe my knowledge of the Lord to the tools I obtained through The Church of Jesus Christ of Latter-day Saints. I have enjoyed every minute of my association with the church, and I intend to remain a faithful member. The current war we face did not originate with blogs or bloggers. The blogosphere is following the battle, not leading it. It began long ago, and the efforts to deal with it here are because of the many losses we have and are suffering. They are needless losses. We just need to be willing to discuss and recognize there certainly are some tough questions. They don't go away.

Tradition's Grip

Assume you are taking a course at the local university on William Faulkner. The book for study this semester is *The Sound and The Fury*. This course does not require you to actually read the book. Instead, the information in this class will come exclusively from your professor. To begin the semester, she will be lecturing and instructing you on 'all things Faulkner.' She will discuss biographical information, including everything she could find about his personal life. She will give lectures on his writing. There will be discussions about literary criticism given his writings and awards he has won. You will listen to audio recordings of Mr. Faulkner reading passages of *The Sound and The Fury*.

As the semester progresses, she will begin to discuss the book. She will tell you about the first time she read it, and what kind of impact it had on her. She will tell you why she decided to teach an entire semester course on this one work of Faulkner's. You will learn what her expectations and preconceptions were before she even began reading. You will hear all her first impressions. She tells you that she thought it was difficult the first time. There will be lectures on the genre, characters, plot, setting, style and structure, point of view, images, symbols, and themes. She will discuss the reception when first published. She will discuss each part of the novel in detail. She will then tell you how her personal reactions have changed as her understanding has deepened. As the semester winds down, she will end with her explanation of the literary significance of this book. With that, the semester is over.

Shortly after the end of the semester, because of this class and the things you learned, you decide to actually read *The Sound and The Fury:*

Do you suppose, with your first reading, you could formulate any thought about this book independent of what your professor fed you?

Could you make your own critical evaluations about characters, plot, point of view, themes, or symbolism?

Could the biographical information you learned about Mr. Faulkner be extricated from your psyche in order to have a blank slate from which to assess Mr. Faulkner's reason for writing this novel?

Could you read this book through your lense?

How much of your professor's impressions, understanding or analysis would you have to completely discard in order to form your own personal conclusions about this material?

How many times would you have to read it before you began to make your own analysis?

Would the professor's framework control your first reading?

Could you ever escape from her views to discover your own?

The Lamanites were unable to convert, even when taught the truth, because of the traditions of their fathers which were not correct.[2649]

"Becoming as a little child" is necessary, because children are able to be taught. They are still open. They want to be filled. For such is the kingdom.[2650] None of the arguments our Lord was required to endure with His fellow-man was ever with a child.

Ignorance Enshrined

A purported group of "over 260 active and disaffected Mormons" claims responsibility for a "95 Theses" document released recently. (The quotes in the preceding sentence are theirs. This is how they self-describe.)

Unlike Martin Luther, they choose to categorize themselves rather than to expose themselves by using their identities. There are only a few who identified themselves. For the most part, they remain unidentified. That betrays a weakness of character and leads to the conclusion they want to complain, but they do not want to be responsible for complaining. A "reform" movement must be made of sterner stuff. They appear only willing to whine; not to do the work or take the risk Martin Luther took when he wrote the document they mimic.

[2649] Mosiah 1:5 "I say unto you, my sons, were it not for these things, which have been kept and preserved by the hand of God, that we might read and understand of his mysteries, and have his commandments always before our eyes, that even our fathers would have dwindled in unbelief, and we should have been like unto our brethren, the Lamanites, who know nothing concerning these things, or even do not believe them when they are taught them, because of the traditions of their fathers, which are not correct."

[2650] Luke 18:16 "But Jesus called them *unto him*, and said, Suffer little children to come unto me, and forbid them not: for of such is the kingdom of God."

I've looked at the 95 Theses. They are largely based on upset stemming from astounding ignorance of our history, scriptures, doctrine, and teachings. However, this is a relatively common condition we find ourselves. As a community of believers in the restoration through Joseph Smith, we've neglected to teach and/or learn the very things that would benefit these "260 active and disaffected Mormons." These people may well be of good faith and honest intent. I'll assume that of them. But they are unable to reconcile some of the things from our past with the things they thought they knew about Mormonism. The problem is that what they thought they knew about Mormonism is not at all what I know and what they should have known about Mormonism. That may not be entirely their fault, but they must shoulder part of the blame.

I understand it from a different perspective because I've paid a price in study, prayer, practice and devotion. In *The Second Comforter* I said: "The truth will scratch your eyes out, and then scratch them in again." I've been through both. These "260" have been only through the first.

They have 11 troubling points about the Book of Mormon. I've discovered many more. I've reconciled them all in my mind.

They have 5 troubling points on the Book of Abraham. I've discovered many, many more. This is a vital topic for study. I've gathered a library of materials on this text. When I was teaching the Priests' Quorum in my ward, I took 4 weeks with them teaching on the Book of Abraham. I wasn't going to let any of them get "poached" by critics because they didn't have enough background information to understand the issues and history. Using the *Documentary History of the Church*, they were shown what Joseph described he translated as the Book of Abraham. They were shown the photographic reproductions of the papyri returned from the Metropolitan Museum of New York to the church. The difference between these scroll documents and Joseph's description did not require a commentary. They saw with their own eyes the difference between the two. No one is ever going to convince them using an argument based on misinformation.

These "260 active and disaffected Mormons" have 11 troubling points about Polygamy and Polyandry. Again, it betrays a shallow understanding of our history and comprises only a fraction of what we should all know about this issue. Until we face this, discuss it openly, and put history and context together in a forthright and honest way, we are vulnerable to upset and distress anytime someone who knows a little more than we know comes along with a "fact" from our history we can't put into context.

This raises enough to make the point:

We're losing the battle with many of these souls. The more honest and intellectually open of our members are being taken in traps precisely because their greatest strengths (confidence and openness) allow the critics to show them our weaknesses. This should not be allowed to happen. Narrow-mindedness and dogmatism, as a result of fierce and unrelenting loyalty to an institution, should not rule the day. The winnowing out, if allowed to continue, will produce a frightening form of Mormonism akin to the more radical political movements currently underway in the world.

When Joseph Smith was alive, Mormonism embraced all truth.

"The first and fundamental principle of our holy religion is, that we believe that we have a right to embrace all, and every item of truth, without limitation or without being circumscribed or prohibited by the creeds or superstitious notions of men, or by the dominations of one another, when that truth is clearly demonstrated to our minds." (Letter from Joseph Smith to Isaac Galland, March 22, 1839; *The Personal Writings of Joseph Smith*, Dean C. Jesse, editor; Deseret Book, 421–422)

I'd like to see that be the case once again.

I've never found a problem in the faith for which I could not ultimately find a solution or answer. The faith is quite resilient. But, oddly, some of the actual answers are thought to be so fearful that they must be ignored, suppressed or denounced. Fear is not only the opposite of faith, but it contains within it the bitterness of hell.[2651] We have become too fearful.

Questions from This Week

Since mentioning it, I've gotten a number of questions about President Eyring's General Conference talk.[2652] Part of his remarks are particularly insightful. After talking about the church's ordinance, he elaborated:

> The way to do that is clear. The Holy Spirit of Promise, through our obedience and sacrifice, must seal our temple covenants in order to be realized in the world to come. President Harold B. Lee explained what it means to be sealed by the Holy Spirit of Promise by quoting Elder Melvin J. Ballard: "We may deceive men but we cannot deceive the Holy Ghost, and our blessings will not be eternal unless they are also sealed by the Holy Spirit of promise. The Holy Ghost is one who reads the thoughts and hearts of men, and gives his sealing approval to the blessings pronounced upon their heads. Then it is binding, efficacious, and of full force."

> When Sister Eyring and I were sealed in the Logan Utah Temple, I did not understand then the full significance of that promise. I am still trying to understand all that it means, but my wife and I decided at the start of our nearly 50 years of

---

[2651] Moses 1:20 "And it came to pass that Moses began to fear exceedingly; and as he began to fear, he saw the bitterness of hell. Nevertheless, calling upon God, he received strength, and he commanded, saying: Depart from me, Satan, for this one God only will I worship, which is the God of glory."

[2652] Eyring, "Families under Covenant", General Conference, April 2012.

marriage to invite the Holy Ghost as much as we could into our lives and into our family.

I agree that men may be and often are deceived about who is worthy and who is not. But the Lord alone will judge righteously. Therefore, He decides who will be sealed and who will not. President Eyring is teaching true doctrine.

The portion of the scroll (which was quite long and included different segments) Joseph translated the Book of Abraham from is described in church history. There are three critical features to this text:

The record of Abraham and Joseph, found with the mummies, is (1) beautifully written on papyrus, with black, and (2) a small part red, ink or paint, (3) in perfect preservation (*DHC* 2:348).

Color Plates of the *Hor Book of Breathings* are available in Appendix A, starting on page 33 of *The Hor Book of Breathings: A Translation and Commentary, Studies in the Book of Abraham*, Vol 2; (FARMS/BYU Press 2002). The contrast between Joseph's description in church history and the photographs of the recovered papyrus requires nothing more than looking at it.

The description "a strong faith and a firm mind in every form of godliness"[2653] involves at a minimum the following:
- Strong faith is obtained by obedience and sacrifice, as explained in the Lectures on Faith. It requires the sacrifice of all things to obtain favor with God. No one attains to this by cowardice or respecting the views of men above the commandments of God.

[2653] Moroni 7:30 "For behold, they are subject unto him, to minister according to the word of his command, showing themselves unto them of strong faith and a firm mind in every form of godliness."

- Every form includes not merely passing acquaintance with the Lord's will, but an earnest search into the things God wants from you. And, as you find His will, then to obey it. Everything must be put on the altar. Whether it be friends, property, or life itself, it must be every form.

- Godliness is different from virtue. It is even different from righteousness. I've explained both previously and won't repeat it. Godliness requires you to become godlike in your sentiments and in your meekness before Him. Whether men understand you or attribute motives to you, the relationship is between you and the Lord. Godliness is when your walk here is along the path He has chosen for you.

––––––––––

Prophecy requires someone to fulfill it before you can know who was being identified. Until the work is done I think it is a foolish thing to speculate about identities. There's probably been hundreds of potential individuals, living and dead, who might have done a greater work than they accomplished here. However, they are blinded by the craftiness of other men, or they fall victim to those who deceive, or they allow traditions to control their understanding and fall short of the glory they might have obtained. Hence the saying that many are called, but few are chosen.

Christ Clarifies His Role

I've been reading the 1830 *Book of Commandments* as reprinted in *The Joseph Smith Papers: Revelations and Translations, Vol. 2*. I've been struck by how many clarifications Christ made of His role to the early saints. It is apparent there were a number of false notions in circulation about who Christ was and what His future role would include.

The Lord clarifies that the saints should: "look not for a Messiah to come which has already come." (Chapter XVI, verse 27).

He later adds that when He does return: "they shall see me in the clouds of heaven, clothed with power and great glory, with all the holy angels." (Chapter XLVIII, verse 37).

If that were not enough to remove the question about His return, He further explains: "the Son of Man cometh not in the form of a woman, neither of a man traveling on the earth." (Chapter LII, verse 21.)

He mentions Enoch, telling us that Enoch and his brethren "were separated from the earth, and were reserved unto [God], a city reserved until a day of righteousness shall come, a day which was sought for by all holy men, and they found it not because of wickedness and abominations." (Chapter XLVIII, verse 14.) Since "all holy men" sought for this city, but found it not, it is apparent that the rule is failure because holy men cannot teach righteousness to the wicked who prefer their abominations, pride, vanity, and errors. The exception is success.

The Lord clarifies there will be success before the world will see Him. He will have a holy city built, which He will call "the New Jerusalem." There, His glory will rest upon these few inhabitants: "it shall be called the New Jerusalem, a land of peace, a city of refuge, a place of safety for the saints of the most high God. And the glory of the Lord shall be there, and the terror of the Lord also shall be there, insomuch that the wicked will not come unto it: And it shall be called Zion." (Chapter XLVIII, verses 59–61).

When He does show Himself to the world again, it will be in judgment: "I the Lord . . . will come down in heaven from the presence of God, and consume the wicked with unquenchable fire" (Chapter LXIV, verse 36).

I've heard some of the same errors discussed among Latter-day Saints who would know better if they read the scriptures. As early as 1830 the Lord explained He was the Messiah, and had already come. He will not return as a man walking on the earth, but will come in glory and judgment when He returns, and that we need not look for another to come in that way.

I am surprised at how difficult it is to hold on to doctrine. It evaporates almost before our eyes. Perhaps the greatest miracle of the ages will be this latter day New Jerusalem. For, despite all the wickedness and abominable beliefs of mankind urging them to vanity and faithless pride, there will be some small group willing to learn and walk in the way of God. That will be a miracle indeed among the people living in this generation.

A Sign

When the Seed of the Woman was born, a new star appeared in the heavens. In like manner, when the Lion of Judah returns, as with his first coming, there will be a new star seen. All the world will note its appearance and shall be troubled at its meaning. When it makes its appearance, you may know His return is soon upon the world. You may also know by that sign that He has given to me the words I have faithfully taught as His servant.

INDEX

42957244R00267

Made in the USA
San Bernardino, CA
11 December 2016